THE FIRST RAPPROCHEMENT

Also by Bradford Perkins

Prologue to War: England and the United States, 1805-1812
Castlereagh and Adams: England and the United States, 1812-1823

RUFUS KING
Portrait by John Trumbull
Courtesy of Yale University Art Gallery

THE FIRST RAPPROCHEMENT

ENGLAND
AND THE UNITED STATES
1795–1805

BY BRADFORD PERKINS

UNIVERSITY OF CALIFORNIA PRESS
BERKELEY AND LOS ANGELES · 1967

UNIVERSITY OF CALIFORNIA PRESS
BERKELEY AND LOS ANGELES, CALIFORNIA

CAMBRIDGE UNIVERSITY PRESS
LONDON, ENGLAND

Library of Congress Catalog Card Number: 55-9468

Second Printing, 1967

For

W. L. P.

Foreword

WHEN HISTORIANS EXAMINE THE DIPLOMACY OF JOHN ADAMS' ADMIN-
istration, they concentrate on the undeclared war with France; when
scholars seek out the threads woven into war by dashing Congressmen
in 1812, they tend at least to trace these filaments back to the 1790's
without properly placing them in the context of that period. Thus for
two reasons an era of generally successful Anglo-American diplomacy is
overlooked. This study attempts to suggest certain limitations in the con-
ventional view of the relations between England and the United States
following the Jay treaty.

As all acquainted with the period well know, controversy and discord
did not come to an end in 1794. However, during the regime of John
Adams and the first administration of Thomas Jefferson, the spirit of
hostility was so powerfully challenged by other forces that the decade
may be characterized as the period of "The First Rapprochement." For
about ten years there was peace on the frontier, joint recognition of the
value of commercial intercourse, and even, by comparison with both preceding and succeeding epochs, a muting of strife over ship seizures and
impressment. Two controversies with France, one under each administration, pushed the English-speaking powers even more closely together.

My primary concern is with these relatively neglected developments,
rather than with more familiar aspects of the decade or the chain of events
culminating in President Madison's war message of June 1, 1812. Historians have largely ignored the important problems of English as opposed
to American opinion, the formulation of constructive British policy after
years of negative obstruction, and the generally satisfactory state of
Anglo-American relations from 1795 to 1804. Upon these matters, I have
concentrated this study, while at the same time attempting to indicate the
importance of the forces holding back the rapprochement.

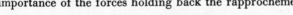

My search for materials was made more successful by the assistance
willingly provided by others. In England, R. L. Atkinson, Secretary of
the Historical Manuscripts Commission, and the late Colonel G. E. G.
Malet, Registrar of Archives, helped me to find elusive manuscript material subsequently kindly placed at my disposal by George Grenville

Fortescue, Colonel Anthony Barnes, and Viscount Sandon. Without Mr. Fortescue's permission to examine the papers of Lord Grenville this study could scarcely have been written, and Mr. Fortescue and Sir Tresham Lever, perceptive chronicler of the Pitt family, have made it possible for me to include a previously unpublished portrait of Lord Grenville. I also owe thanks to President Wilson H. Elkins of the University of Maryland, for permission to use his unpublished study of Anglo-American commerce; to the Research Committee of the Academic Senate of the University of California at Los Angeles; and to others, on both sides of the Atlantic, too numerous to mention.

Many people have aided me with criticisms and suggestions, although I alone am of course responsible for errors of fact and interpretation. Frederick Merk, under whose direction this project was begun, patiently waded through the first drafts. I have also benefited from the comments of Roland D. Hussey, John S. Galbraith, Robert N. Burr, and C. Page Smith, colleagues at the University of California. The penetrating criticism and scholarly example of my father, Dexter Perkins, have been of great value. Historians have nearly exhausted both the banal and the exotic in attempting to thank their wives for assistance, so I shall content myself with saying that the limitless assistance and encouragement provided by Nancy Tucker Perkins have, above all, contributed to whatever merit this study may have.

BRADFORD PERKINS

Harvard, Massachusetts
August 15, 1954

viii

Acknowledgments

LIKE ALL STUDENTS, THE AUTHOR OWES A REAL DEBT OF GRATITUDE TO the various libraries and manuscript repositories in which he has worked, as well as to the staffs of those institutions. In this case, they include the Widener and Houghton Libraries, Harvard University; the Library of Congress and the National Archives, Washington; the Public Record Office and the British Museum, London; the New-York Historical Society, New York; the Library of the University of California, Los Angeles; the Massachusetts Historical Society, Boston; the Scottish National Library, Edinburgh; the University Library, Cambridge, England; and the Bodleian Library, Oxford.

Quotations from various books, chiefly the works and letters of British and American statesmen, appear by courtesy of the copyright holders. They are: George Allen & Unwin, Ltd., for Anna M. Wilberforce, ed., *Private Papers of William Wilberforce*, London, 1897; the American Historical Association, for Elizabeth Donnan, ed., *Papers of James A. Bayard, 1796-1815* (American Historical Association, *Annual Report for 1913*, II), Washington, 1915, and Worthington C. Ford, ed., "Letters of William Vans Murray to John Quincy Adams, 1797-1803," American Historical Association, *Annual Report for 1912*, Washington, 1914, pp. 347-408; Appleton-Century-Crofts, for Lowell J. Ragatz, *The Fall of the Planter Class in the British Caribbean*, New York, 1928; Blackie & Son, Ltd., for Vere Foster, ed., *The Two Duchesses*, London, 1898; Curtis Brown, Ltd., for Bonamy Dobrée, ed., *The Letters of George III*, London, 1935; the Cambridge University Press, for Sir Adolphus W. Ward and George P. Gooch, eds., *The Cambridge History of British Foreign Policy, 1783-1919*, Cambridge, England, 1939; the Carnegie Institution of Washington, for permission to include, in modified form, maps from Charles O. Paullin, *Atlas of the Historical Geography of the United States* (Carnegie Institution of Washington, *Publication No. 401*), Baltimore, 1932; Columbia University Press, for James F. Zimmerman, *Impressment of American Seamen* (*Columbia University Studies in History, Economics and Public Law*, Vol. CXVIII, No. 1), New York, 1925; Constable and Company, Ltd., for Francis Bickley, ed., *The Diaries of Sylvester Douglas (Lord Glenbervie)*, London, 1913, and Walter Sichel, *Sheridan*, London, 1909; the Essex Institute, for *The Diary of William Bentley, D. D.*, Vols. II-III, Salem, 1907-11; Harcourt, Brace and Company, for George Dangerfield, *The Era of Good Feelings*, New York, 1952; Harvard University Press, for

Kenneth W. Porter, ed., *The Jacksons and the Lees*, Vol. I, Cambridge, 1937; the Historical Manuscripts Commission, for Walter Fitzpatrick, ed., *Report on the Manuscripts of J. B. Fortescue, Esq., Preserved at Dropmore*, Vols. I-VI, London, 1892-98, and John T. Gilbert, ed., *The Manuscripts and Correspondence of James, First Earl of Charlemont*, Vol. II (Historical Manuscripts Commission, *Thirteenth Report*, Appendix, Part VIII), London, 1894; Henry Holt and Company, for Allan Nevins, ed., *American Social History as Recorded by British Travellers*, London, 1924; Houghton Mifflin Company, for Henry C. Lodge, ed., *The Works of Alexander Hamilton (Federal Edition)*, New York, 1904; Hutchinson & Company, Ltd., for James Greig, ed., *The Farington Diary*, Vols. I-III, London, 1922-24; Longmans Green & Company, Ltd., for Giles S. H. F. Strangways, Earl of Ilchester, ed., *The Journal of Elizabeth, Lady Holland (1793-1811)*, London, 1908; the Macmillan Company for Edward Channing, *A History of the United States*, Vol. IV, rev. ed., New York, 1927, and Worthington C. Ford, ed., *Writings of John Quincy Adams*, Vols. I-III, New York, 1913-14; the Massachusetts Historical Society, for *Bowdoin and Temple Papers*, *Part II* (Massachusetts Historical Society, *Collections*, Seventh Series, Vol. VI), Boston, 1907; Dr. Samuel E. Morison, for his *The Life and Letters of Harrison Gray Otis*, Boston, 1913; John Murray, Ltd., for Josceline Bagot, ed., *George Canning and His Friends*, London, 1909, and Castalia P. Leveson-Gower, Countess Granville, ed., *Lord Granville Leveson-Gower (First Earl Granville): Private Correspondence, 1781-1821*, London, 1916; G. P. Putnam's Sons, for Gaillard Hunt, ed., *The Writings of James Madison*, Vols. VI-VII, New York, 1906-8; Oxford University Press, for George D. H. Cole, ed., *Letters from William Cobbett to Edward Thornton, Written in the Years 1797 to 1800*, London, 1937, and Anne Fremantle, ed., *The Wynne Diaries*, London, 1935-40; and Mrs. James B. Wilbur, for James B. Wilbur, *Ira Allen, Founder of Vermont*, Cambridge, 1928.

Contents

Illustrations

Maps

About the Notes

The notes will be found on pages 189-220. In the text, referential notes are indicated by superior numbers in roman type; discussion notes by superior numbers in italics. In the note section, at the upper right-hand corner of each recto page and the upper left-hand corner of each verso page, will be found numbers indicating the pages of the text to which the notes on these two pages refer.

xii

Prologue: The Jay Treaty

"WHITHER IS MADNESS HURRYING YOU RESPECTING AMERICA? A WAR with her would be the summit and completion of ruin. England would thereby be more than ever endangered, and the country would be undone both in point of commerce, and perhaps even of internal tranquility." Thus wrote the Earl of Charlemont, in the fall of 1794, to a friend in London.¹ Although in this instance Charlemont's special concern was caused by a garbled newspaper report, America and Britain did seem near war during much of 1794, and many citizens of both countries shared his lordship's fear for the consequences. Fortunately for both nations —though some have regretted the high price America paid—the drift toward war was reversed by the Jay treaty, signed at Downing Street in November 1794. From that day until the spring of 1805, when Sir William Grant handed down the famous *Essex* decision, relations between the two countries were never seriously marred by the threat of war. Through a decade of world war and peace, successive governments on both sides of the Atlantic were able to bring about and preserve a cordiality which often approached genuine friendship.

In the winter of 1795 few men would have dared to predict such a development, yet the perspicacious Talleyrand-Périgord, then a private citizen visiting America, sketched its general outlines. He asserted that, although there was then strong feeling against Britain and sympathy for France,

America is . . . completely English, that is *England still has the advantage over France in drawing from the United States all benefit that one nation can draw from the existence of another . . . .*
The present discontents will pass. The order of November 6th . . . , the manner in which these orders were executed . . . , the Bermuda corsairs [will not be remembered]. . . . Equally forgotten will be the indirect aid given to the American cause by the success of French arms; and the gratitude will be neither more efficacious or longer-lived for the confirmation of independence than for its first achievement.

This would have been obvious to all, the Frenchman added, "had not the English government for ten years done all that it could think of the most likely to alienate the feelings of the Americans."²

In studying the period after 1794, it is easy to emphasize the quarrel with France or treat Anglo-American relations as a mere prelude to the controversies and recriminations which led to the War of 1812. A number of basic problems, notably impressment, seizures, and trade with the

1

British West Indies, were not definitively settled, and later they arose once more to plague the two governments. Yet even in these fields substantial if temporary progress was made, and this progress accompanied important advances elsewhere, most notably a transformation of American sentiment toward European politics. Such developments are too often overlooked, and for that reason the positive aspects of the period deserve special emphasis. However, they cannot be considered by themselves, in isolation from other events and factors. The treaty which paved the way, cultural and economic forces supporting the political settlement, the state of parties in the United States and Britain, and America's relations with England's great enemy are all parts of the story of the first Anglo-American rapprochement.

In 1794 the initial problem was the settlement of outstanding controversies, many growing out of the treaty of 1783. Even where the Canadian boundary was not in dispute, as it was in several areas, the Union Jack flew from forts on the American side of the line. Furthermore, the Indian war then being fought was blamed upon British intrigue among the western tribes. On the other hand, Englishmen protested that Americans refused to honor obligations incurred before the Revolution, often taking refuge behind state laws designed to obstruct the creditor. A Virginian expressed the general attitude of his fellow citizens when he told a Tory who returned to the United States that "he had not the Money, but if he had a House-full he would [not] . . . pay . . . any . . . British Debt."[3] To these various legacies of the Revolution were added new difficulties brought on by American neutrality. In the spring of 1794, a member of the British government wrote:

The neutral nations, as they call themselves . . . , are doing everything that they can do to feed the war. I make no doubt that we shall ultimately find means to discharge the obligation. In the mean time, many of their ships are brought in every day; and I do not believe that many escape the redoubled vigilance of our cruisers.[4]

British Orders in Council reflected the influence of such ideas, and the United States was the chief sufferer. Hearts both faint and bellicose believed that war was inevitable, although the wife of the Governor of Upper Canada took consolation from the fact that "the result must be speedily decisive."[5]

At this critical moment, John Jay was dispatched to London to negotiate a settlement. His dealings with the British government are too familiar to need detailed analysis, but the cautious friendliness of the Foreign Secretary, Lord Grenville, and his colleagues must not be ignored. Britain as well as the United States recognized the seriousness of the tension and was determined not to rush into hostilities. Soon after the American envoy's arrival, George III wrote Pitt advising against a prorogation of Parliament "at least till the Issue of Mr. Jay's negotiation is clearly seen—" Simcoe, commanding in the Canadian West, Governor-General Lord Dorchester, and George Hammond, the minister at Phila-

2

delphia who had become involved in an exchange of acid notes with American officials, all received orders to do nothing that would embarrass the negotiations.[6]

In two instances the Pitt government declined to adopt the suggestions of interested commercial factions which would have made negotiations much more difficult. One of the groups of creditors consulted by the government protested strenuously against the proposal to refer their claims to an arbitral commission. Yet Grenville persisted, preferring this solution to arduous negotiation for a lump-sum settlement, and his plan was embodied in the treaty. Merchants interested in the Canada trade asserted that surrender of the posts, particularly if not postponed for three or more years, would cripple the fur industry.[7] Grenville rejected their arguments, and evacuation of the posts was taken for granted in negotiating the treaty.

In addition to resisting the suggestions of merchant groups, the government showed throughout the negotiations that its attitude was flexible. An important concession was made to John Jay with regard to trade with India, a partial one respecting the British West Indies, leading the historian to wonder if greater gains might not have been secured by a more astute negotiator than the Chief Justice, even granting the obvious disadvantages under which he labored. The Pitt government showed that it was determined to make every possible effort to preserve peace by urging British merchants to proceed with normal commercial operations less than a fortnight after Jay's arrival.[8]

During the negotiations, Grenville circulated through the Cabinet a "Projet of Heads of Proposals to be made to Mr. Jay."[9] The Foreign Secretary knew that some American demands would have to be granted without cavil. His projet authorized surrender of the posts, though not until the summer of 1796. It suggested an arbitral commission to make awards to American shipowners for illegal seizures of their vessels in the West Indies and a similar body to settle British claims against delinquent debtors. Grenville attempted to insert the Rule of 1756 into the code proposed to govern the activities of the seizure commission, and his commercial projet, while generally unexceptionable, included two "jokers": no mention was made of British colonies, although a marginal note raised the possibility of opening the West Indies, and the draft provided that "no New Prohibitions shall be laid in either Country" upon ships or cargoes of any sort, thus preserving Britain's protective system and forestalling American retaliation.

The comments of only two of Grenville's colleagues have been preserved. Henry Dundas made a few minor criticisms, but he wrote, "the principles of your Projet I much approve of. . . . The Draft to Mr. Jay is perfectly right."[10] Lord Hawkesbury, Chairman of the Board of Trade, responded with a detailed point by point analysis which is interesting both because it demonstrates that even the most conservative Cabinet member recognized that American requests could not be rejected out of hand and because it shows that the government's acknowledged commercial expert was overruled in the interest of conciliation. Hawkesbury agreed that the posts must be surrendered, and he supported Grenville's suggestion that traffic across the Canadian-American boundary be free and open. He analyzed in great detail the proposed debt commission, endorsing Grenville's view that full recovery could not be hoped for but pointing out that British merchants had always recognized the dangers of extending credit in America and advanced their prices accordingly: "if the British Merchants should on the present Occasion, recover the whole of their Debts and Interest upon them, they will gain more than they had any Reason to expect." As for the dispute over ship seizures, Hawkesbury felt that there was error on both sides, but he agreed that "it will be wise . . . to bring these Disputes to a Settlement in as speedy and even as liberal a Manner as possible."

His Lordship was less favorably inclined toward commercial concession to the United States. He protested that American discriminatory legislation more than counterbalanced British restrictions. "Such is the State of the Trade: The most unequal and unjust with respect to Great Britain that can be conceived; and yet the Americans complain & there are People in this Country who support them." In response to Grenville's query about opening the West Indies to American ships, Lord Hawkesbury composed a long defense of the existing prohibition:

With respect to general Power and Command, if this Regulation is abolished, the United States will in short Time become Master in Effect of the West India Islands— . . . The Quantity of Shipping & Sailors which the Americans would obtain by the Abolition of this Regulation will add to their Naval Power in Proportion as it diminishes the Naval Power of Great Britain, and it will add to their Naval Power in those Seas where We have most Reason to be apprehensive of it.[11]

Despite Hawkesbury's eloquent protest, the Cabinet decided to permit American ships of seventy tons displacement or less to trade with the Caribbean colonies, provided that the exportation of tropical produce from the United States was prohibited. When Grenville had a draft of the entire treaty ready for Jay, he again asked Hawkesbury to comment. The Chairman of the Board of Trade gave this document, which closely parallels the actual treaty, his general approval. He endorsed all but one of the articles, adding:

I have made no reservations on the Article which relates to the commercial intercourse between the U. S. and the W. Indies. I consider this Point as irrevocably decided, against the opposition I have always entertained and publicly professed. To this part only of the present Transaction I object. . . . I wish for many reasons, that if there is to be any Cabinet on this point, on which we differ, I may not be summoned to it. My attendance may occasion discussion which cannot now be of any use.[12]

Many years later, Lord Grenville wrote, "My own impressions have always been favorable to . . . extended intercourse between the West India Islands and the United States."[13] If this was indeed his position in 1794, Hawkesbury's dogged opposition may have prevented the Foreign Secretary from making more than a partial concession to the United States. In any case, despite the opposition of the most important supporter of the Navigation System, and with full knowledge of the outcries sure to come from the shipping community, Pitt and Grenville pushed ahead. That the Senate declined to pay the required price in no way lessens the importance of the action, for, so far as Pitt and Grenville were concerned, the terms were fixed when the treaty was signed.

The opening of the British East Indies to American ships was not mentioned in Grenville's projet, nor does it seem to have been the subject of Cabinet discussion, although it raised two obvious problems. In the first place, the East India Company had a chartered monopoly, and it was questionable, both legally and as policy, whether this should be violated. Secondly, there was danger that the United States would soon seize the carriage of Indian goods to Europe from the inefficient East Indiamen. Nevertheless, Jay's request was granted; the result was an explosive growth of American commerce with India.

Jay and Grenville reached a final agreement in the middle of November. On the eighteenth, the Cabinet met in Grenville's office for four hours to go over the draft. No major difficulties developed, and the next day the two plenipotentiaries signed the treaty. England promised to evacuate the frontier posts, opened the East and (conditionally) the West Indies to American shipping, and agreed to arbitration of the debt, seizure, and boundary disputes. But the British government declined to end impressment, refused to accept a liberal definition of the rights of neutral commerce, and offered no compensation for slaves carried off during the Revolution.

Far from being completely satisfactory to the United States, the Jay treaty nevertheless was the first proof that independent America was important enough to secure any concessions from a major power. As a matter of fact, Pitt and Grenville were attacked by Charles James Fox for retreating in the face of American protests at the same time that they ignored the equally justified complaints of lesser nations, to which the Minister replied that when the treaty became public it would be obvious that it was not a dishonorable surrender to the United States.[14] But these criticisms came later; the signing of the treaty passed almost unnoticed in London newspapers, although identical articles in two ministerial papers stated:

The American treaty is the most fair, candid and honourable transaction that ever took place between two States, and as such reflects the greatest credit upon the wisdom of the Government of both Countries. Its probable permanency, and beneficial consequences upon such grounds will readily enter into the head of every well-minded man.[15]

Despite the exaggerated comments of the *Sun* and *True Briton*, the effect of the Jay treaty was delayed and cumulative, rather than instantaneous, largely because of the long struggle over ratification in America. But the agreement settled, or at least moderated, controversies which might have led to armed conflict and, most important of all, allowed the London and Philadelphia governments to develop new policies aimed at the solution rather than the exacerbation of Anglo-American difficulties.

Trans-Atlantic Ties 1

To EFFECT A TRUE RAPPROCHEMENT, A POLITICAL SETTLEMENT ALONE was not adequate. The governments had to be aware that national interests would be served by such a development, and contacts between the two peoples had to be strong enough to support it. Fortunately, these conditions were fulfilled in the decade following the Jay treaty, and an impressive structure was built, albeit slowly, to span the broad chasm across which the nations, their soldiers, and their politicians faced one another in 1794. Three of the piers supporting the bridge were close cultural, personal, and economic relations. These were constantly in the minds of the statesmen who guided the destinies of England and the United States.

Culturally, young America was heavily dependent upon Europe, chiefly upon England. In fact, a commentator on the last decade of the eighteenth century scarcely overstates the case when he says, "what is obvious about American culture . . . is that it is a steady, resolute, instinctive reproduction of contemporary English culture."[1] Fine arts, the theater, literature—all reflected the influence of Britain. Ralph Waldo Emerson's plea for America to throw off "the courtly muses of Europe" was still almost half a century away, its fulfillment at least equally remote.

Many of the foremost American painters of this period paid extended visits to England. At home, they could in general find neither the instruction, patronage, nor stimulation by example which were offered in Britain. Furthermore, the American public, in so far as it showed any interest in painting, virtually insisted upon British standards of taste. English influences harmed some artists, notably John Singleton Copley, whose work went steadily down hill after his arrival in London in 1775. Others developed their style and gained their first recognition in London, often through the agency of a fellow countryman, Benjamin West.

West was the favorite of George III and President of the Royal Academy for almost thirty years. A prominent historical painter, he was equally significant as the patron of Trumbull, Peale, Stuart, and Allston. Although he came to England in 1763 and remained for the rest of his life, Benjamin West never lost his affection for America. In 1798 he told a colleague in the Academy that he would return home "if He could obtain payment from the King of the great demand on him." Six years later he told the same friend, rather inaccurately, that the United States thirsted for art and artists:

West in our conversation said that were He 10 years younger *He w^d go to America*, where He was sure much might be done as the people had a strong disposition to the Arts, & it would be easy to encourage a spirit of rivalry . . . between the cities of Philadelphia & New York.—Trumbull . . ., He s^d sh^d settle at the latter place & He at the former, & raise the spirit as high as it could be.[2]

7

As an important figure in his own right, and as an advocate of things and persons American, West helped to improve the reputation of his homeland in Britain.

In the theater, contact was more exclusively in the nature of a one-way street. English plays dominated the American stage—Sheridan's *School for Scandal* was probably the most popular—and actors and actresses of just below the first rank traveled to the United States in a steady stream. Elizabeth (or Ann) Brunton Merry, who had once been thought likely to rival the famed Mrs. Siddons, was probably the most prominent Briton to appear on the American stage. She made her debut as Juliet at Philadelphia late in 1796 and was an instantaneous success, a fact which was soon reported in England and inspired many others to follow her example. The Yankees paid well; one British actress received £400 for a single appearance in the American capital.[3] In general, English commentators remarked favorably upon the interest the young nation showed in drama and music, although the American habit of smoking in the theater came in for occasional harsh comment.

American literature was somewhat farther advanced than the theater, although it often provoked scornful remarks in British periodicals. The *Edinburgh Review* said about all there was to say in its favor:

The truth is, that American genius has displayed itself, wherever inducements have been held out for its exertion. Their party pamphlets, though disgraced with much intemperance and scurrility, are written with a keenness and spirit, that is not often to be found in the old world; and their orators . . . frequently possess a vehemence, correctness, and animation, that would command the admiration of any European audience.[4]

With the exception of some scientific reporting, these were almost the only areas in which Americans were capable of competing upon equal terms with contemporary Englishmen. In general, Britain was substantially in advance of the United States. Charles Brockden Brown, the first important American novelist, came into print during this period, and his stories were closely modeled after the Gothic style so popular in Great Britain. Mrs. Rowson, author of the great success *Charlotte Temple*, lived for some time in England and also drew heavily upon British prototypes.

British novelists and more serious writers were popular in the United States. This was doubtless in part because British publishers were still able to undersell the Americans, according to William Cobbett, in all fields except "Bibles, and other common books." Edmund Burke was particularly widely read, and the memory of his pre-Revolutionary sympathies doubtless gained wider acceptance for his criticisms of the French. Hannah More also had a ready public. When William Pitt learned that a shipment of forty thousand of her anti-Jacobin pamphlets had gone to America, he sought out the author to tell her that "he had not met with anything in a long time that had pleased him more, than that such sort of reading was gaining ground in America." The precise influence of such writings is obviously indeterminable, but the dominance of British literature must have had powerful, if indirect effects. When, in 1801, the British government proposed excises which would have priced English books out of the American market, Cobbett complained with some justification that "thus, while we lose the trade, we shall also lose the minds of the people."[5]

While Americans could learn of Britain from books published in England, their trans-Atlantic cousins were not so fortunate. For information on the United States and the American character, they had to depend upon the reports either of self-constituted experts who had never crossed the Atlantic or of travelers whose predominant motive was, as Allan Nevins observes, utilitarian inquiry and whose comments on general trends were consequently more often shallow than acute.

Although Professor Nevins adds that "Most of the travellers came over hopefully and returned with their hopes confirmed,"[6] this was by no means always true. The widely read work of Isaac Weld, the anti-emigration tract of John S. Hull, and the poems in which Tom Moore attacked America's "love of gold, that meanest rage," were scarcely expressions of faith in the United States. But sometimes such treatments were so unfair that a Whig journal was roused to complaint; thus, when Richard Parkinson, a middle-class farmer, published his report on America in 1805, the *Edinburgh Review* responded with a highly critical review, protesting both against Parkinson's work and extravagant interpretations of it.[7] Then, too, many reporters, particularly those whose work was designed to encourage emigration, were friendly. Henry Wansey, who went to the United States to investigate the production of wool, later published a volume which included scarcely a word of criticism. William Priest's *Travels* were generally favorable, a fact which doubtless incited the Americanophobe *Anti-Jacobin Review* to scorn them as a volume "which has little to amuse, and still less to instruct." John Davis' book, published in 1803 with an authorized dedication to Thomas Jefferson, was generally friendly, but Davis shied away from political comment. Outdoing all others in size and in warmth of feeling was William Winterbotham's work, four volumes whose tenor is adequately portrayed by two representative chapter titles: "Of the Advantages which the United States Possess over European Countries" and "Of the Prospects and Advantages of a European Settler in the United States."[8]

The most important English visitor at the close of the century was certainly William Cobbett, who came to the United States in 1792. As the editor of *Porcupine's Gazette* and the author of pamphlet after pamphlet, he was the chief reliance of the Federalists in the battle with Bache, Duane, and the other Republican publicists. Cobbett's language was colorful and extreme. Robert Liston, the British minister, praised him as a "man of uncommon ability and strength of mind" whose pamphlets had worked "with equal spirit and success." Liston regretted, however, that it was impossible to convince Cobbett to end "that gross personal abuse which has frequently marred their complete effect."[9]

Cobbett's works, usually bearing his pseudonym of "Peter Porcupine," were widely read in Great Britain. In 1800, a combination of legal persecution and disgust with America drove him from the United States. He returned to England; was introduced to government leaders by George Hammond, and started a·London newspaper called the *Porcupine. Porcupine's* first issue proclaimed its anti-Americanism,[10] and this policy was maintained until the journal died at the end of 1801, having cost the editor £450 of his savings. More successful was the *Works of Peter Porcupine*, a collection of his American tracts brought out in 1801. Despite its bulk and high price—twelve volumes for five guineas—the work sold well, finding its way into the libraries of such men as the Foreign Secretary, the Prince of Wales, and Henry Addington. This venture was soon followed by another. With the support of William Windham, an extreme conservative and the self-confessed heir of Edmund Burke, Cobbett initiated in January of 1802 his *Annual Register*, installments of which appeared weekly. Criticism of Henry Addington and William Pitt was his chief stock in trade, but Cobbett found time to insert an occasional jibe at the United States, then suffering, as he conceived, under the rule of the atheist from Monticello.

Since Cobbett and Isaac Weld had the largest audience of all the travelers, it is inaccurate to say that Britons got a generally favorable impression of the United States from these reports. However, the plethora of works which appeared demonstrated a general interest in American subjects, and in the long run interest was likely to lead to greater understanding. Even Weld and Cobbett had to admit that there were some good things about America, and Cobbett specifically attacked American politicians rather than the ordinary citizen. Cobbett, Weld, the *Anti-Jacobin Review*, and their allies were so opinionated on domestic questions that even a moderately intelligent reader could see that their verdicts in other fields as well had to be viewed with caution. These factors, and the considerable opposition offered to the Weld-Cobbett point of view, had their effect. With the exception of a brief period in 1799 and 1800, British public opinion seems to have been favorably inclined toward the United States. Any estimate is necessarily tentative, but the diplomatic rapprochement apparently proceeded hand in hand with a moderate softening of Revolutionary rancor and an improved English attitude toward the United States.

The interdependence of English and American trade also encouraged good relations. As Talleyrand wrote, "the American merchant is tied to England not only by the nature of his business, the need for credit and the weight of credit already attained, but also by the law which the will of the customer irresistibly imposes on him." Alexander Baring told his countrymen that, however great a blow to their pride the success of the

American Revolution might have been, its economic effects were negligible.[11] No other power threatened British primacy in the American market.

Some English concerns had branch offices in the United States, and scores of others established close ties there. The house of Baring was already the most important London firm specializing in American trade; among its correspondents in Philadelphia were Willing & Francis, Stephen Girard, and William Bingham, a trio whose importance can scarcely be over-emphasized. American merchants engaged in trade with Britain were among the loudest advocates of friendly relations. Even Girard, at first a highly vocal partisan of France, changed his tune as time went on; he saw that American commercial interests were best served by an expansion of trade with England. Like other merchants, Girard benefited from the extension of British credit. London houses usually permitted their correspondents to draw two-thirds to three-quarters of the value of their shipments to Britain upon dispatch. This encouraged reinvestment which in turn led to the further expansion of British credit.[12]

British capital was also transferred to the United States in the form of investments in land, although the size of the flow never equaled American hopes. Here, too, the Barings were heavily involved. On a visit in 1795, young Alexander Baring bought over a million acres in Maine from William Bingham and Henry Knox on very favorable terms.[13] Sir William Pulteney and an associate purchased a huge tract in western New York for seventy-five thousand pounds in 1791, and Pulteney later spent nearly three times that amount in promotional schemes, chiefly through the agency of Charles Williamson, a British citizen who moved to America to manage the property.[14] An East India nabob, Thomas Law, came to the United States to speculate in land in the District of Columbia, and even Charles Vancouver managed a modest purchase of sixty thousand acres in Kentucky, although, as he said, they

afford me no revenue; and as the land lies out of the reach of that Society, in which Mrs. Vancouver has been educated and accustomed to, I am extremely unwilling to subject her, to the painful necessity of making it the seat of our future residence—[15]

Although British diplomats in America consistently warned that such investments were very risky, land titles uncertain, and fraud prevalent, capital steadily flowed across the Atlantic in the early nineties. The hope of a European market—and that meant chiefly a British one—contributed to the speculative mania in America. In 1797, primarily because there was a recession so sharp that the Bank of England was forced to suspend specie payment, British purchases dwindled. This in turn ended the land boom in America, ruining many speculators. The American representative in London wrote in 1798:

You w^d be astonished with the accounts that I could give you of the number of Persons now in Europe charged with the Sale of Land—the times are not favorable, and besides so many irregularities have already been practiced, that all the world are upon their guard and full of Suspi[cion].[16]

11

American securities and government paper attracted somewhat more conservative British capital, with the Barings once again playing a major role. United States bonds and bank stock suffered a severe setback in the London market in the spring of 1794, but the success of Jay's mission caused prices to take a sharp turn upward. Thereafter there was a fairly steady demand for United States securities in Britain, and Alexander Baring felt that a few simple changes would have opened up a much larger market.[17] Baring's house carried out the most spectacular transaction, also a very profitable one, when it coöperated with Hope & Company of Amsterdam to finance the Louisiana Purchase. More than half of the stock of the United States Bank was held abroad by 1798, and the proportion rose steadily. In addition to these holdings and to the foreign funded debt of the United States, twenty million dollars of the domestic debt was in foreign hands in 1795, thirty millions by 1801. In 1803, British citizens were reported to own nearly sixteen millions worth of American securities, almost exactly half the total held abroad.[18] Britain had definitely established herself as the largest foreign holder of the bonds and bank stock of the United States.

An even greater hostage for peace was the commerce which flowed between the two countries. This, too, was not long diverted from its normal channels by the Revolution. The United States provided the British Isles and certain colonial possessions, particularly the West Indies, with raw materials which were vital to the imperial economy. In return, England shipped tremendous quantities of colonial produce and finished goods, largely woolens, to the United States. Both countries struggled to capture the largest possible share of the carriage of these cargoes, but there was little argument about the mutual advantages of the trade itself.

American exports to the Empire were almost exclusively raw materials, although manufactures were carried to India. The most spectacular growth during this period took place in the cotton trade, a direct result of Eli Whitney's invention of the cotton gin in 1793. From near zero, the quantity of cotton exported rose to six million pounds in 1796, twenty million in 1801, and thirty-five million in 1804. America's share of British cotton imports, less than one-sixth of 1 per cent from 1786 to 1790, rose to almost 25 per cent a decade later, and in 1802 importation from the United States outstripped that from Britain's own colonial possessions. Most of this trade went to Liverpool, which was thus able to replace London as the most important cotton importing center.[19]

Despite the efforts of imperial authorities to develop British North America as a source of supply, the British West Indies depended upon the United States for food. America provided 90 per cent of the flour and meal imported by the islands, two-thirds of the grain, and roughly half of the salted meat and dried fish.[20] Grain and flour were also exported to the British home islands, chiefly in years of poor harvest there. In times of shortage, both the actual receipt of foodstuffs and the mere

12

announcement that supplies were on their way across the Atlantic helped to bring prices down. When Europe as well as England had a poor harvest, Britain was doubly dependent upon importation from America. Thus, for example, the American minister reported in 1800 that "America is the only Country from which a considerable and certain importation is looked for, and such is the deficiency of Corn that all we can spare and of every Species will find here a high and certain Market."[21] In the worst harvest years, the Pitt government granted subsidies on foreign grain to encourage importation. The rate of subsidy offered to America was substantially higher than that given to Europe. Pitt and Lord Hawkesbury defended this concession against anti-Americans and the advocates of laissez faire, explaining that it was designed to equalize the risk of American and European shippers.[22]

The value of all American exports to the British Empire rose by 300 per cent from 1795 to 1800, and the boom year of 1801 brought a temporary increase even beyond that figure. Then European peace caused a sharp recession, but there was another upward turn when war was renewed in 1803. Exports to France, which topped those to Britain in 1795 and 1797, fell definitely behind thereafter. From 1802 to 1812, an annual average of 45 per cent of all American domestic exports went to British possessions. This was by far the most valuable portion of the American export trade, just as it was the means by which Britain acquired the largest share of her imports.[23]

Similarly, the United States was Britain's best customer. Habit, ready credit, existing obligations, and wartime conditions made it certain that the United States would continue to look first to Britain. The demand was so great that more than one-quarter of all British exports went to the United States in 1800, and from 1793 to 1800 America purchased more goods in England than did all of Europe combined. Even Bristol, though heavily involved in trade with the West Indies, cleared 20 per cent of all outbound vessels for the United States. Close relations between America and Liverpool began in these years, spurred both by the explosive growth of cotton imports and the increasing exportation of finished goods to the United States. In 1793, American tonnage trading with Liverpool was outstripped by that of a number of other nations; by 1805, more than half of all foreign arrivals and departures were American. The aggregate importance of the whole trade is well indicated by the statistics: from 1795 to 1801 the United States imported British goods officially valued at two hundred and sixty million dollars; during the same period, purchases from the French Empire, the next most important source, totaled just over one hundred millions. Even in the period from 1802 to 1804, during part of which Europe was at peace, Britain provided approximately half of all the goods America imported.[24]

Woolens were the largest factor in this commerce, although other English manufactures and the produce of both India and the West Indies were also important. The official value of woolen goods shipped to the United States doubled from 1790 to 1799; during the same period, America's share of British woolen exports rose from 30 to 40 per cent. Agents from firms all over the British Isles, but particularly from the West Riding of Yorkshire, traveled to the United States to capture this trade for their concerns, usually remaining several years and establishing close ties with American merchants before returning home.[25]

This description gives a general picture of the economic relationship between England and America, its size, variety, importance to each country, and extensive ramifications.[26] The obvious question is: Did the trade, or the men interested in the trade, have discernible influence on the political relations of the two nations?

The interest of the American business community in the preservation of cordial relations with England is well known. Commercial influences played no small part in the birth of the Jay mission and the final approval of the agreement made at London. Since England was the United States' most important market, and since the Royal Navy ruled the waves, the commercial interests were particularly concerned that no small differences should cause a break with England. Fisher Ames voiced their general feeling when he wrote, "peace with that power is to be sought most earnestly—as all our floating capital w^d soon fall a sacrifice" in case of a rupture.[27] Throughout this period, the spokesmen for commerce, although often outraged by British seizures, were more favorably inclined toward England than any other group. The political influence of the business community, particularly under the Federalists, was far from negligible, and men like Hamilton, King, Morris, and Adams were well aware of the important role which Anglo-American commerce played in the development of the United States. Jefferson, too, recognized that trade with England was an integral part of the economic structure and, while ready to use it as a diplomatic weapon, did not cast it away lightly.

In England, interested commercial groups also supported conciliation. Businessmen urged settlement with the United States in 1794, for example, and merchants trading to the West Indies were later claimed, by an opponent of the concession, to have been instrumental in getting the government to agree to a conditional opening of the islands to American ships. In 1801, Liverpool merchants engaged in trade with the United States organized under the chairmanship of the American consul, a former Virginian who consistently worked for closer relations. At about the same time, London houses trading with America endorsed a proposed reform of the Admiralty Courts sought by the United States. On the other hand, Manchester, later a stronghold of free trade and conciliation, was staunchly imperialistic as late as 1800, shifting its attitude only when it became apparent that British colonies could provide neither the market nor the raw cotton required by its expanding industry.[28]

In one of his sour moments, William Cobbett wrote from America:

I am afraid of an American faction amongst the British merchants and manufacturers; for though I cannot suppose that Britain will ever have a King and Ministry weak enough to sacrifice the honour and the permanent good of the whole nation to a set of selfish traders, yet I know, that, despicable as these wretches are, in other respects, they may teaze, they may clamour, misrepresent and embarrass. . . . I can assure you, that the people here place no little reliance on the effect of such a noise.[29]

Although men like Baring and Pulteney certainly commanded the respectful attention of the Cabinet, no "American faction" ever brought serious pressure to bear upon the government during this period. As Alexander Baring said, "the great interest in American intercourse is with the manufacturers scattered all over the country, who are never able to act in a body with a weight corresponding to their importance."[30]

On the other hand, the government had to take account of the huge amount of capital tied up in trade with the United States. As Henry Dundas wrote at a time of controversy, "The Americans are egregiously in the wrong, but they are so much in debt to this country that we scarcely dare to quarrel with them."[31] Consuls in America were required to submit detailed reports on the state of trade, and particularly the British share of it. The correspondence exchanged between Downing Street and the legation in the United States is full of consideration of the same subject, and American representatives in London generally found the Cabinet very well informed. As Cobbett stated in 1802, Britannia's statesmen were imperatively concerned in the study of those nations

who have it in their power to contribute to her safety or her danger; and . . . there is no nation upon earth, which possesses this power to so great an extent as the United States of America, a country which, at all times, has the absolute command of nearly ten millions of British capital, which receives nearly one-third of all our exported manufactures, and which has half as much shipping as Great Britain herself.[32]

Since both the Pitt and Addington governments were particularly attentive to the interests of the British economy, they tried to maintain the profitable trade between England and the United States.

A student of a slightly later period has said with a degree of truth that "British industrialism is a constant factor . . . in the shifts and changes of Anglo-American relations. Its presence can be found, more often as a guiding instinct than as a formulated policy, where it might least be expected."[33] This influence, although shadowy in the period from 1795 to 1805, did exist, despite the fact that British industry was just beginning to depend upon America as its chief foreign market and source of raw materials, and despite the fact, too, that businessmen were for the first time finding their way into the House of Commons in substantial numbers. As the correspondence of British statesmen frequently shows, they were well aware of the importance of trade with America, and the record of concessions made by the Pitt government and its willingness to discuss commercial matters freely with American representatives confirms this judgment. Taking note of the volume of Anglo-American trade and its importance to both nations, the journal which spoke for the most orthodox wing of the government commented, "We trust the rulers of the two countries will ever suffer these considerations to predominate in their minds, and to regulate their conduct."[34]

In the years after 1794, through the mists of past bickering, England and the United States began dimly to see that, in the rather rhapsodic and un-Scottish words of Sir John Sinclair, "though our governments are now distinct, the people are in fact the same, without any possible inducement to quarrel, if they know their respective interests, and with every reason to wish each other well, and to promote their mutual prosperity."[35] The gusty winds of nationalism, which have not completely died even in our own day, blew up a new storm cloud after 1805 which temporarily obscured the vision. But, in part because of the force of economic factors, and aided by cultural ties, the diplomats of England and the United States were able for a short time to steer a course in the general direction, at least, of the beacon indicated by the Scottish baronet.

Empire and Republic 2

THE ENGLAND OF 1795 WAS NOT THE POWERFUL AND OFTEN SELF-SATIS-fied Britain of the years after the bloody carnage at Mont St. Jean. The early years of the struggle against France were indeed "Years of Endur-ance,"[1] a harsh epoch of defeat after defeat (save only on the ocean), of the rupture of coalition after coalition, of hardship and scarcity at home. The "consols," a traditional index of Britain's situation, dropped below sixty, finally touching bottom in 1797 at fifty-three, a level never before reached except during the worst days of the American Revolution. Seven-teen ninety-five was a particularly critical year. At home, failure of the harvest forced wheat up to 108s. a quarter, public meetings urged peace and an extension of the suffrage, and George III himself was stoned on the Mall and shot at with an air gun. Abroad, Holland, which had made peace with France in 1794, entered the war against her old ally. Spain, later to follow the Dutch course, retired from the conflict, as did Russia, leaving Britain to shoulder most of the burden alone. By the end of the year it was thought advisable, for both domestic and diplomatic considera-tions, to insert a passage in the King's Speech promising to negotiate with France if the opportunity offered. Even before the worst of the catastro-phies, William Pitt was gloomy and disconsolate. One of his most intimate friends wrote, "his Spirits are not easily affected, but there is enough new[s] in various Quarters to try the best Nerves any Man ever had."[2]

The one stable factor was the parliamentary position of the ministry. The massive weight of royal influence was firmly enlisted on the side of the Cabinet, and, the year before, that wing of the Whig opposition which shared Edmund Burke's fear of the French Revolution had joined the government after a suitable amount of haggling over place and prefer-ment. There were, as always, disagreements within the Cabinet, as well as between that body and the King, but for several years to come Opposi-tion motions in the House of Commons were regularly beaten down by the combined strength of the King's men, Pittites, and Portland Whigs.

The reigning monarch, George III, was far from a mere cipher. He expected to be (and was) consulted by the government on all major de-cisions, and his departure for a summer holiday at Weymouth was a welcome relief from interference at the Foreign Office. The King almost always advocated simple and direct policies, writing on one occasion that "Italian [style] politics are too complicated paths for my understanding." During this period George never lost sight of what he conceived to be the paramount aim of British policy: forcible restoration of the Bourbon monarchy. He refused to support compromise or entertain the fears of faint hearts. "I believe," he wrote, that England should "place some confidence in naval Skill & British Valor to supply want of numbers: I own I am too true an Englishman to have ever adopted the more modern & ignoble mode of respecting equal numbers on all occasions." American affairs apparently did not particularly interest the King. At formal meetings with Americans he was correct and even friendly. In 1797 he spoke to Rufus King "in the most explicit manner of the wisdom of the Amer. Gov. and of the abilities and great worth of the Characters she produced & employed," adding that he believed George Washington to be the greatest of living men.[3] But this was mere levee conversation; the monarch's private correspondence scarcely mentions the United States, and George probably only subordinated and perhaps modified his ancient prejudices in the face of a powerful threat to British security.

William Pitt, Chancellor of the Exchequer and First Lord of the Treasury or, in the jargon of the day, "the Minister," was a handsome if rather haughty man. In 1783 his father's name, crown support, and the political bankruptcy of rival leaders brought him to Downing Street at twenty-four. For ten years he labored with much success to regain the political and economic ground lost during the American Revolution, but the wars of the French Revolution raised new problems with which he found it more difficult to deal. As J. Holland Rose has written, "His nature was far better suited to the decade of reconstruction than to that of revolution." Cabinet colleagues complained that Pitt was too cautious, or that he too often paid inordinate attention to the voice last at his ear. Certainly his war strategy was often ill-conceived and rarely successful. Yet his preëminent abilities and boundless self-confidence preserved his supremacy in the Cabinet and before the nation. Speaking of their disagreements, William Wilberforce once wrote, "The difference arose commonly from his sanguine temper leading him to give credit to information which others might distrust, and to expect that doubtful contingencies would have a more favorable issue than others might venture to anticipate."[4] At the same time, rather paradoxically, Pitt was essentially a pragmatist. His wartime strategy was generally designed to meet immediate problems, and this seems no less true with respect to much of his policy toward the United States.

William Wyndham Grenville, Lord Grenville, Pitt's Foreign Secretary, shared many of the qualities of his chief, to whom he was related both by blood and marriage. Like the Minister, Grenville was a man of great ability. Even more than Pitt, he was cold in appearance and forbidding in personality; the wife of a Cabinet member once complained that during a whole day at Grenville's house she had never exchanged a word with him. The Secretary's chief failing was one which he himself recognized: "I am not competent to the management of men." Many respected him, but few could easily tolerate his argumentativeness, dogmatism, and obstinacy. He scorned public opinion as much as the advice of those with whom he worked. Commenting on the clamor for peace in 1797, he wrote that the government would be able to do much more for the people "if they would be quiet and suffer themselves to be saved." Nevertheless, there is much to be admired in the Foreign Secretary. His service to the nation, unlike that of so many of his contemporaries, was inspired neither by ambition nor place-seeking, but by true patriotism which, "though confined and cold, was pure."[5] In 1794, he cheerfully offered to resign to make room in the Cabinet for the Duke of Portland, leader of the war Whigs. As Foreign Secretary, he devoted tremendous amounts of time and energy to his task, carrying piles of dispatch boxes home to Cleveland Row or Dropmore in the evening. His grasp of detail and apparent good judgment caused the Minister to rely heavily on him. In marked contrast to other men who served as Foreign Secretary under Pitt, Grenville had only once to submit to being by-passed by a private agent reporting directly to his superior.

Although Grenville must bear part of the responsibility for the limitations of British war policy, his attitude toward the United States was imaginative and perceptive. As a young man, though not willing to accept unreservedly Lord Shelburne's vision of Anglo-American reconciliation, he gave "a conscientious Vote in general approbation of the Peace [of 1783]; a judgment which experience and reflection have abundantly confirmed." A decade later, he shared with Pitt chief credit for the renewal of a conciliatory policy toward the United States. His attitude toward overseas trade was generally liberal, which made him more willing to listen to American requests; in his own words, he refused "to give in to Lord Hawkesbury's doctrine that commerce is to be sacrificed to navigation—the principal to the accessory." Grenville's hot temper made him fully capable of losing patience with the United States, as he did in 1799, and after he left the Foreign Office his mistrust of democracy caused him to criticize the administration of Jefferson as "*a Mob Government . . .* too weak to carry its own measures into effect."[6] But as Foreign Secretary, from 1795 to 1801, he directed his country down the path of reconciliation and was probably the major architect of the rapprochement between England and America.

Henry Dundas, the War Secretary, was a man of a very different type. Grenville was reserved, aristocratic, intensely English, the epitome of the austere statesman; Dundas was jovial, democratic (though he always had his eyes on the peerage), obviously Scottish, and the *ne plus ultra* of political managers. His control of Scotland and of Indian patronage were vital factors in the maintenance of the government. Dundas was no orator—"Miserably Scottish in his accent, and inelegant in arrangement and diction"[7]—but, unlike Grenville, he knew how to manage men. In fact, his passion for conciliation and management in part justified the common complaint that he lacked principle.

Dundas' department, which he managed with singularly less succcess than he did India and St. Stephens, had little direct bearing upon relations with the United States. Nevertheless, because Dundas was a member of the inner trio of government, his attitude was important. He had been a follower of Lord North and voted against the conciliation plan of 1778, but fifteen years later Dundas was esteemed a liberal in general, and on American affairs in particular. In 1803, Rufus King wrote of Dundas (then Lord Melville), "he is both liberal and decided, and the latter is a characteristic rarely to be met with in the public stations of this Country."[8] During this decade, Dundas usually supported concessions to the United States, yet it seems evident that this was not a matter of sentiment, nor even a realization of the growing importance of the United States. Dundas' liberality of view sprang chiefly from his belief in pragmatic solutions, his willingness to tamper with the Navigation System in the interest of the prosecution of the war, and his personal feuds with a number of monopoly groups. From the American point of view, the attractive thing about the War Secretary was the fact that he did not allow prejudices and preconceptions to stand in the way of concessions to the United States.

No such compliment need be paid to the Chairman of the Board of Trade, Lord Hawkesbury. Born plain Charles Jenkinson, this gentleman, aided by devotion to duty and conservative principles, became first a baron and then, in 1796, Earl of Liverpool. His second promotion caused a Whig journal to comment that "The Earl of LIVERPOOL has changed his names so often, that one might suspect he was ashamed of them, and, like those who have brought a name into suspicion, changes it for another to which no disgrace is attached."[9] Hawkesbury was cold, grasping, ambitious for himself and his son, and an inveterate placemonger. But his official position, unflagging energy, and wide knowledge of the field gave him great influence in discussions of commercial policy. His hostile spirit and devotion to the tenets of the Navigation Acts were factors which tended to hold back a rapprochement.

Pitt, Grenville, Dundas, Hawkesbury—these were the most important men in the Cabinet, particularly with respect to American policy. Portland, at the Home Office, commanded little respect among his colleagues and had almost no influence in their councils. William Windham was so wrapped up in schemes, usually wildly impractical, for royalist landings on the French coast that he seldom considered relations with the United States. No more attention to America was paid by Earl Spencer, the capable if unimaginative First Lord of the Admiralty, or the lesser members of the Cabinet. With some advice from Hawkesbury, the "big three" made the decisions. It speaks well for them that, despite a rivalry between Dundas and Grenville, policy toward the United States was never allowed to become the football of factional strife.

In 1795, the Pitt government was strong enough to beat back Opposition attacks with little difficulty. "The general Composition of both

Houses," the King wrote, "is such as all friends to the Constitution must rejoice at." The election of 1796 further strengthened the government's position. In the face of this juggernaut, the Whigs committed what G. M. Trevelyan has called "the great derilection of duty known as 'the Secession.' " Meeting at the home of Lord Holland in October 1797, the Opposition decided to quit the House of Commons. Fox retired to St. Anne's Hill and happy domesticity with Mrs. Armistead, and only a small corporal's guard, commanded by Tierney, remained to fight a covering action. The result was virtual one-party government, and an end to stirring debate. As one young blood wrote, "Nothing can equal the insipidity and dullness of the House of Commons in consequence of the secession of Opposition."[10]

Fox, Lord Lansdowne, and their followers, including Richard Brinsley Sheridan, frequently praised the republican United States. Sheridan once remarked, "America remains, neutral, prosperous, and at peace. . . . Observe her name and government rising above the nations of Europe with a simple but commanding dignity which wins at once the respect, the confidence, and the affection of the world."[11] Whig dinners toasted the United States; Whig newspapers supported American complaints against the Royal Navy. Yet one cannot escape the suspicion that the friendly sentiments of the Opposition were paraded chiefly as mirrors in which to reflect an unfavorable image of the government. Although Thomas Jefferson welcomed it, Charles James Fox's return to office in 1806 was not accompanied by a fundamental melioration of British policy, and at least one acquaintance questioned the depth of Fox's friendship for America: "I know that he has a strong prejudice in favor of this country, but I should like to know whether it is not confined merely to the theory of the Constitution which they profess."[12] In any case, sincere or not, Fox and his friends had little influence upon British diplomacy from 1795 to 1801.

Furthermore, government policy toward the United States did not present as attractive a target as it once had. The crisis of 1794 apparently caused the ministry to adopt a policy of conciliation, although of course not all that America demanded in succeeding years was freely conceded, nor anything that would compromise vital British interests. There was much logic behind a policy of limited concession. Events had shown that it might easily be possible to force the young nation into war, something that Britain could not well risk during the conflict with France. The imperative need for American-borne cargoes was a further factor arguing for a reconciliation, as was the steady economic and political advance of the United States following the ratification of the Constitution. Sometime before the French reached the same conclusion, the Pitt government seems to have realized that such a nation could not be handled with contempt and contumely. One cannot state without reservation that Downing Street reasoned in this manner, for nowhere in the official correspondence are these factors weighed and general lines of policy laid down. There is however a mass of evidence, most convincing in the aggregate, that for these or other reasons Pitt and Grenville changed their tack in 1794 or 1795.

A number of well-informed Americans thought that such was the case. Shortly after completing his negotiations, John Jay wrote home, "I do really believe, that this government means to give conciliatory measures with the United States a full and fair trial." Two and a half months later he reported in the same vein to Washington, adding perhaps too hopefully that even Hawkesbury did not oppose this policy. A year later Gouverneur Morris, who knew British leaders intimately, explained to a skeptical John Quincy Adams that the Cabinet was "well disposed to America. . . . They have made their arrangements upon a plan that comprehends the neutrality of the United States, and are anxious that it should be preserved." Rufus King apparently agreed, for he wrote to Washington just before the latter left the Presidency:

I think that I am not deceived in supposing that a sincere and general desire exists in this country to live in harmony and friendship with us. The disposition is however enfettered and enfeebled by Prejudices and Opinions connected with the national commerce and marine, which make the Government slow and cautious in every step which has a reference to these important concerns.[13]

The statements of American Anglophiles, however, are far less impressive evidence of the existence of a policy of conciliation than British testimony, even when it is only indirect, perhaps negative. For example, the Pitt government only mildly rebuked Hammond's successor when, in direct contravention of the colonial system, he permitted an American agent for seamen to go to the West Indies. And when Robert Liston responded that "my opinion is so strong that such is the right way for G. Britain to manage these people . . . [that unless explicitly ordered to the contrary] you must lay your account with always finding me lean to the side of conciliation & kindness & concession,"[14] this expression of principle drew forth no contrary orders, nor even a hint that the ministry wanted Liston to adopt any other course. Three years later Liston's wife, who worried about the Foreign Secretary's opinion of her husband, was reassured by a correspondent who had talked at length with Grenville:

this Country is anxious to keep the Americans in good humour, and the Man through whose *Address this is the best arranged*, must naturally please the most. I only hope that the A[mericans] will not be *too* sensible how much their good will is courted, because should they know *it well* they will be harder to manage.[15]

The existence of a policy of friendship was further demonstrated by criticisms of it in 1799 and 1800. Thomas Maitland, a British general on a special mission to Philadelphia in the spring of 1799, protested against the many concessions made to America, arguing that "by Conciliation you will never effect [your object;] . . . were less solicitude shewn to gain the good Graces of the American Government, We might possibly be more likely to possess it."[16] Grenville himself came, for a time, to share Maitland's feelings. In a stormy interview with the American minister in 1799, he complained that America had taken advantage of England's good will:

Ever since Mr. Jay's arrival here we have pursued . . . measures of conciliation towards the U. S. and have cherished a disposition to overlook every unpleasant occurance we met with, but I must say that we have not seen a like temper & disposition on the part of the U. S. and it is easy to foresee that the spirit of conciliation must exhaust itself.[17]

Several months later, Grenville repeated the same sentiments in a communication giving Robert Liston permission to return to Britain for consultation. The Secretary wrote, "it may become very necessary for us to reconsider our System as with respect to that country." In reply, Liston urged a continuation of the old policy; he stated that "The advantages to be ultimately reaped from a perseverance in the line of conduct which G. Britain has adopted for the last four years appear to my mind to be infallible and of infinite magnitude."[18]

The reports of Americans in England, Liston's consistent policy of conciliation, Maitland's complaints against concessions to America, and the exchange between Liston and Grenville on "the line of conduct which G. Britain has adopted" suggest that there was a definite shift from a rigid, uncompromising policy to one of friendship. Succeeding chapters will show that Britain made conciliatory gestures in a wide range of fields; these actions certainly fit into a pattern which suggests a definite plan. Admittedly, the evidence is not conclusive, but it seems to indicate that, in the words of a secret agent of the British government, "the lights of this day have eradicated every argument which might have opposed my favorite policy towards America— . . . *conciliation & consolidation.*"[19]

This policy was particularly wise since, despite its youth, the United States had already passed from feeble infancy to bumptious adolescence and expected to be treated as an adult in the family of nations. The American nation was already a leading maritime power, its population was rising at the rate of about 35 per cent per decade, and the government was gradually establishing domestic stability, both political and economic. In 1795, the administration was in the hands of the Federalists, who, by and large, spoke for the commercial and maritime interests. They had, at some cost, patched up the quarrel with England and secured an agreement designed to end differences with Spain. In the West, at least for the moment, the army was making headway against the Indians; behind it, and on its flanks, the probing flow of settlement advanced from previously constructed trans-Appalachian bases. In the older sections of the country, economic conditions were generally good, and it was a maxim of Hamiltonian policy that the strength of the American economy and above all of the government's financial system should not be risked by unwise ventures in the field of foreign relations.

In 1795, George Washington entered on the last and probably the stormiest portion of his service as President. Although Federalist in his approach, Washington had generally managed to maintain a position above party strife until the time of the Jay treaty. Then for the first time he came under serious and far-reaching partisan attack. "It was his country and France which gave him fame in defiance of England," a Republican pamphleteer wrote, "and it is his country and France which in defiance of England will take it away again."[20] Even among Federalists, Washington's reserve, the fruit both of intent and natural shyness, made him more respected than loved. His levees were highly formal, perhaps more so than those of George III, and he was rarely known to relax in public. Devotion to his country, moral integrity and determination, and a real capacity for leadership were among the characteristics that made him a great man. "With regard to his intellectual Powers," an English diplomat wrote without great exaggeration,

there was neither the quickness nor the brilliance of genius, which seizes rapidly, and impresses instantly. . . . Perhaps his natural shyness and reserve gave an appearance of hesitation and confusedness to his manner:—perhaps the System of perpetual Caution (for it *was* System) which he imposed on every word and every look, prevented him from exhibiting . . . the indication of a quick and pregnant Intellect. Be this as it may, he was a Man unquestionably of sound sense and of excellent Judgement.[21]

The President shared the general belief that America should remain aloof from European wars. Initially, he looked with favor upon the French Revolution, but he was repelled by the bloodletting and the attack on property which followed in the train of the march on the Bastille. By 1795, Washington had outgrown most of his prejudices against England; he was respected in that country and carried on an extensive correspondence with prominent Englishmen. He supported the Jay mission and accepted the treaty that resulted from it, though regretting a number of the concessions made by the Chief Justice. On the other hand, Washington gave way to no man in his reprobation of British insults against American commerce, and, to the end of his term of office, he attempted to steer his nation between the Scylla of England and the Charybdis of France.

Vice President John Adams, soon to be Washington's successor, had a very different character and was, in a sense, more human. Adams was capable of writing with regret of a rain which spoiled sledding in Philadelphia and with pleasure of an evening at the home of Robert Morris: "A company of venerable old rakes . . . sat smoking cigars, drinking Burgundy and Madeira, and talking politics until almost eleven o'clock."[22] Adams had human foibles, too. The most important of these were an irritable temper, vanity, and self-righteousness so deep that he tended to ascribe bad motives to all criticism directed against him. Later, as President, Adams suffered for his faults. His policies, although usually wise, had less chance of general acceptance because of the tactless way in which he fought for them. Adams' integrity, learning, patriotism, and abilities were beyond question, yet he was a poor leader. As Worthington

C. Ford has written, "Of undoubted courage and ambition, careful of his independence and jealous of others, he stood much alone, and so largely lost the benefit of acting with others."[23] Like his son after him, John Adams was condemned, as President, to struggle in vain against progressive tendencies he neither sympathized with nor understood.

Although he praised the strength of the British system of government, Adams had no love for John Bull. "If I mistake not," he wrote, "it is to be the destiny of America one day to beat down his pride. But the irksome task will not soon, I hope, be forced upon us." He did not share John Jay's optimistic belief in British friendship: "I know better. I know their jealousy, envy, hatred, and revenge, covered under pretended contempt." On the other hand, his opinions of the French Revolution were unreservedly hostile, and he believed it capable of proof that "the French nation derived more advantage from the connection [during the American Revolution] than we did—that she owes her independence as much to us as we do ours to her."[24] The policy of France during his presidency sharpened Adams' feelings against her, and although an uncompromising and independent nationalist he led his country into close coöperation with England.

The Secretary of State at the time of the Jay negotiations was Edmund Randolph, a protégé of President Washington. Randolph presented the rare spectacle of a public man uncommitted to either political party; as Attorney General he had usually sided with Jefferson, but a foreign visitor thought him basically Federalist though torn by the influence of his Virginia background. Many distrusted Randolph because of his independence. Jefferson complained that he was without principle, and French minister Fauchet wrote, "He . . . played the sincere and made me false confidences. My suspicions, however, kept me constantly on the watch."[25] To the orthodox Federalists, Randolph was anathema. In his official station he tried to stiffen Jay's resistance to British demands, and he only reluctantly endorsed the treaty's terms.

Among those who hated Randolph was Timothy Pickering, the Secretary of War. Pickering was a flinty Yankee, "more the true republican in figure, manners, & mode of living than any man I have seen in America," as the British envoy's wife put it. He had been a strong supporter of the French Revolution, and in 1795 George Hammond reported to London that in negotiations with the Indians Pickering's conduct, "whether the occasion required it or not, has been uniformly marked by expressions of the most blind and undistinguishing hatred of Great Britain." Pickering's transformation into a violent supporter of the Jay treaty has baffled even the most recent student of his career, although it is suggested that his appointment to national office and his devotion to the mercantile interest, combined with assiduous wooing by its members, caused him to revise his beliefs in 1794 and 1795. Whatever the reasons, Pickering became a strong Federalist, much to the disgust of old friends like Henry Dearborn, who complained that "soon after you entered on the duties of the departments of war & State [and presumably because of having been given office], your political sentiments appeared to me, & to many of your former friends, to undergo a considerable change."[26]

Pickering did not have Alexander Hamilton for a Cabinet colleague, since the New Yorker had retired in January 1795 to repair his private fortunes. Nevertheless, Hamilton's influence was still important, particularly after Pickering stepped up to the Department of State in the spring of 1795. Secretary of the Treasury Oliver Wolcott was Hamilton's sycophant, as was bumbling, ineffectual James McHenry, Pickering's successor at the War Department. In addition, Congressional leaders, long accustomed to look to the New Yorker for leadership, continued to respect his counsel. John Adams exaggerated in the bitterness of retirement, but he was not too far wide of the mark when he wrote that upon entering office he found that Hamilton was " 'commander-in-chief' of the House of Representatives, of the Senate, of the heads of department, of General Washington, and last, and least, if you will, of the President of the United States." Hamilton of course sided strongly with the British in the European struggle, and he particularly desired, for the safety of the financial system he had established, the preservation of good trade relations with England. Yet Hamilton was not a blind admirer of the British. He protested as loudly as anyone against the provision order of 1795, often exerted his influence to restrain the more bellicose Federalists in Congress, and generally endorsed a policy of isolation. He wrote to Pickering in 1798, "it is of the true policy . . . of our government, to act with spirit and energy as well toward Great Britain as France. I would *mete* the same measure to both of them."[27]

The party of Hamilton, Washington, and Adams, unlike that of Pitt, was not free from challenge in the legislature. The Federalists controlled the Senate until 1801, but since that body had only thirty or thirty-two members the defection of even a handful could be decisive. In the House of Representatives, the opposition had a majority from 1793 to 1795 and nearly attained one in the next Congress. Thereafter, the quarrel with France worked to the advantage of the Federalists, and their hold was relatively secure until the electoral revolution of 1800. The effectiveness of these majorities was weakened by poor party discipline, factionalism, and superior leadership on the Republican side of the House. Resistance often forced the government to modify its plans, whereas the Pitt government was generally able to go ahead without serious challenge. Both regimes recognized this, and it was one reason why Pitt and Grenville did not push the United States toward a closer political understanding.

The leader of the American opposition, Thomas Jefferson, was in temporary retirement at the beginning of the period, but he kept in close touch with his supporters. His influence with Washington had been a valuable brake upon the Secretary of the Treasury during the early years of the republic, and he was one of the chief architects of the system of neutrality laid down in 1793. Jefferson returned from France in 1789 full of enthusiasm for the French Revolution, and until nearly the close of the century this feeling was relatively unimpaired. He believed that England was the aggressor in the European war, and he was convinced that France would be a magnanimous victor. For example, he wrote from Monticello early in 1795:

I sincerely congratulate you on the great prosperities of our two first allies, the French and the Dutch. If I could but see them now at peace with the rest of their continent, I should have little doubt of dining with Pichegru in London, next autumn; for I believe I should be tempted to leave my clover for awhile, to go and hail the dawn of liberty & republicanism in that island.[28]

Jefferson's sympathies for France had limits, however. He handled Genêt as that zealot deserved, and his affection for the republican experiment did not blind him to America's interest in the balance of power. Thus by 1798 he no longer spoke of dining in London with victorious French generals. "The complete subjugation of England," he wrote, "would indeed be a general calamity. But happily it is impossible."[29]

Jefferson's chief political lieutenant was his trusted friend and fellow Virginian, James Madison. Madison could be a bit cold, but an anti-Republican visitor from England a few years later had to admit that he found him "a social, jovial, and good-humoured companion, full of anecdote, sometimes rather of a loose description, but oftener of a political and historical interest. He was [the description continued] a little man with small features . . . occasionally lit up with a good-natured smile."[30] In general, Madison was less emotional than his chief, more devoted to politics as "the art of the possible." He never committed himself as completely to the French Revolution. But he did distrust England and agreed with Jefferson that American commerce could be used as a weapon to exact concessions from the European powers, a point of view in marked contrast to that of most Federalists, who believed that commerce was to be protected by national policy rather than made the instrument of it. Jefferson stated his and Madison's belief most succinctly, writing in 1797, "War is not the best engine for us to resort to, nature has given us one *in our commerce,* which, if properly managed, will be a better instrument for obliging the interested nations of Europe to treat us with justice."[31]

The Federalists, although unwilling to sacrifice trade on the altar of diplomacy, shared with Jefferson and Madison a belief that the United States should stay out of Europe's wars. This was indeed a national sentiment, although in 1793 there had been a burst of enthusiasm for France so strong that even Jefferson feared that it might be impossible "to repress the spirit of the people within the limits of a fair neutrality." At the same time, Americans were confident of their own ability to repel insult; they already held, in the words of a British diplomat, such an "overweening idea of American Prowess and American Talents that they do not scruple to talk of the United States as singly an overmatch for any nation in

Europe." Public opinion gave no support to any idea of an alliance with England during the naval war with France, and Jefferson probably would not have found it easy to lead the American people into the British connection he considered during the Louisiana controversy. As John Marshall wrote, "Separated far from Europe, we mean not to mingle in their quarrels. . . . We have avoided, and shall continue to avoid, any political connections which might engage us further than is compatible with the neutrality we profess."[32]

At the same time, however, most Americans demanded full freedom to cheer, hoot, and even throw occasional brickbats at the European belligerents. The Federalists, who generally endorsed the first, moderate phase of the French Revolution, soon recanted, and they were in 1795 partisans of England. Many justified the shift by explaining that French victories threatened the balance of power. "Every independent power," wrote Fisher Ames, "has . . . a manifest interest in the sufficiency of British force to balance that of France."[33] In general, however, the Federalists were probably more influenced by their respect for the English political system and their mistrust of French democracy and its possible contagious effect upon America. The Republicans, on the other hand, naturally wished no success to the government which they accused the Federalists of using as a model. They remembered the importance of the alliance of 1778 in the struggle for independence. In addition, taking the cue from their leader, Republicans felt that England had provoked the war and was extending it by means of foreign subsidies so that she could make colonial conquests. The party further believed that the Royal Navy was a greater threat to the interests of the United States than French power on land.

By 1795, most men had made their decision. Advocates of England and defenders of France exchanged pamphlets, insults, and blows. But the division was usually merely a re-affirmation of the choice between the Republican and Federalist parties. Few Hamiltonians supported France, few Jeffersonians England. The new controversy was the last manifestation of the basic political struggle, and loyalty generally remained with the party. The true English party, the French faction—they were small. As a discerning Frenchman reported in 1797, "there is a middle party, much larger, composed of the most estimable men of the other two parties, . . . which loves its country above all and for whom preferences either for France or England are only accessory and often passing affections."[34]

The controversy with France brought about an important change in American feeling. The Federalists spoke more openly of their desire for a British victory. A few Republicans changed sides, and many others reëxamined their conviction that French war aims were mild and benevolent, though so late as 1798 Jefferson wrote that France seemed merely to wish "to republicanize . . . [Britain's] government, and to bring her power on the ocean within more reasonable and safe limits."[35] The Republicans fought to prevent a declaration of war, but they also lost much of their old affection for France. The Peace of Amiens, which temporarily ended British violations of American neutrality, the rise of Napoleonic autocracy, and the Louisiana crisis further confirmed the spiritual death of the alliance of 1778. Rival attitudes toward England and France were not to be a criterion by which the American people could be divided in the first years of the nineteenth century. The decline both of sympathy for France and the bitterest hatred of England was an important factor in American politics from 1795 to 1805.

The greater volatility of American public opinion was but one of many contrasts between England and the United States. The leading personalities, like Plutarchian pairs, were strikingly dissimilar—Pitt and Washington (or Adams), Grenville and Pickering, Fox and Jefferson. The war in Europe brought prosperity to America and its merchant marine, but it struck hard at the British economy. Pitt and his supporters brushed aside Parliamentary opposition but failed to provide successful leadership in a desperate war; the American governments were heavily challenged at home, but they managed, although by a narrow margin, to keep the United States out of the European war. These contrasts, and the facts upon which they rested, were all important influences in the development of Anglo-American relations. So too were other factors common to both nations—the benefits to be gained from an extended commerce, the basic community of heritage, and a temporary parallel hostility toward France.

America Accepts the Treaty 3

Reports that Jay had signed a treaty reached America at the end of January 1795. The Philadelphia *Aurora*, a Republican bellwether, expressed no surprise that, immediately after concluding his business, the envoy had left London for Bath: "No wonder he should be short breathed, and have such palpitations as to need the Bath waters to restore him, after subscribing to so dishonourable a treaty as that said to have been concluded."[1] But the *Aurora* was only shooting in the dark, for no one in America knew the terms of the treaty at this time.

Three copies of the treaty had been hastened off from London as soon as possible after the signing at Downing Street, in the hope that at least one would reach Philadelphia before the Senate adjourned. By an error in the Post Office, both British copies were entrusted to the packet *Tankerville*. This ship had the bad luck to be overtaken in mid-Atlantic by a French privateer, the *Lovely Lass*, and the captain threw his weighted dispatches overboard to prevent their capture. Jay's copy of the agreement was taken to America by a Virginian named David Blaney, whose Atlantic crossing took three and a half months. Blaney, too, had some adventures on the way:

The winds blue continually from the westward from the time the ship left England until we came on the course [coast?] of America. . . . I took a small flask of rum to encourage the sailors to keep a better watch, and pay attention to the ship, and promised them all small rewards if the ship arrived at such a time; but we could not alter the contrary winds. . . . [A] French cruiser board[ed] us, and making mention of the treaty . . . search'd every part of the ship, but such care was taken of the treaty it was impossible for it to have been discovered. . . . I landed at Norfolk at ten o'clock at night, hired horses and made all the despatch I could to reach Philadelphia; my first horse founder'd after getting to Richmond, which I did in one day and part the night. . . . In seven days from the time I landed at Norfolk I delivered the despatches to E. Randolph, Esq.[2]

Washington immediately recalled the Senators, who had dispersed only three days earlier, informing them that "Certain matters touching the public good" required their return on the eighth of June.

British minister Hammond believed that the delay caused by the loss of the *Tankerville* was a piece of good fortune, since it allowed several new and friendly Senators to take their seats, but the French representatives were confident that eleven—enough to prevent ratification—would oppose the treaty.[3] The Federalists were strongest, of course, in the Northeast; Massachusetts was represented by Caleb Strong and George Cabot, Connecticut by Jonathan Trumbull and Oliver Ellsworth, and New York by the transplanted Yankee, Rufus King. While these five were the most distinguished, important support was provided by Senators from the South and West, where the Republicans had not yet solidified their control. Both South Carolinians were Federalists, as were James Gunn of Georgia and Kentucky's Humphrey Marshall, whose vote for the treaty ruined his national career. On the Republican side, there were slippery gentlemen like Aaron Burr and Stephen T. Mason as well as respected ones like James Jackson of Georgia and Henry Tazewell of Virginia, president *pro tempore* in spite of the Federalist majority.

With twenty-one members and Vice President Adams present in a sweltering chamber, the Senate began serious consideration of the treaty on June 11. The first skirmish was over continuation of the policy of secrecy President Washington had initiated, but this was already an academic question for at least one member of the Senate, the apostate Federalist, Pierce Butler, who was sending the treaty to James Madison a page at a time.[4] Two proposals to reveal the terms of the agreement to the public were defeated, twenty to nine. One Republican, Alexander Martin of South Carolina, deserted to the enemy, but otherwise this first vote established a pattern. "Bloodworth, Brown, Burr, Butler, Jackson, Langdon, Mason, Robinson & Tazewell" ran the roll of the minority,[5] and these, with Martin, stuck together on every vote which followed.

After a week-end recess, the real battle was joined. The field of conflict was Article XII, which permitted American ships of limited size to trade with the British West Indies but required the United States to forbid the exportation of tropical produce, a provision designed to prevent the development of a reëxport trade in Caribbean goods. So general was the opposition to this article that the treaty's managers postponed its consideration, and before the next day's session, the Federalist leaders doubtless took counsel among themselves. Never before had the Senate attached conditions to its endorsement of a treaty, but the obstacle had to be hurdled in some way. Hamilton urged that the Senate withhold its approval from Article XII, and it seemed unlikely that Britain would take umbrage at removal of a provision to which she had only reluctantly consented in the first place. Therefore, on Wednesday morning someone, possibly Rufus King,[6] laid before the Senate a motion in two parts: first, that the Senate express approval of all the treaty save for Article XII; and, second, that the Senate recommend further negotiation on trade with the West Indies. This motion virtually disarmed criticism within the Federalist party and established the majority in a less exposed position.

The Republicans sought a four-day recess to reorient their attack now that the most attractive target had been removed, but they were overwhelmed by the Federalist steamroller. After several days of debate, and a second week-end adjournment, Aaron Burr moved that "further consideration of the Treaty . . . be postponed, and that it be recommended to the President of the United States, to proceed, without delay, to further friendly negotiations with His Britannic Majesty, in order to effect alterations in the Treaty." Burr's motion included a list of those features of the treaty which Republicans found objectionable, and it was designed to put the party position on the record. The motion had no chance of success, although Burr supported it with a powerful speech, and on Tuesday, the twenty-third, it was voted down by the solid Federalist majority, twenty to ten.

The next day there was a less direct but more threatening attack. South Carolina's freshman Federalist, Jacob Read, moved to amend the motion for ratification to demand compensation for Negroes and other property carried off by British armies at the close of the Revolution. After some discussion, Read was persuaded to withdraw this embarrassing proposal. The Republicans, however, refused to allow their opponents to escape so easily, and John Brown of Kentucky reintroduced Read's motion. This move was aimed at Southern Federalists, and it did temporarily draw them away from the majority. Read and Humphrey Marshall joined the Republicans, and three other Federalists abstained. The motion was defeated by a vote of fifteen to twelve. This Southern defection, the only real threat to party solidarity during the time the treaty was before the Senate, was shortlived. The dissidents immediately returned to the fold to help defeat another oblique attack upon the treaty.

Apparently not one Senator had changed his mind in twelve days of debate. Given the existing composition of the Senate, the final vote, though close, seemed likely to be safe for the treaty if there were no abstentions. Such proved to be the case. By precisely the required vote of twenty to ten, the Senate agreed to advise conditional ratification.

A critical analysis of the Senate's attitude is difficult, since none of the debates were published and only a few letters bear directly upon the subject. Albert Gallatin, certainly in a position to know if anyone outside the Senate did, ascribed the Republican defeat to James Gunn's defection.[7] If so, the desertion came early in the game, for the Georgian voted with the majority on every roll call. Pierre Adet, the new French minister, claimed that both Gunn and Jacob Read had been bribed, although his dispatch was probably a report of sheer gossip, an alibi for his own failure. Gunn's price, Adet said, was an Indian treaty favorable to his home state; Read's, fifteen hundred pounds from the bulging purse of George Hammond. The Frenchman also claimed that the British commander on the American station threatened to sweep American vessels from the seas if the treaty was defeated in the Senate.[8] Adet failed to emphasize the sectional character of the vote. Roughly speaking, Northerners supported the treaty, although John Langdon of New Hampshire and Moses Robinson of Vermont were exceptions. The South provided most of the opposition, but also a handful of Federalist Senators just large enough to make a two-thirds majority.

Although the President still hoped to keep the treaty secret until ratifications had been exchanged, the Republican party, defeated in what Senator Tazewell called "the most uncandid & unfair proceeding I ever witnessed,"[9] took its case to the people. Copies of the treaty had been circulating outside the Senate for some time. Bostonians who had seen it, according to the Federalist *Columbian Centinel,* were convinced that it reflected "the eminent negotiating abilities of the American Minister."[10] In New York there were several copies, any one of which might have fallen into the hands of a newspaper editor willing to print it. It was fitting, however, that the first paper to publish the treaty should be the leading Republican journal of the day, Benjamin Franklin Bache's Philadelphia *Aurora.* On June 29, less than a week after the Senate's final vote, an abstract of the treaty provided by Senator Stephen T. Mason of Virginia appeared in the *Aurora,* and three days later Bache brought out the text in pamphlet form.[11]

Without waiting to observe Philadelphia's reaction, Benny Bache set off for New York with large bundles of pamphlets. He stopped in that city just long enough to arrange the distribution of this politically and personally remunerative publication. Then, scattering a few copies in Connecticut towns as he passed, Bache posted on to Boston, already in a ferment because the West Indian privateer *Betsy* had been set afire by a mob. That hated manifestation of British sea power had burnt itself out before the Philadelphian arrived, but his pamphlets rekindled the political flames. Ever the pessimist, Fisher Ames succumbed to despair; "the Jacobins," he wrote, "have been successful in prejudicing the multitude against the treaty. . . . Our federal ship is foundering in a millpond."[12] The success of the Jacobins seemed proved when on the thirteenth a boisterous crowd, ostensibly a town meeting, howled its approval of a series of resolutions condemning the treaty, while pickpockets operated fruitfully on the fringe of the crowd.

Few Federalists at first defended the treaty on positive grounds, emphasizing instead that in "treating with a great and politic nation (for such is Great Britain, in spite of her misconduct and corruption)" a negotiated bargain and not absolute submission was all that could be expected. But some were not as easily discouraged as Fisher Ames. Stephen Higginson made light of the mass meeting, pointing out that the better citizens had not been present. Both he and George Cabot were certain that the propertied classes solidly supported the treaty and would be able to carry the people with them. Cabot argued against counterdemonstrations: "after all where is the boasted advantage of a republican system over the turbulent mobocracy of Athens if the resort to public meetings is necessary?"[13] The Federalist situation improved by the middle of August, but the treaty continued to arouse strenuous opposition in the Bay State.

In New York, the Republicans imitated Boston and called a town meeting. When King and Hamilton tried to speak, the mob jammed around the steps of Federal Hall booed and stamped. Finally, as Jefferson later wrote with some glee, "the Livingstonians appealed to stones & clubs and beat him [Hamilton] & his party off the ground."[14] Supporters of the treaty prudently declined to contest the field at a second meeting, and Republican resolutions were enthusiastically adopted. It was some solace to the Federalists that the Chamber of Commerce voted by a six to one ratio to endorse Jay's treaty.

In Philadelphia, two of the greatest disorders took place. On the evening of July 4, a mob whose spirits had already been raised by holiday celebration gathered in the suburb of Kensington to burn John Jay in effigy. Officers of the light horse went from house to house calling out their commands, but they were unable to gather enough men to put down the rioters, and both sides suffered a number of casualties. Three relatively calm weeks followed, as the Republicans waited for public opinion to develop. They then called a meeting of the citizens at which a memorial drafted by Alexander J. Dallas was overwhelmingly approved, while Timothy Pickering watched, dour-faced, from the outskirts of the crowd. The mob put the treaty on a pole and marched on Hammond's residence, where the offending document was burned in the street while showers of stones shattered the British minister's windows. This assault was without doubt the high point in the campaign of violence which greeted publication of the treaty. In Philadelphia, as in Boston, time lessened the intensity of antitreaty feeling, although Hammond wrote in mid-August that "a considerable degree of irritability still exists upon the subject."[15] This pattern was repeated elsewhere. It would be inaccurate to say that the American people had swung around to support of the treaty. The initial outburst of rage had quite naturally spent itself, but the treaty was not forgotten, and it remained an object of Republican execration for years.

During most of the hullabaloo, George Washington was on his usual summer vacation at Mount Vernon. Like other Federalist leaders, he recognized the danger of delay and yet was by no means completely satisfied with the treaty. In a letter to Secretary of State Randolph he stated his position:

conditional ratification . . . may, on all fit occasions, be spoken of [to the Cabinet] as my determination. . . . My opinion respecting the treaty, is the same as it was: namely, not favorable to it, but that it is better to ratify it in the manner the Senate have advised . . . , than to suffer matters to remain as they are, unsettled. Little has been said to me on the subject of this treaty, along the road I passed [from Philadelphia to Mount Vernon]; and I have seen no one since, from whom I could hear much concerning it; but from indirect discourses, I find endeavours are not wanting to place it in all the odious points of view, of which it is susceptible; and in some which it will not admit.[16]

Washington's intention to go ahead with ratification was soon changed by news that the Royal Navy was seizing American ships carrying food-stuffs to France. The new Order in Council reflected British fears, induced by the cold, damp spring, for the harvest of winter wheat. Government agents were sent to the Continent to buy grain, but this supply would be some time in coming. Meanwhile, sailing past Land's End, often even touching at Falmouth for information on market conditions, large numbers of American provision ships passed on their way to France. This tempting source of supply was not long ignored. On the twenty-fourth of April, the Privy Council ordered that

the Commanders of our Ships of War shall, till Our further Orders herein, detain all Ships laden with Corn, or other Provisions that shall be bound to France or to the Ports occupied by the Armies of France, or which They shall have reason to believe are proceeding to France, . . . [and they shall] bring all such Ships into . . . [the] Ports of Great Britain.[17]

For months thereafter, American consuls in England dolefully reported the arrival of seized vessels, sometimes as many as eight or nine at a time. The British paid what they estimated to be a fair price for the provisions, then hustled them off to the areas of greatest shortage, particularly London. Other ships, stopped near the coast of France, helped supply the British expedition operating in Quiberon Bay. That the government intended the new order to be interpreted as broadly as possible is apparent from a letter sent by the First Lord of the Admiralty to one of his captains. The hint contained in a previous directive to naval officers, wrote Lord Spencer,

was intended to satisfy them that the Government did not wish them to be over nice or scrupulous respecting the nature of the papers of those ships, as we know the greatest deceptions are attempted to be put into practice, and the present circumstances both with respect to the enemy and to this country are such as to justify a less degree of attention to those delicate points than at another time.[18]

There can be little doubt that England was short of food, particularly grain, in the spring of 1795, but, unless the situation was truly desperate, this move was a very foolish one. A similar order nearly brought war in 1794, and the decree came nearer to defeating the Jay treaty than anything done by its Republican enemies.

News of the confiscation of foodstuffs reached Philadelphia at the end of June. The Republicans argued that the new orders demonstrated what they had always suspected, that Britain never intended to execute the treaty and had merely used the negotiations to lull America into silence. "Surely," stated the *Aurora*, "if they . . . intended to ratify it, they would not thus sport with our most important commercial interests." Even less partisan minds agreed that the new move was serious. Secretary Randolph, who was preparing a careful but not too unfavorable analysis of the treaty for the President, at once added an opinion that "the order for capturing provisions is too irreconcilable with a state of harmony, for the treaty to be put in motion during its existence." Washington agreed and had the Secretary inform Hammond that if the report of a new Order in Council should prove correct, the President would "require a farther Time to determine on the Course of Proceeding, which . . . it may be expedient for him to adopt." All but Wolcott in the Cabinet, and Alexander Hamilton as well, endorsed the President's decision. Hamilton urged the government "to send to our agent the Treaty Ratified as advised by the Senate with this instruction—that . . . he is . . . not to exchange the ratification till the order is rescinded; since the U. States cannot ever give an implied sanction to the principle."[19]

However, the impact of the provision order, threatening as it did both the Jay treaty and the development of Anglo-American understanding, was soon counteracted by an even more startling event. Earlier in the year, the *Jean Bart*, to which Minister Fauchet had entrusted his reports, was overtaken by H. M. S. *Cerberus*. The dispatches were tossed overboard, but a captive British skipper named Goddard, fearing that his ship's papers were in the weighted bundle, jumped into the sea and held the packet until a British longboat picked him up. Of the documents which Goddard saved, the most important was Fauchet's Dispatch Number Ten of October 31, 1794, which for some reason was not even in cipher. The young minister's language was truly Gallic in its rhetoric and highly ambiguous, but Dispatch Number Ten seemed to imply that Edmund Randolph was a partisan of France who would, for money received, perform services for the Republic. This promising document passed through Admiralty channels to the Foreign Office. Grenville, who long before had instructed Hammond to work for Randolph's removal, enclosed the captured documents in a letter to Hammond, surmising that "the Communication of [them] . . . to well disposed Persons in America may possibly be useful to the King's Service."[20]

Hammond's idea of a "well disposed Person" was Secretary of the Treasury Wolcott, to whom he read a translation of Dispatch Number Ten. Wolcott took the original and showed it to Timothy Pickering and Attorney General Bradford,[21] and Pickering then wrote to Washington urging him to return to Philadelphia because of an important, confidential development. The President left Mount Vernon as soon as possible. On the evening of his arrival at the capital, dinner with Randolph was interrupted by Timothy Pickering, who privately told Washington the whole story of Fauchet's dispatch. The Chief Executive gave Randolph no inkling of what had transpired, but the next day he announced to the Cabinet that he was going to ratify the treaty, thus reversing the policy which he himself, Randolph, Hamilton, and most of the Cabinet had earlier advocated. The President forced Randolph to humiliate himself by preparing and presenting to Hammond a memorial which was an explanation of the government's decision and a confession of the Secretary's failure. This the English envoy received with scarcely concealed pleasure. Then Washington finally confronted Randolph with a copy of Fauchet's Number Ten and asked his erstwhile protégé to comment on it. Randolph knew Washington too well to expect to be able to change his mind, so he made no attempt to defend himself and immediately drafted a letter of resignation. Timothy Pickering was placed in temporary charge of the Department of State.[22]

Randolph hastened northward to secure proof of his innocence from Joseph Fauchet, who had gone to Newport to embark for France on the frigate *Medusa*. Fauchet had nearly, and his luggage had actually, been captured in Long Island Sound by H. M. S. *Africa*, which stopped a number of vessels within American waters, but when Randolph reached Newport the Frenchman was still there and the captain of the *Africa* was engaged in a hot controversy with Governor Fenner of Rhode Island. Fauchet promised to give Randolph the evidence he desired, but before he could do so the *Medusa* took advantage of a fog and made good its escape, with Fauchet aboard. Not until months later did Randolph receive from France the proofs Fauchet had promised to provide. Acting Secretary of State Timothy Pickering protested strongly against the activities of the *Africa*, but Captain Home escaped disciplinary action.[23] With the ratification of the Jay treaty, the Royal Navy exercised greater discretion, so there was no naval incident of comparable importance until British cruisers attempted to intercept Jérome Bonaparte in the area around New York almost ten years later.

While Pickering was handling this disagreeable affair, President Washington began his search for a new Secretary of State. At least five persons, including Patrick Henry, Rufus King, and C. C. Pinckney, declined to serve, and Hamilton, still an influential Presidential adviser, reluctantly came to the conclusion that "a first rate character is not attainable. A second-rate must be taken with good dispositions and barely decent qualifications. . . . 'T is a sad omen for the government." Washington at last turned to his Acting Secretary, Timothy Pickering. Pickering protested that he was not fitted for the office, but he finally gave way when the President and Oliver Wolcott buttonholed him at one of Mrs. Washington's Friday receptions and insisted that he accept. A friend, while congratulating Pickering on his promotion, warned the New Englander that "the new station may require more of the *suaviter* to qualify the *fortiter*."[24] Despite his own misgivings, Timothy Pickering managed the Department of State capably for four and a half years. Never, however, was his service distinguished by that "suaviter" which his friend Stephen Higginson had recommended.

While Pickering was still Acting Secretary he drafted instructions for the official exchange of ratifications of the Jay treaty. Thomas Pinckney, the regular minister at London, was negotiating with Godoy in Spain, and William A. Deas, the chargé, was not deemed to have sufficient rank, so the American minister at the Hague, John Quincy Adams, was ordered to cross the Channel to handle the business. Adams was directed to protest vigorously against the provision order—if such a directive actually existed, for the American government still had not seen a copy of it. "But if after every prudent effort, you find that it cannot be removed, its continuance is not to be an obstacle to the exchange of ratifications."[25] Since it was thought important that news of the exchange should reach America before Congress met in December, Deas was authorized to act if Adams did not arrive by October 20. Such proved to be the case, and Deas proceeded to Downing Street for the formal ceremony with Lord Grenville on the twenty-seventh of October.[26]

There still remained two danger spots before the Jay treaty should reach calm water. The lesser of these was a complication arising out of a recent treaty with the Western tribes. In the Treaty of Greenville, which was brought about both by the Jay treaty and Wayne's victory at Fallen Timbers, the Indians promised that all traders who entered their territories without licenses from the United States would be turned over to American authorities. Quite logically, the British felt that this contravened the Jay treaty, which granted traders of both nations unrestricted entry into Indian lands. In January the Governor-General of Canada was informed that "all arrangements taken by your Lordship for the delivery of the Posts, should be provisional only, and dependent on the result on an explanation which His Majesty's Minister to the United States will be instructed to require" on the Greenville provision, and further conditional on the passage of a treaty bill.[27]

The second obstacle, full of foam and froth as well as sharp rocks and ponderous boulders, was the House of Representatives, to which the American government had to go for funds to carry out the treaty. The President did not officially inform Congress of the exchange of ratifications until March 1796, two months after the first news from London, since Deas neglected to send an original of the ratifications with his dispatches. It was perhaps fortunate for the fate of the treaty that he did so, for there appears to have been a further shift of public opinion at this time. One factor in the change was the *Camillus* letters, written by Alexander Hamilton with some help from Rufus King. Urged by the President himself, Hamilton began the series in July 1795. James Madison called the letters "anglomany," Jefferson described them as "an Encyclopedie . . . [of] sophisms," and the Boston *Independent Chronicle* not too unfairly stigmatized them as "proverbial for prolixity and verbosity." But Fisher Ames wrote in a burst of poetry that "Jove's eagle holds his bolts in his talons, and hurls them, not at the Titans, but at sparrows and mice." Jefferson circulated a few copies among his neighbors so that they might see the absurdity of the Federalist position, but he found his fellow Virginians unable to "parry the sophistry" and soon ceased the experiment. Hamilton, he commented to Madison, was indeed a colossus.[28]

The counterattack spearheaded by Hamilton's massive thunderbolts made slow but steady progress. Toward the end of 1795, Timothy Pickering and Rufus King felt that the nation was swinging around to support the President in his decision to execute the treaty, and Washington and the French and British ministers soon observed that the treaty was gaining ground. As the President noted, however, "it requires some time to effect a perfect cure; especially, while there remains a morbid tumor, always working, and difficult to eradicate."[29] Still, the shift was apparent, and it must have been a factor which remained in the minds of Congressmen while they debated the Jay treaty.

The long proceedings in the House filled the *Annals of Congress* with argument both serious and frivolous, with appeals to Grotius, Vattel, and the Founding Fathers, with moments of tedium and moments of excitement. The battle began on March 2, when Edward Livingston of New York moved that the President be requested to provide the House of Representatives with all documents bearing on the Jay negotiations, so that it could weigh the treaty and decide whether or not to vote money to carry it out. Livingston's motion in effect posed a constitutional issue: Is the House of Representatives obliged to appropriate money to implement a compact concluded by the President and approved by the Senate? This important issue arose to plague another administration in 1868, when the House only reluctantly provided the money to purchase Alaska, and came up again in 1950, when Congress debated the appropriations necessary to implement the Atlantic Pact, although here much wider questions of interpretation were involved. In 1796, as in 1868 and 1950, the question was left unanswered, although the *Aurora* argued that a definite decision was necessary since "The liberties of our country under the constitution hang in awful suspense." Jeffersonians believed that the issue was simply "whether the powers of legislation shall be transferred from the P[resident]. Senate & H[ouse]. of R[epresentatives]. to the P[resident]. Senate & Piamingo or any other Indian, Algerine, or other chief." To the Federalists, even to some who had doubts about the wisdom of the treaty, the situation was equally clear: "The Legislature possesses neither expressly nor incidentally any authority to give effect to or oppose the operation of Treaties."[30]

Debate on Livingston's motion raged for three weeks. Albert Gallatin sardonically expressed surprise that the Federalists did not support it, since they had claimed, when the treaty was first under attack, "that the President and the Senate were the best judges, because they possessed the best information; to render this information public, must then answer a valuable purpose." Gallatin's jibe was but a pin prick compared to the speech delivered by James Madison, in which the Virginian skillfully examined the problem from a number of constitutional angles. Fisher Ames denounced Madison's arguments as "spun cobweb," but they had great effect. Madison once thought that the Livingston resolution would pass or fail by a handful of votes, but the tide ran strongly for it, and the final vote was sixty-two to thirty-seven.[31]

George Washington, his Cabinet, and Alexander Hamilton all agreed that the request for papers should be declined. Washington therefore sent a message to the House which stated, in sum, that "a just regard to the Constitution and to the duty of my office . . . forbids a compliance with your request."[32] The President argued, among other things, that the framers of the Constitution had not intended that the House should discuss treaties. To this, framer Madison replied with standard Republican doctrine: the intent of the authors was of little importance as compared to the interpretation which had been given to the Constitution by the people in ratifying conventions.[33] The House declined to accept the President's reasoning and reasserted its right to call for papers and discuss treaties which involved other than purely diplomatic matters.

Following this salvo, the Republicans momentarily broke off the attack, for their position was not as strong as it appeared in the roll calls. Many Congressmen from the South and West hated the Jay treaty and the administration which had made it, but they were unwilling to vote against that agreement for fear that the Federalists would take revenge by blocking appropriations to implement Pinckney's treaty with Spain. The British chargé, Phineas Bond, was hopeful that this would be an important factor. Furthermore, he reported, "to with-hold the requisite Appropriations, might lead to a Dissolution of the Constitution, for which the leaders of the democratic Party, with all that Spirit of Disunion & Discontent, which marks their Conduct are not yet ripe."[34]

Well aware of their danger, the Federalists energetically organized public opinion and brought it to bear upon Congress. Even in western Pennsylvania, the constituency of Albert Gallatin and scene of the Whisky Rebellion, petitions were assiduously circulated, and a friend wrote Gallatin that he could use the pressure from home as an excuse for his own rather moderate opposition to the treaty.[35] In Virginia, the Federalists had not dared to go to the people until the cause seemed so hopeless nothing further could be lost; then they found to their surprise that a majority of Richmond citizens desired the treaty to go into effect.[36] Merchant groups all over the nation were encouraged to unite "in one common prayer to the House . . . that the faith, honor and interest of the nation, may be preserved by making necessary provisions for carrying the Treaty into fair and honorable effect."[37]

"The current appears to be strong with us," Hamilton wrote in April,[38] and others shared his opinion. Federalist newspapers claimed that the Fourth Congress, elected two years before at a time of excitement against England, did not accurately reflect the feeling of America in 1796. As the *Connecticut Courant* put it:

It can be demonstrated that there are members of Congress opposed to the Treaty, who do not represent the real sense of one third of their constituents, nor one *tenth of the property* which is at stake. . . . A vast majority of the people of the United States are in favor of fulfilling the Treaty—and this fact will soon appear.[39]

Republican journals rather feebly denied Federalist claims of popular support. In addition, they fell back upon the claim of unfair tactics which their opponents had used when the current was flowing in the other direction. Under the heading, "Those who change will change again," the Boston *Independent Chronicle* asserted that, although a recent town meeting had endorsed the treaty, a majority remained opposed to it. "The busy, intriguing few . . . pre-occupied the public opinion by their personal influence and dexterity" and thereby railroaded through a vote of approval, the *Chronicle* complained. At Philadelphia, the *Aurora* claimed, the circulators of a well-received petition supporting the treaty took advantage of the fact that they were "armed . . . with all the terrors of Banks and Discounts, and with all the influence wealth can give."[40] Such protests were really a confession of weakness, and a shift of opinion apparently was evident. Even if the Federalists overestimated the magnitude of this change, it was still substantial enough so that timid, protreaty Congressmen who would not have dared to flout the overwhelming popular feeling which had existed a year earlier were emboldened to support the agreement.

In the House, the Federalists took the offensive in the middle of April. Theodore Sedgwick presented a resolution that the treaties with Algiers, Great Britain, Spain, and the Indian tribes be carried into effect by law. The Federalists, of course, wanted to tie the Jay treaty to the more popular agreements. Robert Goodloe Harper, a South Carolina supporter of the administration, stated the ostensible logic of this position:

The Power with whom we had the most complex and embarrassing dispute to settle, was a Power possessing great influence over all the others. . . . How then could they [the House] possibly consider, separately, subjects which appeared to be so closely connected? Was it not evident that an accommodation with Great Britain was the foundation—the corner-stone—of our arrangements with all the other Powers on which the prosperity of our country—the security and extension of our commerce, so greatly depend?[41]

The House, however, resisted Harper's arguments and voted separate approval of the other three treaties. The Republicans were elated (although of course the Federalist Senate could still politely blackmail them), and in New York Alexander Hamilton laid plans for countermeasures should the House defeat the Jay treaty.[42]

Just before the end of the debate, Fisher Ames delivered one of the most famous speeches in the history of the House of Representatives. He denied that the treaty violated our alliance with France; indeed, previous treaties were specifically recognized and respected in the Jay treaty. He denied that public opinion was any longer opposed to the treaty, as it perhaps had been in the spring of 1795. "The alarm [then] spread faster than the publication of the treaty. There were more critics than readers." Now passions had cooled, and a majority supported it. How gruesome would be the prospect, said Ames, if the victims of spoliations were denied the opportunity to recover their losses! How threatening the prospect of the frontier if the delivery of the posts to the United States was blocked. "I can fancy that I listen to the yells of savage vengeance and the shrieks of torture; already they seem to sigh in the western wind; already they mingle with every echo from the mountains." Ames carefully avoided any sentiments that might be construed as Federalist truckling to or affection for Great Britain. But, said he, should the House refuse funds, "The disputes of the old treaty of 1783, being left to rankle, will revive the almost extinguished animosities of that period." The result would be cataclysmic; in such an event, Ames proclaimed, "even I, slender and almost broken as my hold upon life is, may outlive the government and constitution of my country."[43]

The day after Ames' monumental effort, the effectiveness of which was recognized even by the *Aurora*, the House voted in committee of the whole. The tally revealed a tie, and all eyes turned to Frederick Muhlenberg, who sat in the chair. Visibly tense, non-Federalist Muhlenberg hesitated, mumbled an explanation, then voted "aye," and the victory was won.[44] The next day, in a roll call vote which was really an anticlimax, the bill passed by a vote of fifty-one to forty-eight. More than two-thirds of the "nays" were cast by representatives from south and west of the Potomac.[45]

While Federalists and Republicans fought bitterly in the House chamber, Phineas Bond and Timothy Pickering had little difficulty straightening out the tangle over the Treaty of Greenville. In accordance with his instructions, the British chargé asked Pickering to prepare an explanatory article confirming the rights of traders in the Indian domains. Pickering, Wolcott, and Hamilton all felt that an explanatory article was unnecessary and that a Presidential declaration should be satisfactory,[46] but they gave way with good grace to Bond's request, and the text of an agreement was easily settled. Bond then wanted to delay the actual signing until Hammond's successor, Robert Liston, arrived, and Pickering agreed to wait until the fifth of May. Vice President Adams was planning to leave for home shortly after that time, and the Secretary feared that his absence, coupled with possible arrivals of Republican Senators and Federalist departures, might jeopardize ratification. On the day of Pickering's deadline, Bond heard from New York that Liston had at last arrived. However, the Secretary of State declined to wait any longer, and Bond consented to sign the explanatory article. As it turned out, Pickering's fears were not justified, for the agreement sailed through the Senate by a vote of nineteen to five less than a week later.[47] This action, clearing the way at last for execution of the treaty, came almost exactly two years after a handful of Federalist legislators put the train of events into motion.

The treaty cannot be judged solely upon its merits as the fruit of diplomatic discussion, weighing the concessions of John Jay and Lord Grenville against one another to see which gained more for his country. The subsequent effect of the agreement is at least equally important. Under its aegis, comity was restored for the first time since the Revolution, bringing with it extensive material benefits for the United States. The Royal Navy, which was far more capable of sweeping American ships from the seas than the raiding frigates and privateers of France, handled shipping with greater care and consideration. As a result, American commerce prospered to a degree which would have been impossible if the asperities and conflicts of 1794 had not been checked. The chief natural channel of trade with Europe was to or through Great Britain, and this channel remained open until the days of the Embargo.

On the other hand, the treaty helped to bring about a serious controversy between America and France. The new European republic was outraged by the apparent treachery of her ally. But, though the Jay treaty naturally gave umbrage to France, peace between the old allies was still possible, and, indeed, Federalist administrations twice sent missions to France to negotiate a settlement. Had the Directory been half so perspicacious as was the Pitt government in 1794, no serious quarrel would have developed. However, motivated by revenge, an emotion which nations can seldom afford to indulge, France's "Young Turks" provoked the United States almost to the point of war. Friendship with France would have been but little help in case of trouble with England, but British cordiality could and did greatly aid the American government when it became involved in controversy with France. As a result, the ties which bound the English-speaking peoples were strengthened. Coming as it did only twenty years after the first volley at Lexington Green, the increasingly cordial relationship of England and America was the best possible testimony to the wisdom of John Jay and William Wyndham, Lord Grenville.

1796: New Envoys, New Policies 4

THE POLITICAL SKIES, SO STORMY IN THE EARLY DAYS OF 1794, WERE gradually clearing, but many legacies of the unfortunate past remained. George Hammond was one of them. He had served his king through several bitter years in America, and his retirement was almost a *sine qua non* to improved relations. Just after signing the treaty, John Jay suggested Hammond's replacement, since "official Darts have frequently pierced thro' official character, and wounded the *man.*"¹ Although Hammond was his personal protégé, Grenville agreed that he must be replaced and in December 1794 sent off a letter of recall. With it went a personal note assuring Hammond that the government appreciated his work in "a difficult and disagreeable situation" but adding that "a better chance may possibly be given to the operation of a System of Conciliation by the Communications passing thro' another Channel and being carried on by a person unmixed in the late Discussions."² The Foreign Secretary promised Hammond a good position when he returned to England. This turned out to be a place as Undersecretary of State in the Foreign Office, where Hammond's colleague was the fledgling George Canning.

Grenville realized that the Philadelphia post demanded extraordinary diplomatic talents, and he had furthermore been urged by Jay to send "A discerning minister, true to your Lordship's conciliatory views, and possessed, if possible of your prudence and self command." Unlike Hammond, who had been young and inexperienced when sent to America, the new minister came from the very top of the scale. He was Robert Liston, a plump, able, friendly Scot who began his career as a tutor in classics, law, and dancing but soon shifted to diplomacy. Hard work and the support of a few prominent Scottish families carried Liston up the ladder, and by 1795 only those who bore titles—Whitworth, Auckland, Malmesbury—ranked higher in the foreign service. In August Grenville offered to transfer Liston to Philadelphia from Constantinople, where he found it difficult to make ends meet. It was a step down from ambassador to minister, but Philadelphia was "a more active situation" and the salary was two thousand pounds, no small sum in a country where ceremonial played a much smaller role than at the Sublime Porte. Liston speedily accepted the new post, but with some misgivings; *"entre nous,"* he wrote to a friend, "I would much rather go anywhere else. A severe climate, hard work, and being surrounded with ill-disposed Yankee doctrinaires will, at my time of life, probably finish me off in a year or two."³

The new minister reached New York in May 1796, "after a stormy but not unprosperous passage, of nearly six weeks."⁴ Federalists there were then celebrating final victory of the treaty in the House of Representatives—surely a good omen for the beginning of a mission—and the city's leading citizens and foremost politicians warmly greeted Liston and his bride, a younger woman whom he had married during his stopover in Britain. Mrs. Liston was particularly impressed by their reception; huge crowds, she wrote home, came to be introduced, and her husband was a real success, "particularly as his Predecessor Hammond was extremely unpopular, both here, & at Phila[delphia]." At least one American witness confirmed this not impartial opinion.[5] The Listons proceeded overland to the capital, where there was some difficulty about housing. Consul Bond had only engaged temporary bachelor quarters, he told Liston, "not having been apprized of your having changed your Condition."[6] This was by no means enough for the Listons and their five servants, and two other members of the ménage, the young and able Secretary of Legation, Edward Thornton, and Lord Henry Petty Stuart, a youth whose father had been a sponsor of Liston. Within a short time, however, the housing problem was solved, and the Listons settled into the Philadelphia routine.

The new minister did well at the American capital, confirming Thomas Pinckney's earlier report that he was "a Sensible well informed Man, of pleasing manners and dispassionate Temper . . . [whose] Prepossessions are in our favor." Within a month after the Listons' arrival, Washington asked them to visit Mount Vernon, an invitation that was often repeated, and a year later a Federalist wrote that the envoy was "peculiarly gifted with those rare and valuable qualities, which at the same time remove every distrust and strengthen a growing friendship. Mr. & Mrs. Liston are much liked, so much so as to be, in the eyes of the Jacobins, *dangerous* people."[7] This was not mere whimsy, for Citizen Adet had just reported to Paris that the Briton was a formidable adversary. Liston seldom quarreled with Timothy Pickering, but the Secretary of State's craggy nature precluded a warm friendship. Furthermore, Pickering seldom went abroad in Philadelphia society. He once explained this to Liston in a letter which, however, indicates something more than a purely formal relationship:

M^r and Mrs Pickering have received the invitation of M^r and Mrs Liston to dine with them . . . , which would be accepted with pleasure; but that Congress do not allow persons holding *executive* offices . . . (unless they possess private fortunes) to have any convivial intercourse with foreign ministers; and scarcely admit of it with the most intimate of their fellow citizens.—It is deemed honor enough for executive officers to toil without interruption for their country, and indulgence enough to live on mutton, mush and cold water.[8]

Liston's misgivings about his new station did not last long. After less than a week in the United States, he informed his friend and banker, Thomas Coutts, that he found the country "extremely fine, and I flatter myself that my situation will not be disagreeable." A few days later he wrote Hammond that "Everything begins very smoothly. . . . Nothing is

wanting . . . to keep this country on a footing of peace & good humour
. . . , except a degree of civility and attention to Justice on the part of
our Sons of Neptune."⁹ On this note of cautious yet friendly optimism,
the rotund Scot began a successful four-year career in Philadelphia.

About a month after the Listons arrived at New York, the new
American minister to England sailed from the same port. He was Rufus
King, a man of far greater eminence in his homeland than Liston but,
like him, urbane, largely self-made, and as later events demonstrated, an
able and conciliatory diplomat. King represented Massachusetts at the
Constitutional Convention, but he soon moved to New York—some said
because he failed of election to the Senate from his native state—and
was duly chosen for the upper house. There he was a staunch Federalist,
one of the behind-the-scenes instigators of the Jay mission, and a defender
of the treaty. In 1796, tired of Senatorial service, King successfully
applied for the London post through Alexander Hamilton, who forwarded
his request to Pickering with a comment that "If we had power to make
a man for this purpose, we could not imagine a fitter than Mr. King."¹⁰

Since the summer season had already begun when King reached London, he did not at first meet leading members of the government and
society, although an introductory audience was hastily arranged before
George III left for Weymouth. George Canning was the only important
Foreign Office official in town, and even he rushed off to visit Pitt at
Holwood whenever possible. But later on, when King did meet Britain's
leaders, he developed valuable personal friendships. The Duke of Portland was sufficiently impressed to recommend the American for an hon-
orary degree from Oxford, and by the winter of 1797 King was being
entertained at small and intimate dinners made up chiefly of members
of the Cabinet. One of his close friends was Sir William Scott, a government legal expert and the jurist who handed down the *Polly* decision.
Another was William Wilberforce, who later served King as a channel
of informal contact with the government.

King became quite friendly with Lord Grenville and paid several
visits to Dropmore. The Foreign Secretary was almost incapable of personal
warmth, and Rufus King never allowed friendship to interfere with
diplomacy, but the two men understood, respected, and trusted one
another. Furthermore, they had similar attitudes on the most important
question of the day. When Grenville forwarded a copy of one of his
speeches on France ("I have thought your friendship to me would give
it in your eyes more interest than it would otherwise be entitled to."),
King thanked the Foreign Secretary and expressed his complete agreement with the sentiments of the speech. It is, he wrote, "only by this
animated, firm and explicit manner of treating the detestable principles
which threaten the existence of every society, as well as of human happiness, that we can expect to see a proportionate and successful re-

sistance."[11] Small wonder that Jeffersonian journals asserted that King was "an Englishman at heart!"

The appointments of Rufus King and Robert Liston contributed to the steady improvement during 1796. Liston himself assisted the rapprochement by urging British officers in American waters to use press gangs as sparingly as possible and intervening to secure liberal regulations controlling Canadian trade with the United States.[12] Before his arrival, the British government gave safe passage to American cargoes and even specie sent from England to Holland to meet interest charges on the American debt, although the Netherlands was under French control.[13] The United States, too, showed its cordiality, particularly by the ready manner in which it enforced the articles of the Jay treaty circumscribing the rights of Britain's enemies in American harbors. Chief Justice Ellsworth prevented the sale of two prizes brought into Charleston by French privateers, and the courts of Northern states usually acted as the treaty required. To make doubly sure, however, at Liston's request Pickering issued a circular to customs' officials directing them to permit no French prizes to enter American ports.[14] Very few were seen thereafter. Like William Bingham's gift of the famous Stuart portrait of Washington to Lord Lansdowne, which also took place in 1796, these incidents were perhaps but straws in the wind. The wind, however, was blowing in the right direction—toward cordiality between the two countries—and the new envoys took up their posts with every expectation, not of fighting old quarrels anew, but of developing good relations.

The dramatic transfer of frontier posts from British to American hands aided this process. Lord Grenville in 1794 had readily agreed to surrender these forts, but this was later made conditional on developments in the United States. At last, in May 1796, with the supplementary article approved and the treaty bill on the President's desk, the British chargé at Philadelphia informed Canadian authorities that the way was cleared for the execution of this part of the treaty. James McHenry, Pickering's successor as Secretary of War, soon dispatched Captain Lewis to Quebec to make arrangements with Lord Dorchester. Dorchester was ready to evacuate the posts on schedule, but the United States Army was finding it difficult to gather sufficient forces to garrison all the posts, and Lewis requested that, to prevent depredations by the Indians, British forces remain in the forts temporarily. Dorchester assented.[15]

Actually, the British forces did not have long to wait, for the Americans occupied the posts as rapidly as they could. In July, Colonel John Hamtramck, commanding advance elements of the army north of the Ohio, received orders from General Wayne to take over Detroit and the post on the Maumee, near which he was encamped. Although Wayne had warned Secretary McHenry in February that he lacked sufficient troops "to give a proper impression,"[16] Hamtramck had only five hundred men under his command. A sixty-five man detail was all that he felt able to spare, and this force, commanded by Captain Moses Porter, accepted the transfer of Detroit on the eleventh of July. On the same day, Hamtramck himself occupied Fort Miami, and four days later, far to the eastward, Oswego was surrendered to the Americans. By the beginning of August, only Niagara and Michilimackinac remained in British hands, and on the eleventh American troops coming by lake from Oswego arrived at Niagara.[17] General Wayne had reached Detroit by this time, and he speedily arranged the departure of an expedition to Michilimackinac. Not enough supplies could be spared to carry the detachment through the winter, so Wayne borrowed fifty barrels of salt pork from the British commander across the Detroit River,[18] and the expedition sailed north to take possession of the last of the posts remaining in British hands.

The smooth exchange of the frontier posts was hailed in both countries. Little success attended scattered Republican attempts to minimize the transaction, perhaps because the opposition had been particularly vociferous on this subject two years earlier. Federalist journals were ecstatic. "IMPORTANT. PLEASING. AUTHENTIC. . . . *What think ye of the Treaty now?*" crowed one of them; "The Posts are taken, and not one drop of blood shed! Eternal praises to the God of Peace and Negociation, thanks to his servants." When Timothy Pickering heard of the surrender of Niagara, he wrote Rufus King, "The *Posts* have been delivered up by the British in a manner perfectly acceptable; and at present we have peace on all our borders, accompanied with internal tranquility." Grenville was very pleased to hear of the transfer and of the "Acts of mutual civility and attention so highly creditable to His Majesty's Government of Canada and that of the United States."[19] This happy condition along the Canadian-American frontier lasted about a decade, the harbinger of over a century of generally peaceful contact following the War of 1812. No single result of the Jay treaty was so fundamental to good relations as Britain's surrender of the forts, for the highly developed *amour-propre* of a new nation could hardly be expected to tolerate the presence of redcoats on American soil.

Although the complexity of the problems faced by the arbitral boards precluded any such spectacular success as had been achieved in transferring the posts, the machinery of all of them was put into motion in 1796. The St. Croix boundary commission was the first to get under way and the first to complete its task, to determine which of the rivers flowing out of Passamaquoddy Bay was the true River St. Croix and thus—in accordance with the treaty of 1783—the international boundary. The United States claimed the Magaguadavic, Britain the Schoodiac, two streams which were about nine miles apart at their mouths but much more so further inland.[20] Since the eastern boundary of Maine ran up the river to its source and thence northward, there was in dispute not only the area between the rivers but also a strip of land, possibly fifty miles wide, all the way north to the (largely mythical) highlands dividing the Atlantic and St. Lawrence watersheds. Many thousands of square miles were at stake, including small but growing farm communities, chiefly American, in the area near Passamaquoddy Bay as well as the British military road and settlement along the upper reaches of the River St. John. (See map, page 50.)

The English choice for this commission—the third member was to be chosen by the other two, or by lot—was Thomas Barclay of Annapolis, Nova Scotia. Barclay was an American Loyalist who served as a colonel during the Revolution, then moved to Nova Scotia and resumed the practice of law. He was a member and later speaker of the provincial assembly. As a British official and possibly as a holder of lands in the St. Croix area, Barclay had an interest in the way the dispute was settled. but he proved to be a satisfactory arbitrator.

The first American nominee was General Henry Knox, a bad choice, for Knox was one of the largest speculators in Maine lands and was already known to be on the brink of bankruptcy. To say the least, self-interest would have severely tested his impartiality. Fortunately, Knox's speculative activities so occupied his time that he informed the government he would be unable to accept unless the first meeting could be postponed until 1797, and Pickering decided to look elsewhere. After conversations with Rufus King, George Cabot, and Fisher Ames, the choice fell upon a Rhode Islander named David Howell. He was, Pickering reported to the President, "a member of the old Congress— . . . a judge, & is now a practicing lawyer. . . . And all agree in opinion of Mr. Howell's integrity, abilities, great learning, & perseverance in whatever he undertakes."[21]

The choice of a third member proved less difficult than some had feared. At the first official meeting in Halifax, Barclay agreed to accept one of David Howell's nominees. He was Egbert Benson, a New York lawyer of distinction whom the American government had considered for a position on the debt commission. Although Pickering had even hinted at a promotion from the New York bench to the Supreme Court if Benson would take up the arduous task in Philadelphia,[22] he was still available for service on the boundary commission. Barclay claimed that he only accepted Benson because he was unwilling to trust to the luck of the draw,[23] but the New Yorker cannot have been too unpalatable to him or he would have insisted on his right to have the third member chosen by lot.

In October, Barclay and Howell met Benson at St. Andrews, on the shores of Passamaquoddy Bay, and the commission got off to a smooth start. The trio held one official meeting, examined the coastline of the bay, and then adjourned until the next summer to allow time for the gathering of evidence and surveying of Passamaquoddy Bay and the streams which ran into it. Long before, Phineas Bond had sent Liston documentary evidence which he rightly described as presenting the British case "by a Train of forcible, tho' prolix, Reasoning."[24] Unconsciously,

ST. CROIX RIVER

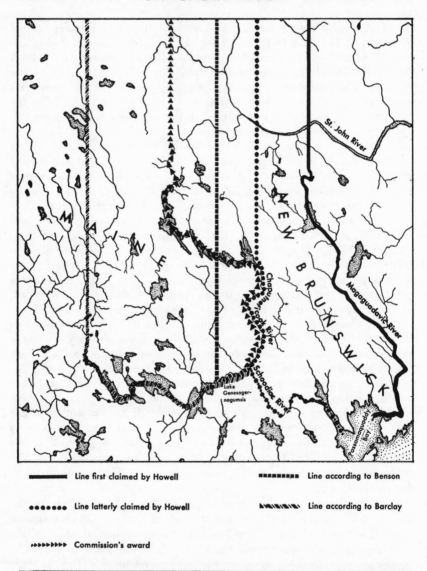

——— Line first claimed by Howell	▪▪▪▪▪▪▪▪ Line according to Benson
●●●●●● Line latterly claimed by Howell	▶◀▶◀▶◀ Line according to Barclay
▶▶▶▶▶▶ Commission's award	

Adapted from Charles O. Paullin, Atlas of the Historical Geography of the United States (*Carnegie Institution of Washington*. Publication No. 401, *Baltimore*, 1932), *Plate 91C.*

Bond was describing equally well the character of the arguments which the agents, Ward Chipman and James Sullivan, presented to the board at its Boston meeting—and, indeed, at all those which followed. Several warm summer days were spent listening to these presentations, one more on a trip to Braintree to question John Adams on the intentions of the negotiators at Paris, and then the board again adjourned, this time to meet in Providence in June 1798.

This recess was made necessary by the slowness of the surveyors, who found it a particularly arduous task to determine the exact longitude and latitude of the head of every stream which might be suggested as the main branch of the St. Croix. To speed things up, the agents before the board suggested that the two countries agree merely to mark the source decided upon with a permanent monument. Barclay endorsed this idea, although he was a bit troubled by the thought that someone—probably a speculator in Maine lands—might move the marker. The American government ordered Rufus King to settle this matter at London. An agreement was reached in March 1798,[25] and Senate approval was secured in June. Thus, in less than five months this minor problem had been smoothly and easily settled, and the way was cleared for a final decision.

The St. Croix commission began its last session at Providence in August. Since 1796 each government had been assiduously searching for evidence that might bolster its case—on the American side, the library of the Vice President was tapped for a rare volume, and the Secretary of State himself sought information in the Philadelphia library—and as a result it was not until October that Sullivan and Chipman at last conceded that they had nothing further to present. Both governments apparently felt that a preponderance of the evidence favored the British case. English authorities said as much, although they promised to accept any decision with equanimity. Pickering hinted to James Sullivan, as he already had in 1797, that a compromise would be acceptable. If the decision established either the Magaguadavic or the main branch of the Schoodiac as the boundary, he wrote, "one party will certainly be extremely dissatisfied." On the other hand, "the North branch of the Schoodiack would be an eligible boundary, as it leaves a large portion of the contested land to each."[26]

In October, when the board began to discuss an award, it was discovered that each member had a different opinion. Howell, the American representative, at first argued for the Magaguadavic, but he soon abandoned his position and shifted to the Chaputneticook, the northern branch of the Schoodiac, up to the point where that stream issued from a group of lakes wandering off in a northwesterly direction. The British member, Barclay, and the third member, Benson, held that the western Schoodiac was the true St. Croix, but they disagreed on the source of this river. Barclay insisted on its headwaters, which would have pushed the boundary almost fifty miles due west, but Benson argued that the river's source was the point where it changed from a regular stream into a series of lakes, the first of which bore the tongue-twisting name of Genesagernagumsis. Barclay was annoyed by this sophistry, but he finally agreed to adopt Benson's view in order to secure an award favorable to Britain. Howell of course refused to make the decision unanimous, and when his colleagues drew up an award he not only refused to sign it but insisted upon his right to include a dissent in the official records. Thereupon, as Howell later reported to the Secretary of State, "Some Altercation, rather unpleasant, took place between my friend Benson & myself in private; Col. Barclay seemed to keep himself on the reserve & to push our Friend Benson forward."[27]

At this point, in the course of his usual summer travels, Robert Liston arrived in Providence and took a hand in the discussions. The American agent, James Sullivan, pointed out to him that, while the award contemplated by Barclay and Benson gave Britain a large area near Passamaquoddy Bay already peopled by American settlers, the source of the Chaputneticook actually lay to the west of Lake Genesagernagumsis. Thus the Chaputneticook line, if extended through the lakes at its head, beyond the point suggested by Howell, would actually be more favorable to Great Britain in the area of the St. John River, where land had already been granted away by colonial authorities. Sullivan thought that he could induce Howell to push the line on to the upper headwaters of the Chaputneticook if the other two commissioners abandoned the Schoodiac. Liston agreed to support this compromise, and, as Howell later reported,

something like a negotiation, started by Judge Sullivan &, I believe, assented to by Mr. Liston, . . . carried them [Barclay and Benson] to the North branch, & induced me to agree with them in our final result—to induce me to which Judge Sullivan read to me your Letters to him in which you contended that the Sources of a river must be the most remote waters which flow in it. . . .

I considered it as a fortunate circumstance that all the claims of Individuals are quieted; and the Satisfaction expressed by both agents gave reason to hope that the parties more immediately interested would readily acquiesce in our result.[28]

Both countries were satisfied with this compromise. The board's English secretary wrote gleefully, "As it is, we lost not a single British settlement. A few miserable Frenchmen at Madawaska on the route to Canada fall within their territory."[29] Although the St. Croix decision did not fix the entire northeastern boundary, much of which remained in dispute for almost half a century, the successful demarcation of a portion of the Maine boundary was a credit to both governments. The success of this first arbitration was in no small part due to the fact that they allowed the commission to do its own work with a minimum of outside interference. In general, they limited themselves to advice and encouragement sent to the agents, and both expressed a willingness to accept any award that was made. Finally, when the natural nationalistic inclinations of the commissioners brought about a tense situation, the wise voice of the British envoy tactfully supported a compromise settlement which proved satisfactory to the members of the board and to their countries.

The debt commission never equaled the success of the St. Croix board, nor did it even make as much progress in 1796, although at the time this did not seem particularly ominous. This body, which had the job of examining the claims of British subjects who were unable to collect debts incurred by Americans before the Revolution, had five members. Each country named two, and the fifth was to be mutually agreed upon or chosen by lot. The American nominees were Thomas FitzSimons and James Innes. FitzSimons had been a member of Congress under the Articles of Confederation and the new national government as well as a representative of Pennsylvania in the Constitutional Convention. He was a Federalist and a successful businessman. James Innes, a Virginian, was well known in his home state as a lawyer, having gained part of his reputation in a celebrated struggle against the attempts of a British creditor to collect debts owed to him. Although Innes' residence in Virginia and his part in this case opened him to possible charges of prejudice, he played a creditable part in the proceedings at Philadelphia until his death in 1798, and the British members of the commission never complained that he showed undue bias.

Lord Grenville was somewhat slow in making his choices for the Philadelphia commission, and when he did turn his attention to the problem he had difficulty finding men who would take the job. Finally, in September 1796, Thomas Macdonald and Henry Pye Rich were appointed. The American minister in London, Rufus King, thought that they were good choices:

the former is a Barrister of some eminence; the latter is a Merchant who has resided for more than Twenty years in Holland, and was the British Consul there at the commencement of the war between this and that Country.—They are both esteemed to be liberal and upright men wholly unconnected with the business of the Commission, and well disposed to cultivate a good understanding and friendly intercourse between the two Countries—[30]

Macdonald made a hasty trip to Scotland to see the principal creditors and then, after some altercation with the Admiralty over the size and quality of the ship which was to carry them across the Atlantic, he and Rich sailed in "a very small & old 28 Gun Frigate which had never got a thorough repair."[31] Six hundred miles at sea, heavy weather forced the ship to turn back. The two appointees soon reëmbarked, but they did not arrive in the United States until long after the end of the year. The commission had its first meeting in May 1797.

By this time, the London counterpart of the debt commission had long been at work. This body, authorized by Article VII of the treaty, made awards for seized American vessels unfairly treated in British courts as well as for British ships lost because of some violation of America's neutral obligations. Any incident occurring prior to the exchange of ratifications could be raised before the board. Thus the long delay before ratification greatly multiplied American claims, already much larger than the British, by bringing seizures under the provision order of 1795 before the commission for adjudication.

The United States again made its appointments first. Alexander Hamilton was considered—a fair indication of the board's importance in American eyes—but the actual choice fell upon two young attorneys. Christopher Gore of Massachusetts was a successful speculator and lawyer who had been considered for the post of Attorney General. But he much preferred a sojourn in London to one in Philadelphia, and many influential friends supported his application for this position. The other man chosen, William Pinkney, had served in the Constitutional Convention and been active in Maryland politics. He apparently owed his appointment to his friend James McHenry, the Secretary of War.[32]

On arriving in England, Gore and Pinkney found that their British colleagues were to be John Nicholl and Nicholas Anstey. Both of these men were well-known experts on maritime law; in fact, throughout their service on the board they also filled other positions in this field for the British government. Grenville looked upon the caliber of the nominees as further proof of the friendly attitude of His Majesty's Government. "Both Dr. Nicholl and Mr. Anstey," he wrote John Jay, "are known (in some degree) in America, . . . and I trust the appointment has proved the spirit in which it is made." Christopher Gore thought that the appointment of Nicholl, who had often represented American claimants before British courts, was particularly fortunate; "there is good reason to hope from his general character for integrity, candor & soundness of intellect, that he may not be unfavorable to a true & liberal exposition of the rights of neutral nations—"[33]

In order to lighten the commission's burden, even before it met the British government suggested noncompulsory arbitration of some of the more straightforward cases by the King's Advocate and an expert to be named by the United States. These two could make an award which would be binding if accepted by both sides; otherwise, the case would return without prejudice to the docket of the commission.[34] When the United States accepted this proposal, the British named Sir William Scott to represent them, and Rufus King chose John Nicholl—a good indication of the confidence which he commanded. Nicholl and Scott got to work in October 1796 and were able to fix awards totaling almost eighty thousand pounds.[35] This scheme, initiated by Great Britain, speeded up payment and lessened the pressure on the London commission.

The fifth member of the commission had to be chosen by lot, since each country insisted upon nominating its own citizens. Luck favored the Americans, and John Trumbull's name was drawn. The painter had been in London since 1794, when he served as John Jay's private secretary but had little to do with the negotiations of that year. Trumbull had no legal training and only a rudimentary knowledge of diplomacy or business, and yet, for the final drawing, the British chose him from among the names presented by Pinkney and Gore. They might have made a different choice had they known of the vigor with which Trumbull castigated the Royal Navy in private conversations, but, as it turned out, he was a conscientious and fair-minded member of the board. Like everyone else, Trumbull failed to foresee that this work would take almost a decade; in accepting his appointment he wrote to his colleagues, "it may be in our power to fulfill the intention of the Treaty by an accomplishment of our Duty so prompt as shall not seriously interfere with my wish of an early return to my Country—"[36]

The board had hardly begun to function before it struck a snag which threatened to destroy it. The American agent, Samuel Bayard, asked that the "illegal and unjust decree" of the High Court of Appeals in the case of the ship *Betsey* be overthrown.[37] The British members took umbrage at Bayard's language. They also contested his assertion that the board could reverse judicial decisions and at the suggestion of the British proctor announced that, if the Americans continued to support Bayard's interpretation, they would by seceding deprive the board of a quorum. Fortunately both sides agreed to postpone further discussion while the British members consulted Lord Grenville.

Rufus King, righteously indignant at Proctor Gostling, had already raised the matter at Downing Street. Lord Grenville poured oil on the troubled waters, condemning Bayard's extreme language but adding that "the Kings Gov^t are not bound to support the Positions taken by [the proctor] Mr. Goseling."[38] He suggested that King consult the Lord Chancellor, and Loughborough, a man not ordinarily noted for his tact, worked out a compromise which saved the face of both sides while giving the substance to the United States. He categorically repudiated Gostling's contention that the board could not review British court decisions; these, he said, "are the very cases which it was intended should be examined and decided by the Commissioners."[39] The board, Loughborough added, was competent "to Examine the Questions which have been before the H. Court of Appeals . . . and to afford Redress, not by reversing the Decrees already passed, . . . but by ascertaining the Damage that the Claimant had sustained . . . and by awarding Payment thereof to be made by his M. Government."[40] In other words, while the court's decision might have been justified by British decrees in force at the time, it was still possible for a shipowner to have a claim in equity—and the treaty used this word—against the British government, a claim which the board could consider. Loughborough's common-sense decision ended the controversy. The arbitrators resumed their meetings; eventually, the owners of the *Betsey* were awarded sixty-seven hundred pounds, and the board thereafter was able to adjudicate virtually any case that it felt to be within the purview of the treaty. This settlement was a fitting end to a year of great progress. In twelve months, Congressional approval of the Jay treaty and the successful execution of much of it had drawn Britain and the United States closer together.

In riposte, the French opened a diplomatic counteroffensive. The old friends of America—Brissot, Paine, Lafayette—no longer held positions of responsibility, and younger and less experienced rulers were encouraged, even intoxicated, by the astounding series of victories which crowned French arms. By the end of 1796, France had overrun Holland, driven Prussia from the war, and enjoyed the fruits of Bonaparte's first Italian campaign, while at home the accession of the Directory promised a more stable government. It is small wonder that these events led the Republic's leaders to believe that no power on earth, certainly not a young, faction-torn nation with neither an army nor a navy, would dare to oppose them. Acting on this hypothesis France assumed an attitude of menace which brought her to the very brink of open warfare with the United States.

Although there were rumors of French plans for armed action against the United States when news of the ratification of the Jay treaty reached Europe,[41] the Directory first adopted a policy designed to make this unnecessary. Urged on by their envoy in the United States and, it was said, by James Monroe, the American representative at Paris,[42] the French government determined to intervene boldly and openly in the coming Presidential election. Since the Federalist government seemed to have no desire to come to an agreement with France—no instructions went to Monroe during the first six months of 1796—France would cause the administration to be replaced by a friendlier one. Adet was directed to announce his recall and the suspension of diplomatic relations with the United States. "I have," Monroe commented on this development, "detained them seven months from doing what they ought to have done at once."[43] Adet was further ordered to proclaim that the election was in effect a choice between a quarrel with France and the friendship of that old ally. By combining a threat with an appeal to former comrades in arms, the Directory hoped to defeat the Federalist candidate—Adams was no more palatable than Washington—and secure the triumph of Jefferson.

This French policy was a blunder born of self-confidence and contempt for America. The Federalists immediately seized upon it. Answering Adet, the *Connecticut Courant* asserted, "You must needs lug into your address the very name of Jefferson, for no earthly purpose but to discover the real object of it! And now there is not an elector this side the Delaware that would not be sooner shot than vote for him." Resentment at foreign interference was strong, but an even more effective answer to the French was Washington's Farewell Address, released to the American people in September. In later epochs the sections referring to foreign affairs were applied to relations with Great Britain or other powers, but in the fall of 1796 no one could misunderstand the meaning of Washington's warning against permanent alliances; no one could fail to see the contemporary application of his assertion that "nothing is more essential than that

56

permanent inveterate antipathies against particular nations, and passionate attachements for others, should be excluded; and that in place of them, just and amicable feelings towards all should be cultivated."[44]

The Farewell Address, which reached England in November, first drew the attention of London papers to the campaign in America. On the ninth and tenth all the major dailies gave it top billing, printing the text and adding extended comment. Washington's message dominated the pages of the newspapers for almost a week, a remarkable demonstration of interest in American affairs which encouraged one enterprising Londoner hastily to prepare and put on sale copies of John Trumbull's portrait of the President.

London journals all agreed that Washington was a distinguished statesman and that his message was important, but beyond that political prejudices inevitably resulted in different interpretations. The *Morning Chronicle*, the Opposition paper which carried most comment, praised Washington for providing the rare spectacle of a man voluntarily abandoning power: "It is a grand and most affecting sight, thus to see a virtuous and exalted man prove by his conduct that it was not to serve private avarice or ambition—not the thirst of power or of aggrandisement that moved him to depart from domestic ease." Perhaps fearful that some would not appreciate the domestic applicability of this lesson, the *Chronicle* followed it up with a sally at "the tribe of Placemen and Pensioners" who supported Pitt's government. "They cannot," the paper reported, "believe it possible that a man should voluntarily abdicate the dignities and privileges of office merely for the good of the country."[45]

Tory papers naturally declined to accept this interpretation, and all regretted that Washington had decided to retire. Since any change of policy might fatally affect "the prosperity of their infant State, and diffuse still more widely the flames of War which now desolate a great part of Europe," said the *Sun*, "his Resignation . . . becomes a circumstance of general import, and of general concern." The staunchly Pittite *True Briton* agreed, writing that the President's retirement was "an event that must be deeply deplored, not only by every friend of America, but by every man who feels an interest in the general happiness and welfare of Europe."[46] Government papers, however, took some consolation from Washington's attack on factionalism, and they attempted to apply this part of his message to British and European politics. The *Times*, already one of the big guns of English conservatism, argued:

General WASHINGTON'S Address to the People of the UNITED STATES, is the most complete comment upon English Clubs and Clubbists, upon Factions and Parties, and factious Partizans. The authority of this Revolutionist may be set up against the wild and wicked Revolutionists of Europe, if not as Altar against Altar at least as Altar against Sacrilege.[47]

By this time, the American political campaign was in full swing, and it was closely watched both by Robert Liston and Pierre Adet, who was still in the United States although his official functions had been suspended.

An important battleground was Pennsylvania, where both sides threw their full force into the struggle. Threats, bribes, illegalities, and slander —all played their part, and Liston wryly remarked that, "if the infant state of the Society is taken into consideration, the advances made by the members in the road towards corruption will be found to be fully as rapid as was to be expected."[48] Rumors that British gold bought votes for Adams were constantly repeated, and Liston felt that they had some effect. At any rate, thirteen Jeffersonian electors were chosen, only two for Adams. Although the Pennsylvania election was a sharp blow to Federalist hopes, they rightly refused to concede defeat. As many had predicted to Liston, Pinckney's presence on the ticket helped cut into the Republican majority in the South. One vote each from North Carolina and Virginia, success in the Middle States other than Pennsylvania, the two votes there, and a solid North all combined to gain Adams the victory by three votes.

British newspapers maintained their interest in the campaign until the end, distorting it, as usual, to suit their own political purposes. Thus the *Times* described Adams as the political heir of Washington, a man "attached to a mixed Government, particularly to that of Great Britain, . . . [whose] private character is of the most irreproachable kind." On the other hand, said the paper, applying what was intended to be a devastating parallel, "Mr. JEFFERSON is considered as the LANSDOWNE of America. . . . His talents are said to be inferior to those of Mr. ADAMS, and are thought to possess more shew than solidity."[49] Across the political fence, the *Morning Chronicle* chose to emphasize different aspects of the election, picturing the republicanism therein displayed as a magnificent example of the middle road between anarchy and despotism:

What a scene has America displayed! The election of a President . . . has taken place with less disorder than the election of a Member for a popular Borough in England, and certainly with much less immorality and expense. [Liston and other observers might well have contested this statement.]

The event has put the Constitution of America to the test, and it has come forth pure and unsullied—an example to all people of the value of consistency and steadiness in principle. The result . . . ought to be a warning . . . to the parasites of arbitrary power . . . that no people can be truly secure in the enjoyment of the blessings of peace, who have not an essential voice in the Councils of their Government.[50]

The victor in this exemplary campaign, wearing a new suit of pearl-colored broadcloth, was sworn into office on the fourth of March, 1797. "He assumed on this occasion," wrote Robert Liston, "what, compared with the usual simplicity of his appearance, might be looked upon as a degree of state:—a new carriage,—liveries,—and a sword and cockade." Liston had already analyzed the probable effect of Adams' succession in terms which bore some resemblance to Adet's famous characterization of Jefferson, though less forceful and more hopeful. Adams' victory, he said, seemed to be a gain for Britain, "not because I perceive in Mr Adams

any partiality of sentiment towards Great Britain, but because he de-
tests . . . our enemies, and because the firmness of his character removes
all danger of his being *bullied* into measures which he does not approve."[51]

The inauguration of Adams may be said to mark the end of the first
phase of the rapprochement. Three years of capable diplomacy had thrust
the danger of armed conflict into the background, and, with new and able
ministers at each capital, there was every prospect for the development of
real cordiality. The much maligned Jay treaty had at last been firmly
seated as the keystone of American foreign policy, and the benefits it
conferred were already impressive. Since passions had run high in 1794
and 1795, citizens of the United States of course continued to breathe
sentiments other than sweetness and light toward Great Britain even
after the Jay treaty went into effect. Nevertheless, as many observers
remarked, the change in public opinion had been truly remarkable. By
1797, the heyday of Benjamin Franklin Bache had passed, and a simple
appeal to Anglophobia was scarcely an adequate political stock in trade.
In retirement at Mount Vernon, Washington may well have reflected with
satisfaction on these developments. He and all supporters of Anglo-
American friendship could afford to look hopefully to the future.

The Press Gangs 5

B Y THE NARROWEST OF MARGINS, JOHN ADAMS SUCCEEDED WASHINGTON as President of the United States. At the same time, across the Atlantic, William Pitt gained an easy victory in the Parliamentary election of 1796. After sharing for four years responsibility for the maintenance of good relations, Pitt and Adams left office at almost the same time in 1801. During these years, Pitt led his country, none too successfully, through years of war and creaky coalition, for this was the era of Rivoli and Marengo and Hohenlinden, of the Mutiny of the Nore, of the Eighteenth Brumaire and the rise of Bonaparte. England's beleaguered state encouraged Pitt and Grenville to continue a conciliatory policy toward the United States, while in America the controversy with France that Adams had inherited from his predecessor flared up into an undeclared war and impelled him in the same direction. There were few disagreements until the President opened negotiations for peace with France and exposed the schism within the Federalist party, which took to its deathbed—the fatal illness was prolonged—in a spasm of treachery and recrimination.

Anglo-American relations during these years fall into two categories, each reflecting a different aspect of the struggles against France. While engaged in an undeclared war, the United States worked out with Britain a system of mutual assistance. This was as important as the dramatic Franco-American naval clashes taking place at the same time. The other side of the story, meriting equal attention, was the whole complex of problems arising out of the neutrality of the United States during a major European war—impressment, the position of neutral commerce, and the degree and manner in which the British Navigation System was to be modified under the pressure of war.

Impressment was one of the most important issues threatening Anglo-American friendship in the years after the Jay treaty. In countless ports of the Empire, press gangs swooped down to gather in American seamen enjoying a few hours of bibulous shore leave; at sea, British men-of-war ordered American merchantmen to heave to while arrogant boarding officers examined the crew for able-bodied seamen who might or might not be British subjects. If a few American citizens were impressed by mistake, said Britain, that was regrettable. But war makes harsh demands, even upon neutrals, and impressment was the only effective means by which the Royal Navy could recruit men. Conditions on board His Majesty's ships virtually precluded voluntary enlistment, since able-bodied seamen were paid about ten shillings a month, seldom received shore leave, and almost always had to serve until the end of the war. Harsh discipline was necessary to keep the ships functioning efficiently, and the principal reliance was on the cat-o'-nine tails, which occasionally caused death, although one seaman was reported to have survived 157 lashes.[1]

Naturally, there were many desertions from the King's service. Lord Nelson once placed the total at forty-two thousand in the period down to the Peace of Amiens.[2] Large numbers of men deserted either in the ports of the United States or to take service in American ships in other parts of the world. The frigate which brought Macdonald and Rich to the United States lost twenty men by desertion as soon as she reached port, and such happenings were not rare. Consul Barclay reported in 1799 that the crew of a captain's barge was invited to desert in the presence of the skipper, and Barclay went on to state that "His Majesty's Packet Boats invariably lose a part of their crews every time they enter this Port by desertion. . . . The enormous pay allowed by the Americans to Seamen is too great a temptation for our Sailors to resist."[3]

Some conflict with the United States was inevitable, and it was high-lighted by disagreement on two important issues, the national rights of a merchant vessel at sea and the indefeasibility of allegiance. Britain claimed it to be a "great and fundamental principle of maritime jurisdiction . . . that ships upon the high seas compose no part of the territory of the state." Grenville argued that a belligerent had an incontestable right to search neutral vessels for enemy soldiers and property, "a right incon-sistent with every idea of territory," and that there could therefore be no doubt that "it also has the right to take its own subjects found on board of a foreign vessel on the high seas."[4] The United States govern-ment refused to accept this principle. It insisted that the American flag, at least to a degree, protected ships from foreign interference, but the precise amount of protection conferred by the Stars and Stripes was not defined in this period, either by Federalist or Republican administrations.

Similar differences existed over the definition of citizenship. Again the British position was clear, the American vague. The common law held that citizenship was indefeasible. Pitt's government clung firmly to this principle, refusing to grant that Britons who moved to the United States and were naturalized could thus avoid the responsibilities of English citizenship, including service in the Royal Navy. Replying to a naval officer's request for a definition of American citizenship, the Admiralty's secretary stated that "no British subject who was not an Inhabitant of America on or before the Separation of that Country, can be regarded as a Citizen of the United States if liable to be impressed."[5] American officials did not consistently endorse the principle of voluntary expatria-tion during this period. However, a series of naturalization acts conferred full citizenship upon newcomers to the United States; one law, that of 1790, required a waiting period of only two years. The Federalist admin-istration never formally insisted that Great Britain recognize these naturali-zation proceedings, however. Pickering was particularly liberal in his attitude; Robert Liston reported that "he seems to be sensible that the admission of the effect of naturalization, if it ever takes place, must be a concession on the part of Great Britain, and the fruit of amicable negotiation for that purpose."*⁶*

Although a few American seamen were taken by press gangs at the time of the Nootka Sound controversy, impressment did not become a serious problem until near the close of the Washington administration. Down to the end of 1795, Thomas Pinckney asked the release of only thirty-two impressed Americans,⁷ but early in 1796 new factors pushed impressment to the fore. British ports had been swept clean, and the merchant marine had surrendered as many men as it could spare, but still the Royal Navy complained that it was short of men. Consequently, impressment from American ships in British ports increased markedly, and for the first time the Royal Navy began to seize men from vessels sailing on the high seas. The reaction of the United States was strong, and there was little that Robert Liston could do to stem it. He attempted to mollify the Secretary of State, and he wrote letters to British captains in which he "suggested the propriety . . . of forebearance and moderation, and . . . exhorted our officers to adopt the maxim that it is better that the guilty should escape than that the innocent should suffer."⁸ Neither move had any appreciable effect.

In fact, it was already too late. As early as February the House of Representatives requested the President to send agents to England and the West Indies to work for the release of impressed Americans. Republicans, led by Robert R. Livingston, agitated for further action, and were supported by party journals. "The patriotic Livingston, the SAILORS FRIEND, will, we trust, accomplish some effectual plan to check the base conduct of the British," wrote the *Independent Chronicle*.⁹ After a short interval, a bill was introduced into the House providing funds for agents for seamen and establishing a system of certification so that Americans could prove their citizenship.

This bill provoked acrimonious debate in the House. Conservative Federalists protested that Congress had no right to direct the Executive in the field of foreign affairs and claimed that the certificate system was full of loopholes. Some Republicans denied these charges and attempted to brand the Federalists as a party uninterested in the fate of ordinary Americans, while others, notably Livingston, did not even bother to conceal their hatred of the British and their desire to twist the lion's tail. Moderate members of the House supported the bill both because of the pressure of public feeling and because they felt that something had to be done to protect American seamen from indiscriminate if not malicious impressment by the British Navy. The bill passed by a vote of seventy-seven to thirteen; only the most determined Federalists, men like Roger Griswold, Uriah Tracy, Theodore Sedgwick, and William Vans Murray, dared to vote against it. There was some wrangling with the staunchly

Federalist Senate, which attempted to tighten up the bill, but the upper chamber did not hold out for long. Congressional action was completed in May, and President Washington soon signed the Act for the Relief and Protection of American Seamen.[10]

Lord Grenville's reaction confirmed warnings by those who had insisted that the bill was loosely drawn. Down to this time, England had tolerated an informal system whereby American consuls issued protections when presented with far more detailed proof than that required by the new law. Now, however, the Foreign Secretary asked Thomas Pinckney what evidence the consuls would henceforth demand and implied that consular protections would no longer be accepted unless the old standards were maintained. Neither Pinckney nor his successor, Rufus King, was willing to admit officially that the Act for the Relief and Protection of American Seamen was not satisfactory. They therefore permitted the consuls to act under it. Grenville soon complained that certificates were being issued to Englishmen and requested King to "notify to the Consuls that they are in future to abstain from a proceeding which far exceeds the limits of their office . . . [and is] an act . . . injurious to the authority of the King's government."[11]

From this time on, no protections were issued by American consuls in Britain, for King was unable to get Grenville to permit a return to the old system arranged by Pinckney. The Act of 1796 was so carelessly drawn, fraud so prevalent, and the sale of documents to Englishmen so common that only a few months after John Adams came into office Lord Grenville informed the Admiralty that even protections issued in the United States were no longer acceptable proofs of citizenship.[12] Since new legislation in 1799 did not materially tighten the regulations, Britain continued to refuse to recognize the certificates. Until the end of the war, the Royal Navy usually released American seamen only upon receipt of an authenticated representation from the Secretary of State or a sworn statement signed by the collector of customs in the seaman's home port. The ill-advised legislation of 1796 not only failed of its purpose but destroyed as well a workable, though limited, arrangement.

The appointment of agents for seamen in England and the West Indies, the original conception of the House of Representatives, was more successful. The first American representative in the Caribbean was Silas Talbot, a Revolutionary privateersman and former member of Congress who later commanded U. S. S. *Constitution*. Although Britain generally refused to admit foreign officials into her colonial possessions, Robert Liston sanctioned the appointment and gave Talbot letters of introduction to officers serving in the Caribbean. However, Grenville lost no time in informing Liston that His Majesty's Government did not intend to make an exception in this case. Pickering declined to end Talbot's mission, although he did direct him not to spend all his time at Jamaica but to travel from port to port.[13] The British government tolerated this arrangement, a much less serious violation of the traditional prohibition than acceptance of a resident agent.

Silas Talbot arrived in the West Indies in the autumn of 1796. During the next six months he visited most of the British possessions. Admiral Bligh at Jamaica, Admiral Harvey at Martinique, the governors of Barbados and Jamaica, and some lesser officers assisted him as much as possible. From March to May, 1797, Talbot and his assistants secured the release of well over a hundred men, and his presence in the area made British officers much more cautious when impressing seamen who claimed to be Americans. Unfortunately, this was not the whole story. Many British captains were uncoöperative. They were more concerned about the efficient operation of their ships than the diplomatic reverberations of impressment. What was more serious, however, was that Admiral Sir Hyde Parker, who exercised over-all command in the area, adopted a rigid and unfriendly attitude. Parker, later to achieve a dubious fame as the commander whose recall signal Nelson refused to see at Copenhagen, was an irascible officer nicknamed "Old Vinegar" by his subordinates. Soon after Talbot arrived, Sir Hyde refused to permit him to interview seamen on board British warships.[14] This order was not universally enforced, but it made the agent's task much more difficult. Furthermore, many of the captains who served under Parker, made aware of his attitude, refused to release any men claimed by Talbot.

By spring, the American's patience was exhausted. He applied for writs of habeas corpus against captains of ships which had Americans on board, and for a while this move was spectacularly successful. Over the protests of the King's Solicitor, the court ordered Captain Pigot of the *Hermione* and two other commanders to surrender seven sailors. The men from the *Hermione* told Talbot that four more Americans were on board, so recourse was once again had to the courts, and these too gained their freedom. Then, as Talbot reported, "the other Captains began to be somewhat alarmed . . . , and they gave out that I need not take out writs against them, for they would discharge all the Americans upon my application, and giving proof of their citizenship." Using the lash of court proceedings on recalcitrants, Talbot secured release of forty-seven seamen in six weeks.[15] Unfortunately for Americans on board British ships, there was no way to prevent news of these proceedings from reaching Admiral Parker, who was then with a squadron off the coast of Santo Domingo. In May, Sir Hyde directed his subordinates to ignore writs served at Talbot's request. Parker had previously warned Talbot that he felt himself directly responsible to His Majesty's Ministers, "to whom only, I hold myself accountable for my conduct, whatever may be the consequences."[16] The consequences for Parker in this instance were not serious, since Jamaican judges declined to contest the matter with the admiral. Silas Talbot's card had been trumped.

Although the American agent sadly reported to Philadelphia that "there is a total stop Put, to all effectual means that I have been able to devise for the release of our Citizens" and went on to predict that "no more seamen will be discharged during the time that Sir Hyde Parker may have command in these seas,"[17] events did not turn out quite so ill as Talbot feared. Parker continued to demand almost impossible proof of citizenship, but Admiral Harvey was more understanding, and impressment, which the American had feared would be speeded up after Parker's refusal to respect habeas corpus proceedings, was for some time carried out on a moderate scale in the West Indies. In 1798, Talbot resigned his office to take a naval command and was replaced by William Savage, a British subject and Jamaican magistrate who carried on the controversy with Parker until Admiral Seymour replaced Sir Hyde in 1800. The change in command, Savage reported, brought about a situation "widely different on the Score of Humanity."[18]

After Parker blocked action in the theater where impressment was most common, the only hope for impressed sailors lay in appeal to the Admiralty through American officials in London. The first man appointed agent in the capital was John Trumbull, but he declined to add this work to the burdens of the seizure commission. Rufus King himself forwarded weekly requests to the Admiralty until David Lenox, Trumbull's replacement, reached England in May 1797 to take up a post which he filled unobtrusively and well for five years. It was a thankless, wearisome task—long labors to get proof of citizenship, carefully copied lists sent to the Admiralty, laconic notes in reply announcing the release of a handful, close watch to see that even these got their freedom—but certain circumstances made the agent's work less arduous than it might have been. Although very conscious of the requirements of protocol, Lord Grenville allowed Lenox to bypass the Foreign Office and correspond directly with Evan Nepean, Secretary to the Lords Commissioners of the Admiralty, thus eliminating one step in the ordinary procedure. Nepean was reasonable and not unfriendly. He and the agent worked out an arrangement that eliminated the worst red tape, and for at least the first years of his mission Lenox did not complain of the British attitude.[19]

If a chart were made of the pressure impressment put upon Anglo-American relations, it would not show a steady rise from zero in 1793 to explosive heights in 1812. There were sharp ups and downs, and this was a final factor which eased Lenox's task. For purely military reasons, from 1797 to 1803 impressment was not as widespread as it had been in 1796 or was to be again when the British navy was rebuilt upon the renewal of war against France. "During the residence of Mr. King in England," John Quincy Adams later recalled, "there was much intermission of the practice [of impressment]."[20] In a negative way, because attention was not so frequently directed to the problem, this contributed to the easing of Anglo-American tension.

This point must not be exaggerated. The American agent found plenty to keep him busy, both in handling new cases and in attempting to secure the release of those who had been caught in the heavy press of 1796. Lenox's first official act was to present a list of seamen whose release had already been asked by Pinckney and King. Thereafter, he sent Nepean numerous requests; at least once, the list contained over five hundred names. When at the end of the war, he prepared a chart summarizing his activities, it showed a total of more than two thousand applications to the Admiralty. Although there is no indication of the years in which these men were first impressed, it is obvious that the problem did not cease in 1796. Lenox secured the release of 1042 men, roughly 47 per cent of all applications made. In 552 cases the Admiralty categorically refused to consider discharge; in another 624, Nepean declined to accept evidence forwarded by the American agent and asked for further proof.[21]

Cold figures scarcely reveal the tragic side of the story. Some Americans were killed fighting Britain's battles, and even those who eventually gained release often served many months or even years before they were able to appeal to Lenox. When discharged, these men were given the pittance owed to them as wages, perhaps some prize money (occasionally a very substantial sum), but no indemnity for the hardships suffered was offered by the Admiralty or demanded by the American government. Nor did Britain ever take decisive steps to control the naval commanders who most viciously practiced impressment or violated the rights of neutral ships. Occasionally, and only in those rare instances when the United States protested against a ship or her commander by name, the officer was recalled to England to explain his actions, but more often than not this made little difference to his subsequent career. Thus the British government appeared to condone the activities of the harshest commanders, those who used press gangs without stint or scruple. The impressment of even one native-born American citizen was justification for the most extreme protest; the seizure of twenty-five hundred sailors who at least presented some proof of American citizenship (for Lenox eliminated obviously fraudulent applications before forwarding the rest to Nepean), a number proportionate to some seventy-five thousand Americans today, was a flagrant invasion of sovereignty which would have justified almost any reprisal the United States chose to make.

In justice to Britain, and particularly to the Pitt government, a few words must be added. The Empire was engaged in a desperate war for survival against an enemy as powerful as the Germany of Kaiser Wilhelm or Adolf Hitler, and in the 1790's Britain's only potent weapon was the fleet flying the White Ensign. To keep this force manned, and, equally important, to discourage desertion to American ships, rigorous impressment was deemed necessary, both by naval officers and the civil officials who were their superiors. Malice did not enter into the picture, at least as far as the Cabinet was concerned. The ponderous machinery of the

Admiralty, the distances involved, and primitive communications made it difficult for the government to impose its desires upon captains at sea. The advantages that inertia conferred upon the old routine, unwillingness to tamper with a system which proved its worth from a military point of view—these, too, discouraged government intervention, and none of the administrations serving George III during two decades of war made major changes in impressment policy. In time of war, the piecemeal handling of individual cases was all that Britain felt she could offer to a neutral power, even to one with whom relations were generally cordial. Impressment was one field to which Pitt and Grenville were unwilling to apply fully their general policy of conciliation, and only a reduction of the Admiralty's voracious demand for men and the surprising restraint of the American government postponed the development of a dangerous quarrel.

On the diplomatic front, Britain fended off American attempts to negotiate limits to the practice of impressment or tied these negotiations to a program for the restoration of British deserters which, if carried out with vigor, would have served England's purpose almost as well. The tone was set in one of Rufus King's first conversations with Grenville. "I have no reason," the new minister wrote, "to doubt the sincere desire of this Government to cultivate our esteem. . . . I do not think they would for a slight cause disagree with us. But their colony trade and marine are topics intimately connected with their prosperity and security and more deeply with their commerce."[22]

Seven months later, and apparently at Pickering's suggestion, Robert Liston reported to London that it might be possible to negotiate a convention for the mutual restitution of deserters. Impressment had become a less explosive issue as the number of incidents declined and popular anger turned in a different direction with news of Pinckney's rebuff at Paris. Even if imperfectly enforced, the convention would be a warning to would-be deserters that they could not expect even the tacit protection of the United States government. America, with minuscule armed forces, would gain little directly, but if the Royal Navy was able to reduce the number of desertions fewer Americans would be lost to the press gangs. Lord Grenville hastily drafted the projet of an agreement. To put teeth into it, he included a provision giving consuls authority to have deserters arrested and confined until called for by representatives of the armed forces. To prevent the United States from claiming as deserters men impressed from American ships, the Foreign Secretary inserted an article stating that volunteers and those "compelled to enter" the naval forces of their own country were not to be covered by this agreement.[23]

Grenville's attempt to protect the practice of impressment sealed the fate of the proposed agreement. Liston warned that he had small hope of success even before he took up the matter with Pickering at Trenton, where yellow fever drove government offices during the summer and fall of 1797. In October, the Secretary told Liston that Grenville's draft was unacceptable, and friends of England, including Alexander Hamilton, warned the British minister that, even if it wished, the administration could not afford to give its sanction to any concessions which would add fuel to Republican assaults on the "Anglo-Feds." The Foreign Secretary accepted his rebuff without rancor and instructed Liston to suspend negotiations for a general agreement, although giving him power to arrange an informal exchange of deserters between the land forces along the Canadian frontier should the United States desire one. It would not be wise, the Foreign Secretary felt, to give the pro-French faction in the United States anything to use for propaganda purposes, particularly since "in a very short time the disputes between France and the United States will [possibly] terminate in actual hostility; in which event the latter would soon perceive it to be for their interest to enter into some engagement with His Majesty."[24]

The progress of the XYZ negotiations, of which Rufus King kept the Foreign Secretary informed, doubtless encouraged Grenville in this hope, but things did not work out as he expected. America never declared war on France, never suffered seriously from desertions, and for some time the convention remained in the background, occasionally mentioned in correspondence but never the subject of negotiation. When, in 1800, Britain again raised the matter, Pickering stated that the English projet was as inadmissible as before and countered with a draft which included an article aimed at preventing impressment on the high seas.[25] Even Liston, who regretted the necessity of impressment and constantly urged moderation on naval officers, felt that such an agreement was impossible, and his opinion was, of course, endorsed by commanders on the American station. On the American side, in the first detailed instructions he sent to Rufus King after becoming Secretary of State, John Marshall wrote that the problem "deeply affects the feelings and honor of this nation."[26] Between the positions of the two nations, as reflected by Liston and Marshall, no agreement was possible.

A convention for the mutual return of deserters was at best an oblique approach to the problem. In 1797, when Britain tried to broaden the agreement to protect impressment, and in 1800, when the United States tried to limit the practice, negotiations were killed by the appearance of the basic issue. Britain saw the danger of injecting impressment into American domestic politics, yet could not afford to end the practice. The Federalists seem to have recognized that impressment was vital to Britain's war effort. They were ready to complain strenuously against the seizure of Americans, to fight for their release, and even to attempt to cajole England into agreeing to confine the practice to ports of the Empire, but they declined to exert full pressure against Britain, particularly while the two nations were struggling against a common enemy. Both countries, then, had their reasons for holding back. The result was peripheral action, a refusal to face the real problem, and no substantial progress.

How does this record fit into the general story of impressment during the administration of John Adams? Although the diplomats failed to eliminate this source of friction, impressment was a smaller issue at the end than at the beginning of Adams' regime. The Royal Navy was under less pressure and could afford to exercise a bit more restraint; the agents for seamen, particularly David Lenox, were able to secure the release of large numbers of men; and heinous crimes committed by the French diverted America's attention. The complete elimination of impressment as a source of controversy was an almost impossible task in wartime. To push the subject temporarily into the background might well be considered a success. This cost the freedom of a large number of American seamen. Yet it can easily be argued that the policy of the Adams administration was every bit as successful as the one of bluster and recrimination later adopted by Thomas Jefferson. Even war was not enough to make the British government promise to end impressment.

Merchantmen and Merchant Commerce 6

ALTHOUGH THE PRESS GANGS BROUGHT THE WAR HOME TO AMERICA MOST cruelly and directly, European hostilities affected the nation's sea-borne commerce in other ways as well. The seizure of merchant ships was the most obvious of these, yet the war brought good fortune as well as bad to shipowners. It stimulated the market for many commodities, destroyed peacetime sources of some, and virtually created the American reëxport trade. At the same time, hostilities forced both Britain and France to open their colonial trade to ships of the United States, for many of their own merchantmen were diverted to wartime tasks or lost to the enemy.

England's relaxations of the old colonial system were never as sweeping as those of France, primarily because the supporters of the Navigation Acts were still immensely powerful. The elder Lord Hawkesbury was an indefatigable defender of things as they were, and he occupied a key post at the Board of Trade. Lord Sheffield was an assiduous and influential propagandist for the old system, and shipowners and monopolists generally could be counted upon to resist any wholesale change. As in all matters, Pitt was not so deeply devoted to principle, and he recognized that the war made certain relaxations inevitable. The Minister was supported loyally by Lord Grenville and with enthusiasm by Henry Dundas, who was an earnest advocate of the commercial as opposed to the shipping interest. Since Pitt, Grenville, and Dundas dominated the Cabinet, their attitude insured a moderately liberal policy toward the United States as long as the war continued. American commerce benefited in the two areas it most desired to penetrate, the British West Indies and India.

In 1794, John Jay was instructed to secure formal British approval of trade the United States was already carrying on with India. Although Jay had uneven success in other fields, he did get Grenville to agree to admit ships of the United States into "all the Sea Ports and Harbours of the British Territories in the East Indies" on equal terms with British merchantmen. The only conditions were that American vessels should not engage in coastwise trade within British India or "carry any of the articles exported by them from the said British Territories to any port or Place, except to some Port or Place in America."[1] Thus the Jay Treaty legalized American trade with British India, challenged the restrictive philosophy that had a powerful hold on English thinking, and in effect exempted the United States from the provisions of Pitt's India Act of 1784, which confirmed the trading monopoly of the East India Company. American shipowners were put on a more favorable basis than private British shippers, for the latter were still forbidden to trade with those portions of the subcontinent under the control of the East India Company.

The Company was threatened in two ways by the treaty of 1794. The opening of Indian ports to American vessels was a powerful lever in the hands of opponents of the monopoly, including Henry Dundas, who could argue that privileges granted to foreigners should not be withheld from the general body of the King's subjects. Furthermore, the treaty gave a great impetus to the so-called Clandestine Trade against which the Company was struggling in vain. The nabobs who amassed wealth in India had originally sent their loot home in the form of bills drawn upon the Company, but the drain on its exchequer caused the monopoly to outlaw the practice. The nabobs, looking for ways to avoid this control, exported goods to foreign nations where drafts on London could be purchased, or sent them indirectly to the banks of the Thames itself. By 1794, American shippers had procured a share of this illegal trade for themselves, and the Jay treaty made it easier to carry on. Despite this dual attack upon the Company's position there was scarcely a murmur of complaint when the terms of the Jay treaty were first revealed. The *Morning Chronicle*, a Whig standard-bearer, expressed the only public criticism when it attacked the government for assuming "a right to *purchase peace* of a foreign state, at the expence of exclusive privileges, which have been previously sold and guaranteed, to certain of its own subjects, without their consent or indemnification."[2]

However, the Company soon awakened to its danger, and the Court of Directors attempted to have restrictive provisions placed in the Trade with India Bill of 1797. The treaty required a direct inward voyage to the United States. The Company asked that the outward leg, too, be required to be a direct one, and it further requested that foreign trade be limited as much as possible. Henry Dundas answered for the government. Dundas did not, as is often supposed, control the workings of the East India Company; he merely headed a key faction which could usually apply important leverage.[3] On the Parliamentary side, however, his position was decisive, and his answer to the Directors therefore settled the matter. Dundas stated that it was unwise to talk of restricting foreign trade when victory might well depend upon Britain's ability to "convince other Nations of the liberality of our commercial Principles." Furthermore, he emphasized that "the Americans whose amity with us is at least as desirable as that of any other nation would probably consider themselves hardly dealt with" if new trade limitations were imposed so soon after the conclusion of "a solemn and well considered treaty." Finally, he rejected the Directors' request for a ban on indirect outward voyages, warning the Company not to expect insulation from all foreign competition, but rather to depend upon its huge capital, monopoly of Britain-to-India carriage, and "a judicious and well devised System of commercial Policy."[4] This letter— incidentally an excellent example of the pragmatic Pitt-Dundas approach

—ended all chance of restricting by legislation what had been granted to the United States by treaty. The government refused to jeopardize improved relations with the United States by making concessions to a group with which it had been carrying on guerrilla warfare for some time.

The Pitt ministry gave further evidence of its liberal attitude when the legality of an indirect outward voyage was questioned. The American ship *Argonaut* was seized by the Royal Navy while en route to India after a stop in Europe. Initially, Lord Kenyon condemned her on the ground that, by implication, the Jay treaty demanded an uninterrupted voyage in both directions.[5] The government forced a new trial and Grenville meanwhile let it be known that he and Jay had not intended such to be required. In November 1798 Lord Kenyon reversed himself, thereby illustrating the extent of political influence in British courts of the period.

That the party insured [said the justice] might have come from *America* to other countries in *Europe* and bought goods and carried them back to *America*, and from thence to the *East Indies*, seemed to be admitted. Then, in point of reason, why may not that which may be done indirectly be done directly? and on fair construction of the words of this article we think that this objection cannot prevail.[6]

The requirement of a nonstop return to America was destroyed by evasion. In 1797 the captain of the ship *Elizabeth* sailed upriver from Calcutta to the interior Danish port of Serampore, from which he cleared for Europe. Since the Jay treaty only banned a coasting trade within British India, and since it specifically allowed a ship to pick up cargo at different ports, the departure for Serampore was perfectly legal. Clearance from Serampore to Europe was a manifest evasion of the spirit of the treaty, and Calcutta authorities had to decide whether or not to condone it. The captain had the letter of the law on his side, and to enforce the spirit of the treaty might easily divert American ships to foreign ports in India. The *Elizabeth* was allowed to hire a Calcutta pilot to help her reach the open sea,[7] and a precedent was established which shattered the restrictions imposed by the Jay treaty. In this way—or, occasionally, by transshipment at sea—American ships obtained a virtually unhampered trade with British India.

As American trade with India grew, the East India Company became more and more alarmed. In 1799 the Directors requested Grenville to prevent indirect voyages via Serampore, but the administration declined to do more than mention the matter to Rufus King. Again, in 1800, the Company asked that the United States be urged to check the Clandestine Trade, but Dundas argued that no international agreement could possibly be effective, and nothing was done.[8]

Although the British Government aided the American merchant marine in its penetration of the Indian trade, efficient management and the advantages of neutrality—lower insurance rates, fewer convoy delays, and so on—were probably more important. American ships charged about half the freight rate of the Company and astounded Indian officials by the speed with which they handled cargo. They were backed by large amounts of British capital provided either by nabobs or disgruntled London houses without a share in the monopoly. In line with its traditional policy, the British government refused to permit the establishment of consulates in India, but this was the Americans' only major handicap.[9]

Energetic Yankee shipowners made the most of their opportunity. In 1795, America's portion of the foreign trade of Calcutta, the principal port of entry, was only about one third, but after the treaty went into effect the United States outstripped all other non-British powers combined. As early as 1796 a Boston paper, reporting that forty ships from Salem alone were employed in the India trade, predicted that "The American commerce to the East; will ere long rival England."[10] This optimism was not misplaced; by 1801, American ships had captured about 70 per cent of foreign trade with India and probably carried about as much as the Company itself.[11] Americans reëxported Indian goods to Europe, threatened the Mediterranean and West Indian markets of the East India Company, and sometimes even carried goods from London to British India. It is not surprising that the Company was worried by this growing menace.

Nations are not inclined to thank other nations for favors bestowed upon them, and America's reaction to the opening of India was no exception. Aside from the various ways in which self-interest was served, England would have to be satisfied with a negative success. Commercial relations are a thorny business, as the American struggle to penetrate the British West Indies was to show, but in this instance a possible object of controversy was removed. Trade with India became an important source of wealth for the United States and particularly for the shipowners of Salem and Providence. The wise and friendly attitude of the Pitt ministry lay at the base of this commerce.

The British government showed greater caution in the case of the West Indies, though trade with these islands was even more tempting to the acquisitive eye of Americans. The inner Cabinet was not hostile, and West Indian property holders, English manufacturers, and capitalists who financed them were all interested in cheap freight rates. But their support was by no means important enough to embolden Pitt to act positively and openly; the opposition, led by Lord Hawkesbury, was much more strongly entrenched than the East India Company. Therefore, it was by temporary and partial concessions, rather than a general overthrow of British commercial principles, that the West Indies were opened.

Provisions from the United States were a vital factor in the economy of the islands, permitting the Negro labor force to be employed almost exclusively in the cultivation of more valuable tropical produce. British legislation, fairly effectively enforced until 1793, confined the carriage of these cargoes to imperial vessels. When the war diverted merchant ships and allowed England to expand its holdings by conquest, the possibility of dangerous shortages threatened the West Indies. An obvious remedy was to open them to American shipping, and this step was taken, though in an indecisive and halting manner. By annual proclamation of the colonial governors, almost all of the British islands permitted American provision ships to trade with them throughout the Anglo-French war. Grenada, Barbados, Jamaica, Dominica, and St. Vincent's welcomed ships from the United States as early as 1793, and Tobago and the Leeward Islands soon followed suit. The governors' justifications of these proclamations were carefully examined by the Board of Trade. Although they were warned not to extend similar privileges to any other neutral, the governors were seldom rebuked for opening their islands to provision ships flying the Stars and Stripes, and annual legislation relieved them from penalties under the Navigation System. The closest student of the subject concludes that, although British law theoretically remained in force, "through its repeated temporary suspension by the governors . . . , traders from the United States enjoyed free entry for practically the whole period of the war."[12]

Although at first American ships were only allowed to bring provisions to the islands, they soon managed to avoid this restriction and carried to the West Indies manufactures and other goods, some of them reëxports originally purchased in Great Britain. As a result, the value of British exports to the West Indies was cut in half from 1793 to 1795, and the level remained low thereafter.[13] The governors allowed Americans to exchange their cargoes for colonial produce, usually sugar and coffee. But London could see no reason why exports to America should be allowed to aggravate the shortage in Great Britain, and in 1796 the Colonial Office issued a circular forbidding the export of sugar in American bottoms. Coffee came under a similar prohibition. Evasions were frequent, however, and usually supported by gubernatorial proclamations, so in 1799 the government warned that no indemnity would be given for such concessions, and cautioned that "any Breach of the Laws of Trade and Navigation is highly penal."[14] Nevertheless, the traffic in sugar and coffee continued until the end of the war. The United States reëxported only twenty-one million pounds of sugar in 1795, but not less than fifty million pounds annually from 1798 through 1801. The role played by British produce in this expansion was very substantial.[15]

Since the British West Indies were one of the most important markets of the United States, taking roughly one quarter of America's annual exports to the British Empire, relaxation of the Navigation System was a great boon to the American merchant marine. For example, in 1790 and 1791 only about twenty-two hundred tons of American shipping a year went to the British West Indies, but in 1794, after the first proclamations had been issued, the total was nearly fifty-nine thousand tons. Soon ships of the United States virtually monopolized the carriage of provisions to the West Indies. In 1793, American vessels carried 16 per cent of the grain exported to British Caribbean possessions; the next year, the share carried by Americans was 88 per cent, and the United States maintained a firm hold thereafter. This pattern was a common one, duplicated in the carriage of flour and of lumber and cooperage materials, two other important exports to the Antilles. The carriage of dried fish, a staple part of the slaves' diet, was shared somewhat differently, since British North America furnished about half the supply and this naturally remained a monopoly of British ships, but only in 1797 did the American merchant marine fail to carry as much as 90 per cent of all fish shipped from the United States.[16]

The repeated, virtually continuous opening of the West Indies to American ships relieved pressure on the diplomats. The United States did not press strenuously for a modification of the Navigation System by treaty, although Rufus King sailed for England in 1796 with instructions to secure the unlimited opening of West Indian ports. British fears that the United States would capture the carriage of tropical goods from the British merchant marine had already been expressed in the rejected article of the Jay treaty. To allay these fears, Pickering authorized King to agree to put trade with the West Indies on a virtual barter basis, limiting the value of goods that American ships could carry away from the islands to the value of those which they brought.[17] When King presented the American offer to Lord Grenville, the Foreign Secretary promised to consult his colleagues, but negotiations were never joined. The British government was well satisfied with the existing system of proclamation, a system which did not rouse conservative opposition in England and left Britain free to close the islands if such a move became desirable. There the matter rested till the close of the war, equally happily for the American merchant marine and the wartime needs of Great Britain.

Since the British government often permitted American vessels to carry cargoes from enemy islands directly to Great Britain,[18] the only part of the West Indies trade involving Britain which was never opened to ships of the United States was that between the home islands and the colonies. This would have been too great a flouting of traditional principles, and it does not seem to have been seriously considered at any time. However, just before the Pitt government left office in 1801, Henry Dundas did suggest that it might be "politic at the present moment to communicate to America during the War a direct trade between Great Britain & our colonies." Dundas argued in his usual pragmatic manner, pointing out that it "would be a very great Douceur to America and would preserve them in a state of amicable Neutrality" and, by diverting American shipping from the less profitable and more hazardous business of carrying the goods of the enemy's colonies to Europe, would also "greatly tend to diminish the resources of our Enemies."[19] But William Pitt was essentially a cautious statesman; his mind shrank from bold departures. His successor, Henry Addington, compounded these defects and lacked imagination as well. So the United States had to be satisfied with the concessions that had already been made. Doubtless America was less critical of British policy because no one dreamed that such a policy as Dundas proposed would ever be considered. Actually, with India and the Antilles open, the United States had little reason to complain of Britain's attitude toward American trade with the Empire.

Large and important as the trade with England's overseas possessions was, it was dwarfed by that between the United States and the British home islands. Since each nation was the other's best customer, the carriage of this trade was naturally important to both of them. Shortly after the Revolution, English ports were opened to American merchantmen, and Article XIV of the Jay treaty reaffirmed this, stating that "There shall be between all the Dominions of His Majesty in Europe, and the Territories of the United States, a reciprocal and perfect liberty of Commerce and Navigation." By Article XV, both nations were granted most-favored-nation treatment, with one important exception. Britain was allowed to establish special tariffs and tonnage duties, so that, despite American legislation discriminating against foreign shipping, British vessels would be on as favorable a footing as those of the United States.[20]

The clause permitting these so-called "countervailing duties" caused a certain amount of friction during the administration of John Adams, and Rufus King twice intervened to request changes in proposed British legislation. The matter first arose when the American Treaty Bill was finally presented to Parliament in May 1797. The delay was caused primarily by the Board of Trade's decision not to establish a flat 10 per cent discriminatory duty like the American one, but rather to work out a detailed, varied schedule of charges on all types of goods. Rufus King kept as close a watch as possible upon the proceedings of the Board, but, to play it safe, he asked for and received from Lord Grenville permission to see a draft of the bill before it was introduced.[21] The draft by no means satisfied King. In a series of notes to Grenville and Undersecretary Canning, he objected that the bill effectively banned American carriage of some goods. King also argued that the countervailing duties were too high, particularly because they left out of account extra lighthouse duties paid by foreign ships in the British Isles.[22] The Board replied with a paper which demonstrated, at least to the satisfaction of the British government, that the countervailing duties were well within the treaty limits. Grenville and Pitt declined to make any major changes in the bill.[23]

The American Treaty Bill soon came before Parliament. In introducing it, the government spokesman, Dudley Ryder, expressed confidence that the House of Commons would enthusiastically approve a bill to carry out "a Treaty which the recollection of former friendships, as well as the surer ties, perhaps, of mutual interests and events promised to render as permanent, as it was advantageous to both parties."[24] Most of the House apparently agreed, for, although there was some Whig criticism of the government for not opening the British West Indies, Commons approved the bill only three and a half weeks after Ryder's opening remarks. It became law, despite King's reiterated protests.[25] The American minister was unhappy, but he had been given repeated opportunities to make his views known, and he did secure a number of minor concessions. When the act was laid before Congress, there was some criticism of it. Thomas Jefferson, with a rare solicitude for shipowners, ruefully noted that the countervailing duties "will confessedly put American bottoms out of employ in our trade with Gr. Britain."[26] As was the case with so many of Jefferson's Cassandra-like predictions, this one was not fulfilled.

A year after passage of the Treaty Act, King intervened more successfully in support of American shipping, this time to bring about modifications of proposed convoy and tonnage duties. The minister reported to Philadelphia in March 1798 that, although framed as specific rather than ad valorem duties, a "Bill will soon be brought before Parliament, imposing a 2½ per Cent Impost upon Exports & Imports of Great Britain [carried in foreign bottoms] . . . to afford Convoys to the trade" and balance the convoy fees already charged British ships.[27] In May, Pitt and Grenville received King at Downing Street to hear his complaints. The meeting was lengthy and spirited. Most of it was devoted to a technical discussion of the rates of the convoy duty, which King claimed discriminated against American vessels, but he also objected that proposed new tonnage duties unfairly burdened the shipping of the United States in its competition with the British marine. King rested his case primarily on the Jay treaty, and this provoked a heated exchange in which Pitt and his adversary each expressed a belief that the other nation benefited most from the compact's commercial articles. Pitt finally had to admit that he was not familiar with the terms of the treaty—an amazing admission!—but promised that if King's statements were correct substantial changes would be made. On this note the conversation ended, and the American was well satisfied.[28]

The second draft of the bill failed to embody many of the revisions King had requested, but, after further consultations between Pitt, his chief revenue adviser, George Rose, and probably King himself, a third was prepared. This one made major concessions, and Rose wrote the American:

I cannot bring myself to think that the Measure as at first proposed trenched in the slightest Degree either on the Letter or the Spirit of the Treaty rightly understood, but if the Sacrifice we have made of Income shall tend to prevent Mis-conceptions or Mis-representations in America I shall rejoice that you succeeded.[29]

The new bill reduced the tonnage duty, eliminated proposed imposts on sugar and coffee from the United States passing through England as an entrepôt, wiped out the export duty on finished cloth (half of all exports to the United States), and lowered the charge on cotton imported from America.

Rufus King welcomed these changes. He reported to Pickering that, although the export and tonnage duties were still not quite all that could be wished, the levies on imports were in every way acceptable. King's dispatch was cautiously phrased, but in the privacy of his journal he frankly exulted at his success.[30] Even in cases when the Cabinet refused to admit the justice of his criticism, important changes had been made because of his intervention, even though these alterations might have a harmful effect upon the prosperity of the British merchant marine. Furthermore, the relatively moderate rate of duties allowed Federalist journals to explain and justify them as being "for the express purpose of defraying the expense of convoys, rendered necessary by the depredations of the French on *neutral* commerce."[31]

Commercial legislation was but one factor among many affecting maritime trade between the United States and Britain, and its importance is impossible to assess. It can, however, be stated with confidence that, despite the fears of such diverse personages as William Bingham and Thomas Jefferson, British legislation definitely did not greatly reduce America's share of the carriage between England and the United States. The number of British vessels engaged in the direct trade grew steadily from 1796 on, but American ships outnumbered them at least ten to one until the end of the war. It is true that in 1796 more American ships were engaged in this trade than in any other year down to 1800, but 1796 was out of line when compared with the more representative years of 1794 and 1795; against these, the years from 1797 to 1801 more than hold their own. During this period, nearly 18 per cent of the tonnage of foreign vessels trading in British parts was American. This share was larger than that of any other power, a remarkable tribute to the maritime capabilities of the young American republic and the perception of Pitt and Grenville.[32]

The steady increase of trade was at least as important as the manner in which its carriage was shared. American exports to Britain rose steadily from 1797 to 1801; imports from England likewise climbed to a new peak in the latter year. American purchases of English manufactures increased by one third, and from 1797 to 1801 the United States never took less than 27 per cent of these exports.[33] It is small wonder that in speaking of "the most perfectly good Understanding . . . between this Country & the United States," George Rose should go on to say, "I have a clear & strong Conviction that it is to the Interest of both to maintain that. . . . We may, and I hope we shall, be a Tower of Strength to each other."[34]

The growth of American trade with the British Isles, like that with other parts of the Empire, was stimulated by the war. This branch of commerce was the most important single trade of both countries; it played a major role in the prosperity of the United States and the maintenance of the British economy under the strains of war. By and large, the attitude of the two governments was as understanding here as it had been in dealing with colonial commerce. Strong economic ties by no means made quarrels, even war, impossible, as the next two decades were to show. But while the commercially minded administrations of Pitt and Adams remained in power, it was a near certainty that neither nation would cripple or destroy the lucrative trade across the wide Atlantic, in the Caribbean, or to the Orient. The economic bonds which tied the two peoples together were allowed to grow with little interference.

Britannia's Rule of the Waves 7

IN THE DIARY OF A YOUNG NAVY WIFE TRAVELING THROUGH THE MEDIterranean on her husband's vessel in 1796, there may be found the following entry:

SUNDAY, FEBRUARY 5TH. Took a prize in the morning a ship under American colours laden with grain from the coast of Barbary bound to Marseilles tho the Master, Captain Richard Smith swears he was going to Genoa, his papers and letters prove the contrary. A great bore to examine these papers . . . we cannot make out who she belongs to now, it is a great confusion and potheration.[1]

Although in this case the American skipper soon admitted that his voyage was illicit, in most ways the incident was a common one. All over the ocean, from time to time and with varying frequency, American ships were halted by the Royal Navy. Often a prize crew was put aboard, and the merchantman sailed for a port where there was a British prize court, there to be plunged into the labyrinthine processes of admiralty law.

Altogether, such incidents caused the diplomats a great deal more trouble than impressment or trade relations. Americans were outraged when they read, for example, the *Aurora's* doleful account of a merchantman taken to St. Pierre by the Royal Navy:

There her sails were cut up to make trowsers for the British sailors, the vessel eaten up with worms, and the cargo by the British. The American vessels there were allowed to beat to pieces against each other—some fun—and some drifted to sea; their people were kept on prisoner's allowance, and many compelled to enter on board the British men of war.[2]

It was not Republicans alone who remonstrated after reading such stories, embroidered or not, although it would be easy to cite their protests by the score. President Washington referred to the British privateers as pirates, and in 1796 young John Quincy Adams angrily asserted, "The maritime law of nations recognized in Great Britain is all comprised in one line of a popular song, 'Rule Britannia! Britannia rule the waves.' "[3]

There was, unfortunately, justification for all but the most extreme protests. Hundreds of American ships were taken in the spring of 1795 alone, under the secret provision order, although most of these were released after receiving prompt if not always adequate compensation for their cargo. In 1795 and early 1796, privateers preyed voraciously on merchantmen trading with the French West Indies. Thereafter, chiefly because American commerce with France was greatly reduced, the number of seizures declined. But in 1799 the Caribbean was again a trouble spot, and Timothy Pickering felt that conditions were worse than they had been for five years.[4] This was, however, an exception to the general

WILLIAM WYNDHAM GRENVILLE, LORD GRENVILLE

Portrait by John Hoppner

rule. By comparison with the years preceding the Embargo, the period from 1796 to 1800 was fairly quiet. After the United States made peace with France, a really threatening outbreak took place, and not until August 1801 was the British chargé able to report that American anger had cooled.[5] Two months later, the armistice between England and France allowed American merchantmen once again to roam the seas without fear of molestation.

The fluctuating incidence of seizures was not the result of any major changes in British policy, for until 1801 England fairly consistently maintained the principles with which she began the war. A basic principle, and one generally accepted, was the right of a belligerent to seize contraband of war bound to enemy ports, but the application of this rule caused friction, for no satisfactory definition of contraband had ever been worked out. Far more important for Anglo-American relations, however, was British interference in trade between Europe and the enemy's colonies, particularly those in the West Indies. Strongly influenced by mercantilist thought, England attempted to deprive the enemy of a source of gain while maintaining and expanding her own commerce, even at the expense of neutral powers. Broadly speaking, she did this in two ways. First, Britain claimed the right not only to capture enemy vessels but also to seize enemy property when carried in neutral bottoms, so that her opponents could not continue a profitable international trade simply by consigning it to nonbelligerent vessels. Secondly, Britain enforced the Rule of the War of 1756, an English declaration that neutrals were not to be allowed to carry on in wartime a trade which had been closed to them in time of peace. This was really a concomitant of the previous point, for belligerents attempted to save their colonial trade by opening it to neutral shipping.[6] It was these two points—the attack on trade in enemy property and enforcement of the Rule of 1756—which caused most of the discussion between England and the United States in the war years.

The difficulty sprang from the tremendous growth of the reëxport trade. In 1790, the value of transshipped foreign produce totaled less than 3 per cent of all American exports. With the outbreak of war in Europe, reëxports skyrocketed. In 1796 they were worth more than all goods shipped from the United States six years earlier, and they reached a peak value of forty-six million dollars in the last year of the war. The financing and carriage of this commerce was very lucrative.[7]

Britons believed that the reëxport trade was largely based on fraud and deception. They felt that Americans were violating the spirit if not the letter of the Rule of 1756, carrying on via the United States a trade that had not been open to them before the war. In addition, they suspected that a large proportion of the goods thus transferred never actually became American property, but rather that a false veneer of American ownership was added to protect the cargoes from capture. Thus, for example, Admiral Vandeput, no enemy of the United States, complained in 1797, "there is scarcely an American Vessel which comes from the Havannah to any of the States, but what it is partly laden and frequently wholly so, on the Spanish Account, tho it is very difficult to bring it to Proof." Even Secretary of State Pickering had to admit that "to favor the French, and acquire great profits in trade, many American merchants have prostituted every fair principle of commerce, and put their captains on taking such deceitful oaths, as to render suspicious the papers of innocent merchants, to their vast injury."[8] Evidence was difficult, almost impossible, to obtain on the high seas. This was one reason, and an understandable one, why British ships brought so many American merchantmen into port for adjudication.

Widespread fraud was not, however, a valid excuse for the harshness and incompetence of many Vice-Admiralty Courts. The Federalists sometimes claimed that these tribunals became less stern after 1795; one party newspaper declared that "since the exchange of the treaty, a very material alteration in the conduct and disposition of the judges . . . in our favour, is very visible."[9] Such a change was, however, not visible to all witnesses, and the courts rightly remained distrusted throughout this period. Their failure is most eloquently demonstrated by the record of their decisions carried to the High Court of Appeals. This record shows that, out of 225 decrees involving Americans reviewed by the High Court down to 1801, 179—80 per cent of the total—were reversed to grant relief to American shipowners.[10] West India courts were the worst offenders. On a single day the High Court reversed seven decisions made by the court at St. Kitt's, and in fifty-three out of fifty-nine cases the Bermuda judges had their verdict against American vessels reversed or sharply modified.

Most seized ships were probably eventually freed, either by a favorable decision somewhere in the judicial hierarchy or because the captors realized their case was weak and declined to prosecute. This was, however, but partial satisfaction to the United States. Long delays took place in any case, but particularly in the appellate process, and during that time the ships were either tied up in British ports or released only upon the posting of heavy bond. Appeals carried to the High Court commonly took four or five years; often the delay was longer, and in 1801 four American cases originating in 1793 and twenty-six dating back to 1794 were still on the docket. Experienced British statesmen were not unaware of the feeling that was likely to be aroused. One top diplomat wrote in 1797, "The Appeals are become of great moment. . . . They are terribly accumulated at present; and nothing would give a more merited credit to the whole Character of Government, than an expeditious and able course of Decisions."[11]

It is to the credit of the British government that during this whole period a moderate and malleable attitude was maintained toward the complaints of the United States. Britain was fully aware of the amount of fraud covered by the American flag, equally aware of the benefits France derived from trade that evaded the spirit of the British maritime code. She was also firmly determined not to abandon the principles she had established; indeed, she went to war with the powers of the North to maintain them. Within these limits, however, Pitt's government gave positive though often belated evidence of its willingness to act favorably upon the complaints of the United States.

There are two substantial exceptions to this generalization. Rufus King was unable to establish a definition of contraband, and he was likewise unable, down to 1801, to get the British government to agree to consider American vessels trading with the New Orleans deposit in the same light as ships from ports on the Atlantic coast. At the time of the Jay negotiations, Lord Hawkesbury argued against including definitions of contraband in the treaty; neither belligerent nor neutral, his Lordship felt, would abide by the definition.[12] In general, the Jay treaty recognized this fact, as, for that matter, did the treaty John Quincy Adams negotiated with Prussia in 1799. In that year, however, Timothy Pickering directed King to seek a formal article on contraband. After step by step negotiations with subordinate officials, King presented a draft to Hammond, but nothing came of it, and in November he was ready to concede failure. The matter died, only to be resurrected briefly and equally unsuccessfully by Marshall's long instructions of September 1800.[13]

Negotiations over New Orleans were scarcely more satisfactory. In 1799, Pickering directed King to point out to the British government that the deposit area should be considered an extension of American territory, since goods passed through it without paying any duty or in any way coming under Spanish sovereignty. As with contraband, however, King was unable to secure an agreement, perhaps because relations deteriorated in 1800. Marshall's renewal of the claim in the September instructions caused a flurry of activity, and King got Grenville to accept the American contention, only to have the government fall before formalities were completed. Finally, in the very month that Louisiana was purchased from France, Britain belatedly agreed to consider the deposit area part of the United States as far as the regulation of shipping was concerned.[14]

There was, fortunately, substantial success in more important fields. Britons knew that overzealous, ignorant, and grasping officers, particularly in the privateering service, often seized American ships unjustifiably. Shortly after his arrival in America, Robert Liston urged positive action to reduce the number of unwarranted seizures, and Lord Nelson once wrote directly to the King's first minister to protest against the activities of privateers flying the Union Jack: "with very few exceptions they are a disgrace to our country. . . . Such horrid robberies have been committed by them in all parts of the world, that it is really a disgrace to the country which tolerates them."[15] Because these failings were recognized, the British government and judiciary often intervened to assist American shipping.

Several representative incidents illustrate England's attitude. In 1799, Rufus King complained that privateers and warships under Sir Hyde Parker's command were seizing American ships trading with Spanish colonies, although British merchantmen engaged in similar commerce were not molested. Grenville brusquely directed the Admiralty to put a stop to such practices and demanded an investigation so that he might "receive His Majesty's Commands as to any further step that His Majesty may judge fit to be taken for the maintenance of the good understanding and friendship prevailing between His Majesty and the United States." On another occasion, in a decision delivered one day after King raised this particular point with Grenville, Sir William Scott stated that American ships should be given particularly favorable treatment when bound for blockaded ports because of the length of time it took for news of blockades to reach the United States. "That the *Americans* should . . . send their ships upon a fair conjecture that the blockade had, after a long continuance [been lifted] . . . and for the purpose of making fair inquiry whether it has so [terminated] . . . is I think," said Scott, "not exceptionable." The Addington government continued this policy. Eight merchantmen taken when they attempted to enter Le Havre were freed when King raised the matter, and the new First Lord, St. Vincent, promised that in the future special warning would be given to American ships arriving off blockaded ports.[16]

Britain occasionally recalled commanders who were particularly offensive to the United States. There was no general policy in this regard, and indeed much more might have been done. In justice to the Pitt government, it must be added that the ministry's generally favorable attitude slowly trickled down to commanders on the seas and that, furthermore, the United States generally failed to name offenders when protesting against seizures. In 1801, a particularly obnoxious commander—Captain Pellew of H. M. S. *Cleopatra*—was recalled at Rufus King's behest. When his superior officer allowed Pellew to proceed first to the West Indies, he too was ordered home to answer for his conduct and to explain "the persuasion that he has participated too much in the avaricious passions of his subordinate Officers."[17] King was assured that neither officer would serve in American waters again.

In a further attempt to meet justified complaints, the government improved the character of condemnation proceedings. At the time of the Jay negotiations, Grenville wrote the Duke of Portland that a reform of the court system was fundamental to good relations, "for let us make what regulations we please by treaty, the West India and Bermuda privateers will continue their depredations . . . as long as they find the West Indies Courts disposed to countenance their proceedings." After some delay, Portland took up the matter with the Admiralty, which admitted that "Irregularity & Inconvenience" had been caused by the proliferation of Vice-Admiralty Courts and the low caliber of judges appointed. As a remedy, the Admiralty suggested that all courts be eliminated except those in the most important islands. This was done, and Grenville wrote to Jay, "Knowing, as I do, how much evil has been produced by the multiplication of these courts, I look to this reduction with very sanguine hopes."[18] The policy of concentration was maintained for the rest of the war. When John G. Simcoe established a Vice-Admiralty Court in Santo Domingo, appointing as judge one Richard Cambauld, who had, according to Pickering, "an extraordinary facility in condemning,"[19] Rufus King complained to the Foreign Office, and orders from London put Cambauld and his court out of business. Appeals against the verdicts of West India courts were cut by five-sixths between 1794 and 1796, although much of this reduction was caused by the falling off of seizures themselves.

When, in 1800 and 1801, large numbers of ships were again condemned, American complaints recommenced. In March 1801, King made an indirect approach to St. Vincent through Thomas Erskine, and the new First Lord replied that one of his first aims was "to reform the Courts of Admiralty in the Colonies with a view to check the vexations which the American commerce has been subject to." A month later, Sir William Scott informed King that he was working on a bill to lay before Parliament. Sir William discussed his draft with King, embodied in it some suggestions made by the American, and received his approval of its final form.[20]

Scott's bill was essentially a further application of the concentration principle. Since judges were dependent upon fees for their livelihood and captains could take prizes to any port they chose, there was a great temptation to convict and thus attract the custom of naval commanders. Scott hoped to end this abuse by reducing the number of courts in the western hemisphere to three—one each at Jamaica, Martinique, and Halifax. (In the House of Commons, the bill was amended so as to do away with the fee system altogether.) Only one M. P. attacked the measure as too liberal a concession to America, while the Whigs argued that it came too late and failed to strike home at the corruption which had been rife in the West Indian courts. "Mere error," said one Opposition member, "could not account for the great number of sentences which had been reversed upon appeals to this Country."[21] But the Whigs joined with government supporters to pass the bill.

Although long overdue, the general overhaul of the court system was none the less welcome. The complaint of a Barbados agent that it would destroy the "privateering spirit" and the gratification expressed by President Jefferson were eloquent testimony to its wisdom.[22] Scott's bill was probably a result of the wave of complaints which swept across the Atlantic from America, Thomas Jefferson's accession, and the fact that at this time England was coping with a new Armed Neutrality that it was feared the United States would join.[23] In any event, the government took a step which went a long way to meet the complaints of the United States.

Since, however, the act came into force only a few months before the end of the war, it was more important for its indication of the attitude of the British government than for any direct benefits it conferred upon American shipping.

Although the motives and honesty of appellate courts seldom came under attack—from the highest naval court there were appeals by captor and owner in about equal numbers—the long delays were a frequent subject of complaint. In 1797, when American irritation threatened to break down the London claims commission, the Court of Appeals ordered procedural changes which speeded the activity of all courts. Later in the same year, Rufus King complained about Sir James Marriott, a justice in the High Court of Admiralty, who was a feeble old man, unable to keep up with the court calendar. When Marriott refused to resign unless given a very large pension, Grenville ordered that public criticism be directed at him. Almost literally forced out of office, Sir James retired in November 1798. His conduct had been so bad that the representatives of other nations, claimants before the court, and even captors added their complaints to those of Rufus King, but his interference was the most important factor which spurred the government to action.[24]

Removal of Marriott, elimination of a great majority of the Vice-Admiralty Courts, and corrective interference in the activities of the Royal Navy and privateers were all significant contributions to the cause of amity. British policy toward the United States was not generous—there was no general overhaul of the system of command—but neither was it grudging and obstructive. As a result, American commerce was more leniently treated than that of any other neutral, and there was never any serious danger of a clash resembling that between Nelson and the Danes at Copenhagen in April 1801.

Even more fundamental than action at this level was the tenor of the general maritime policy that was laid down. At the outbreak of the war, according to his own account, Sir William Scott told Pitt that the government would have to decide between a harsh and a mild policy toward neutrals. Since he expected the war to be short, Pitt chose the latter course.[25] What Britain considered a restrained policy never seemed overgenerous either to the American government or to the owners of vessels taken by the Royal Navy. There was a basic disagreement on neutral rights which was avoided rather than settled, and the United States maintained that many seizures were illegal confiscations of American property. But, within the limits of the Rule of 1756 (which, however, the United States never recognized), England's policy toward American commerce was legal, justifiable, and not immoderate. Particularly harsh action, when it occurred, was owing to erring subordinates or overwhelming necessity and ran counter to general government policy.

The first major statement of Britain's position, the Order in Council of January 1794, directed the seizure of vessels bound from the French

West Indies to any European port and of French property bound from those islands to any port whatsoever. Nothing was said about neutral property being carried away from the French possessions or about French colonial produce bound from the United States to European ports, so long as it was bona fide American property. Thus, the Order of 1794 tacitly approved indirect trade between the French colonies and Europe via the United States. At a Cabinet meeting in November 1797 it was determined to maintain this policy, and the Order of January 1798 reaffirmed British acceptance of the broken voyage. As a result, American reëxport trade grew by leaps and bounds. An attempt was made to direct this trade to British ports by the so-called Dutch Property Acts, granting favorable importation and storage terms to products brought from the West Indies via the United States, and, in sharp violation of the Rule of 1756 and the Navigation System, American ships were allowed to bring goods directly from French colonies to Britain.[26]

The United States had always given duty drawbacks upon reëxport. At New York, rebates were given for only 4 per cent of all duties collected in 1792; they increased to 25 per cent in 1795 and 33 per cent in 1798 as the reëxport trade grew. In March 1799 a new procedure was instituted. Upon the entry of cargoes intended for reëxport, a duty was no longer collected. Instead, the importer posted a bond which was returned to him when the goods left on the second stage of their journey. The clearances then given did not differ from those issued for domestic exports.[27] This change clearly encouraged purely ceremonial importations to evade British regulations. It caused a stir in England. Lord Chatham, Pitt's brother and Lord President of the Council, suggested a new Order in Council,[28] but the government did not retaliate against the American legislation.

It was left to the courts to warn the United States that Britain would watch the reëxport trade closely. In 1799 this was begun by Sir William Scott in the case of the Hamburg ship *Immanuel*. The *Immanuel* was engaged in commerce between her home port and Santo Domingo, perfectly legal under the Order of 1798, but Captain Eysenberg took his ship into Bordeaux en route and there exchanged a portion of her cargo, thus in effect entering the direct trade between France and Santo Domingo. After leaving Bordeaux, the *Immanuel* was taken by a British cruiser and brought in for adjudication. Sir William Scott began his decision in this case by reaffirming the Rule of 1756, and he condemned the cargo taken on at Bordeaux, since trade between France and her colonies had not been open to foreign shipping before 1793. Britain's foremost maritime lawyer then proceeded to establish the doctrine of continuous voyage, a tenet which was to lie at the heart of future discussions of American rights. Sir William freed the goods shipped from Hamburg, holding that the whole voyage and not the component parts was what was important. Trade between Hamburg and Santo Domingo was legal; therefore, to carry it on via intermediate ports was also permissible.[29] Applied here in favor of a neutral, the doctrine had greater potential importance as a check on the reëxport trade. Commerce between the enemy and her colonies was illegal when carried on directly; it was, by the doctrine of continuous voyage, also illegal when carried on indirectly. In other words, there must be a bona fide importation into America before Britain would admit the legality of reëxport to her enemies.

The next problem was to define bona fide importation, and this task also rightly fell to Scott, in the case of the ship *Polly* (1800). The *Polly* was taken in the North Atlantic while en route to Bilbao, Spain. She had on board a cargo consisting chiefly of fish from Massachusetts but also including sugar which the *Polly* herself had brought from Havana a few months previously. The sugar was the only part of the cargo that the captors claimed, and the Halifax court refused to condemn this. The case was appealed to the High Court of Admiralty, where crown counsel, appearing for the captors, pointed out that the sugar had been purchased by the skipper of the *Polly* with a bill drawn upon the same house to which that part of her cargo was consigned in Spain. Thanks to the bonding provision of American law, there was no proof that the way stop in the United States had been more than a merely formal landing and spurious payment of duties. The captors argued that these facts made it logical to suppose that the sugar was Spanish property. But even if this were not so, and the sugar belonged to Americans, the cargo should be condemned as a violation of the Rule of 1756, since trade between Cuba and Spain had not been open to American ships before the war. A "mere transshipment in *America*" was not sufficient to break the voyage; there must be proof of a real intent to market the goods there, and this was lacking.

Scott refused to accept this line of reasoning and upheld the Halifax tribunal. He agreed with crown counsel that the crux of the matter was the existence of importation in good faith, but he went on:

It is not my business to say what is universally a test of *bona fide* importation: It is argued, that it would not be sufficient, that the duties should be paid, and that the cargo should be landed. If these criteria are not to be resorted to, I should be at a loss to know what should be the test; and I am strongly disposed to hold, that it would be sufficient, that the goods should be landed and the duties paid.

In such a situation the burden of proof that the shipper intended to evade the maritime code rested with the captors. The evidence they presented was inconclusive, said Scott, and the ship and sugar were ordered discharged from custody.[30] Sir William did not absolutely rule out other tests of intent; he merely established landing and payment of duties as the two paramount tests. Nor did he modify the Rule of 1756 or the doctrine of continuous voyage, and intent to violate them still justified condemnation. But the burden of proof was on the captors, and such proof was difficult to obtain. For this reason, the *Polly* decision greatly aided American commerce.

Scott's pronouncement, which governed British admiralty law until

1805, was endorsed by the government. Shortly after his decision, the Admiralty received orders to permit indirect trade as long as the colonial produce was "without fraud and colour intermediately imported" into the United States; the Cabinet directed that such cargoes should not even be brought in for examination unless they were bound for the mother country of the colony of origin.[31] Some months later, the Nassau Vice-Admiralty Court—soon to be wiped out by the reform act—condemned American ships carrying Spanish produce. When Rufus King called attention to this, the new Foreign Secretary, Lord Hawkesbury, acted quickly, not even insisting that the offensive decisions pass through the appellate process. He asked and soon received a legal opinion from the King's Advocate, Christopher Robinson, declaring that the Nassau court had acted illegally. Robinson's report, later forwarded to King for the guidance of American shippers, expressly stated, "the produce of the Colonies of the Enemy may be imported by a Neutral into his own Country, and may be re-exported from thence even to the Mother Country of such Colony" so long as the voyage is broken by bona fide importation.

What . . . amounts to an intermediate importation into the Neutral Country, may sometimes be a question of some difficulty. . . . But the High Court of Admiralty has expressly declared, (and I see no reason to expect that the Court of Appeal will vary the rule,) that the landing the goods and paying the Duties in the Neutral Country breaks the continuing of the voyage, and is such an importation as legalizes the trade, although the goods be reshipped in the same Vessel, and on account of the same Neutral Proprietors, and to be forwarded for sale to the Mother Country, or the Colony.[32]

The *Polly* decision, Robinson's paraphrase of it in even more explicit language, and the provisions of American law all meant that shippers could carry on a scarcely interrupted trade between France and Spain and their colonies. Official British acceptance of a very liberal interpretation of the Rule of 1756 was a marked concession to the United States, and when the *Essex* case ended this interpretation in 1805 it helped light the fuse that eventually led to the War of 1812. Seizures continued after the *Polly* case, of course, chiefly because the ownership of the cargo was in question, because the nationality of the owner was contested, or because either the British commander or American skipper was acting contrary to maritime law as it was interpreted by England. The Boston *Independent Chronicle* fairly regularly ran a column, devoted to seizures and confiscations, which it sarcastically entitled "Evidences of British Amity." But the reduced number of seizures brought a consequent decline in the intensity of American complaints.

While British actions reduced tension between the two countries, England also benefited from the rising tide of American protests against the maritime excesses of France. In the first years of the war, France's attitude toward American commerce was uncertain and wavering, although a stock Republican argument against the Jay treaty was that it would provoke the French into retaliation. Federalists scoffed at this: "The letters and whispers about French resentment come from our own Jacobins, who *wish* and *court* that resentment, to verify *their own predictions*, and to make our government odious." But the opposition was correct; news of the approval of the Jay treaty and recall of James Monroe caused French policy to harden. The Republicans argued that "We have now become the unhappy victims of our own folly"; they thus attempted to explain rather than to justify French actions. Most Americans were angered by the new attack upon their merchant marine. In February 1797 Alexander Hamilton wrote to Rufus King, "The conduct [of France] is making the impression which might be expected though not with that electric rapidity which would have attended similar Treatment from another power."[33]

Worse was still to come. Just before Adams' inauguration, the Directory denounced the "free ships, free goods" provisions of the treaty of 1778 and yet announced the enforcement of legalistic articles of that agreement which allowed French ships to seize large numbers of American merchantmen. Early in 1798, the French government decreed that any British goods found on board a neutral vessel would subject the entire cargo and the vessel itself to condemnation. Lord Grenville expected that this would cause the United States to declare war,[34] and well it might have, for the effect upon American commerce was truly devastating. When John Quincy Adams reported Prussian interest in a new league of neutrals, Timothy Pickering answered that the United States might consider coöperation against France. But, he said, "it would be highly impolitic to embarrass *Great Britain* by any maritime combination. For . . . the little finger of *France*, in maritime depredations, is thicker than the loins of Britain."[35]

The growing importance of French crimes was the last of many influences that transformed Anglo-American relations after 1794. The Jay treaty ended the immediate threat of war and wiped away a number of controversies, but it also left many questions unsettled, including sources of friction which later helped bring about the War of 1812. It is to the credit of both nations that they were able to lessen the tension caused by these issues. Least was done to settle the problem of impressment, but even here—though largely because of changing exigencies of war—British outrages lessened, as did harsh statements on both sides of the water. Seizures continued to be the expensive price of neutrality, but unfairly captured vessels were usually ultimately released, and the Pitt ministry laid down rules for neutral commerce, far more liberal than those of France, that encouraged the growth of the American merchant marine and reëxport trade. In addition, American ships were permitted to enter the ports of India and the British West Indies and allowed to establish a near monopoly of carriage across the Atlantic. On its part, the Federalist government, while firmly pressing for what it believed to be American rights, declined to engage in a war of bombast and menace designed to take advantage of Britain's beleaguered state. A firm base was prepared for the coöperation that was to come when the American quarrel with France led to armed hostilities.

Shortly after they signed the treaty of 1794, John Jay wrote an emotional letter to Lord Grenville in which he used two distinct, if somewhat hackneyed, metaphors:

The Storm I hope & believe will soon cease, but the agitation of the waters will naturally take some Time to subside—no man can with Effect say to them. Peace be still. By casting *oil* upon them, they will doubtless be the sooner calmed—Let us do so. . . .

To use an Indian figure—may the Hatchet be henceforth buried forever, and with it all the animosities which sharpened, and which threatened to redden it—[36]

Perhaps appropriately, since Jay knew less of the frontier than of the sea, his first metaphor proved most applicable to Anglo-American relations in succeeding years. The hatchet, though less fiercely brandished, was not buried; animosities between the nations did not come to an abrupt end. But, on the other hand, oil was applied with good effect to the storm-tossed waters. The agitation that remained was of less moment than a new storm on America's horizon.

Foes of France 8

A MERICA'S UNDECLARED NAVAL WAR WITH FRANCE BROUGHT ABOUT close Anglo-American collaboration. Since that time, and particularly in the three great crises of the twentieth century, the awareness of common peril has had a similar effect. A study of coöperation in the 1790's is valuable because this was the first such concert, has been largely ignored by historians, and contributed powerfully to the development of good relations. Although there were no precedents to guide them, the Pitt and Adams governments worked out a scheme of mutual assistance with ramifications in a surprising number of fields. Many of the concessions to American interest already mentioned were a reflection of this system, but they were concessions to America as a neutral power rather than coöperation with the United States as a co-belligerent. The collective action undertaken against France was at least equally important.

When John Adams was inaugurated in March 1797, American relations with France were near the breaking point. News that Charles Cotesworth Pinckney, Monroe's successor, had been rebuffed by the Directory was already on its way across the Atlantic, and French seizures were multiplying, with a consequent effect upon American public opinion. A month after the inauguration, the wife of the British minister wrote home:

the change that has taken place in the minds of the People of this Country within a twelvemonth is not to be described, like a torrent for a time stopped in its course, it rushes with double violence, indeed the French have laboured for some time past to disgust, & we to please, both seem to have succeeded even beyond their contemplations.

So strong was feeling against France that Liston himself jokingly asked his friend Hammond "whether you would prefer a Treaty offensive & defensive or wish a defensive one only."[1]

Nevertheless, the President, Federalist though he was, thought first of sending a new mission to France. His decision was endorsed, partly for reasons of domestic politics, by leaders like Hamilton and King. Robert Liston wisely made no attempt to dissuade Adams, nor, thanks to Pickering's wise advice, did he carry out a tactless plan to present an official note emphasizing his "hope and trust" that the new mission's instructions would adequately protect British rights.[2] The three commissioners, Pinckney, John Marshall, and Elbridge Gerry, reached Paris in October. Talleyrand declined to see them, but gentlemen who claimed to be his emissaries demanded, as the price of a settlement, the payment of a douceur. The demand was firmly refused, but its very presentation made France's attitude apparent. Marshall and Pinckney concluded that a settlement was highly unlikely and thereafter devoted their efforts to establishing the American position on the record, a course Gerry followed with much reluctance. Lord Grenville soon learned of these developments, probably from Rufus King, and in January 1798 he wrote to Liston about "this new Situation of Affairs," informing his subordinate:

It will be the object of His Majesty's Government to improve it by every means which can best tend to unite the two Governments, and to prove to the people of America that their Interests when independent no less than their former bonds of connection lead them to look to Great Britain as their most natural Friend and support.[3]

In March, reports from the American envoys reached Philadelphia, and on the fifth John Adams sent one of them to Congress without comment. There was a loud explosion. Leading Federalists talked of war. Robert Goodloe Harper urged his constituents to "rouse once more the spirit of '75," and another Federalist wrote, "We must reconcile our minds to a few moments of Warfare. It will not hurt us."[4] The Republicans blindly but hopefully asserted that the one dispatch sent to Congress did not fairly represent the situation, and they called upon the President to reveal the rest of the correspondence. John Adams dutifully forwarded the dispatches, revealing to the world France's attempted extortion.

Anti-French meetings swept the country, and the Republicans found their backs to the wall. Some denied that Talleyrand had played any part in the business. Others like Abijah Adams, editor of the Boston *Independent Chronicle*, blamed Jay's treaty for the new developments and claimed that "The conduct of France needs no apology. They *do* as they have been *done* by." (Probably more Republicans would have endorsed Albert Gallatin's statement a few months later that "Whatever differences of opinion may formerly have existed on the subject of our differences with France, I believe there is but one sentiment on their late conduct.") More impressive was the argument that a war with France would be hazardous and expensive, while mere bluff could serve no useful purpose. As the *Chronicle* put it:

The parade *on paper*, with no money, and but little force to carry it into execution, it cannot be supposed will intimidate the French, as they have already had combined powers fully united to oppose, and in the controversy they have brought the *whole*, excepting England, to submit to their terms. . . . Let this be a caution to America.[5]

Although the Republicans fought to the end, they were unable to prevent abrogation of the French alliance and the initiation of large scale preparations for defense. "Hail Columbia" made its debut, sung to the tune of "The President's March," and John Adams became a genuinely popular figure for the first time.

Henrietta Liston was exhilarated by the new developments:

the tide is turned, & I look with astonishment at the violence with which it flows.—
the President went to the Play last night for the first time. He is a Presbiterian
[*sic*] & goes seldomer into publick than Washington did:— . . . nothing could equal
the noise & uproar, the Presidents March was play'd, & called for over & over again,
it was sung to, & danced to, some poor fellow in the Gallery calling for sa ira,
was threatened to be thrown over. When I tell you that five years ago the *Mania* was
as strong in favor of the French you will say, that a cold national character is no
security against madness. the Democrats are silent, some indeed seem to recant, whether
convinced, or waiting a fit moment to rally, I know not. but at this moment the
British are extolled as the first people, /next to themselves I mean,/ for having so
long resisted the Tyrants of France. an Alien-bill is to be brought in to the Senate
immediately, a Secretary of the Navy is to be appointed, Frigates are fitting out,
Men & Money voted, & every Man speaking with a degree of violence at which I
often stare with astonishment.

Robert Liston reported that the government, though still determined to
avoid war if possible, expected it to come; "they look forward to an
eventual concert and cooperation with Great Britain."[6]

The XYZ dispatches reached Europe in May and caused a great
stir. Close observers of the Irish scene reported that the Franco-American
quarrel had a decisive effect in Ulster, destroying republican sentiment
which had previously existed even among Protestants. At London, George
III went out of his way to tell the American minister how greatly he
respected the steadfastness of the envoys at Paris.[7] Newspapers of both
parties united to attack the French; even Opposition journals professed
to be shocked by "a scene of unprincipled corruption," although one
slyly noted that "whatever the French may think, *we* know that America
is not easily conquered." Pittite organs, after liberally insulting the French,
often interpreted the affair as further proof of the futility of negotiations
with France, a conclusive demonstration that "there is *something in the
present French System, which is incompatible with the Peace and Security
of any other Power in the World.*" It was hoped, even asserted, that the
Americans realized that "they have no other means left for escaping the
universal disaster, than to make a common cause with the only European
Power which has successfully combated these tyrants."[8]

The British government's view was much more cautious than that
of London newspapers. In February Lord Grenville had expected war
between America and France, but now he was not so certain. He questioned Adams' motives in first sending only one dispatch to Congress
and, although encouraged by the popular reaction, regretted the lack of
energy and decisiveness which he felt marked the proceedings of Congress.
In May, referring to a minor squabble with Rufus King, he commented,
"I suppose we shall not find it difficult ultimately to settle these points
if Am.^ca really goes to War with France." Grenville's doubts were shared
by his subordinate, George Hammond, but, at least in public, William
Pitt expressed a contrary view. He told Rufus King that "If . . . there is
any one count more than another that could inspire the Eng. Nation
with a confidence and enthusiasm in the present struggle, it w^d be to find

themselves engaged with America ag^t a common Enemy—"[9]

The United States soon became involved in a naval conflict with France, although, as Grenville had anticipated, there was no declaration of war. While building armed forces of her own, America necessarily depended upon England for assistance, and a helping hand was frequently extended across the Atlantic. As a result, the period from the publication of the XYZ dispatches to the Mortefontaine convention was marked by common action and mutual assistance in the military field that was not equaled for more than a century. This was particularly true with respect to military supplies, since, with the exception of Eli Whitney, American manufacturers were incapable of the mass production of implements of war.

Perhaps the most dramatic contribution—and one often remarked upon in recent years—was what has been called the first "lend lease,"[10] a British gift of cannon for harbor defense. These guns, originally the main battery of a French man-of-war taken during the Seven Years War, had been mounted at Charleston but were carried away to Halifax at the close of the Revolution. They fired a twenty-seven pound ball, not standard in British ordnance, and therefore were lying idle in Nova Scotia, so Timothy Pickering asked if it would be possible "either to *beg* or BORROW or *buy* these guns, to be once more transported to Charleston."[11] Prince Edward, commanding in Nova Scotia, agreed to lend the cannon and eighteen hundred shot to the United States. "It gives me great satisfaction, Sir," wrote Liston to Pickering, "to be able to furnish this proof of the desire entertained by His Majesty's publick officers, and especially by one so nearly connected with the Throne, to render every service to the United States that is within their power."[12]

Ships were soon dispatched to Halifax to pick up the cannon. The royal prince's deputy made some show of handing over an extra artillery piece and seventy-six extra shot, and the guns were carried off to the United States. Pickering next asked if they could not be made an outright gift, and in January the Foreign Secretary directed Liston to return the official receipt for the guns and shot to the United States government. As Pickering said, the loan and then gift of the cannon was important "not so much for their intrinsic value (though that is not inconsiderable) as that they are ready for immediate service; & that we want them."[13] The twenty-seven pounders never fired a shot against the enemy, but Britain's prompt, friendly action was gratefully noticed in Philadelphia and made a substantial addition to American coastal defenses.

The transfer of military supplies, however, was usually handled on a business basis. Even when arms and equipment were purchased in England, the United States was dependent upon British good will, since the export of military supplies was generally forbidden by law. In June 1798 Grenville informed Liston that, despite these regulations, export permits would be granted for most items unless they were urgently needed by

Britain's armed forces.[14] During the conflict with France, England permitted the United States to procure sails, bunting, and anchors for naval vessels; Indian saltpetre, a vital ingredient in gunpowder; plans for artillery pieces; and a number of other military necessities, even such apparently simple things as cartridge papers.

Naval cannon were among the most imperative needs of the United States. The British had a large supply, partly because of the many captures made by the Royal Navy, and were quite willing to turn a penny by selling some of them to the United States. Large shipments went off to America, sometimes as many as two to four hundred pieces at a time. In addition, scores of merchantmen armed themselves in British ports, particularly after offensive armament and privateering commissions were authorized toward the close of 1798. So many ships fitted out to cruise against the French that at least one consul ran out of the forms Rufus King had forwarded to him.[15] It seems a fair guess that an overwhelming proportion of the guns with which American vessels fought or menaced the French were acquired in Great Britain.

Small arms were more difficult to procure because there was a shortage in England so serious that it was only barely possible to supply Royalist expeditions against France, but in November of 1798 the Board of Ordnance promised to deliver two thousand muskets immediately and five hundred per month thereafter.[16] Copper sheathing for ships' bottoms was also in short supply, and King was able to obtain only a small quantity for the United States Navy before permission was rescinded at the end of 1798.[17] With this single exception, the British government permitted the United States to purchase all types of military supplies in England.

Far more important than the acquisition even of large quantities of supplies from Britain was the support of the Royal Navy. At the beginning of the war, American commerce was almost completely dependent upon Britain for protection—"Shield, still Britannia, shield from harm, / The Nations with thy naval arm," cried a Federalist pamphlet[18]—and even at the end of hostilities most of the burden was borne by England's walls of oak. The Royal Navy's American squadron was reinforced as French activities off the coast of the United States increased, and the sight of British warships in American waters was, for a change, a welcome one. Meanwhile, an American navy was built as speedily as possible, and in August 1798 a British government newspaper patronizingly commented, "the Navy of America, though not in a situation to bear a comparison with the Fleets of Great Britain, is yet respectable as the effort of an infant State, struggling in defense of its Liberties."[19] This new fleet soon developed close relations with the Royal Navy.

Convoy protection was fully as important in the nineties as it is in our own day, and it was much easier to provide. Since most of the French ships at sea were commerce raiders operating alone, a single frigate was adequate protection for an almost unlimited number of ships, and most convoys actually did sail with no more than a frigate and a sloop. As early as January 1797, Grenville authorized Liston to "express His Majesty's Willingness to afford a naval Protection to the Commerce of the United States" if a rupture between America and France took place or seemed imminent. Liston occasionally asked individual captains to take ships under their wing until, in April, Admiral Vandeput ordered his commanders to provide all possible protection to American shipping. The effect on public opinion, Liston happily reported, "exceeds the expectation I entertained respecting it & I cannot avoid expressing an anxious wish that it may be carried to the utmost possible extent & that with this view an addition may be made to the Naval Force on this Station."[20] Liston's dispatch crossed outbound instructions from London directing Vandeput to "afford every protection in his power to the Commerce of the United States."[21]

Meanwhile Rufus King was wrestling with the problem of trans-Atlantic convoys. At first, he hesitated to take any action which might prejudice the success of the mission to France. But finally, in 1798, learning of a new French decree that made even the smallest amount of British cargo grounds for confiscation of a ship and all its contents, King decided to act. With his concurrence, Grenville wrote to the Admiralty that "the Commanders of such Neutral Vessels, bound to the Ports of the United States, as may choose to avail themselves of the Convoys, . . . may be at Liberty to do so for the present." The first spring convoy, said Grenville, should sail "even though there should be no British Vessels ready to avail themselves of it." King soon distributed a circular letter urging American skippers to join convoys, and the Admiralty ordered a sloop and a frigate to leave Spithead on March 1, touch at Cork, and then proceed to the United States with all vessels that desired protection.[22]

Most unarmed merchantmen traveled in convoy from this time on, although, as George Cabot put it, "the idle desire of each [captain] to be first home . . . [caused] some intractable spirits [to] break away & get captured."[23] Sometimes American naval vessels provided the protection, occasionally ships of both nations shared the task, but by far the greatest part of the work was done by the Royal Navy alone. The British force at Martinique regularly convoyed American ships until they were out of the Caribbean danger zone. Vandeput's squadron protected merchantmen going to the West Indies, and the admiral sent Robert Liston the departure dates of convoys bound for Europe, thereby overcoming American reluctance to request British assistance. If the testimony of the admiral's successor may be trusted, Vandeput even allowed convoyed American ships to avoid search merely by stating that there was no contraband aboard, a policy definitely reversed upon orders from London in 1800. In European waters, American vessels trading with the

German coast were allowed to join British convoys. Thus in all the major areas where French raiders were to be feared, American skippers were sheltered by the Royal Navy. Such protection was not extended to the merchantmen of any other power that did not have a formal military alliance with Britain.[24]

There was little friction. When the Americans established their own convoys, Robert Liston feared that Great Britain's insistence upon the right to search vessels even when under convoy would lead to trouble with the United States, just as this determination helped cause the clash with Denmark in 1801. Liston's fears never materialized. In 1799, Stephen Decatur told a British commander that had his force been larger he would have prevented the search of vessels under his protection, but the British minister was assured that Decatur would be ordered to allow ships to exercise the right of search.[25] In general, the convoy system worked smoothly and to the immeasurable benefit of both countries. When unconvoyed merchantmen of either nation did fall prey to French raiders they were often recaptured and restored to their owners by ships of the other country.

American authorities realized that the tiny navy—fifteen vessels in 1798, a dozen more in 1799—would be of little use if spread thin over the entire ocean. They therefore decided to let Britain hold the line in most areas and concentrate in the Caribbean, where frigates and smaller vessels were of particular value in the struggle against French corsairs. In December 1798 all but one of the ships at sea were in that theater; in mid-1800, twenty-two out of twenty-five. Even in the Caribbean, the United States had more freedom in stationing its vessels because of the large British forces based on Jamaica and Martinique. Orders given to Captain Alexander Murray, for example, authorized him to cruise anywhere in the Caribbean but suggested that it was "presumed that the British will attend sufficiently to the Island of St. Domingo."[26]

Since both navies often used false colors, there was increasing danger of an accidental clash as American forces grew. Shortly after the frigate *United States* narrowly avoided a duel with a British ship of fifty guns in July 1798, the American government proposed the exchange of recognition signals. Admiral Vandeput made some slight changes in the list of lights, hails, and flags suggested by Secretary of the Navy Stoddert, but he welcomed the idea and in fact later claimed credit for it. The signals were soon in use throughout the Western Hemisphere.[27] The system was not foolproof. At the end of 1798, the American ship *Aurora* shifted from French to American colors too late to avoid a broadside from H. M. S. *Latona*, and U. S. S. *Enterprise* later fought a night action with the schooner *Louisa Bridger*, the latter probably a British privateer not privy to the signals. There are the only such incidents on record, however, and the signals performed useful service throughout the war.

In other ways, too, contacts between the two navies reflected the closeness of their governments. Formal salutes were exchanged whenever American ships visited British ports; on one unfortunate occasion the garrison of Martinique lost six men when a cannon exploded while answering the salute of the *United States*. At the Cape of Good Hope, Captain Preble of the *Essex* was well received, and one of his leave parties spent a night in British accommodations ashore when the ship's launch sank in a sudden squall. Port Royal, Jamaica, was a frequent port of call, and at least one captain carefully spruced up his ship in order to make the best possible impression on veteran British sailors there. Captain Truxtun took the *Constellation* into Port Royal after her bloody action with the *Vengeance* and received hearty congratulations from Admiral Parker and other British officers. Earlier, the *Constellation's* victory over the *Insurgente* won for her skipper the gift of a piece of plate from Lloyd's committee of merchants engaged in the American trade, a reward reprobated by the *Aurora* as paving the way for an increase of British influence, since "votes of *plate* and *guineas* are not mere things of compliment."[28] Victory in single ship duels with the French raised the reputation of the United States in the eyes of a nation that put a high value on sea power.

There was only one major clash between the two navies, and the captains involved were rebuked and punished. In November 1798 H. M. S. *Carnatic,* commanded by a Loyalist emigré named John Loring, stopped the American sloop *Baltimore* and removed fifty-five seamen, although most of the men were returned when Captain Phillips of the *Baltimore* protested that he had not been left enough men to sail the ship. The irate American government courtmartialed Captain Phillips, and commanders were ordered not to permit impressment unless compelled to do so by force. Several months later, Captain Thomas Tingey refused to surrender any man to a British boarding party, and the claim was not pressed. The First Lord, Earl Spencer, and Lord Grenville were unhappy about the publicity given the *Baltimore* incident in the United States, but the Admiralty ordered Loring relieved of his command and sent home. King noted that Spencer's attitude was "liberal and friendly, tho' sufficiently guarded."[29] That this affair was the only clash between the arrogant Royal Navy and the aggressively cocksure young forces of the United States is in itself a good indication of the existence of a rapprochement on the seas as well as in the chancelleries.

The military rapprochement was made more effective by coöperation in the fields of intelligence and intrigue. It is no exaggeration to say that Anglo-American relations in this semi-clandestine sphere were close and respectful, if not always open and ingenuous, and the Pitt government promptly disavowed Robert Liston's only major indiscretion, a connection with the Blount Conspiracy. Late in 1796, the British minister was approached by John Chisholm, a middle-aged government agent among the Indians, who suggested a scheme whereby a motley army of former Tories, frontiersmen, and Indians, based on American soil and aided by Britain, would seize the Gulf Coast and other Spanish dominions. Liston forwarded the plan to London, although he had many reservations about it, and a short time later approved Chisholm's request to cross the Atlantic. Passage was paid for out of secret service money, although Liston admitted that he knew too little about Chisholm to have complete faith in him.[30] His confidence by no means increased when Chisholm disappeared on the eve of his departure, forcing His Majesty's envoy and an aide to make a frantic search in Philadelphia taverns. The assistant extricated Chisholm from a barroom brawl at one in the morning and carried him off to his ship. Grenville had already categorically declined to connect Britain with the scheme, writing Liston early in April not to allow Chisholm to come to England:

I think it merely necessary to observe that, exclusively of the inadequacy of the means to the end proposed, the two Objections which have occurred to yourself—the necessity of employing the Indians—and the impropriety of originating within the United States any hostile expedition against a Nation with which they are at peace—are of sufficient magnitude to counter-balance the advantages which are likely to result from the execution of such a plan.[31]

But Grenville's warning was much too late, and Chisholm soon arrived in London, where he had an unhappy series of adventures. The government was by no means lavish in providing him with funds, and a combination of debts and liquor several times caused his incarceration in Newgate prison. The Indian agent finally returned to America, so chastened by his experiences that Timothy Pickering felt it safe to give him back his old job.

While Grenville's instructions arrived too late to prevent Chisholm from setting out on his futile errand, they nevertheless served a valuable purpose, helping Liston to extricate himself from difficulty. A compromising letter written by Senator William Blount, the leader of the conspiracy, fell into the hands of the American government. It mentioned the departure of Chisholm to arrange British support. Pickering and Adams declined to suppress the letter, although Liston urged them to do so, but they did permit him to prepare an explanatory note, minimizing the British role, which was submitted to Congress with the other documents.[32]

In the face of a storm of protest encouraged by the Republicans and the Spanish minister, Liston decided to reveal Grenville's orders categorically disavowing Chisholm and his friends.[33] This unorthodox move somewhat reduced the pressure. Liston's willingness to admit his part and even to reveal confidential instructions from his government, as well as the nature of those orders, made an impression on the Secretary of State and could not fail to lessen American suspicions. Furthermore, his conduct contrasted favorably with that of the Spaniard, Carlos M. d'Yrujo, who unwisely allowed himself to become involved in a paper war with the Secretary of State. This new quarrel diverted attention from Liston's relations with Chisholm and, through him, with Blount. The envoy had learned his lesson. Never again did he engage in dubious intrigues in America.

Much more satisfactory, though less publicized than the Blount affair, was the coöperation between Liston and Canadian officials on one side and the American government on the other to hamstring French intrigue in the West and in Canada. The United States declined to be lulled by assurances, forwarded through Monroe, that "there did not exist in a breast of a member of the [French] government an intention or wish to disturb" the American West,[34] and Adet's attempts to strike at Canada were sufficiently obvious to keep British authorities on the alert. Grenville directed Liston to suggest coördinated action, including pressure on Indians on both sides of the line to surrender agents who stirred up plots against Canada or the United States. In May 1799 Pickering and McHenry agreed to have American army officers keep a close watch on French schemers, exchange information with Canadian forces, and act with them if military action should break out along the border. This friendly American attitude was most important, for the chief planner of Upper Canadian defense, Alexander McKee, stated that his arrangements were based upon the assumption that the United States would cover all routes of invasion save that up the Mississippi.[35]

The same coöperative spirit governed relations in the East. Once, when a French agent sold out to Liston, he and Pickering tried to use the turncoat to steal information from Adet and Yrujo, but their amateurish scheme failed. On many other occasions, however, information provided by the United States materially aided authorities in Canada. There the *habitants* had exhibited an ugly mood in 1794, resisting an attempt to call out the militia, and French agents frequently slipped across the border to lay the groundwork for filibustering expeditions from the United States.

One of these agents was David McLean, who visited Montreal and Quebec in the fall of 1796. McLean's plan, a twelve-thousand-man invasion from Vermont and New York, was too elaborate to succeed. But the spy was capable of causing serious trouble in Canada, and Robert Liston went to Pickering and McHenry for help as soon as the scheme reached his ears. He came away well satisfied, reporting to London, "I have mentioned to the American Ministers the suspicions entertained with respect to the people of Vermont; and I think we may rely upon their taking every measure that the nature of a federal Government will permit to prevent the Assembling or Arming of Troops within the Territory of the Union."[36] Closely watched by American authorities, David McLean was unable to organize a force of any consequence, and on a second trip to Canada he was betrayed to the British, captured, and executed. His plot never had much of a chance. Most Canadians were as unwilling to take arms against as for the British, however much some might grumble at foreign rule. The United States government was on the alert, and, as the Secretary of State put it:

Whatever might have been done three years ago when we were suffering under British spoliaitions and saw threatening appearances of hostility from that power, France can form no reasonable hopes of assistance in the U. S. except from a few corrupt men, a few desperate adventurers, and a few, who apparently would be willing to sacrifice even their own country to their malignant passions."

Canada was quiet by the fall of 1797, and never again did French plans seriously threaten her peace.

Britain continued to keep a close eye on McLean's fellow conspirators. When one of them, Louis LeCouteulx, unwisely crossed the boundary, he was promptly incarcerated. He remained a prisoner at least until 1801, although Liston reported that "he was an inoffensive and even amiable man in private life; . . . incapable not less from disposition than from mediocrity of understanding, of forming any serious plan against the peace and order of His Majesty's Provinces."[38] Great Britain anticipated firm American demands for LeCouteulx's release, but none seem to have been made. The United States had little interest in men who threatened good relations between the two countries and peace along the frontier.

The same attitude is evident in the handling of the Ira Allen affair. In 1796, Ira Allen, one of two surviving brothers in a famous clan that originally numbered six, went to France, where he purchased a huge quantity of small arms. Deserters from the *Olive Branch*, which was to carry the arms to America, crossed the Channel and reported the impending shipment to British authorities, who suspected—rightly, it would appear from evidence now obtainable in French archives—that the arms might really be for use against Canada. The Royal Navy was alerted, and after eight days at sea Allen was stopped by a British seventy-four and taken into Portsmouth.

Rufus King forwarded Allen's protests to Grenville, but at the same time he wrote Pickering that it might be advisable to investigate the matter. This Pickering did, but even before receiving answers to all his inquiries he wrote King both official and private letters stating his belief that the arms were indeed for use against Canada and that Allen was not only a villain and a liar but a thief. Pickering's only concession to the lack of evidence to support his position was the reservation of his harshest adjectives for the private letter. Subsequently, the Secretary received information supporting Allen's story, and he then sent King instructions to intervene in the Vermonter's favor. But the wording of these instructions was weak, and most of the evidence came from Republicans, whose testimony Pickering may have expected King to discount.[39]

Rufus King seems to have shared British misgivings about the destination of the arms, for he accepted the ministry's plea that it could not interfere in the processes of Admiralty courts and did not even intervene when Sir James Marriott condemned the shipment in December 1797. By this time, all danger of an attack on Canada had passed, David McLean was dead, and the arms were beginning to deteriorate from improper storage, facts which doubtless helped Allen get them released on bail in 1798. The case dragged on for years, partly because Allen was thrown into prison when he visited France to gather evidence. Finally, in 1804, long after the close of the Federalist regime, Allen won his case. For eight years, and particularly in 1797, when alone the arms might have been of much use against Canada, the United States refused to exercise its full diplomatic strength in Allen's behalf, even though Sir William Scott admitted that it would be difficult to prove any connection between Allen and the French.

In a somewhat similar episode, Britain was called upon to forswear an adventurer whose activities threatened the United States. He was William Augustus Bowles, an ex-Loyalist who had already twice failed in filibusters against Florida. After escaping from a Spanish prison ship, Bowles visited London in 1798 and then came to America. He was put ashore on the Florida coast by H. M. S. *Fox*, procured his own election as Director-General of all the Creek tribes, and ordered white men out of the Indian lands. The United States was alarmed for several reasons, but largely because the appearance of Bowles in a British ship after a favorable reception by West Indian officials seemed to indicate that England was attempting to establish a new pawn in the American chess game.

To soothe American sensibilities, Robert Liston took it upon himself, for he was without instructions, to declare that His Majesty's Government would not support Bowles in any designs harmful to the United States. In this he was soon more than technically correct, for London ordered that no financial support be given to Bowles. Lord Grenville expressed acid surprise that the United States should request assurances but authorized Liston to inform American authorities that "His Majesty's Ministers are entirely unacquainted with any hostile Designs which Mr. Bowles may meditate in the Indian Territory, and that he has no authority, commission, Instruction nor Promise of support from His Majesty's Government."[40] England could not deny having some connection with the leader of the Creeks, and thus with his anti-American activities, but her final decision to abandon Bowles was as firm as, if less speedy than, her rejection of Blount's schemes. In America there was peace and concert which hardly suggested that in a decade plots and counterplots would again be the rule in the American West and along the Canadian boundary.

Although opportunities for coöperation of this nature were far fewer, even in Europe there was an extensive exchange of information, and Americans, including several in official positions, directly aided the British war effort. Thus, for example, David Parish, American consul at Hamburg though a British subject, handled the disbursement of British subsidies to Continental powers until the French complained and he was removed from office. The American consul in London gave England first-hand reports on the situation in Ireland, Germany, and America. In 1798 Rufus King, as interested as Lord Grenville in Nelson's Mediterranean chase of Bonaparte, forwarded private letters which he apparently hoped would help solve the mystery of the French general's destination. Timothy Pickering gave the British American consular dispatches describing developments on the important Ile de France, where Britain had no reliable informants. On his part, Lord Grenville frequently forwarded to King secret information on European politics, and in 1798 George Hammond told King that his government would assist the United States in getting intelligence from France after the ejection of the American envoys.

More important and interesting than any of these incidents were the activities of Gouverneur Morris, whose recall as American minister to France was demanded in 1794. Morris crossed the Channel to England, where he became a popular figure because of his antirepublicanism and picturesque character, and perhaps too because of an inaccurate report that his peg leg was the result of a tangle with a tiger. Morris dined at intimate dinners with Pitt and Grenville—"The wines are good and the conversation flippant," he confided to his diary—[41] but soon had more than social activities to occupy his time, acting as a channel for unofficial exchanges between George Washington and Lord Grenville. The American also offered Grenville a firsthand report on conditions in France and Germany, with particular emphasis on the means by which France evaded the British provision blockade.[42]

Morris' information and grasp of politics so impressed Grenville that in the summer of 1796 the Foreign Secretary asked him to go to the Continent to play the role of informant, observer, and informal British propagandist. Morris' first stop was at Berlin, where George Hammond was attempting to bring Prussia into the war, but their joint efforts were unsuccessful, and Morris moved on. From Vienna, he sent long, detailed reports to London. To solidify the support of European monarchies, he urged Britain to declare the war a crusade of self-defense and antirepublicanism: "This kind of crusade will not indeed be so wonderful as that which was produced by the preaching of Peter the Hermit, but it may answer better purposes." Morris suggested the use of Lascar or Croat soldiers, already accustomed to similar climates, in an attack on Latin America if Spain entered the war. He added, half jocularly, "If, as is said, the Pope means to declare a holy war against France and *her allies,* he might give you a detachment of monks, supplied with the due quantities of bulls and such-like ammunition."[43] The American's reports to Grenville, all forwarded without signature to prevent embarrassment should one fall into enemy hands, continued into 1797. In addition, Morris tried to convince Continental statesmen that security could be won only by a decisive victory over the French, but the Austrians and Prussians, already sadly battered, refused to accept the logical conclusions of this reasoning. According to John Quincy Adams, Morris finally made himself "very obnoxious" at both courts.[44] He sailed for home late in 1798, more than three years after his first report on European conditions.

While Gouverner Morris aided Britain as a private citizen, at least once official American representatives offered their assistance to the Pitt government. William Vans Murray, whose wife was English, was the American minister to the puppet government at the Hague. He carried on an extensive correspondence with Rufus King; the parts that seemed important were turned over to Grenville by King, and, not satisfied with that, the British intercepted and decoded much of the remainder. In the spring of 1798, Murray reported that the Dutch underground was ready to attempt a counterrevolution if proper arrangements could be made. Through Murray, King forwarded the terms upon which Britain would coöperate; "England desires to see and would gladly assist . . ." was the way he began his letter. Negotiations continued until November, when Grenville finally told King that Britain could not deal with the Dutch patriots execpt on the basis of restoration of the Prince of Orange and the stadholderate.[45] The failure of these clandestine negotiations only slightly lessens the significance of the action of Rufus King and William Vans Murray. With America virtually at war with France, they were ready to assist in embarrassing that enemy under cover of their diplomatic positions.

The variety and extensiveness of intelligence coöperation, like union of action in the military field, is impressive evidence of the closeness of Anglo-American relations. In 1794 the British government dispatched ships of the line to keep watch on the United States, and John G. Simcoe wrote, "The first object of my Heart would certainly be, with adequate force and on a just occasion, to meet . . . [Washington] face to face."[46] By 1799, Simcoe was denying the truth of public reports that he was anti-American, his successors in Canada were coöperating closely with the United States, and the Royal Navy's American squadron, acting in conjunction with the naval forces of the United States, concerned itself only with the problem of French privateers and commerce-raiders. Furthermore, instead of conducting rival intrigues among tribes in the American West, the United States and Britain jointly endeavored to preserve peace in the area, exchanging information on suspected French designs there as they did with respect to so many other matters. Without British assistance, American resistance to France would have been much less effective. Conversely, American participation in the war brought both moral and material benefits to Great Britain. Only formal allies could have done much more for one another than did the United States and England at this time.

Toussaint, Miranda, Alliance 9

MILITARY COÖPERATION WAS SO SUCCESSFUL THAT THE BRITISH AND American governments were led to consider more far-reaching schemes. The only such project which came to fruition was the development of a common policy toward Toussaint L'Ouverture. In the crucible of war, self-interest molded agreement out of what had previously been contrasting attitudes and conflicting economic interests. Before 1793, French Santo Domingo produced as much sugar as all the British West Indies, but a Negro revolution and guerrilla fighting on the island brought the export trade to a halt. The British colonies enjoyed a great boom. England therefore had little interest in encouraging trade with Santo Domingo unless she herself gathered in the profits. The United States, on the other hand, looked greedily to the island as a potential source of less expensive tropical produce. Politically, the idea of an independent Negro Santo Domingo was not attractive to England or America, since both feared that the virus of freedom would infect slaves in their own possessions. But the United States was by no means enthusiastic when, in line with a consistent wartime policy, Pitt's government chose conquest as an alternative, since an English victory would place the island behind the bars of the Navigation System.

British forces entered Santo Domingo late in 1793, but the easy triumph that had been anticipated did not materialize. Within three years over seven thousand English soldiers were killed in action, and many more succumbed to disease. Henry Dundas himself was forced to admit the bankruptcy of British policy by the end of 1797; the costs, he confessed, far exceeded present or prospective gains.[1] Dundas had no alternative to suggest, and Grenville continued to express horror at the idea of an independent Negro state, but the facts of the military situation were running against them.

At first, the United States subordinated economic interests to a desire to see the slave rebellion crushed; at one time, Pickering even hinted that the United States would assist British forces struggling against Toussaint. But by the winter of 1798 it was obvious both that a decisive British victory was impossible and that, on the other hand, Toussaint was virtually free from French control. Pickering began to feel that it would not be too difficult to prevent the infection from spreading to slaves in the United States, which was, after all, a good deal farther removed than Jamaica, and he saw that a native regime was more likely to favor American commerce than was Britain or, in normal times, France. With these thoughts in mind, the Secretary of State told Liston that the independence of Santo Domingo might meet with American approval. Liston's report so alarmed Grenville that he sent copies of the dispatch to other government departments and expressed his abhorrence of the idea to Rufus King.[2]

At this critical point, news from Santo Domingo radically altered the situation. A young English lieutenant colonel, Thomas Maitland, had assumed command there when his superior became ill en route from Europe. Although his own position was uncertain, Maitland boldly decided to withdraw British troops from advanced positions and concentrate them at Môle St. Nicholas and Jérémie. Then, without waiting to learn the government's reaction to this unauthorized step, he signed an agreement with Toussaint providing for the complete evacuation of Santo Domingo. In retiring, Maitland made good terms with the Negro chieftain, who promised not to support armed attack or political intrigue against Jamaica and also agreed to open his ports to English shipping.[3]

Although the Cabinet tried to keep the agreement secret while debating its acceptance, rumors were soon so widespread that Rufus King asked for information, expressing confidence that America's interest in the island would "excuse what might otherwise seem a mere matter of curiosity."[4] When, at the Foreign Secretary's suggestion, King examined Maitland's correspondence at the War Office, he raised an obvious question: Had Maitland recognized Toussaint as the head of an independent state? If so, America had an equal right to trade with him. If not, she could not permit British ships to carry cargoes from the United States to Santo Domingo, for American law banned trade with French dominions. Hammond, William Huskisson, who showed King the documents, and Grenville were all unable to give him a clear answer, so King turned to Dundas. He pointed out that provisions which England exchanged for Haitian sugar and coffee might be used to outfit privateers preying on American commerce. As Maitland's negotiations were unauthorized and not binding, King asked the War Secretary to have the convention rejected or amended to protect American commerce, like the British, from privateers based on Santo Domingo. Dundas replied cordially, promising to "direct Col° Grant [Maitland's intended successor] to propose an additional Article to this Effect, and to inform Gen¹ Toussaint that unless it shall be accepted and strictly observed, he must not expect that the Convention can be ratified or executed by this Country."[5]

While Dundas' promise was encouraging, a more definite agreement on policy seemed needed. Grenville suggested that the best way to restrain Toussaint's pesky privateers and his dangerous doctrine of Negro freedom was to limit his contacts with the outside world by establishing an Anglo-American monopoly to trade with Santo Domingo. This concern would "furnish no manufactures but from the British Territories, and no articles of Produce or live stock but from America." Trade would be funneled through Port Républicain (Port-au-Prince), making it easy to control, and Toussaint would be required to help the outside powers enforce his own isolation and their monopoly of his trade.[6] King pointed out that this scheme was politically and constitutionally impossible in the United States. He suggested instead that the trade be opened generally to British and American merchants, who could be closely watched by their governments. Grenville grumbled a bit, but Pitt was ready to consider King's plan. He agreed that "concert in this business . . . was . . . of the first importance; that if the best Plan was inconsistent with concert, one must be devised that will secure this primary object and as many others as possible."[7] Thus died the monopoly scheme, another sacrifice in the interest of coöperation with America.

King, Pitt, Grenville, and Dundas agreed that a British agent would have to be sent to Philadelphia, and Thomas Maitland was the obvious choice. Dundas framed instructions for him which stated the government wishes in great detail, but in essence Maitland was directed to accede to the desires of the United States in all regards as long as the principle of limited, supervised intercourse was maintained.[8]

Meanwhile, American merchants had begun to clamor for a share of the lucrative trade with Santo Domingo. In November, Pickering sent word there that American cargoes would probably be forthcoming if the ouster of Hédouville, the French agent, really meant that "General Toussaint and the other chiefs will . . . assume the direction of the affairs of the Island."[9] Congress soon authorized the President to reopen trade with French colonies which showed a spirit of independence and restrained privateers. Although stated in general terms, "Toussaint's clause," as Jefferson called it, was designed to refer to Santo Domingo alone, and Pickering rebuffed an emissary from Gaudeloupe who sought to have it applied there. Robert Liston was alarmed, fearing that "dazzled by the prospect of . . . immediate and brilliant advantages," the United States would overlook the dangers of Negro republicanism and the possibility of serious disagreement with Great Britain.[10] Liston's concern was justified, for the pressure upon John Adams steadily mounted. Even the Federalist *Columbian Centinel* blamed delay on a fear of France, urged formal recognition of Toussaint, and predicted that if this were not done "we shall see, though reluctantly, the commerce of that rich and populous Colony fall exclusively into the hands of the British."[11]

Fortunately for Anglo-American concord, news of Maitland's appointment soon arrived, closely followed by the envoy himself. The first proposal of Liston and Maitland, that one port be opened to ships which would be required to get a passport from the British minister at Philadelphia, was rejected by Pickering. But, after a fortnight of give and take, with Oliver Wolcott joining Pickering on the American side of the table, the conferees reached an informal agreement that took the form of "Heads of Regulations" to be proposed to Toussaint by Maitland upon his arrival in Santo Domingo. The direct trade was to be opened to British and American ships, but neither Toussaint nor any other foreign power would be permitted to carry goods to or from the island. As a compromise between the American wish for unrestricted entry and Britain's desire to channel trade through one port, several of the most important ports were to be opened, and at these official points of entry merchantmen could get permission to engage in the coastwise trade. This was a major concession by the British, although the procedure provided for more supervision than the original American proposals. Finally, it was agreed that no inhabitants of Santo Domingo, except representatives of Toussaint on missions to England and the United States, would be allowed to leave the island, and no Frenchman would be permitted to land there without the consent of the Negro chief.[12]

Liston and Maitland felt that the Americans had driven a hard bargain, an impression that the satisfaction of Timothy Pickering and John Adams somewhat justifies, but they argued that better terms were not attainable. Liston admitted that the "Heads of Regulations" did not end the threat to Britain's black colonies, since the volume of trade would make it impossible to prevent intrigue if Toussaint chose to attempt it. But, said Liston, "the great and unanswered argument always recurs to the mind." Toussaint was virtually independent; it was impossible to turn back the clock and deal with him on any other basis. The agreement at Philadelphia was the best possible compromise between the existing situation in Santo Domingo and the interests of Britain and the United States.[13] Maitland agreed, although he was more critical of the Americans, writing that "no Consideration of political danger weighed at all with them, when even the hope of a precarious Mercantile benefit appeared to be within their reach." On the other hand, "The principal benefit after all will be derived from acting together . . . and in getting the American Government on the one hand nearer to Us, and on the other nearer to a positive declaration of War with France."[14]

The Englishmen would doubtless have been somewhat more pleased if they had seen the instructions Pickering sent to consul Edward Stevens at this time. Stevens was on the point of concluding an agreement with Toussaint opening the island to American shipping, but Pickering directed him to suspend negotiations until Maitland presented the "Heads of Regulations" to Toussaint. The Secretary of State noted that the proposed restrictions on commerce went far beyond those contemplated in Stevens' first instructions, but he added:

we consider the prospect which has been opened to us of a lucrative trade to St Domingo, is to be ascribed in a great degree to the operations of the British; and . . . the continuance & protection of that trade rest chiefly on the Naval Superiority of Great Britain. We are bound then, by a direct regard to our commercial interests, and considerations of political Safety against what may justly be called a common enemy, to act in perfect concert with Great Britain."[15]

General Maitland, who sailed from Philadelphia on H. M. S. *Camilla* late in April, reached the Cap three weeks later. Accompanied by Edward Stevens, he went to Gonaives to meet Toussaint. Since the Negro chieftain had no love for the British and did not desire to strengthen rumors that "St Domingo was to be sold to the british Government, and once more brought under the Yoke of Slavery," Maitland kept in the background for five weeks while Stevens worked to induce Toussaint to accede to the demands of the white powers. The agreement took the form of a secret convention between Toussaint and Great Britain, although it was chiefly the work of an American and applied equally to British and American commerce. Toussaint absolutely refused to receive a permanent British agent, so Edward Stevens consented to handle English affairs. "My Efforts in favor of the british Interests," he wrote Pickering, "will become more difficult, and my situation more unpleasant. You may be assured, however, Sir, that I shall not omit any Thing that lays in my Power to promote the joint Interests of both Countries."[16] Maitland thanked Stevens for his generous action.

One more hitch, potentially a serious one, developed before trade with Santo Domingo was finally resumed. The Philadelphia agreement took effect on August 1, and the negotiators understood this to mean that English and American ships could first enter Toussaint's ports on that date. But Stevens, who misunderstood the purpose of his superiors, insisted that no ships could leave their home ports for Santo Domingo until the beginning of August. He convinced General Maitland, British squadrons in the Caribbean were so informed, and ships that left the United States in July, intending to reach Santo Domingo after the end of the month, were thus exposed to capture. At Pickering's request, Robert Liston hurriedly wrote Sir Hyde Parker and circularized all the British commanders he could reach, explaining the error of Maitland and Stevens. In addition, he provided American skippers with protective passports. Liston's prompt action prevented any serious difficulty.

The way was thus cleared for the resumption of a limited trade with Santo Domingo, a trade, incidentally, that never proved quite as lucrative as American merchants had hoped. Subsequently, a number of minor disagreements developed between the United States and Britain,[17] but all of them were successfully smoothed over. In this whole affair, despite Thomas Maitland's misgivings about American selfishness and shortsightedness, despite some American fears of the British, both countries clearly recognized the advantage, the near necessity, of a common policy toward Toussaint's rebellious colony. Their coöperation eliminated a potential source of serious controversy and demonstrated the ability of the two nations to work in close harmony when dealing with major problems.

Other important projects were considered in a manner providing further evidence of Anglo-American intimacy, but all of these schemes eventually failed, showing that there were fields in which, unlike Santo Domingo, the plant of coöperation would not flower. One of these was Latin America, where the situation differed markedly from that in the Pearl of the Antilles. In the latter, a revolution existed and demanded recognition, but in the Spanish colonies internal seethings and expatriate intrigue were only faintly cracking the incrustations of three centuries of European rule. Tempted by commercial advantage as well as by the opportunity to strike a blow at the vassal of France, many Englishmen and Americans cast their glances southward.

In most cases, their attention was directed thither by the indefatigable Francisco de Miranda, first of the great Latin American revolutionaries. Fleeing from his homeland in the eighties, Miranda reached London at the time of the Nootka Sound controversy. William Pitt rejected his plan for revolutionizing South America, so Miranda went to France, where rebels found better favor. He became a general officer but fell from power with his friends, the Girondists, and was cast into prison. Luckily escaping with his life, Miranda slipped across the Channel to Britain in January 1798. There he attempted for years to secure English and American support for an expedition to free Spanish America.

The connection between Miranda's fantastic plans and Anglo-American relations, if not the plans themselves, calls for some comment. It is significant that neither British nor American supporters of Miranda considered coöperating with him unless the other power would also assist him. Rufus King, for example, argued in 1798, "The destiny of the new world . . . is in our Hands: we have a Right, and it is our Duty . . . to act . . . as Principles,"[18] but never once did he advocate support of Miranda without British concurrence. Similarly, Alexander Hamilton, who somewhat tardily endorsed Miranda's design and probably hoped to command American troops participating in it, showed no desire to "go it alone" in South America. Britain's position was even more definite. In 1798, Grenville stated that no expedition would depart for Latin America unless and until the United States was consulted.[19] Unilateral action was too risky and too likely to involve England and America in quarrels to be seriously considered on either side of the water.

Furthermore, many English and American leaders shared a common horror of revolutions, even when they were in enemy territory. In 1799, when Britain mistakenly suspected that the United States was about to aid Miranda, the Cabinet discussed the situation. Grenville opposed any extension of "the spirit of revolution." So did his colleagues, although

Windham and Dundas were willing to consider joining the Americans, not so much to further their plans as to direct them into safer channels.[20] The British might have spared themselves this concern, for John Adams was just as firmly opposed to the idea of spreading revolution. In 1798 he declined to answer a letter from Miranda. Late in life, the ex-President expressed surprise that Pitt and Miranda should have thought that a man who had already witnessed so many revolutions would "be desirous of engaging myself and my country in most hazardous and bloody experiments to excite similar horrors in South America."[21]

Alexander Hamilton, although eager to take part in a broad attack on Spanish possessions, had earlier warned Miranda that "I could personally have no participation in it, unless patronised by the government of this country."[22] Lesser men continued to dream of filibusters, but the possibility of government action in South America was, at least for the time being, buried in 1798 and 1799. There were too many "ifs" in the equation. If the Directory rather than the Empire had occupied Spain and directed its colonial policy, if America's troubles with France had expanded into war with the ally of France, if the reluctance of key figures in Britain and America had been overcome, Miranda might have sailed for his homeland under Anglo-American auspices. As it was, the temporary enthusiasm of William Pitt and Rufus King fell far short of bringing the project to fruition, and the adventurer's schemes remain an interesting but undeveloped episode. When the emancipation of Latin America was achieved, it owed little to the activities of emigrés scheming for foreign support, infinitely more to the organizers of native forces.

The joint venture for very high stakes advocated by Miranda's backers was not the only extension of Anglo-American coöperation considered at this time. Several years later, William Cobbett confidently stated that "To have formed that defensive and offensive alliance . . . which I urged . . . , there wanted nothing but the hearty good will of this [i. e., the British] cabinet."[23] As was so often the case, Peter Porcupine was not completely fair; closer union was prevented not by the coolness of Pitt and Grenville, but by the feelings of John Adams and his advisers. Questions posed by the President to his Cabinet in 1798 clearly reveal his own feelings:

Will it not be the soundest policy, even in the case of a declaration of war . . . , for us to be totally silent to England, and wait for her overtures? Will it not be imprudent for us to connect ourselves with Britain, in any manner that may impede us in embracing the first favorable moment . . . to make a separate peace? What . . . can we expect from England by any stipulations with her, which her interest will not impel her to extend to us without any? . . . On the other hand, what aid could we stipulate to afford her, which our own interest would not oblige us to give without any other obligation?[24]

Even the more partisan Federalists in the Cabinet shared the President's view that informal agreement was preferable to treaty commitments. After consulting Hamilton, James McHenry forwarded the New Yorker's views to Adams with little change, agreeing that "Mutual interest will command as much from her as Treaty. . . . 'Twill be best not to entangle." If Pickering handed in a written response, it has been lost, but a few weeks later he told Hamilton that he did not favor an alliance at that time, although feeling that "provisional orders should be sent to Mr King."[25] Despite Jefferson's brokerage of rumors that an alliance had already been signed, no such idea was seriously considered by the government.

Comprehensive instructions were finally sent to Rufus King in April. Pickering wrote that it was not deemed "expedient at this time to make any advances to Great Britain," and that even if war were declared the President would not consent to an alliance pledging America not to make a separate peace. On the other hand, Pickering continued, "the United States will not be wanting in the exertion to support . . . [the] common interest . . . [and] may from time to time agree on such co-operations, as circumstances should require." Specifically, following a suggestion originally made by Hamilton, the Secretary of State asked if Britain would lend a dozen warships to the United States and strengthen naval forces in American waters when war broke out. In return, the United States offered to move ground forces to positions covering all approaches to Canada from the Mississippi region and to provide "a competent body of troops and militia" to meet invasion or insurrection in British North America.[26]

Grenville's response took the form of lengthy instructions to Liston. The Foreign Secretary somewhat disingenuously argued that the United States had most to gain from close political ties; otherwise, France might offer terms so attractive that Britain could not turn them down and "the United States might be left, though against the Wishes and Interests of this Country, yet still unavoidably, exposed to the Resentment of France—" But if England were bound by an alliance she would certainly fulfill her engagements "with that scrupulous good Faith which has distinguished the Measures of His Majesty during . . . this Contest, and in the midst of the most disgracefull Conduct on the Part of other Powers."

The Foreign Secretary agreed to consider a loan of surplus warships, but he noted that "His Majesty would expect in Return . . . some Aid and Advantage . . . , and particularly that the American Government would furnish Him with a certain Number of Seamen," a *quid pro quo* that certainly doomed this particular project. King had mentioned the possibility of an attack on Louisiana, and this, said Grenville, far from being "any Cause of Jealousy, would certainly be a Matter of Satisfaction," but he implied that the United States would be expected, in return, to accept a British conquest of Santo Domingo, of which there was then still hope. In closing, Grenville told Liston that uncertainty as to America's wishes alone prevented more concrete proposals. "You may with the fullest

Confidence assure the President that any Proposals . . . will be cordially received."[27] On balance, Grenville's instructions manifested a friendly spirit. True, he asked a high price for British warships. But on the other hand he offered to expedite the supply of military equipment and to give careful consideration to American suggestions. There was no harsh language, no attempt to force John Adams' hand. With the American situation still unclear, the Englishman can hardly be blamed for not taking a more positive stand. Doubtless he later felt that events justified his reserve.

Pickering seemed unwilling to discuss the specific suggestions made by Grenville, so Liston raised them with the President during a summer visit to Braintree. Although Adams had "little or no reserve in talking of political subjects . . . [and] conceived it to be the interest of this country as well as that of Great Britain to enter into mutual agreements," Liston was unable to pin him down. The President said that until American public opinion firmly supported an arrangement with Great Britain, which he had confidence it would in time, nothing could be done.[28]

Public opinion never crystallized as Adams expected, or said that he expected. Rumors of alliance continued to excite opposition, and they were aided by Republican wile and the ignorance of many citizens. A Republican journal in Boston, for example, printed an account of the purported alliance, admitted that so far the story was mere rumor, but closed by stating that the report might have begun with Federalists who "intended to familiarize the citizens to so fascinating an idea!" In Pennsylvania a Federalist judge on circuit was told by German farmers that they were strongly opposed to "the *alliance* and sedition bills. By the alliance (when desired to explain) Mr Adams, a son of the President, was to marry a daughter of the King of Great Britain;—and General Washington was to hold the United States in trust for that King!"[29] The idea of, perhaps, John Quincy Adams married to one of George III's numerous progeny was indeed an engaging vision.

Thus affairs drifted along in the fall of 1798. Robert Liston was forced to play a waiting game, meanwhile demonstrating Britain's friendly attitude by offering convoys and other assistance. Liston sometimes feared that Lord Grenville might expect something tangible in return, so he privately asked George Hammond if Downing Street approved of his course. In an official response, Grenville commended Liston's actions and directed him to repeat that further aid would be forthcoming if the United States declared war. To scotch widespread rumors, Liston was authorized to declare publicly that Britain had no desire to bind the United States in "a permanent System of Alliance for general Purposes."[30]

Once again Grenville's invitation failed to elicit a response at Philadelphia, in large part, ironically enough, because Nelson's magnificent triumph at Abukir relieved some of the pressure on America. We "congratulate the citizens of the *United States*, on the event," a Boston editor wrote, "as every proceeding which tends to lessen the naval forces of *France*, diminishes the ability of that Republic to plunder our commerce, insult our flag, or menace our Independence." An American diplomat put the matter more simply: "For the United States it is unequivocally and positively a grand blow against France, and for us!"[31] When the news reached Philadelphia, William Cobbett was astounded to hear an enthusiastic crowd sing "God Save the King" under the very windows which not too long previously had been shattered by angry mobs protesting the Jay treaty. Preparations for war continued, but America felt more secure, and closer ties and alliance were not again the subject of diplomatic correspondence. All in all, the story of American relations with Britain during the undeclared war against France seemed to show that most Americans felt as did John Marshall, who said in 1798, "it would be madness and folly not to endeavour to make such temporary arrangements as would give us the aid of the British fleets . . . ; but I would not, even to obtain so great and so obvious a good, make such a sacrifice as I think we should make, by forming a permanent political connection."[32] Alliance—no; cordial coöperation—yes.

A Brief Drift Apart 10

D URING THE LAST YEAR OF THE PITT AND ADAMS REGIMES, THE CAUSE of friendship suffered a serious check. Though muffled during the years after 1795, some potentially dangerous issues were not eradicated, and seizures, for example, again became a serious problem in 1800. But, at this time, new and not old frictions contributed most to the drift apart. One was the restoration of peace between America and France, the other a quarrel within the commission considering pre-Revolutionary debts.

The breakdown at Philadelphia was particularly regrettable since the other Jay treaty commissions had been so successful. The St. Croix award was completed in 1798, and the seizure commission made steady progress—a real tribute not only to the temper of its members but also to the wisdom of British and American officials. This body, which had earlier avoided one serious obstacle, successfully surmounted another in the summer of 1797. Although the treaty authorized review of all cases arising before the exchange of ratifications, the British government expected the board to deal primarily with West Indian seizures. However, ratifications were so long delayed that confiscations under the secret provision order were brought within its scope, and in June 1797, in the case of the *Neptune,* the commission held that this decree was not a legitimate exercise of belligerent rights and that the owners had been inadequately compensated.[1] Under this precedent, more awards were made than for any other cause, and Britain's acceptance of the decision clearly demonstrated her good faith.

The arbitrators made steady progress, limited only by the slowness of the American agent and insufficient documentation provided by the claimants, until a serious difficulty arose early in 1798. The treaty required claimants to exhaust all possible legal remedies, but many cases were apparently irretrievably buried in the appellate courts. Therefore, when, on the last day permitted for the introduction of claims, the American agent before the board presented memorials on all cases pending, he naturally included many cases—actually 390—still before the courts, as well as some in which claimants were still trying by judicial means to collect restitution ordered paid to them. The British members threatened to secede if their colleagues insisted upon hearing cases still *sub judice.* The first compromise suggested by the Americans was rejected, and for a short time it seemed that no agreement was possible.[2]

However, as in the *Betsey* case eighteen months before, the British government conceded the major point at issue—the slowness of the judicial process—although this time asking for a *quid pro quo*. Under pressure from Downing Street, the Lords Commissioners of Appeals directed a speedier presentation of evidence, and the pace of all courts soon quickened. This order was communicated to the board. At the same time John Nicholl announced that, as a further concession, the British members would consider cases in which restitution had been ordered but not collected and even "pass awards on the Exchequer, the British Government . . . taking upon itself to recover the property from the hands of the Captors." In return, the Americans were expected to refrain from passing upon claims still before the courts. This compromise was accepted by Trumbull, Gore, and Pinkney, and the commission resumed business in August 1798. But for difficulties in its sister board at Philadelphia, the London group would probably have finished its work without incident. A major part of the credit lay with the British government, which had, as Rufus King said, constantly "shewn a real inclination to remove difficulties, and to cause the Treaty to be executed with good faith and liberality."[3]

The commission on prewar debts, meeting at Philadelphia, had a much stormier career, although it began smoothly enough. The British representatives, Thomas Macdonald and Henry Pye Rich, were well received when at last they landed in April 1797. Grenville had instructed them to insist upon nominating one of their own countrymen for fifth member, as the Americans had done at London. The suggestion of their colleagues, James Innes and Thomas FitzSimons, that Fisher Ames be chosen by mutual consent was therefore rejected, and the British members nominated John Guillemard, a merchant visiting America who was believed to be "distinguished for the union of talents and information with uncommon modesty, candour and urbanity." Guillemard was then formally chosen by lot, although Liston regretted that Grenville's orders had made it necessary to resort to this expedient. Fisher Ames, nominated by the Americans, Liston reported to London, was "known to add to very brilliant parts so much liberality of sentiments and so fair and friendly a disposition toward Great Britain" that his choice would have been a happy one, both for its effect upon public opinion and for the efficiency of the board.[4]

The commission's business was very complicated. It had to decide whether legal impediments, usually state laws, blocked the creditor's efforts and whether the debtor was solvent when collection was attempted. If both questions were answered in the affirmative, the board scrutinized the wildly inflated claims of the British merchants and made an award. At first, the arbitrators examined each case individually, but they soon became bogged down in details. Thomas Macdonald therefore suggested a radical change in approach. In the first place, said he, the simplest definition of legal impediments should be adopted: "*Every* cause of delay is an *impediment*. Every cause of delay arising *positively* out of the oper-

ation and effect of law, or *negatively* from defect of *law* is a *lawful impediment.*" Macdonald also suggested that the claimant be required to prove
only three things: existence of the debt at the time of independence,
presence of a legal impediment, and the impossibility of a fair settlement
in American courts. To defeat a claim, the United States would have to
show that the debt was not bona fide or did not exist, that the debtor
was insolvent, or that there had not been due diligence on the part of
the creditor in his attempts to collect.[5]

From the date of the presentation of Macdonald's paper, the board
became an acrimonious debating society rather than an arbitral commission. The Americans refused even to consider his suggestion. The
majority persevered, however, and matters came to a head in August,
when the board heard the claims of William Cunningham & Company, a
merchant house which had extended credit to Virginia planters. Applying
Macdonald's rule, the British commissioners and Guillemard found that
Cunningham & Company was entitled to satisfaction. James Innes was
on his deathbed, but FitzSimons vigorously dissented. Two days later he
threatened to secede to prevent a similar decision in the case of Daniel
Dulany, once a pamphleteer against taxation without representation but
later a Loyalist exile. The usual summer epidemic of yellow fever intervened at this point. Instead of making use of the recess to seek a compromise, Timothy Pickering concerted plans for a secession with Fitz-
Simons and Samuel Sitgreaves, a Federalist lawyer who had been appointed on Innes' death, while Attorney General Charles Lee prepared an
immoderate statement denouncing Macdonald's rules.[6]

Shortly after the resumption of business, Macdonald, Rich, and Guillemard attempted to force a decision in the case of Charles Inglis, former
bishop of New York. Although the clergyman had never tried to collect
through the state courts, the majority held that he was entitled to compensation since any such attempt would certainly have been fruitless. The
American commissioners seceded three times to prevent a decision, reporting to Pickering, in a tone that left little hope for the future of the board,
"there is on the part of the majority but little observance of Decorum with
regard either to our nation or ourselves, and as little of the liberality,
candour, and moderation, which we deem essential to the attainment of
. . . justice."[7]

The climax came in July, touched off by the case of Andrew Allen,
a member of the Continental Congress who resumed his British allegiance
in December 1776. The key question was that of his citizenship. The Americans claimed that the United States became independent in July 1776,
and that Allen was liable to punishment—the confiscation of his property
—when he deserted to the British side. The majority held that independence was not established until 1783 and that Allen was therefore entitled
to restitution. After heated argument, FitzSimons and Sitgreaves seceded

and sent word that they would no longer meet with the board. They did, however, return for one more meeting at the end of July. Following an exchange of personal comments, Macdonald read his forceful, lengthy decision in the Inglis case. At three o'clock the reading was finished. After a further exchange of insults, FitzSimons and Sitgreaves angrily left the room. Never again did they return. "Thus ends," wrote John Guillemard, "this Chapter of events—in which Great Britain has been duped, and a sacred and important Treaty broken."[8] The Philadelphia breakdown caused Lord Grenville to suspend the seizure commission.

Why did the board at Philadelphia fail? A number of answers to this question were suggested, and doubtless there was some truth in almost all of them. The British blamed their American colleagues, whom they called "men of the most turbulent and untoward disposition, of most envious and irritable vanity, of most unconquerable prejudice and most bitter emnity, and most lax and unwarrantable principles." Pickering and the American representatives were inclined to fix the responsibility on Thomas Macdonald "and the apparent incompetency of his colleagues to act an independent part," and even Liston had to admit that Macdonald was "ardent and tenacious in argument, and disposed to press his victory over his antagonist to the utmost."[9] But Liston felt, as did many Englishmen, that the size of the claims was a much more important factor. The sum asked was nearly double the annual American budget, and the Republicans did not fail to make the most of this. Early in 1799, for example, the old Virginia patriot, Edmund Pendleton, attacked the London commissioners for niggardliness and those at Philadelphia for attempting to saddle America with a huge burden. "I am inclined to think," Pendleton said, "the U. States would have a good bargain to discharge both classes of commissioners, and set the spoliations . . . against the assumed British debts; although probably not a shilling on that account was justly due from the Union."[10] Robert Liston suspected that, in the face of such criticism, the Federalists were unwilling to risk the political consequences of paying even a substantial portion of the total. The United States denied this, claiming instead that unjustified interpretations of the treaty—and Jay's own opinion justified this—had expanded the claims far beyond the intent of the negotiators.[11]

Probably the chief blame should fall on Timothy Pickering and Robert Liston. They stood on the sidelines while trouble developed and then plunged into the fray, not as mediators but as participants. As so often in his career, Pickering allowed his emotions to blind his judgment. Unfortunately, Liston was equally unimaginative, and by the time he learned that Lord Grenville inclined toward a negotiated settlement it was already too late. When Grenville heard of the final suspension of the board, he sharply pointed out to his subordinate that the whole affair was in striking contrast to the manner in which he and Rufus King had settled problems of equal difficulty in London.[12]

The problem now became a full-fledged diplomatic one. A settlement was not made easier when Thomas Macdonald published a bitter attack on America that had a predictable reception in both countries. The *Anti-Jacobin Review,* for example, stated that the administration had "connived at, if not encouraged" the secession, which was supported by "the dishonest part of America, among whom, unfortunately, are to be included some members of her government."[13] Such bitter feeling helped to make work for a compromise, in John Adams' opinion, "the most snarling, angry, thorny, *scabreux* negotiation" that ever a government had to undertake.

Lord Grenville and Rufus King naturally tended to support the positions of their own countrymen, but neither had a closed mind. In May, before the final collapse, they agreed that "constructions in either extreme must be given up" if they threatened Anglo-American harmony,[14] but King unfortunately was without instructions. He remained so, because of almost incredible slowness on Pickering's part, until February 1800. At that time, although with little hope, he presented the draft of an agreement framed by the Secretary of State that laid down the rules of procedure for the debt commission. In April, Grenville returned the expected answer: the proposals were "in no respect explanatory of the Treaty, but in manifest contradiction to it" and could not be accepted by Britain.[15] A fortnight later, Rufus King visited the Foreign Office to see what could be salvaged from the wreckage. At first the conversation followed familiar and unproductive lines. Then the American asked if Grenville's casual mention, at an earlier meeting, of a lump sum settlement meant that the Pitt government would consider this means of ending the quarrel. The Foreign Secretary replied that, while he himself did not favor it, his colleagues thought that this might be the best way out, and he volunteered an opinion that the creditor's claims were wildly swollen. Rufus King hurriedly reported this development to Philadelphia, adding his own belief that it might "lead to the satisfactory conclusion of a most difficult business."[16]

Once again King and Grenville had opened the way to an amicable settlement. The Foreign Secretary presumably would have preferred to fight for Britain's rights within the board, but in the interest of conciliation he accepted the advice of the Cabinet and dropped the hint picked up by Rufus King. From this moment on, there was steady progress toward a settlement. Although John Adams was very annoyed at the "spleen and ill humor" Britain had shown, he gave the idea his approval, and in August the new Secretary of State, John Marshall, told King that the United States was prepared to pay up to one million pounds.[17] King had promising conversations with Grenville, Hammond, and Nicholas Anstey, whom Grenville appointed to work out the details, but just as negotiations seemed on the verge of success the Pitt government resigned. Shortly thereafter John Adams quitted office, and the problem of the treaty commissions was left to new administrations. Already it had contributed powerfully to the cooling of relations.

Britons were particularly irritated by developments in Philadelphia because they suspected that these were connected with the departure of a mission to negotiate peace with France. As the *Anti-Jacobin* put it, "The new embassy . . . is a subject of general conjecture and general expectation [in America]; . . . all . . . hope that it will produce a state of things that will enable America to set *Britain* and *British debts* at defiance." Such suspicions were natural but unfounded; the coincidence in time was purely fortuitous, and the only connection between the two was the common effect they had upon English relations with America. John Adams had never given up hope that an honorable peace could be made with France. When the Directory approached him through William Vans Murray at the Hague, the President surprised the nation by nominating Murray to negotiate a settlement. Federalist journals objected that "Negociation with France is an invariable prelude to national ruin, and misery,"[18] and party leaders protested vigorously, but all they were able to achieve was a broadening of the mission to include Chief Justice Oliver Ellsworth and former governor William R. Davie of North Carolina.

In April, when reports of the new mission reached England, they did not cause a great stir since the campaigns of Jourdan and the Archduke Charles, as well as the raging issue of Irish union, monopolized space in the newspapers. Government journals allowed the *Anti-Jacobin Review*, which swung into an attack upon America with its usual zest, to express their disappointment. The *Review*, seeing the new appointments as proof that "The conflict of parties is over, and the French faction is everywhere triumphant," accused the President of having "forfeited his own character for consistency, and paved the way for the degradation, if not the ruin, of the country." The ministry was almost equally displeased. In October, Rufus King wrote to Philadelphia that, since the appointment of Murray, "I have observed . . . a coldness towards the U. S., an indifference to their affairs, a disposition to give unfavorable interpretations to their conduct, and in my ordinary intercourse with the Gov^t . . . more difficulties than I had before been accustomed to experience."[19]

Meanwhile, the mission had been delayed, primarily through the efforts of Timothy Pickering and Oliver Wolcott, who headed the administration while the President was absent in Massachusetts. John Adams became impatient. Late in September, he hurried to Trenton, whence yellow fever had again driven the government. At the temporary capital, Adams found not only the Cabinet, but Hamilton, Ellsworth, and Davie as well. In addition, Liston was expected within a few days, a circumstance even Pickering realized would be suspicious. "If the mission . . . be suspended," he wrote Washington, "the *Aurora* will ascribe it to British influence and the efforts of the British faction, as we shall in this case be called anew altho' the arrival of Hamilton . . . & the passing of Mr. Liston are purely fortuitous."[20] Whether a cabal or not, even

121

this battery of talent was unable to change the mind of the President, and on October 16 he ordered Ellsworth and Davie to leave for France. They reached Paris in March, after being assured that the new consular government would receive them, but for some time negotiations dragged, since Bonaparte was absent—this was the spring of Marengo—and Talleyrand was busy arranging the retrocession of Louisiana by Spain.

While the emissaries waited for Talleyrand to give them his attention, a political explosion took place at home. Adams had long been aware that Pickering, McHenry, and Wolcott gave far more obeisance to the retired Secretary of the Treasury than to himself, and by May 1800 he had had enough of their intrigues. McHenry's resignation was requested and received. Summary punishment was not dealt out to the less bumbling and more oleaginous Oliver Wolcott, but when Timothy Pickering declined to resign, saying that his personal finances would not permit it, Adams dismissed him with a curt note: "Divers causes and considerations, essential to the administration of the government, in my judgement, requiring a change in the department of State, you are hereby discharged from any further service as Secretary of State." Republicans hailed the end of Pickering's regime at the Department of State. As the *Aurora* put it, in language not much more extreme than that used by its journalistic allies, "If ever a man went out of a public station loaded with the universal execration of an injured country, it is Mr. Timothy Pickering, . . . [whose career shows] the mischief that may be done . . . , even by small and contemptible talents and a narrow mind, when set on fire by malignity."[21] At the other extreme of the political spectrum, the high Federalists, whose already slim confidence in Adams had been shaken by the mission to France, abandoned him. Led by Hamilton, they were soon engaged in open warfare with the President, who finished his term of office under fire from both sides of the political fence.

Timothy Pickering retired temporarily to the frontier. As Secretary of State, he had been far from a complete success. For one thing, he was a poor subordinate; years later he wrote that he did not believe Cabinet officers should be bound by the maxim of *"implicit obedience or resignation.* On the contrary, I should think it their duty to prevent, as far as practicable, the mischievous measures of a wrong-headed President."[22] In addition, Pickering was unfitted by temperament for an office that requires, if not urbanity and tact, at least self-control. Still, his service to the nation had not been negligible. His very forcefulness fitted him for the task of answering the pronunciamentos of Yrujo, Fauchet, and Adet. He helped to lead his country into a close connection with England without forfeiting American freedom of action. Never a large man, he was a conscientious and strong-willed one, so devoted to the Federalist cause that he allowed this to blight his attitude toward everything else, including John Adams.

To succeed Pickering, the President chose John Marshall, the most prominent Virginia Federalist after the death of Washington. Marshall had led the defenders of the Jay treaty in Virginia, spearheaded the XYZ mission, and then temporarily resumed the practice of law, but soon, at Washington's request, he ran for Congress and was elected. He won Adams' respect by demolishing the Republican attack on the President for surrendering Thomas Nash to Great Britain.[23] Remembering Marshall's opposition to the Alien and Sedition Acts, some Federalists regretted his promotion; "I sometimes . . . think," complained Benjamin Goodhue, "that none of the Virginia Federalists are . . . better than half-way Jacobins." In England, too, Marshall's appointment was not favorably received. Pickering had been an earnest advocate of resistance to France, while the new Secretary was a Virginian, an attorney, and, Englishmen thought, doubtless a delinquent debtor. The *Sun* believed that the change was "a kind of sacrifice to the people who are anxious for peace with France" and the *Morning Post,* in an amazingly inaccurate article copied by the *Times,* reported that "Mr. MARSHALL is said to be . . . attached to the French Republic, to which he was lately an Ambassador."[24] But, although his tenure was cut short by the Republican victory in 1800, Marshall proved to be an able, balanced Secretary of State.

Pickering's dismissal, the debt commission controversy, and the mission to France all contributed to the development of friction between England and America, but, in addition, the climate of opinion was changing in each country. Britain's military outlook temporarily improved after the battle of the Nile; first Nelson, then Archduke Charles and Suvorov, provided happy news for Downing Street. The temporary change of fortune encouraged England to be less considerate of neutrals. A renewal of Armed Neutrality, Bonaparte's coup d'état, and his second Italian campaign soon weakened England's position, but the full effect of these events was not felt until the end of the year. Meanwhile, there were important changes in the American situation. The least anti-British of all factions, the extreme Federalists, lost ground because of their advocacy both of war with France and of the Alien and Sedition Acts, and John Adams for the first time strongly challenged the ultras for party leadership. The dissipation of Federalist strength, a decline of feeling against France, machinations of interested politicians, and a renewal of seizures probably account for the new spate of Anglophobia that appeared in 1800. Many Americans were alarmed by the situation, and they hoped British policy would not play into the hands of England's enemies. "There never existed," wrote Theodore Sedgwick, "two nations which had a stronger interest in mutual confidence & amity than that country and this. It is in her option whether they exist, or the reverse take place."[25]

Ominously, it appeared for a short time that Britain would lose sight of this postulate of nineteenth-century Anglo-American relations. Early in 1799 Thomas Maitland had protested against widespread concession to America, arguing that this "line of conduct . . . will never answer any good end, or tend in the smallest degree to forward the views for which it is adopted." As time went on, government organs shifted toward Maitland's position—the *Times* endorsed Cobbett's prediction that the whole American fabric was about to collapse, and the *Anti-Jacobin Review* analyzed the situation in the United States "to prepare our countrymen for a *controversy,* if not a *contest,* which, we foresee, must speedily occur." In February 1800, Grenville gave Liston permission to return home, saying that American developments "highly injurious to our interests both there & in Europe" might make it necessary "to reconsider our System as with respect to that country." He added, rather threateningly, that "where we cannot controul events, we must as well as we can regulate our conduct according to them."[26]

Liston was so affected by Grenville's change of attitude that he composed a highly emotional plea for continuation of the old policy. He believed that the United States would weather the present storm and steadily grow in wealth and power—"God forbid that it should be to our detriment and to the triumph of our enemies." All disputes could be solved, the envoy felt, except that over the claims of creditors, and "we perhaps had better consent to indemnify them ourselves than resolve on a war," for war would bring the loss of Canada, extensive attacks on British commerce, and "the propagation of enmity & prejudices which it may be impossible to eradicate."[27] Whether this plea had any effect we do not know, but Grenville did not carry out the radical change he had considered. Relations slowly improved, and the spring of 1800, when the Grenville-Liston exchange took place, may be said to mark the nadir of Anglo-American relations between the Jay treaty and the *Essex* case.

Already two developments, the handling of the Nash-Robbins affair and England's reaction to the death of Washington, had indicated that the trend was about to be reversed. Thomas Nash was a petty officer on H. M. S. *Hermione* in 1797, when her commander, Captain Pigot, announced that the last man down from the yards would be flogged. In their haste, two men fell to the deck and suffered broken bones. Pigot ordered them thrown overboard as useless "lubbers." That night the frigate's crew mutinied, murdered the officers, and set a course for a Spanish port. There they scattered, and many found their way into the American merchant marine and navy. Nash, who joined the crew of the merchantman *Tanner's Delight,* was arrested when his ship called at Charleston, South Carolina, early in 1799. He readily admitted that he had been on the *Hermione,* but claimed to be an American citizen impressed by Captain Pigot, exhibiting a protection issued in the name of Jonathan Robbins, of Danbury, Connecticut, to support his assertion. At Liston's request, President Adams investigated the case and, after satisfying himself that the protection was fraudulent and that Nash was really a British subject, requested Federal Judge Bee to have him turned over to the Royal Navy. In time, the mutineer was condemned and executed.[28]

The Republicans, led by the *Aurora*, attempted to make political capital out of the affair, and Philip Freneau, their poet laureate wrote an emotional "Epitaph of Jonathan Robbins,"[29] but the public was never aroused as it would have been in earlier years by the surrender of any seaman—British or American—to the summary justice of the Royal Navy. By the time the House of Representatives took up the case, early in 1800, the Republicans were willing to let the matter die without debate, knowing that no political advantage could be wrung from it. But confident Federalists insisted that the motion to censure the President be put to the ballot and defeated as it deserved. It was, handily, after a very effective speech delivered by John Marshall on the final day of debate.[30] The whole affair demonstrated that simple and unsubstantiated appeals to Anglophobia would no longer arouse a majority of the populace.

On the other side of the Atlantic, only a few months earlier, England had learned of the death of Washington. Here was a man who had led his nation in a revolutionary struggle against the British crown, who had been the chief figure in a contest bearing some resemblance to the French Revolution, who had once been considered by Englishmen as the epitome of all that was base in mankind. Yet, as early as 1797 Rufus King reported from London, "The King is . . . very popular . . . among the People of this Nation: it would be saying very much to affirm, that next to him, General Washington is the most popular character among them, and yet I verily believe this to be the fact." When Washington died, Liston penned a eulogy which summarized the reasons for Britain's changed attitude. "His love of peace and good order," Liston wrote, "his marked aversion to the extravagance of democratic principles, . . . [and his] opposition to the system of the present rulers of France, must render his death an object of regret even in distant countries."[31]

Only Cobbett, the court, and the *Anti-Jacobin Review* seem not to have shared Liston's feeling of a deep loss. The editor was annoyed to see British officers march in a memorial procession at New York, particularly since they followed cannon taken from English forces during the Revolution, and, when London learned of Washington's demise early in January, the court declined to take any notice of it. The dyspeptic *Anti-Jacobin Review* also declined to go into mourning for the ex-President, but even its comment is proof of the general esteem in which Washington was held. "Curious indeed is the fact," said the *Review*, "but it is nevertheless a fact, that in no country has this man so many admirers as in that against which he was guilty of treason and rebellion."[32]

The *Anti-Jacobin's* surprise was understandable, for, as Rufus King noted, "The Newspapers . . . all announced the General's death & in a manner honorable to his memory."[33] As a matter of fact, the leading London journals seemed almost to vie with one another in the extravagance of their praise. The *Morning Post* got off to a slow start because it at first doubted the accuracy of the report from America and declined to comment, until confirmation was received, on "so great a loss to the cause of liberty, at a moment when it stands in need of every assistance." A few days later the *Post* entered the contest of eulogiums, but the other papers were well off the mark. The *Post's* Whig stablemate, the *Morning Chronicle,* had already printed an effusive panegyric on the day news first reached London:

The whole range of History does not present to our view a character upon which we can dwell with such entire and unmixed admiration. The long life of General WASHINGTON is not stained by a single blot. . . . His glories were never sullied by those excesses into which the highest qualities are apt to degenerate. . . . His fame, bounded by no country, will be confined to no age.[34]

Much to the amusement of the *Chronicle,* which pointed out that many who were now Pittites had opposed concession to the American colonies, the government newspapers joined in the chorus of praise. Overriding its own warning that "any encomium on this truly distinguished character would be superfluous," the *Times* devoted itself to the attempt. Washington was said to have displayed "the rare combination of talents at once military and pacific, that would do honour to the first General and the first Statesman of any age or country." Furthermore, since his private life was one of unblemished virtue, characterized by "the most endearing manners, he has also enjoyed the almost exclusive happiness of dying in full possession of his reputation and glory."[35] Other government journals copied the *Times'* item or expressed similar sentiments, and a life of the ex-President running through four issues of the *British Magazine* as well as the various prints advertised for sale at this time—an engraving of the famous Lansdowne portrait for one and a half guineas, others at prices from a few shillings on up—show the interest and affection Washington commanded in England.

Neither the mourning for Washington nor the Nash-Robbins affair was important in itself, but each was an indication that the United States and Britain were not bound for another 1794. Matters soon took a pronounced turn for the better. In April, King and Grenville initiated a new approach to the debt commission problem. Marshall's omnibus instructions, sent in September, were well received in London, and early in 1801 King reported that "not only the Justice of our demands but the present posture of Europe [i.e., the impact of Marengo and Hohenlinden] ought to have their proper influence in favour of a speedy and satisfactory adjustment [of our affairs] with this country."[36]

The Franco-American convention and the visit to England of one of the negotiators tested the Pitt government's attitude. The convention put a final end to the hope that America would become an ally, and it included a code of neutral rights that directly opposed British principles. These articles did not bind third parties, of course, but they were a public if indirect attack upon English maritime doctrine and might have caused trouble if the United States had attempted to press them upon Britain. Many Americans, including Jefferson, feared that the convention of Mortefontaine would "endanger the compromising us with G B,"[37] and England's moderation was the more significant because it was unexpected after the acerbities of the previous year.

Although British newspapers did not attempt to conceal their chagrin that an agreement had been reached, they generally adopted a moderate tone. The only exception was William Cobbett's new journal, which promised to expose the envy and malignancy of "both our open and secret enemies; . . . a striking instance of which is exhibited in the Convention between France and America," and added, speaking of the latter nation, "we have too intimate a knowledge of her resources to deprecate her anger, or dread her hostility." More representative was the comment of the *Times,* which found the agreement "satisfactory, as none of the Articles infringe upon the late Treaty concluded by Mr. JEFFER-SON [*sic!*] with our Government, of which some apprehensions were entertained, as it had been so frequently the subject of cabal in America."[38] The ministry's reaction was equally conciliatory. Grenville commented unfavorably on only one of the articles in the maritime code and told Rufus King that otherwise "he saw nothing in the convention inconsistent with the [Jay] Treaty . . . , or which afforded any ground of complaint."[39]

A short time later, Oliver Ellsworth reached England. The Chief Justice had one rare advantage: Thomas Macdonald admitted that he was an honest man, "possessed of a certain delicacy of sentiment and conduct which must give him a cast of singularity [in the United States] —I understand he is ignorant of the world, but not assuming—another uncommon combination in America."[40] Doubtless for weightier reasons than Macdonald's recommendation, British officialdom welcomed Ellsworth more cordially than any other American visitor during this period, despite the fact that he had been one of the negotiators with France. The Speaker escorted him to the House of Commons, and at the Law Courts he was invited to sit next to Chief Justice Kenyon on the bench. As far as his health would allow, Ellsworth passed a pleasant winter in English society at London and Bath. Rufus King was certainly correct when he reported home that Britain's reaction to the convention of Mortefontaine and "the distinguished manner in which Mr. Ellsworth has been received by the Court has a tendency to show that, at present, it has no animosity nor unusual prejudice against us."[41]

Since the American government had no desire to widen the chasm, the brief drift apart appeared to have been checked. Perhaps too much had been attempted too rapidly. Perhaps some reaction was inevitable, since the United States had shifted so rapidly from the brink of war with Britain to a near alliance against the first friend the young republic ever had. Yet all the troubles and bickering of 1799 and 1800 could not conceal the fact that permanent gains had been made, and by the end of 1800 the way was open for resumed cordiality. This path was followed, with only a few sidewise wanderings, for some years to come; the next quadrennium even provides the edifying spectacle of a Republican President seriously considering military alliance with Great Britain. That such a thing was possible is powerful evidence of the success of the Pitt and Adams regimes. Reservations remained on both sides of the Atlantic; prejudices engendered by a fratricidal war could not be obliterated in a short term of years. But, by and large, the *British Magazine* was not incorrect when it noted in 1800 that "unfortunate differences which once subsisted between Great Britain and America have not prevented the two powers from forming an intimate and cordial friendship."[42] The preservation and improvement of this cordiality was the responsibility of the governments succeeding those of John Adams and William Pitt.

Jefferson and Addington Step Forward 11

IMPROBABLY ENOUGH, AN ERA OF INCREASED CORDIALITY OPENED IN 1800 with the triumph of historically anti-British forces led by Thomas Jefferson. Shortly afterward the Pitt government collapsed and was replaced by a ministry which made peace with France in the fall of 1801. Following these changes, from 1801 to 1805 Anglo-American relations passed through a cycle very similar to that opened by the Jay treaty. Beginning with the settlement of disputes between the two countries, this phase of the rapprochement reached a peak when the United States felt itself threatened by France, then faded away in the face of assaults from several directions.

The election of 1800 was one of the closest, most bitterly contested campaigns in American history. The Republicans were fortified with powerful issues, but they owed their victory at least as much to the schism within the Federalist party. Adams and the mass of the Federalists were ranged against Hamilton and many other party leaders; the President accused the Hamiltonians of being a "British faction," and the former Secretary responded with a bitter pamphlet calumniating John Adams' public career. Such disunity was fatal in the face of the highly organized efforts on behalf of Jefferson.

The first major test was the New York election in May, for the legislature then chosen selected the state's presidential electors. Both sides recognized the importance of the contest, but the Republicans, led by Aaron Burr—"To Colonel Burr we are indebted for everything," wrote one Republican—made the greater exertions and carried the city of New York, and thus the state, by the narrow margin of 250 votes. Just before the election, H. M. S. *Cleopatra* brought two captured American vessels into New York harbor, a circumstance which, according to Robert Liston, contributed powerfully to the final result when properly exploited by Burr and his minions.[1]

The Federalist loss in New York cost Adams twelve votes, more than enough to assure a Republican victory if Jefferson could maintain his 1796 strength elsewhere. The Federalists fought furiously to regain the lost ground. By political blackmail they secured six more votes in Pennsylvania than they had obtained in the last election, and in New Jersey, taking advantage of an old law which allowed women to vote, Federalist gentlemen "proceeded to the Hustings, followed by their daughters, their housekeepers, their female relations and dependents" and delivered such a large vote that the state was easily carried by Adams and Pinckney.

But a renewal of British seizures, called by Liston "perhaps the most efficient of all the causes of the approaching triumph of the Democratick interest,"[2] provoked a wave of feeling against England, and in December returns from South Carolina confirmed that the Federalists would not be able to make good the loss suffered in New York.

Reports of the Republican victory, forwarded to London by the British chargé d'affaires in a specially chartered vessel, caused a decline in the "consols," already shaken by bad news from Europe. The *Anti-Jacobin* predicted the collapse of the American government, but drew some consolation from the fact that its ruin would show "the modern reformers, the framers of cheap-governments, the constitution-mongers . . . the folly and danger of departing from settled rules, fixed notions, and established principles." The *Anti-Jacobin,* still enraged by America's supposed perfidy in the matter of the Philadelphia debt commission, added that if the United States continued to break faith, "if supported by British capital she seeks to throw off British connection . . . , her ruin is rather 'a consummation devoutly to be wished,' than a calamity to be deplored." As usual, the *Anti-Jacobin's* language was exceptionally harsh, although administration organs shared its fears. The *Times,* for example, commented that "The result is certainly unpleasant towards this Country, as Mr. JEFFERSON is the life and soul of the French faction in America."[3]

Actually, while most Jeffersonians still disliked England, this concept of a "French faction in America" was, to say the least, out of date. The Franco-American quarrel had its effect, even upon Republicans. As the Jeffersonian *National Intelligencer* said in a review of the period, "The partiality of our citizens for the French Republic began to decline [in 1796 or 1797]. Its declension was rapid and decisive." Attacks upon American commerce, plus accounts of the "numerous and tragic excesses committed by succeeding parties," prepared the way for an even greater shift when news of the Eighteenth Brumaire reached America. This event —"the gloomy spectacle of the bayonet dispersing the depositaries of . . . public confidence"[4]—virtually destroyed the last vestiges of Republican political ties to France. The reaction of the *Aurora,* a leading party journal, is a case in point. At first this paper refused to credit Paris reports of a coup d'état. Then, hopefully but not confidently, the *Aurora* wrote, "Let us consider Bonaparte still worthy of his past fame. Let us suppose some causes which we have not yet heard of may hereafter justify the outrage he has done to the government of his country. Then indeed would the prospect to France and to mankind be transcendently splendid," since Bonaparte could be expected to bring new vigor to the prosecution of the war.[5] But only a day later this Republican newspaper abandoned even this hope and surrendered to despair. Others in the party underwent the same change, though less rapidly and often without the necessity of public explanations, and the rare Republican defenders of Bonaparte in 1800 justified his seizure of power only as a necessary prelude to a stable democratic government. But in England all of this was unknown or ignored, and the *Times'* lament was fairly representative.

Jefferson, who was well aware of the mistrust, largely mistaken, with which he and his party were viewed in England, did his best to dissipate this feeling. Before the inauguration, he had a series of talks with Edward Thornton and assured the chargé, Liston's successor, that the new administration would be every bit as friendly as the Federalist government. Jefferson admitted that Republican campaigners had insulted England but said that "he hoped henceforward that language would be used no longer, . . . [since] there was nothing to which he had a greater repugnance than to establish distinctions in favour of one nation against another." Thornton was so encouraged that, the day after the inauguration, he sought another interview with Jefferson to discuss specific problems—the debt commission, impressment, seizures, and trade with Santo Domingo. The President's attitude was moderate, and as Thornton rose to leave Jefferson reiterated his hope that the British government would ignore the reports of "newspaper *trash*" that he was anti-British and a friend of France. The chief executive admitted that "For *republican* France he might have felt some interest," but he emphasized that "there was assuredly nothing in the present Government of that country, which could naturally incline him to show the smallest undue partiality to it at the expense of Great Britain."[6]

Secretary of State Madison apparently felt the same way. His first detailed instructions to Rufus King ran over the issues between the two countries in some detail and hinted at retaliation if Britain did not change her course. At the same time, however, the new Secretary carefully refrained from directing King to make a strong *démarche* to the British government and noted with satisfaction the various minor concessions England had made. The next day, when Madison had occasion to discuss relations with England in a letter to James Monroe, he strongly emphasized the good side of British policy and took comfort from the fact that "the present policy of the British Gov^t treats the U. S. with more respect & conciliation than heretofor notwithstanding the prophetic alarms sounded on this subject agst the election of Mr Jefferson."[7]

The moderation of Jefferson and Madison surprised British authorities. Early in 1801, Lord St. Vincent—like some Federalists—feared that the Republicans would lead their country into the new Armed Neutrality, and Rufus King felt it necessary to deliver to Lord Grenville a long lecture on America's determination to continue its neutrality, concluding with a prediction that "unless farther & new causes of complaint should arise, . . . the good understanding between the U S. & Eng. would [suffer] no diminution" under the new regime.[8] King's judgment proved to be correct, and within a year after Jefferson's inauguration, Britain generally recognized that the Virginian's election had not been the catastrophe that was first feared. In America, there was a noticeable lessening of anti-British feeling, and in the fall of 1801 a devoted Jeffersonian wrote to his chief, "I do not believe that any event wou'd produce more mischievous consequences to the U. S. than a rupture with G. B. either in a political or pecuniary point of view."[9]

Meanwhile, across the ocean, Pitt laid down the cares of office at almost the same time that news of Jefferson's triumph arrived in London. Pitt's fall sprang directly from the Irish question. After the Act of Union in 1800, he proposed to pass Catholic emancipation through the new Parliament of the United Kingdom, both to assure domestic peace and support of the war among the Irish and to redeem pledges which Lord Castlereagh had made to Hibernian politicians to secure their support. The Cabinet split on the issue, and, when one of the opponents of emancipation revealed Pitt's plan to the King, George III announced that his coronation oath would not permit him to give it his approval. After some delay, Pitt faced up to the problem of royal opposition, although he characteristically declined to make an outright fight for emancipation. He offered to shelve the project for the duration of the war if the King would prevent agitation against it in his name. The monarch's answer did not satisfy Pitt, and in February 1801 he sent in his resignation.

George III chose Henry Addington, Speaker of the House of Commons, to succeed the fallen Minister. Pitt approved and promised to support the new government, which included the Duke of Portland, Lord Eldon, and the Earl of St. Vincent, whose name added ornament to the Admiralty. For the Foreign Office, after considering a number of candidates, Addington chose Robert Banks Jenkinson, Lord Hawkesbury; "only think of Jenky as Secretary of State. I cannot endure that, nor will you I think, easily," wrote the wife of Britain's foremost diplomat.[10] The selection of this young and untried man, son of the defender of the Navigation System, to face the problems of war and a new Armed Neutrality was a measure of the weakness of the administration, and the public's reaction was not a good augury for its success. A Whig paper pretended to think that the whole thing was a rather bad joke, since the appointment of a man like Addington was impossible. Even the administration journals were cautious; the *Sun's* praise was labored, and the *Times* expressed anxiety in contemplating "a Government which appears so weak as to depend upon the precarious support of the Ministers it has displaced, or a Coalition with the opponents of both." Grenville scornfully referred to the new Cabinet as being composed "out of the under actors of the same Company."[11]

The unprepossessing character of Henry Addington himself was the chief cause of public skepticism. "The Doctor," as he was called because he dabbled in medicine and his father had been royal physician, had no illusions about his own abilities; he accepted office only after being strongly urged by the King and Pitt. He was a conscientious, unimaginative politician who had been a good Speaker of the House, or, in the words of two friends, "a good sort of man, but not of such weight as to be able to stand against any vigorous attack made upon his Adminis-tration."[12] His attitude toward America is practically indiscernible, although in 1812, before rejoining the government, he made sure that it intended to suspend the Orders in Council.

For Lord Hawkesbury, Addington's choice to succeed Grenville, this was the first big step upward in a career leading to Number Ten, a residence he occupied longer than any other premier after Pitt. In *Coningsby*, Disraeli castigated Hawkesbury as "the Arch-Mediocrity," but this is not quite fair. Hawkesbury had no great talents, and he perhaps inherited too much of his father's placemongering ambition, but he was also a loyal, moderate, and honest Cabinet member with a knack for preserving harmony among his colleagues. Furthermore, despite an aspect in debate which made one observer say that he looked "as if he had been on the rack three times and saw the wheel preparing for a fourth,"[13] Hawkesbury was the best speaker on the government side in Commons, and in 1803 he was transferred to the Lords to provide sturdier opposition to the thrusts of Grenville and other enemies of the government.

As Foreign Secretary, Hawkesbury was not a great success, and Brougham's comment, in 1803, that "Jenky seems now to be suspected of talents as he has long been convicted of industry, activity, and some information," stands almost alone. It was soon apparent·that his chief fault was the slowness with which he worked. Rufus King was not the only one to find this annoying; the veteran Russian diplomat, Count Woronzow, told a friend that important communications languished for two or three weeks on the Foreign Secretary's desk and stated, "most solemnly, that Lord Hawkesbury is absolutely incapable of transacting business. . . . On the whole, there is an actual imbecility in his Lordship, as a man of business."[14] Woronzow exaggerated, but there is no doubt that Hawkesbury's failure to drive the Foreign Office at a faster pace was his major failing.

The advent of Addington and Hawkesbury did not arouse as much concern for the future of Anglo-American harmony as had the triumph of the Republicans. Rufus King feared that the new government would provide weaker leadership in the struggle against France, and he regretted that Pitt and Grenville had gone out of office just as a solution to the problem of the debt commission appeared to be in sight. But he did not complain of the attitude of the Addington ministry; indeed, his first interviews with Hawkesbury, with St. Vincent, whom he consulted on impressment, and with Addington ("He expressed sentiments such as an Eng. Min' ought to entertain respecting America.") were eminently satisfactory.[15] King's attitude was shared by the new American government, and a year later Secretary of War Henry Dearborn expressed the general opinion of his colleagues when he wrote:

the British government at no time since our revolution has discovered so friendly a disposition towards this country as they do at present. It is evident that they are at last convinced that such a friendly intercourse with this country as will secure a great part of our trade is in a considerable degree essential to their own existence as a great & powerful nation.[16]

In 1804, just before the fall of the Addington ministry, Madison agreed that "the present administration in G. B. appears more liberal & cordial toward the U. S. than any preceding one."[17]

Neither new government made immediate, large-scale changes in the diplomatic corps. The post of Robert Liston, who left America at the end of 1800, remained vacant for more than two years, and Rufus King was permitted to continue at London, although, in the event of a Republican victory, he had expected to be replaced, a prospect which he regarded philosophically: "Presidents, Secretaries, Generals and Ministers—myself among them—may be removed, still the machine will move on!"[18]

Robert Liston had begun to hint a desire to return home as early as 1799. The stated reason was poor health—he had a circulatory ailment in one leg—but there can be little doubt that the deterioration of relations and stiffening attitude of Lord Grenville played a major part in his decision. In February 1800 Grenville sent Liston a leave of absence and an assurance that he would not be asked to return to the United States.[19] That spring, Henrietta Liston happily began preparations for a return to Scotland. She and her husband gave a party for the children of Philadelphia—we may presume, despite her statement to the contrary, that the invitation list was carefully compiled—and sold their furniture. They spent the summer traveling up and down the country, ranging as far as Monticello and Niagara Falls. A visit to Timothy Pickering, at work hacking a home out of the wilderness on the Pennsylvania frontier, was omitted, since, as Liston put it, "such a journey would have given a better handle than has yet been afforded to the brutal attacks which continue to be made upon your character and conduct by the abandoned editors of the Democratick Prints."[20] In December, the Listons embarked at Norfolk in H. M. S. *Andromache,* bound for Antigua, where the retiring minister hoped to regain health during an extended stay with his wife's relatives.

Liston's service in the United States had been a credit to himself and his country. Incautious involvement in the Blount conspiracy and failure to anticipate the explosion within the debt commission were the only major mistakes that could be charged to him, and on the other side of the ledger there were much more substantial entries. His intervention settled the St. Croix issue in a most satisfactory manner, and he showed consistent sympathy for American complaints against proven outrages by British naval officers. His able handling of the problems raised during America's war with France was particularly praiseworthy; he took advantage of all opportunities to develop American friendship while at the same time avoiding any appearance of forcing the United States to move

SIR ROBERT LISTON
Portrait by Gilbert Stuart

farther or faster than it wished. He helped to work out the agreement on Santo Domingo, perhaps the most significant and important example of coöperation during this period. Above all, though heartily disgusted with the United States at the time of the debt commission breakdown, he did not throw his hands into the air; he remained hopeful that an agreement could be worked out and confident that a provocative, bellicose policy toward the United States would be the height of folly. Finally, in marked contrast to his predecessor, Liston earned the respect of most Americans and the enmity of few—this was not the least of his many contributions to the Anglo-American rapprochement.

When Liston left America, Secretary of Legation Edward Thornton became chargé d'affaires. The *Anti-Jacobin Review* urged the ministry to ignore diplomatic usage (which limited the rank of Britain's representative to minister since that was King's title) and send as Liston's successor "an Ambassador of the first rank;—a man of opulent fortune, and of a liberal and enlightened mind," but such innovations did not appeal to Addington and Hawkesbury, who allowed Thornton to keep his position while they carried on a leisurely search for a new minister. A former tutor, like Liston, Thornton was, we are told, "a *quiet*, sensible, well-informed man, without brilliancy or elocution. Well-educated, and full of information, which he details slowly from a natural impediment in his speech." He was on friendly terms with Jefferson and had a generally favorable attitude toward the United States. When at last he was relieved, the *Aurora*, a Republican journal which had not succumbed to the charms of Robert Liston, paid him a rare compliment, asserting, "had all the Ambassadors who have preceded Mr. Thornton acted with the same decorum which has marked his deportment for upwards of twelve years, while he resided here, less jealousy and more good-will would have subsisted between the two nations."[21]

Even the most talented and decorous chargé, however, is not often allowed to undertake important negotiations, particularly when there is a minister in residence at the other court. Such was the case between 1800 and 1803, when Rufus King virtually monopolized the handling of important business between the two countries. In some ways, these were the most interesting years of his mission, but at first King had little luck with the Addington regime. Hawkesbury was not only slow, but for many months his time was fully occupied, first in completing a settlement with Russia which confirmed the demise of the Armed Neutrality, later in negotiating peace with France.

Peace seemed imperatively demanded in 1801, for England was exhausted after eight years of warfare. In December of the previous year a member of the Pitt government wrote, "God only knows how we shall weather our present difficulties. I confess that for a long time I have been given to despond."[22] With such an attitude fairly common in high places, it would have taken a strong government to continue the war.

And this the Addington ministry was not. So, during the summer of 1801, secret negotiations were opened through Louis Otto, the French representative in London, and in October preliminaries of peace were signed. The terms, later confirmed by the treaty of Amiens, were not particularly favorable to Britain, since France was allowed to keep Belgium and some other territory she had occupied, whereas England restored almost all of the conquests upon which Dundas had expended so much blood and treasure.

Nevertheless, the peace was enthusiastically received, particularly by the poor, who had suffered most from shortages, the recruiting sergeant, and the press officer. That staunch Gallophobe, William Cobbett, found that in London as in Philadelphia it was unwise to refuse to put candles in the windows when the mob howled in celebration; every pane of glass in his house was broken. When General Lauriston arrived a few days later with Bonaparte's ratification, the horses were unhitched from his carriage, and a swarm of noisy, boisterous, thankful Londoners hauled him through the streets to the door of Otto's residence on Portman Square. Politicians were not as enthusiastic as the populace; Sheridan said that "It is a peace every body is glad of and nobody is proud of," and Rufus King reported that many felt that it merely marked "the end of the first punic war."[23]

The armistice between England and France of course completely altered the diplomatic stage. It did not cause an immediate change of cast, for the Addington government easily won the election of 1802, defeating many opponents of the peace, including William Windham. But the Pitt coalition had already been shaken by the defection of Grenville and his followers, who formed a "New Opposition," independent both of the government and the Whigs. Now there were further desertions, and even Pitt himself only reluctantly endorsed the peace. His support, cool though it was, royal patronage, and the forbearance of the Whigs allowed Addington to maintain himself, but it was an uncomfortable situation, and any important change was almost certain to bring down the government. Addington and Hawkesbury had always to take account of their uncertain political position in handling relations with foreign powers. On the other hand, there was of course no longer any possibility that the United States would join England's open enemies or the almost equally troublesome Armed Neutrals. The end of the war removed this potential weapon, insubstantial though it may have been, from the Jeffersonian diplomatic armory.

The Peace of Amiens also caused powerful changes in the volume, character, and carriage of British and American commerce. News of the preliminaries of peace upset American business: "The effect . . . of the Peace in *Europe,* has been an immediate fall of country produce; and a stagnation of commercial pursuits." Nor was recovery by any means immediate; a prominent Boston merchant wrote, early in 1802, "Business is here almost at a stand. Vessels have fallen prodigiously in value, there are very few Sales made except at prices very much below those that existed before the Peace—"[24] The war's end freed ships of America's maritime rivals from the risk of capture at sea, from the expensive necessity of traveling in convoy, and from heavy wartime insurance rates. England, with the world's largest merchant marine, benefited the most. Whereas in 1800 only seventy thousand tons of British shipping reached America, in 1802 the total was over one hundred thousand tons, a 500 per cent increase over the low point in 1796.[25]

In addition to restoring competition, the armistice crippled the reëxport trade. France and Spain regained many of their colonies and the normal channels of commerce were reopened, thus greatly reducing the demand for American reëxports, which fell in value from forty-seven million dollars in 1801 to only thirteen and a half million in 1803. Domestic exports were not so harshly hit, and in 1803 they reached a peak only surpassed by the record year of 1801, but the direct trade between England and America suffered severely. British exports to the United States declined as a result of the reopening of Continental markets, and when her own export trade slackened America found it more difficult than ever to pay for purchases abroad. Imports for domestic consumption dropped off nearly 40 per cent in 1802, although almost half that loss was regained the following year.[26]

A realization of the probable commercial consequences deeply affected the attitude of the United States toward the peace. An entry in William Bentley's diary records the general feeling:

This day the Agreable News of the signing of the preliminary articles of

PEACE

between Britain & France reached us. . . . The evidence of the fact was official and yet no news of such importance could be received by all parties with greater silence, or more mixed emotions. All rejoiced at the sound of peace, & all recollected the great commercial advantages of our Country in the late war. Passion & Judgment struggled without victory.[27]

Peace in Europe was the last new factor altering Anglo-American relations in 1801. In addition to powerfully affecting the commerce of England and America, the armistice had important political effects. Thus the agreement between Otto and Hawkesbury was of far greater importance than the changes of government in the United States and England. In 1801, however, one could not confidently have predicted this. The character of the new era was yet to be seen.

Two Conventions 12

RUFUS KING REMAINED AT LONDON SOME TIME AFTER THE JEFFER-
sonians came into office, despite James Monroe's brief and rather petty
attempt to have him removed.[1] Alone among those most intimately connected with Anglo-American diplomacy, the New Yorker's career spanned
the transfer of authority in both countries. By 1801, he had spent half a
decade in the British capital, was well-liked and eminently well-fitted to
carry on negotiations with the new government. It is to the credit of
Jefferson and Madison that they declined to replace King and, instead,
used him as an agent in attempting to solve important problems. Throughout these negotiations, on such varied matters as the Jay treaty commissions, impressment, the Canadian-American boundary, and discriminatory
commercial practices, Rufus King maintained a firm but friendly attitude
which protected the interests of his country without seriously straining
relations between England and the United States.

The Philadelphia debt commission controversy, so near settlement
just before the Pitt government fell, was the first topic King raised with
Lord Hawkesbury. The British representative in earlier negotiations,
Nicholas Anstey, provided Hawkesbury with a long memorandum out-
lining the subject, minimizing the claims of the creditors and urging
the government to retreat from a demand of one and a half or two
million pounds, "it being perhaps more politic with a view to an *amicable*
adjustment to preserve the Character [of the United States government
rather] . . . than to urge facts unnecessarily which cannot even be . . .
mentioned without reflecting on the American government." But Hawkesbury ignored these recommendations, and even the conversations Anstey
was carrying on with Rufus King, so King broke off discussions with
Anstey and entered into direct negotiations with the Foreign Secretary
and Henry Addington. The delays made him furious; correspondence
with Hawkesbury, a conference with "the Doctor," and the rallying of
Grenville to his support all failed to bring progress. In May, the Foreign
Secretary said that he personally favored accepting a fixed sum in lieu
of the debts, but that it had as yet proved impossible to find time to
thrash the matter out in Cabinet.[2]

Meanwhile, the Republican government confirmed King's basic
assumption, that the change from Adams to Jefferson would not affect
American policy. In April, preliminary instructions were sent to King
ordering him to continue along the lines sketched out by Marshall. In
June, Thomas Jefferson and his Cabinet unanimously agreed to an offer

of six hundred thousand pounds, and Madison soon sent instructions to King informing him of this decision, which was conditional on a renewal of the seizure commission.[3]

These instructions reached King a few days before he at last received notice from Henry Addington that the Cabinet would meet in a few days to make a final decision; "it is a relief to me to be assured myself, and to be able to state to you that your suspence will soon be terminated." King knew the British government too well to put much stock in this promise, so he was not surprised when a month elapsed before he received Britain's decision from Hawkesbury. In an interview at Downing Street, the Foreign Secretary told him that the Cabinet felt that two million pounds was a fair figure, but that, from a strong desire for "an amicable and final Settlement of the Business, it had consented to accept the Sum we had offered, if the Terms of the payment could be satisfactorily adjusted, and Provisions made that the American Courts should be open in future."[4]

The end seemed at last to be in sight, and in September Lord Hawkesbury asked George III's approval, writing that "Your Majesty's confidential Servants are of opinion that, under all the circumstances of the case, it is wise to close with this [American] offer."[5] This should have been the penultimate step, but it was not. There was, first of all, a brief flurry over the article respecting American courts, for the Cabinet felt it did not guarantee fair treatment for creditors in the future. Then the preliminaries of peace intervened, distracting attention from lesser business. And, finally, Hawkesbury's colleagues discovered something he had not made clear, that the London seizure commission was to be reactivated. King was outraged to have a new objection raised at so late a date, and he was doubtless also irritated to find that the Cabinet was so poorly informed as to think that the creditors' claims outweighed those against the Royal Navy by any such sum as six hundred thousand pounds.[6]

Although he almost lost hope, King continued to bombard the Cabinet with papers urging that the convention be signed. His efforts were supported by merchants trading with America, who threatened to raise the matter in Parliament if the government did not arrange a speedy settlement, and by Lord Grenville, who informed Hawkesbury he had always intended that the London commission should carry out its task.[7] In the middle of December, as King recorded it in his diary, "Not hearing from L[ord] Hawkesbury [I] went . . . to D[ownin]g Street and desired to see him—his Lord^P saw me and told me that he was in hopes we sh^d be able to settle the business."[8] But Hawkesbury went on to suggest a very complex method of payment that King found unacceptable, and it was several weeks before the American was able, in conversations with Lord Chancellor Eldon, to get this ill-considered, last minute addition deleted.

Finally, early in January, almost a year after King first raised the matter with the Addington government and nearly three years after the final rupture at Philadelphia, the Foreign Office informed King that the convention was ready for signature. It was short and concise. The United States agreed to pay six hundred thousand pounds as compensation for claims before the debt commission and promised that the courts would be open to British creditors in the future; in return, it was stipulated that the London commission should reconvene immediately.[9] A few days later, after sending official reports of his success to Madison, King wrote to his former superior, John Adams:

No one knows more thoroughly than you do, the source of those difficulties, often discouraging and sometimes disgusting, which continue to encumber our negotiations with this G[overnment]: the affair of the Debts, of all others, was the most likely to revive feelings and prejudices not yet extinguished, and which have been suffered to do such real disservice to both countries. I have notwithstanding persevered, and waded through; whether meritoriously or otherwise is a question, that I must refer to those, whose Province it is to decide.[10]

The British merchants who were to be recompensed out of the six hundred thousand pounds grumbled a bit; one told Rufus King that they expected to recover "no more than half a crown in the pound, considered the settlement to have been a mere political one, and intended to petition Parliament for a compensation for their losses, as soon as the Convention was ratified—" Several months later, in an open letter to an American correspondent, William Cobbett adopted this view:

The debts due to British creditors amounted to about *three millions,* in lieu of which we have obtained *six hundred thousand pounds.* . . . In diplomatic transactions this country is ever out-witted, but by no nation has she been out-witted more glaringly than by America. Observe, that, while we forego all the advantages of the treaty of 1794, you forego none of them. While the decisions of the [debt] board . . . are wiped away, because they operate against the wishes of America, those of the board, constituted to examine and decide on the claims of Americans, are to have their full effect.

In general, however, British journals supported the convention, though Opposition papers pointed out the good bargain America had secured. The *Morning Post* suggested that only a realization that most of the claims were fraudulent could have induced the government to agree to settle for such a small sum.[11]

In due course the convention arrived in America, where it was endorsed by the administration, though with little enthusiasm. Remembering the battle over an earlier agreement with Britain, King and Marshall later agreed that this one "would have met with a different Reception . . . had the administration remained in the hands of those from whom it has been lately removed."[12] On the other hand, some Federalists objected that the interests of the South alone were served by the settlement: "It is said the *Virginia* planters are perfectly satisfied with the Convention. . . . No wonder—when four-fifths of the debts due to British subjects, for which we are to pay 600,000l. were due by *Virginians,* who have now got rid of them in the modern mode—by not paying them."[13] The Senate requested to be informed how much the United States would have had to pay if the commission's majority had its way. But since the total was estimated to be twenty-four million dollars and the proposed payment to Britain was roughly one-tenth of that amount, the Senators apparently concluded that the bargain was a good one. Although Jefferson expected real opposition, the convention sailed through by a vote of nineteen to two less than a month after it was presented. The nays were cast by two Republicans, George Logan and Thomas Sumter,[14] both well known for their independent voting records. Otherwise, Federalists and Republicans alike endorsed an agreement conceived under Adams and brought to fruition under Jefferson.

A bill appropriating funds for the first installment to be paid to Britain was rushed through both houses before the end of the session; since the payment was not due until the end of the year, Madison hoped that the British would accept this action as further proof of the administration's friendly attitude. In succeeding years, the remaining payments were made with a minimum of fuss and every evidence of cordiality on both sides. At America's request, the last was paid through the house of Baring in London, for the two previous installments had seriously reduced the supply of specie in the United States.

The British government appointed the three British members of the Philadelphia commission, Macdonald, Rich, and Guillemard, to apportion the six hundred thousand pounds among British claimants, and the merchants' threat to seek Parliamentary redress was not carried out. In 1804, when the trio closed the application books, more than sixty-one thousand "debts and transactions," totaling five and one-third million pounds, had been brought to their attention. The claims were of course wildly inflated, and, since there was a fixed sum to be divided and not an unlimited one to be extracted from a foreign government, Macdonald, Rich, and Guillemard went over the papers with a fine tooth comb. Only about 21 per cent were accepted as legitimate claims.[15]

While the commissioners struggled with their paper work at an office on Great Marlborough Street, the seizure board, which had reassembled in February 1802, continued business at its old quarters on St. James Square. For a year, progress was steady, but then a new difficulty arose out of the American contention that interest should be allowed for the period during which the commission's proceedings had been suspended. The British resisted this proposal, arguing, as Hawkesbury put it, that "as this Suspension had taken place in consequence of the suspension of the Commission in America," for which it was claimed that the United States was responsible, "it did not appear . . . that the Board here had authority to allow Interest for this portion of Time."[16] As in 1796, King was referred to the Lord Chancellor. Once again the Chancellor overruled the British members of the commission, but this time the Foreign Secretary, as well, was forced to abandon his original position. In April 1803 the commission resumed its sittings, and King reported that "there is reason to believe that no farther difficulty is likely to occur in the satisfactory conclusion of the Business of this Commission."[17]

Rufus King did not often allow himself to indulge in official optimism, and when he did so it was usually ill-judged. But this time he proved an accurate prophet. All American appeals, save only twenty or thirty still before the courts, were decided by the middle of July 1803. British claims, a small number of cases arising from breaches of American neutrality, lagged somewhat, but by the end of August agreement in principle had been reached on all of them. For some months thereafter the board met only sporadically; John Trumbull went to Bath, and Nicholas Anstey took part in the feverish militia activity accompanying the resumption of war with France. Finally, on the twenty-third of February, 1804, the last case was finished, and the commission "closed with perfect Harmony."[18]

During its career, the London arbitrators awarded nearly one and a third million pounds (about six million dollars) to American shipowners, and, in addition, Sir William Scott and John Nicholl arranged payments of nearly sixty thousand pounds in preliminary settlements designed to take some of the load off the commissioners' shoulders. Awards to British claimants came to about one hundred and ten thousand dollars. The overwhelming majority of all payments was ordered after the board resumed business in 1802.[19]

Success reflected credit on all concerned, not merely on the members, although they played their roles much more creditably than Macdonald and his colleagues at Philadelphia. It was, of course, easy for the United States to accept the commission's decisions, for the fifth member was an American who often cast the deciding vote in favor of his countrymen. The British government, on the other hand, was asked to and did accept in good grace the huge and unanticipated sum charged against her, even though many of the awards were for provision seizures brought within the jurisdiction of the commission by the long delay in American ratification of the treaty. Furthermore, twice, when its members appealed against the opinions of the majority, the Lord Chancellor and the government refused to support these protests. British officials watched alertly for danger signals, at least until Hawkesbury came to the Foreign Office, and exerted themselves to remove difficulties before they became serious and deep-rooted.

Rufus King must also receive a share of the credit. He kept a careful watch on the proceedings of the commission and successfully upheld the American position in discussions with the British government. In negotiating a settlement after the breakdown in 1799, he showed real skill, persevered for months in the face of exasperating delays on the part of the Addington ministry, and was finally able to conclude a settlement. His determination and self-control paid impressive dividends, and his part in the accommodation of the connected problems of debts and seizures was perhaps the most important contribution to Anglo-American harmony made by any individual from 1795 to the end of the War of 1812.

The seizure commission's success was a valuable illustration of the utility of the arbitral method. The St. Croix proceedings demonstrated that arbitration could work, for the United States was prepared to accept any award before Robert Liston's intervention brought about a more palatable decision. The work of the London body, delayed though it was, proved that arbitration could succeed when applied to more important problems. But its history also showed—and this unfortunately had not been recognized at Philadelphia—that constructive governmental intervention might be necessary when personal and conceptual conflicts within the arbital commission became really serious. Arbitration, then, was shown to be a useful tool, but not a panacea.

Recognizing the limits of the practice, the British and American governments did not attempt at this time to apply it to sections of the Canadian-American boundary still in dispute. Instead, they carried on negotiations for a direct settlement, largely but not completely ignoring some gaps in the boundary—northern Maine, for example—and concentrating on two important ones. The first lay between the Lake of the Woods and the Mississippi River, an area about which little was known since, for reasons that remain unclear, the international survey authorized by the Jay treaty had never even been begun. The other gap was the line· of demarcation between British and American possessions in Passamaquoddy Bay. The American agent unsuccessfully requested the St. Croix commission to draw this line in 1798, and the ownership of Deer, Moose, and Campobello Islands, as well as lesser islets, was still uncertain.

Madison raised the curtain on boundary negotiations in the summer of 1801, asking King to have exploratory conversations with the British government. As in the debt negotiations, Rufus King discovered that the British government's lassitude was the chief bar to a settlement. Being without formal, explicit instructions, he could not press the matter and soon reported to Madison, "the subject being one with which he was entirely unacquainted, I have no reason to believe that [Lord Hawkesbury] . . . has thought of it again from that time to this: no progress can be made until your farther Instructions are received."[20]

King's report prodded Madison into action. He consulted James Sullivan, the acknowledged expert on Maine boundaries. Sullivan said that American claims to all but Moose Island were weak, and he confirmed Madison's suspicion that the channel between Campobello and the American mainland was navigable only at high tide. Free navigation of the entire bay he felt to be the most practical and easily attainable means

PASSAMAQUODDY BAY

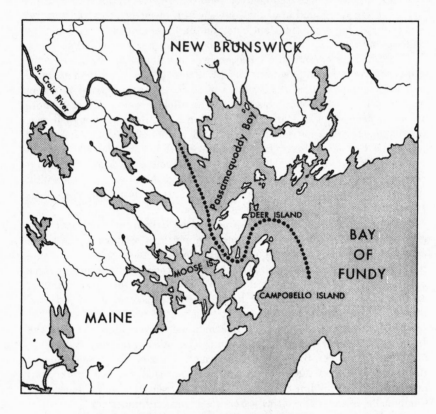

•••••' BOUNDARY ACCORDING TO KING-HAWKESBURY CONVENTION
(Campobello Island reserved to Great Britain)

Adapted from Paullin, Atlas, *Plate 92A.*

of protecting America's water-borne commerce in the area. In instructions soon sent to King, Madison asked for Campobello, but he enclosed Sullivan's letter and authorized King to fall back upon free navigation of the bay if necessary. In the Northwest, the Secretary wanted the line to run from the source of the Mississippi to meet the western shore of the Lake of the Woods on a tangent, then along the edge of the lake to its northwest corner.[21]

Before King received these instructions, he had a somewhat disquieting interview with George Hammond. The Undersecretary showed him

THE NORTHWEST CORNER

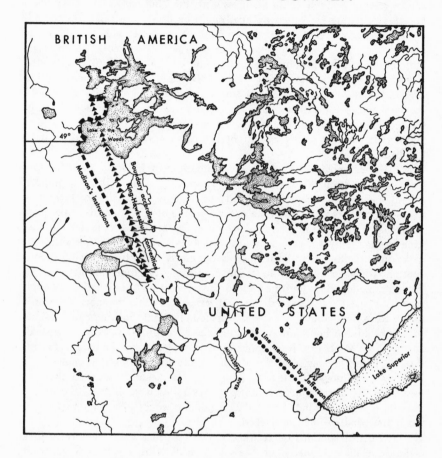

Adapted from Paullin, Atlas, Plate 93B.

Thornton's account of a conversation during which Thomas Jefferson expressed an opinion that the simplest way to settle the line in the Northwest would be "to run a course from the western extremity of Lake Superior by the shortest line wh. would reach the Mississippi—the lands in that quarter were remote & whether they belonged to Cana[da] Louisiana or the U. S. was both uncertain and a matter of no consequence—"[22] Fortunately, the British did not make too much of this report. Had the negotiations been more difficult, the President's indiscretion might have proved expensive.

Madison's orders reached London a few days after Rufus King left for a well-earned holiday on the Continent. Lord Hawkesbury at first rather testily declined to do business with the American chargé, Christopher Gore, telling Gore that nothing could be done "until Mr. Hammond, the under Secretary of State, should come from the seaside," as he knew most about it.[23] Some progress, however, was made during the summer, although when King returned in the fall he was asked to discuss the Passamaquoddy question with Thomas Barclay, who was then visiting England. But Barclay was out of town, and not until February 1803 did the two men get together. They easily came to an agreement on all but Campobello Island, and Barclay even privately reported to the Foreign Office that future controversy might best be avoided by conceding it to the United States.[24]

King was hopeful, for he had no intention of insisting upon Campobello, and he wrote Madison that "at present I foresee nothing to impede a Settlement . . . except the difficulty of engaging the Minister to bestow upon the Subject sufficient time to understand it."[25] After his experience in the debt negotiations, King must have felt himself fortunate that this time he had only to wait a month and a half for Lord Hawkesbury to make up his mind. By April, they had agreed upon the draft of a convention which differed little from Madison's original instructions. In Passamaquoddy Bay, the line ran north and east of Campobello, although the island itself was reserved to Great Britain; in this manner, Madison's desire for a navigable channel was satisfied. Two interlocking commissions to fix the Maine boundary were authorized, roughly as Madison wished. In the Northwest, the draft convention provided for a boundary to run directly from the source of the Mississippi to the northwest corner of the Lake of the Woods. Since both King and Hawkesbury believed that the source of the Mississippi was about thirty miles west of the Lake of the Woods, it was anticipated that this boundary would not differ materially from that Madison had described.

The draft remained on Hawkesbury's desk for a month before further action was taken. Finally, on May 11, Rufus King received word from George Hammond that the Cabinet would make a final decision on the matter that evening. The Undersecretary added that his chief was confident that the decision would be favorable, and this turned out to be the case. The next day, near the very close of King's mission, he and Lord Hawkesbury signed the engrossed copies prepared by Foreign Office clerks.[26] King had every reason to be satisfied with his achievement, for the agreement promised to remove a number of small but vexing and potentially more irritating problems.

News of the Louisiana Purchase arrived in London just three days after the signing of the boundary convention. No one anticipated that the contrast in scale between the two agreements or intrinsic conflicts in their terms would cause any particular difficulty for the boundary settlement in the United States. In instructions handed to the new British minister to the United States, Anthony Merry, Lord Hawkesbury scarcely considered the boundary convention since, as he put it, that "will I presume have been ratified by the Government of the United States previously to your arrival in America."[27]

Such was far from being the case. Although Albert Gallatin urged the President to praise it in the Annual Message that heaped extravagant compliments upon France for the sale of Louisiana, Jefferson's reference to the agreement was short and cold.[28] Soon afterwards, he cast it to the Senatorial lions. Opposition immediately arose. It was directed chiefly at Article V, which fixed the northwestern boundary. Senators feared that the King-Hawkesbury line, which dropped the boundary southward (by eighty miles, though the Senate did not know the exact distance), would weaken American claims to territories north and west of the Lake of the Woods. Britain, some claimed, would insist that the line described in Article V marked the boundary between Canada and the United States, Louisiana Purchase or not. Of course, if it could be shown that neither King nor Hawkesbury knew of the Purchase at the time they drew up the convention, much of the strength of this position would be destroyed, although the way would still be open for the British to claim that the westward extension of the boundary should begin at the end of the line fixed in the convention. America's answer would have to be that the United States' claim to territory beyond the convention line was based upon claims transferred from France by the Purchase, and that while the convention recognized the boundary as between American and British claims, it did not, and could not, settle disagreements which had at that time existed between France and Britain.

With these thoughts in mind, the Senate named John Quincy Adams chairman of a committee to investigate the problem. At his request, Madison asked Rufus King for information. The retired minister, who had just reached home, stated that the text of the convention had been drawn up weeks prior to the conclusion of the Louisiana Purchase and had been signed before news of the Purchase reached London. This information was embodied in a report delivered to the Senate by Adams. It was a short report, and its conclusion was indecisive: "not having the means of ascertaining the precise northern limits of Louisiana, as ceded to the United States, the committee can give no opinion whether the line to be drawn . . . would interfere with the said northern limits of Louisiana or not."[29] Thus the Adams report refused either to endorse or to deny the claims of the opponents of Article V, nor did it discuss the argument that the King-Hawkesbury convention would affect claims held by a third party when this agreement was drawn up.

The administration apparently decided to support conditional ratification, and Madison confidently stated to Merry that the Senate would approve the convention with the exception of Article V. The vote, early in February, confirmed Madison's prediction. A motion to approve Article V was lost, nine to twenty-two, and then the remainder of the convention was unanimously approved. On the first ballot, all but two of the New England senators voted for Article V. They showed more concern for their section's interest in good relations with England and in the settlement of the Maine boundary than for claims in more distant areas, and they were unwilling to jeopardize the rest of the agreement by eliminating Article V. The Republicans, on the other hand, voted almost solidly against this article. Timothy Pickering accused Jefferson of desiring to take advantage of Great Britain's setbacks in the new war with France to press for further concessions,[30] but there is no proof that this was so. It seems more likely that the Republicans honestly felt that the convention weakened American claims to the northern parts of Louisiana (and many believed, inaccurately, that the Treaty of Utrecht had fixed the northern boundary of that territory at forty-nine degrees), despite the fact that the two agreements had no direct relationship. Of course, the fact that Rufus King was a possible Federalist candidate for the Presidency in 1804 made the alteration of his handiwork a far from unpleasant task for Republican senators.

Anthony Merry, who dabbled in projects for New England secession, urged his government to reject the conditional ratification. Such a step, said Merry, by depriving New Englanders of the gains they envisaged under the convention, might "prove to be a great exciting Cause to them to go forward rapidly in the steps which they have already commenced towards a separation from the Southern part of the Union."[31] Merry's argument may have had some influence upon Lord Harrowby, Foreign Minister in the new Pitt government, but it seems much more likely that pique at a presumed violation of good faith caused the British government to decline to accept the convention as modified by the Senate. The matter provoked a good deal of discussion, most of it bad tempered, between Harrowby and Monroe, the new minister at London.

The labors of Rufus King had been in vain. But for the slowness of the Foreign Office, the convention might have been signed several months earlier, and ratification would have been easy if it had arrived in America before spring. As it was, the Republican regime offered up this convention as a sacrifice to the acquisition of the Louisiana province. Its reasoning did not completely lack validity, for ratification would have strengthened the British claim to a transcontinental strip, eighty miles wide, with its southern limit at the level of the upper Mississippi. There is no certainty, however, that this would have been a decisive factor, for American claims to both the eastern and Pacific portions of the region rested on other bases. In other words, it need not be assumed that any line would have run due west from the terminus of the boundary drawn by King and Hawkesbury. Even conditional ratification, however, left the way open for an unexceptionable settlement of the remaining problems with which

148

the convention dealt, and far greater discredit is owing the second Pitt government for rejecting this than to the Jeffersonians for modifying the agreement in the first place. We may understand Harrowby's irritation at the American practice of conditional ratification, but we need not condone his willingness to let temper affect government policy.

To describe the later fate of the boundary convention, it has been necessary to pass beyond that great dividing point, the summer of 1803, when the barometer began once again to waver in the direction of stormy weather. These discussions have no direct bearing upon Rufus King's mission or Anglo-American relations during his last years at London. Until it became entangled in outside events, the convention seemed to be a promising settlement of issues between the nations, and the attitude of both governments during the King-Hawkesbury discussions was a further demonstration of their common support of conciliation and moderation. This same spirit had been of vital importance in the negotiation of the debt convention of 1802, which ended a much more dangerous, complex, and highly charged controversy. All in all, in the spring of 1803, Anglo-American relations were in excellent condition, in large part because of the conventions negotiated by Rufus King and Lord Hawkesbury.

Rufus King Closes His Mission 13

WHILE THE TWO KING-HAWKESBURY CONVENTIONS WERE HIS MOST important achievements, Rufus King carried on a number of other negotiations during the closing years of his mission to London. His mixed success reflected the change in Anglo-American relations: the structure of cordiality was no longer being improved at the rapid pace that had marked the previous half decade, but neither was it being torn to bits by dissension between London and Washington. In all cases, whether or not agreement was reached, sincere efforts were made to avoid fanning the embers of discord into flame.

British countervailing duties, intricately calculated charges designed to offset America's 10 per cent tariff discrimination in favor of her own ships, again attracted attention during the Addington regime. In 1797, Rufus King protested against the weight of these duties, but during the war they had little effect and were almost forgotten. The return of peace altered the situation by restoring competition on the high seas, and shortly after news of the preliminaries reached America Madison directed King to point out to Hawkesbury that the British duties unfairly burdened American commerce. The simplest way to restore equity, said Madison, seemed to be to replace the countervailing duties with a flat 10 per cent discriminatory export duty on goods carried from Britain in American bottoms. The Secretary did not suggest a repeal of discriminatory duties, which would confer gratuitous benefits upon third parties, but he noted that Representative Samuel Smith of Maryland, a prominent Jeffersonian, planned to introduce a bill along these lines.[1]

Just before King raised the subject, Lord Hawkesbury received a report from Edward Thornton, who believed that Smith and his supporters were wrong in thinking that the removal of discrimination would strengthen the position of the American marine. Thornton argued that if England maintained a monopoly of West Indian carriage, the most lucrative part of the triangle trade in the Atlantic, removal of all other restrictions on trade would benefit British shipping rather than American.[2] Perhaps influenced by this report, Hawkesbury told King that the British government recognized the inequities of the existing system but would rather end discrimination altogether than levy a 10 per cent export duty. The American minister had no authority to consider such a proposal, but he concluded from Madison's comments on the Smith bill that the Secretary of State would be willing to consider it and suggested to Hawkesbury that Parliament pass permissive legislation that could be put into effect by the Crown if the United States reciprocated.[3]

Only a fortnight after King's first conversation with Hawkesbury, Nicholas Vansittart, the government's commercial expert, gave the House of Commons notice of his intention to introduce legislation along these lines. This bill, drawn up after a number of conferences with Rufus King, provoked a certain amount of opposition. In the *Annual Register*, William Cobbett as usual attacked concession to America, and he warned that the abolition of discrimination would leave "the navigation of the two countries to a rivalship in *cheapness of freight*, in which she is sure to surpass us. Never, from the day that our countervailing duties cease, will there be a single shipment, from America to Europe, in a British bottom."[4]

The bill came up for a second reading on March 5, having been delayed by Henry Addington's illness, and the ensuing debate is one of the few on American affairs in this period that was reported in detail. The chief speaker against the proposal was General Isaac Gascoyne of Liverpool, whose opposition Rufus King stated to be an election maneuver,[5] probably designed to assure the support of the still dominant shipping interest there. Gascoyne emphasized the threat to British shipping posed by the spectacular growth of the American merchant marine. He assailed the bill as a threat to the Navigation Acts, "which, next to the great charter of our liberties, ought to be kept inviolate," then closed with an attack upon American shipping, American good faith, and the United States generally. Gascoyne was supported by Cobbett's patron, William Windham, and by Dr. French Laurence, but, although they attacked the bill, this pair used the debate chiefly as a scaffold from which to paint in somber colors a picture of the commercial war with France brought on by the cessation of military hostilities.

On the government side, Vansittart scoffed at Gascoyne's argument that the Navigation Acts were threatened, pointing out that no new trade was opened to vessels of the United States. He asserted that repeal would encourage American importation of British manufactures—a statement Laurence deprecated as "making a distinction between our mercantile interest and our Navigation Act"—but added that shipping would also benefit since the lessening of port charges would confirm England's position as the entrepôt through which American produce reached the Continent. Vansittart also pointed out, in justifying the proposed experiment, that existing law had failed to prevent American domination of the carrying trade. All these arguments were repeated by Addington and Hawkesbury in speeches showing little more than a general knowledge of the problem.

Toward the close of the debate, a Whig member congratulated the government for bringing forward legislation, "the effect of which would be to draw into a closer connection this country and America; a policy of the soundest kind." He expressed the hope that, if Jefferson had any lingering predilection for France, the bill would help to erase it. This provoked from Hawkesbury a rather ponderous but significant statement, one he was by no means forced to make:

I am aware [he said] it is a dangerous thing to undertake to answer for the disposition of the Government of a foreign Country; but I think it due to America to state, that from the conduct of the Government of that Country for some months past, there is reason to believe, that next to the consideration of her own interests, which of course is her first object, her views and intentions toward this country are fair and honourable, and there is nothing in her disposition that ought to give us distrust. I believe, that like every other country, where her interests and ours clash, she will prefer her own; . . . but I can see nothing in the conduct of America that ought to inspire us with distrust.[6]

The bill, which was to have force for one year, soon became law. Too late, Lord Sheffield penned an angry protest; he claimed that the United States, learning that a discriminatory policy would not force Britain to open the West Indies, wanted the countervailing duties removed so that she could complete her monopoly of the trans-Atlantic carrying trade.[7] Sheffield's tardy argument was ignored, for the ministry had already laid out its course of action. Doubtless it hoped to assist British manufactures in maintaining their hold on the American market, now opened to Continental rivals by the end of the war, and also felt that British shipping could not lose and might well benefit if discrimination were ended. For these reasons, and because it believed that prompt action would show America the basic friendliness of Great Britain, the Cabinet rushed repeal through Parliament and sat back to await American approval.

Meanwhile, there had been a serious hitch in the United States. Madison wrote King in April that "a mercantile current that appeared to set against it" had induced Smith to postpone discussion of his bill. "There is reason to believe," said the Secretary, "that owing to ignorance and jealousy, this current has not even yet entirely ceased."[8] A month's delay did not weaken the opposition, and much to the regret of Madison, who now favored complete repeal of discrimination, Smith was forced to abandon his bill for the current session.

Urged on by Gallatin and by King, who argued that rejection of the British offer would imperil further commercial negotiation, the President spoke favorably of the English offer in his next Annual Message. But Jefferson was not willing to make repeal a party issue to be supported by the full strength of the administration. He explained to Thornton that the Northeast, which opposed the proposal, had to be given special consideration since it was the section most concerned.[9] Shipowners feared that the proposal was "intended to operate as a small bounty on *Virginia* tobacco, . . . [at] the expense of the navigation of the U. States" and argued somewhat more logically that they could not successfully compete with Great Britain while the West India trade remained closed. A Massachusetts Federalist, for example, suggested to a member of the Cabinet that, behind a mask of friendship, the English might well be plotting a carriage monopoly.[10]

152

In January 1803, the House Committee on Commerce and Manufactures issued a report on British discriminatory legislation. This report, written by Samuel Smith, while admitting that as yet there had been no harmful effects, predicted that countervailing duties would eventually strangle American shipping. The committee said that the United States must choose between the abolition of discrimination and new legislation to balance British levies. It favored the former,[11] but Congress took no action upon the report, and before long the resumption of war in Europe assured the prosperity of the American merchant marine.

Once again, as in the case of the boundary convention, Rufus King had been the victim of bad luck, and if, in either instance, he felt that he had reason to complain it was because of weak support by his own government or the slowness of the British rather than because of any bad spirit shown by Addington and Hawkesbury. King's work to reduce commercial barriers proved abortive because the Jeffersonian government declined to support a project it had encouraged. Self-interest, as it was seen at the time, of course played a part both in the British offer and the American rejection of it. Perhaps Thornton and his superiors were right, perhaps the American merchant marine benefited more from discrimination than the British. So shipping interests in the United States felt, and they had their way.

In other fields,[12] King had more success, notably in securing the return of Maryland bank stock. In 1775 the colony of Maryland owned many shares in the Bank of England. At the end of the Revolution, Maryland's commercial agents declined to surrender this stock until their own claims against the new state were settled. Appeals to the court proved unavailing, and finally Rufus King was directed to see what he could do. He almost secured release of the disputed securities in 1797, but at the last moment new claims against the state blocked his efforts. After the changes of government in 1801, King again raised the matter. Addington and Hawkesbury were not unsympathetic, but only after a great deal of prodding did the Foreign Secretary initiate judicial proceedings to transfer the stock to the Crown, which in turn could deliver it to Maryland. This process, too, proved to be a long one, and, just before leaving London, Rufus King asked for formal British assurances that the bank shares would be given to Maryland as soon as they were recovered from the legal morass. In April 1803 Hawkesbury signed an order to the Attorney-General drafted by King and Lord Chancellor Eldon, stating the government's intentions as King desired. "I flatter myself, Sir," Hawkesbury wrote to King, "that this Communication will be regarded . . . as a new Proof of his Majesty's disposition to consult and promote the Interest of the United States."[13] The envoy's perseverance had paid a handsome return; thanks to a steady reinvestment of dividends, Maryland finally recovered stock worth about two hundred thousand pounds.

Earlier, the outbreak of war between the United States and Tripoli gave the Addington government an opportunity to show its cordial attitude. Soon after becoming President, Thomas Jefferson dispatched a squadron to the Mediterranean to protect American commerce from Tripolitanian corsairs. At about the same time, the Bashaw declared war upon the United States. Thornton soon reported that the conflict was likely to improve relations between the United States and England since there were no American bases in the Mediterranean and "the necessity of a frequent recurrence to the British ports will at least ensure a certain degree of harmony between the two flags," and for once the Addington government was on the alert. Even before a Madisonian request for assistance reached Britain, the Minister and Lord Hawkesbury informed Rufus King that His Majesty's Government would gladly extend the use of British naval facilities to the American squadron. Supplies would be furnished to Commodore Dale at cost.[14]

In the United States, this action had the result that Addington and Hawkesbury no doubt anticipated. Madison felt that while the British offer was not disinterested—England had no love for Barbary either—it was further evidence of a friendly policy, and Jefferson only slightly more grudgingly noted that "This, with some other indications, gives us to hope that that government may be disposed to treat us with more justice & respect."[15] The assistance extended to the United States Navy was considerable. Dale's squadron underwent a general overhaul at Gibralter before opening the campaign against Tripoli, and in succeeding years supplies were frequently taken on at Malta and Gibralter, powder was occasionally left in storage there to dry, and American sailors spent their shore leave at Valetta or in the shadow of the Rock. In 1805, when relations with England were again strained, a Federalist journal pointed out that "our officers receive every support and civility in the power of the British administration . . . to give; and this too by order of that British government, which Mr. JEFFERSON's hireling editors . . . are in the daily habit of abusing by every blackguard epithet in their power to bestow—"[16] Even the press gangs respected American seamen, although many were British subjects liable to impressment.

Negotiations on impressment, in the guise of a convention for the mutual return of deserters, had been broken off in 1800, but soon after taking over the Department of State James Madison directed King to raise the subject once again. In a series of interviews, King and Lord St. Vincent made substantial progress. The new First Lord even accepted an article which specifically banned impressment from ships at sea. Hawkesbury accepted this proposal, doubtless because it tacitly recognized the right of impressment in British ports and was tied to an agreement to return deserters.[17] But Britain can never have been enthusiastic about a proposal which went to the very roots of her maritime supremacy, and the conclusion of peace, bringing impressment to a halt, gave Downing Street a plausible excuse for postponing a settlement.

RUFUS KING CLOSES HIS MISSION

By the spring of 1803, war clouds were again on the horizon, and King therefore made one last effort to settle the problem by negotiation. With assumed confidence he forwarded to Hawkesbury "the article relative to our seamen, to which we had agreed a little before the close of the late War." It read:

No Person shall be impressed or taken upon the high seas out of any Ship or vessel belonging to the subjects or Citizens of one of the Parties, by the private or public armed Ships or Men of War belonging to, or in the service of the other Party, and strict orders shall be given for the due observance of this Engagement.[18]

Hawkesbury referred the matter to the Admiralty. St. Vincent immediately responded, with at least a grain of truth, that as King's draft stood it "would deprive this Country of all her Seamen." He suggested important modifications and then returned the ball to the Foreign Office, writing a friendly letter to King wishing him *bon voyage* and stating that he had forwarded the information in his possession to Hawkesbury, who would doubtless be able to conclude an agreement before King sailed.[19]

Since business brought on by the renewal of war with France overwhelmed the Foreign Secretary, however, King soon turned again to the First Lord. "Did I not know," he wrote, "that the object in itself is of small, very small importance to this Country, I should hesitate in urging it, notwithstanding the great embarrassment it has produced, and will continue to create in America." St. Vincent's reply was sufficiently encouraging so that, in concert with Nicholas Vansittart, Rufus King hastily drew up a convention to which the First Lord made only a few minor objections. The proposed agreement was changed to meet these criticisms, but then King was dealt a crushing blow. St. Vincent returned his draft "with a few alterations, which have occurred, since I had the honor of conversing with you upon this Subject this morning."[20] Among these changes was an amendment specifically exempting from the agreement seamen and ships traveling in the "Narrow Seas," water around the British Isles that his lordship said had been "immemorially considered to be within the dominion of Great Britain."[21] King responded that it was unnecessary to include any mention of the Narrow Seas, "which are or are not within the Dominion or jurisdiction of Great Britain—if they be within, the addition is not requisite as the Jurisdiction is already excepted; if they are without, they are high seas and should not be excepted."[22] Amazingly enough, St. Vincent gave way before this reasoning and approved the convention.

Since this was the very day of his departure from London, King did not have time to see Sir William Scott, whose approval Hawkesbury had earlier told him would be necessary. He asked Hammond to see Scott, have Hawkesbury sign two copies, and send them to Great Cumberland Place for his own signature. By one-thirty, King had not heard from the Foreign Office, so he hastily wrote Christopher Gore, requesting him to go around to Downing Street to clear up the difficulty, and then left for

155

Cowes to take ship for America. Not until the next morning did King learn from Vansittart that "Sir W. Scott has stated very serious objections . . . [to] the little plan which we arranged in Downing Street," notably the omission of all mention .of the Narrow Seas.[23] The government declined to act without Sir William's approval. Thus ended negotiations for the limitation of impressment.

Even as originally framed by Rufus King, the convention would not have rooted out the impressment issue. The agreement would have ended the most provocative and humiliating invasion of American rights —impressment on the high seas from ships flying the flag of the United States—and, by limiting impressment to seaports, made it easier for seamen who were trapped by the press gangs to initiate appeals for release. However, King's draft did not outlaw impressment in British harbors, a less contestable exercise of national sovereignty but also the means by which large numbers of sailors were forced into service. Still the British government was not satisfied; it devised a means whereby the Royal Navy could recover seamen whose ships never entered British ports. Even this must have been only reluctantly extended, for Addington and Hawkesbury accepted with relief the opportunity to end negotiations provided by King's departure.

When Rufus King declined to accept Britain's claim to sovereignty over the waters surrounding the British Isles, it was once again demonstrated that the two countries were negotiating from positions so far apart that no real settlement was possible. King himself thought that, given time, he could have secured an accommodation,[24] but this is highly unlikely. None of his successors came as close to getting an agreement on the subject, although in 1806 British negotiators gave informal assurances that the practice would be closely regulated if agreement was reached on other matters. With the return of war, impressment soon became a real issue between England and America, far more important than it had been during the earlier Franco-British conflict. For once, King's perseverance had failed to pay dividends. But this failure was not typical of his mission as a whole, and when he sailed from Britain in May 1803 relations between the two countries were generally good.

King's departure was not hastily planned. Early in 1802, he began to weigh the pros and cons of resignation, by February rumors of his retirement were circulating in London, and in August he requested permission to return home the next spring. The same day, writing to John Marshall, he expressed gratification at the administration's reception of the debt convention, but also mentioned his earnest "wish that on other and still more important concerns its sentiments had been equally correct."[25] What these other concerns were, King did not say. The boundary convention had not yet been scuttled (or even signed), so the Federalist envoy probably referred to the handling of the countervailing duty offer, perhaps to Jefferson's indiscreet conversation with Thornton on the subject of the Northwest boundary, and almost certainly to Madison's habitual reserve, which left King ignorant of the administration's general policy, in marked contrast to the situation while the minister's own party was in power. When King's decision became known in London, merchants trading with America organized an impressive farewell dinner which was reported in all the leading newspapers. The *Times* wrote:

Saturday a grand dinner was given at the London Tavern by the American Merchants, to RUFUS KING, Esq. the American Ambassador to this Court, who is on his return to America. The CHANCELLOR of the EXCHEQUER, Lord HOBART [undersecretary at the Foreign Office], and several other distinguished characters were present. Mr. INCLEDON, Mr. DIGNUM, and Mr. SEDGEWICK, entertained the company with a variety of songs &c.[26]

In order, the guests drank toasts to the King and constitution, the Queen, the Prince of Wales, Rufus King, "Prosperity to the United States of America," and "Perpetual Friendship between the United Kingdom and the United States, &c. &c."

King's baggage was loaded aboard ship in April, but he delayed his departure for some time, despite the skipper's impatience. The boundary and impressment negotiations at London, as well as those of Livingston and Monroe at Paris, and his desire to observe at first hand the political effects of the renewal of the war all caused the retiring minister to linger in Britain. Not until the middle of May did King have his leave-taking audience with George III, who told him:

he had entertained but one Determination since the separation of America, which was to cultivate peace and friendship with the states, and that he never would change his disposition. He added .that it gave him pleasure to declare that he foresaw no occurrence that would be likely to affect the present good understanding and friendship between him and the United States.[27]

As an historical analysis of the policy of George III and his ministers since 1783, this declaration left something to be desired. But as a statement of present British policy it was a good omen for the future and merited the extensive quotation with which King favored Madison.

A few days later, the American sailed from Cowes. On his arrival in New York, Madison rather brusquely told him that he need not come to Washington to report, but King was able to make his views known to Jefferson through Albert Gallatin, then visiting New York. He told the Secretary of the Treasury that the Addington government was "the most favorable that has existed or can exist for the interests of the United States," but one whose days in office might be numbered. The ex-minister had little respect for the personnel of the British Cabinet; Gallatin reported to Jefferson that "Mr. King himself . . . called them 'little men.' "[28]

Rufus King had taken advantage of both the weakness and the friendliness of the Addington government to negotiate the settlement of several problems. In dealing with this regime, as with the previous one, his path was smoothed by a number of factors. Generally speaking, he enjoyed cordial support and wise direction from Philadelphia and Washington, under Republican as well as Federalist governments. His own obvious friendship for England and support of the British cause also contributed to his success, securing him a more ready hearing at Downing Street. Finally, his personality was admirably adapted to the London station. Possessed of some of the aristocratic spirit, urbanity, and strength that characterized men like Grenville, he was well fitted to become their cordial associate. Even Lord Hawkesbury, whose idleness often called forth strong language from the American envoy, bore him no ill will; a year after King's departure, the Foreign Secretary toasted him at a diplomatic dinner.

Thus favored, Rufus King's mission to the Court of St. James was truly distinguished. As Channing says, he was "one of the most effective representatives the United States ever had at London."[29] During the administration of John Adams, he helped to complete the bridge of reconciliation whose scaffold had been erected by John Jay. In addition, he handled with skill and tact his share of the problems of neutrality and quasi-war. When Thomas Jefferson succeeded Adams, King remained at his post to help keep the bridge in good repair. Several of his contributions were declined by the Republicans, but King settled for once and all the knotty problem of the pre-Revolutionary debts and contributed powerfully to the preservation of Anglo-American comity. As a London daily remarked several months before his departure, "Mr. King has exercised the functions of the important station he filled so much to the advantage of both countries, that his departure is the subject of general regret."[30]

W HEN RUFUS KING SAILED FOR AMERICA, HE CARRIED WITH HIM THE first news of the Louisiana Purchase, which had been completed by Livingston and Monroe only a few days before. Napoleon's decision to sell the territory he had only recently acquired from Spain was a wise one, for it had long been an axiom of American policy that the rusty empire of the dons was the only foreign power that could be tolerated in Louisiana. If Napoleon had persisted in his dreams of overseas empire, he would certainly have brought on a serious clash with the United States at a time when warfare was being renewed in Europe, and he might well have forced America into the arms of his greatest enemy. As it was, the last phase of the Louisiana question, which began with the treaty of San Ildefonso in 1800, briefly seemed about to effect a revolution in Anglo-American relations.

France had been seeking the return of Louisiana for some time, and in 1798 rumors of a retrocession caused a number of Americans to advocate a "strike first" policy and evoked from Lord Grenville a statement that Britain would welcome an American descent of the Mississippi,[1] but it was not until the autumn of 1800 that Spain finally promised to deliver up the territory. This agreement was supposed to be kept secret, but its general outlines were soon known. Hawkesbury and King discussed the matter in June 1801, at a time when it seemed probable that the Floridas as well as Louisiana were to become French property. The Foreign Secretary, who saw in this a serious threat to Canada and the West Indies, hinted that Britain might have to undertake preventive occupation of the Floridas, at least. King immediately responded with standard American doctrine, "taking for my text the observation of Montesquieu, 'That it is happy for trading Powers that God has permitted the Turks and Spaniards to be in the world since of all nations they are the most proper to possess a great Empire with insignificance.' " In other words, said King, "we are content that the Floridas should remain in the hands of Spain, but should be unwilling to see them transferred except to ourselves."[2] The proposed British expedition was not mentioned again during the few months before the end of the war.

Rumors of a Franco-Spanish treaty reached the United States from so many quarters in the spring of 1801 that, by May, Madison was able to afford the luxury of returning a report forwarded by Alexander Hamilton without a word of thanks, unkindly adding that the data "had been previously signified to this Department from several sources."[3] But it was not until fall that Madison received a copy of the agreement, forwarded to him by Rufus King, which definitely confirmed the rumors that had been flying. This may or may not have come to him from British sources, but it was certainly owing to English good offices that he was able to inform Washington of French assurances to Britain that the expedition about to depart for America had in view the reconquest of Santo Domingo and not the establishment of a new domain in the American interior.[4] This apparent respite was short-lived, however, for the administration soon received information showing that Bonaparte had not lost sight of the more distant prize, and Jefferson and Madison were forced to turn their attention to the problem.

Jefferson's point of view was essentially a continuation and modification of policy he had helped to formulate as Washington's Secretary of State. As early as March 1802, in conversations with Edward Thornton, he stated that he had warned the French and Spanish representatives in Washington that "the inevitable consequences" of French occupation of Louisiana "must be jealousy, irritation, and finally hostilities."[5] A short time later, the President composed the long private letter to Robert Livington, American minister to France, that is among his more famous compositions. In it, he stated, "The day that France takes possession of N. Orleans fixes her sentence which is to restrain her forever within her low water mark. It seals the union of two nations who in conjunction can maintain exclusive possession of the ocean. From that moment we must marry ourselves to the British fleet and nation."[6] Pierre S. du Pont de Nemours, a Frenchman about to return to his homeland, was allowed to read this letter and entrusted with its delivery. In a covering note, the President urged du Pont de Nemours, who had many influential friends in Paris, to bring the French government to its senses; "this measure," Jefferson wrote in a characteristic vein, will soon "cost France . . . a war which will annihilate her on the ocean, and place that element under the despotism of two nations, which I am not reconciled to the more because my own would be one of them."[7]

By summer, Jefferson was stating that threat even more openly. At public gatherings, Thornton reported, he "makes no scruple to say, that if . . . the United States should be unable to expel the French . . . , they must have recourse to the assistance of other powers, meaning unquestionably Great Britain." The chargé noted that administration papers, as well as the President himself, excoriated the "usurpation of Bonaparte"; the whole situation led him to conclude that, although the Republican party might not be cured of its "bitterness against Great Britain, . . . its predilection for France scarcely exists even in the name." A short time later, Thornton suggested that Jefferson's attitude might be further improved if London periodicals could be induced to include complimentary references to his talents, particularly in the field of science.[8] What more the chargé can have hoped for from the President at this time is a mystery. Their contact was already so close that the French representative, Louis Pichon, was alarmed.

What appeared to be Presidential indiscretions were probably actually calculated parts of a general policy. The administration wanted to make it clear to France that even the most pacific of American governments would resist the transfer of New Orleans by any means that came to hand; the hints of an alliance with Britain were part of this warning. As yet, however, no approaches were to be made to Great Britain. Rufus King received no instructions to consult the British government, and he actually learned of the administration's attitude only when Hawkesbury permitted him to read dispatches from Thornton. In 1802, Jefferson and Madison still hoped to negotiate with France or Spain, and they held the British card in reserve. In May, Madison instructed Livingston to warn France that "the worst events are to be apprehended" if New Orleans should change hands. France could prevent such a development either by agreeing to leave Spain in possession or by selling New Orleans and the Floridas to the United States.[9] Thus, by the end of 1802, Jefferson and Madison had formulated American policy—a threat to oppose French occupation of Louisiana by force coupled with an offer to settle the problem by diplomacy.

Britain's position was by no means so clearly established during 1802. For Jefferson and Madison the problem was fairly simple and obviously of overriding importance, but for Addington and Hawkesbury, Louisiana was only one facet of a larger problem, or even two larger problems—relations with France and with America. The Addington government, as has been shown, worked for good relations with the United States. But, for most of 1802, at least, the Cabinet hoped that peace with Bonaparte could be made to last, and this hope affected its thinking and attitudes. As a result, British policy drifted.

William Cobbett and William Windham attempted to prod the government into action. Early in 1802, Cobbett stated his position in the first issue of the *Annual Register,* and he maintained it with typical Porcupinian tenacity until the very end. The editor believed that the threat to Canada and the West Indies and the economic importance of Louisiana (he proclaimed it to be potentially the best cotton area in the world) were sufficient reasons in themselves for Britain to block French designs. But, to his mind, there was a third, and even more important factor, the effect of retrocession upon politics in the United States. France, he said, wanted possession of Louisiana "to form a balance against that military and naval influence which Great-Britain has by the possession of Canada, New Brunswick, and Nova Scotia," a balance that would enable her to obtain "a domineering influence in the councils of the federal city, which councils are already but too much disposed to favor those plans, which she has laid for destroying the commercial and naval preponderance of England.[10]

In the fall, Cobbett enlisted the support of William Windham. Windham wrote directly to Addington, arguing that there was little difference between refusing to deliver up Malta to France and preventing the transfer of Louisiana to the same power. If Britain were willing to risk the consequences of the first, as the Addington government held that she must, she might as well risk those of the second, particularly since possession of New Orleans and Louisiana would give to France "nothing less than the command of two Continents." A small squadron and a regiment or two would suffice to forestall the French, a serious strategic threat would be ended, and the "counsels & good wishes [of the United States] would probably be completely engaged to us, by such an act of rescue." But the government must act promptly, for "It is really a point on which may turn the fate of the world."[11]

Early in 1803, a staunch Addingtonian named George Orr, otherwise known only as the author of a slim paper on the techniques of chimney sweeping, joined Cobbett and Windham in urging the government to take positive action. In a pamphlet entitled *The Possession of Louisiana by the French Considered,* Orr pointed out the political importance of Louisiana to England and America, emphasized the cultural and racial ties between the two countries, and urged a general political alliance which should begin with joint action to prevent French action against New Orleans.[12]

Despite the fire falling upon them from numerous directions, neither the government nor its newspaper supporters were willing to admit that there was anything in the situation which called for action. The *Times,* apparently nominated to duel with Cobbett, attempted to put a gloss of high statesmanship on the government's inactivity. In May 1802 it commented:

The rapid progress which America has made from the advantageous circumstances of [neutrality] . . . made it necessary for this Country to keep a watchful eye on her proceedings; whereas by bringing the restless power of France to her very back, we shall be relieved from our anxious and active vigilance, as the Americans will be fully employed in attending to the designs of their new, ambitious, and enterprising neighbors.[13]

The *Times'* language in the early months of 1803 differed from that of the previous year only in that the anti-American note had disappeared. In one typical editorial it argued that "The usurpation of *France* in *Louisiana* . . . may . . . promote a cordial and brotherly re-union between our late Colonies and this Country." After considering this topic at some length, the paper concluded, "The affection and kindness of the Greek Colonies for the Metropolitan Country, after centuries of complete independence, fill some of the most delightful pages of history."[14]

Both positions, that of the *Times* and that of Cobbett and his allies, were somewhat wide of the mark. The disputants did not realize that no American government would tolerate French occupation of New Orleans.

Unlike Cobbett, however, John Walter, the editor of the *Times*, failed to see that Britain would get little thanks for playing a negative role when the presence even of a few men-of-war might have decisive importance. Walter attempted to characterize as a positive, intelligent policy what was really the fruit of governmental lassitude or, at best, cynicism. For, despite the cannonading on a number of fronts, Lord Hawkesbury refused to define British policy. He could feel little concern about the interior of Louisiana, once commenting that "it must be a very long time before a country quite a wilderness could become of any considerable value."[15] Rufus King was unable to get him to budge. Not a single instruction sent to Thornton in 1802 mentioned Louisiana in detail, and there is no evidence that the members of the government discussed it at London. Quite consciously, to avoid making negotiations for a definitive peace more difficult, the Louisiana question was excluded from the discussions at Amiens.

The whole situation was transformed when, late in 1802, the Spanish Intendant at New Orleans issued a proclamation revoking the right of deposit. If enforced, this decree would cripple the commerce of the Western states; furthermore, by clearing the title of encumbrances, it seemed to foreshadow the transfer of the region to France. When the text of Intendant Morales' decree reached Washington at the beginning of December, the *National Intelligencer* valiantly attempted to prevent a stampede of public opinion, asserting among other things that, "From the steps, no doubt taken by our government, national expectations may be entertained that the decree will be revoked before it can have operated extensively to the injury of our trade." Nevertheless, there was an explosive outburst of public sentiment. Phineas Bond soon reported to London:

Scarcely any Thing has happened since the Revolution . . . , which has so much agitated the minds of all Descriptions of People in the United States as this Decree: the democratic Party hesitates not to reprobate in the most acrimonious Terms the evil Effects of a temporizing Policy in this Government upon this Occasion; while those who have always seen and known the great Advantages to arise from a close Connexion and Friendship with Great Britain, date, from this moment, the first Symptom of an universal Disposition to establish a firm and powerful Alliance between Us.

Thornton endorsed Bond's report, adding that "I find men, formerly the most vehement in their politics, asserting in the most unqualified terms the necessity of an union among all the members of the civilized world to check her [France's] encroachments, and to ensure the general tranquillity."[16]

Jefferson was alarmed. Rumors of war, or at very least an armed *coup de main* carried out by Westerners under Federalist auspices, were common topics of conversation. The President and Madison acted promptly and wisely, announcing the appointment of James Monroe as a special emissary to France. This nomination was made because of Monroe's great reputation in the West, and, as Jefferson frankly stated, it was aimed at reducing "the fever into which the Western mind is thrown by the affair at N. Orleans stimulated by the mercantile, and generally the federal interest."[17] The Federalists were outraged. A promising political issue was snatched from beneath their very eyes, and the instrument of their embarrassment was to be James Monroe, who in defending his own conduct in France had attacked the immortal George Washington. The Federalists fumed that this was a Jeffersonian trick designed to conceal an impending surrender to Bonaparte. They fought with all their might to prevent Senate confirmation of Monroe, but the appointment was approved by the narrow margin of two votes.

Edward Thornton wisely showed no pique at this new development, and he offered to hold the monthly packet to carry Monroe to Europe. Jefferson seemed pleased, so the chargé rather boldly asked whether Monroe would proceed to London if his mission to Paris ended in failure. Jefferson replied that no decision had yet been made, but he assured Thornton that the United States would never give up her right to use the Mississippi and "should they be obliged at last to resort to force *they would throw away the scabbard.*" Madison told Thornton that, while the United States might settle for free navigation of the river, the only really satisfactory solution would be the sale of commanding territory to the United States.[18] This was generally the view expressed in joint instructions for Livingston and Monroe handed to the Virginian on March 2.

To aid Monroe in his mission, a secret appropriation bill, authorizing the expenditure of two million dollars for the purchase of New Orleans, was pushed through Congress. As the British chargé reported, the United States still hoped to acquire New Orleans "*in an honest way* (to use the expression of a Senator in the confidence of the Administration) that is by purchase." Thornton was by no means confident that this was possible, but as no "immediate member of the government" broached the subject of an alliance, he contented himself with saying in public that whatever country incurred the enmity of France "acquires by that act alone the friendship of Great Britain; and that, where the relations are so intimate as they are between her and the United States, this must be speedily followed by her active co-operation."[19]

Actually, although it was a closely guarded secret, the administration was seriously considering alliance with England if Monroe and Livingston were rebuffed at Paris. Jefferson raised the subject at a Cabinet meeting in April, and a majority was willing to bind the United States not to make a separate peace,[20] a far more important restriction on American freedom of action than any responsible Federalist had considered in 1798. Instructions along these lines were sent to Paris at the end of April. Madison told the envoys that, if France seemed determined on war or had "formed projects which will constrain the United States to resort to hostilities," they were to open conversations with the English. Notwithstanding American reluctance to become entangled in European politics, said the Secretary, "the advantages to be derived from the co-operation of Great Britain . . . at this period . . . are too obvious and too important to be renounced." Since the administration could have no idea of the "price which she may attach to her co-operation," Monroe and Livingston were given only general instructions in this regard. A pledge not to make a separate peace and, despite Cabinet reluctance, special concessions to British trade in Louisiana were approved, but English occupation of the trans-Mississippi territory was "altogether repugnant to the sentiments and the sound policy of the United States" and would not be tolerated. Madison went on to say that it was hoped that "sound calculations of interest, as well as a sense of right, in the French Government, will prevent the necessity of using the authority expressed in this letter." If France only insisted upon ending the deposit, Livingston and Monroe were directed to open consultations with the British while awaiting a decision between peace and war. But, "if France should avow or evince a determination to deny to the United States the free navigation of the Mississippi, your consultations with Great Britain may be held on the ground that war is inevitable."[21]

Meanwhile, there had been a number of developments in Europe. Reports that the First Consul was determined to take over the Floridas as well as New Orleans, despite the dangerous situation of the forces in Santo Domingo, threw Robert Livingston "in[to] the utmost consternation." The American, who had previously ignored Lord Whitworth, Britain's ambassador at Paris, began to have conversations with him which were designed to, and did, arouse "a considerable degree of jealousy" in Talleyrand. These visits, although sedulously repeated, somewhat baffled Whitworth, who reported, "I have certainly of late found Mr. Livingston more than usually cordial, and although not very confidential yet professing that his instructions strictly enjoined him to be so." Whitworth's dispatches reached Hawkesbury shortly before John Hookham Frere reported from Madrid that Charles Pinckney, the American representative there, had similarly approached him and even hinted at joint Anglo-American action to block Bonaparte's plans.[22]

A month later, the Foreign Secretary received important observations from Edward Thornton in Washington. Thornton's dispatches during this whole period reflected his alert mind, skillful handling of President Jefferson, and long observation of the American scene. To these was added the virtue of a sprightly style, and this combination of factors must have made the reports of interest to even so languid a mind as that of Lord Hawkesbury. Until early in 1803, perhaps because of his low rank, Edward Thornton had not presumed to suggest policy to His Majesty's Government. Toward the close of 1802, however, the rising tide of anti-French opinion in America and widespread support for the idea of an expedition to seize New Orleans caused him to change his attitude. On January 3, 1803, he wrote Hawkesbury that a tremendous opportunity was staring Britain

165

in the face, an opportunity which it would cost little to develop.

I should hope, My Lord, that by having some share in the delivery of this Island of New Orleans to the United States, which it will be impossible to keep from them, whenever they chuse to employ force, His Majesty's Government may hereafter attach still more this country to our interests, and derive all the advantage possible from the intercourse with that important part of the world.[23]

Thornton's dispatch, the reports from Whitworth and Frere, and Rufus King's obvious concern finally prodded the Addington government into wakefulness. Three days after the receipt of Thornton's letter, Hawkesbury encountered Lord Malmesbury at one of the King's levees. He told the crusty old diplomat that the Americans "were much alarmed, and drawing towards us." Possibly they had already seized New Orleans, a development which "would enable us to come forward with great advantage." Malmesbury was interested, but he urged caution—he could not forget that the Americans had gained independence by a revolution against the British crown. Hawkesbury heard him out, answered politely, but made no promises.[24]

Since a renewal of the war with France seemed inevitable—the first militia calls were issued early in March—many of the government's objections to the constantly reiterated arguments of Cobbett were made null and void. If the United States seized New Orleans, as seemed likely, Britain could of course "come forward with great advantage." There was, however, a more promising course, the Thornton refinement of Cobbett's original scheme. At small cost, England could take Louisiana from the weak Spanish regime and hand it over to the United States. Britain's interests would be served in two ways. All chance of a French base on the American continent would be brought to an end, whereas if Britain waited for the United States to act it was still possible that Bonaparte would be able to establish himself in the area along the Gulf coast. Furthermore, the United States could not fail to appreciate British assistance; she might offer special commercial concessions in the newly acquired territory and would certainly be more sympathetic toward Britain as the war recommenced.

Only three weeks after the receipt of Thornton's dispatch, a new British policy was put into operation. In a letter obviously based on confidential discussions with the Foreign Secretary, Rufus King told Robert Livingston that England was considering the dispatch of an expedition to Louisiana. What did Livingston think of this?

Should we like to see the English at New Orleans? not with the view of keeping it, but to prevent its going into the hands of France—or perhaps to assist us in acquiring Title to, and the possession of it?—If you are authorized to negotiate a purchase, would not the occupation by the English benefit your bargain, it being well and previously understood that if we obtain the Title they would give us the Possession?[25]

Lord Malmesbury, who had some influence with the government, still had doubts about the wisdom of the new policy. In a letter to a Cabinet member he complained about "the giving Louisiana to America"; Malmesbury hated Americans, "a mean illiberal, shabby people," and still believed that the best policy was to encourage a quarrel between France and America.[26] Nevertheless, the government persevered. Early in April, King for the first time hinted at the British shift in a report to the Secretary of State. The American envoy told of a conversation with Addington during which the premier said that, if war came, "it would perhaps be one of their first steps to occupy New Orleans." "The Doctor" assured King that it Britain took over the area it would be merely to keep it out of the hands of France. Britain regarded American possession, he said, as the best solution to a difficult problem.[27]

The policy chosen by Addington and Hawkesbury was, from all points of view, the wisest that Britain could adopt, particularly because it recognized the most important factor in the equation, that the United States would fight rather than see a new power take over Louisiana. Doubtless the most sanguine hopes for American gratitude would have been disappointed, but delivery of New Orleans could not have failed to have a powerful effect in the United States and, furthermore, it was as certain to involve America in conflict with France as the old, "hands off" policy. The decision was an imaginative one, a rarity in Addingtonian annals, and also further demonstrated the favorable attitude of the British government. If Addington and Hawkesbury had looked upon America as a spiteful brat which might yet turn upon its parent, they would never have adopted this policy, nor indeed would it have had any point. Their decision shows a clear understanding of the situation and realization that it was possible to work in concert with Thomas Jefferson.

The only trouble with British policy was that it developed too late. On April 11, just as news of James Monroe's arrival at Le Havre reached Paris, the First Consul directed Barbé-Marbois to arrange the sale of Louisiana. Two days later discussions were opened, and on the fourteenth Lord Whitworth reported to his superiors that "America is the first to reap the fruit of our discussion with this Government, in consequence of which Mr. Munroe finds the difference which occasioned his mission nearly adjusted."[28] There was some haggling, with Livingston alone and with both Americans, but shortly after the end of the month the three documents making up the Louisiana Purchase agreement were signed.

The transaction passed almost unnoticed in London newspapers, whose columns were full of news of the resumption of hostilities between England and France. When rumors first reached London, the *Morning Chronicle*, which had earlier expressed confidence that "The Americans are not base enough to buy a peace from France," publicly doubted that the measure had actually taken place. The *Chronicle* soon ate its words— in a very small item. The other papers commented in about equal detail; only the *Morning Post* showed any enthusiasm. Cobbett, who still had his sights trained on Lord Hawkesbury, announced his satisfaction that

America was to get Louisiana, but he blamed the Foreign Secretary for acting so slowly that Britain got no credit while France gained great influence in America and several million pounds to boot.[29]

A number of British officials expressed approval of the transfer. Lord Hawkesbury, doubtless stifling a bit of disappointment and yet gratified that French designs in America were at an end, drafted a cordial letter to Rufus King informing him of "the pleasure with which his majesty received this intelligence." A few months later, Alexander Baring told Timothy Pickering (as the Yankee remembered it in 1821) that "his government would rather have paid the purchase money out of the public treasury, than not have the transfer to the U. States effected." And James Monroe, who certainly had no deep affection for Britain, reported toward the end of the year that the English reaction was generally favorable; "Castleray" and Hawkesbury had expressed special pleasure to him in informal conversations.[30]

Privately, however, many Britons must have shared Cobbett's regret that England had not been able to gain positively as well as negatively from the controversy between America and France. Hawkesbury and Addington moved too slowly, and Bonaparte, seeing that Britain was not prepared to give way on Malta and other issues between them, accepted the gage of battle and disposed of Louisiana as one means of clearing the decks for action. Had the Cabinet acted with greater speed, it would not have been possible for Robert R. Livingston to write, as he did in the fall of 1803, that "Tho' the war had much effect in accelerating the business, we derived no aid in the transaction from the interference of Britain—"[31]

News of the Louisiana Purchase, borne from Europe by Rufus King, caused a storm of political activity in the United States. Following some struggle with his constitutional scruples, Jefferson convened Congress, which after a sharp debate approved the bargain and provided the purchase money. "The enlightened Government of France," the President told the legislators when they first met, "saw with just discernment, the importance of such liberal arrangements as might best and permanently promote the peace, interests, and friendship of both [nations]," and therefore sold Louisiana to the United States. Not all members of Congress saw it this way. "The King of Great Britain . . . at this crisis I take to have been by far the most able negotiator we had," said one Representative during the course of the debates. This was undoubtedly true, in the sense that Congressman Purviance meant it; the hardening of British policy toward France was a factor in Bonaparte's decision to sell the territory to the United States. Everyone recognized, despite the words of Jefferson's message, that this had not been an act of benevolence on the part of the First Consul, and France gained little credit in America for its action. "I believe, sir," one Representative said without challenge from his fellows, "that there is not within these walls an admirer of the present Government of France."[32] If Britain's slowness to awaken to the possibilities

168

of the situation deprived it of a chance to make political capital, so too did Bonaparte's obvious reluctance to sell Louisiana reduce the credit he got in America when he finally decided to do so.

The Louisiana convention provided for the transfer of American bonds to the government of France, but the First Consul had no desire to hold United States securities as an investment. He wanted cash. French banks declined to try to float such a huge bond issue in Europe. Therefore, at the suggestion of Livingston and Monroe, the French government opened negotiations to sell the stock in England and Holland through Hope & Company of Amsterdam and Francis Baring & Company of London.[33] The houses of Baring and Hope were the largest European handlers of American securities and thus natural candidates for the job. Although hostilities between England and France had already commenced, Alexander Baring, the future Lord Ashburton but then a cadet of the London house, traveled to Paris in company with P. C. Labouchère of Hope & Company. The two bankers easily reached an agreement with Barbé-Marbois. Simply stated, it provided for an exchange of stock for specie in three installments. Baring and Hope agreed to pay fifty-two million francs for securities with a face value of sixty millions.[34]

Before going to the United States to receive delivery of the first portion of the stock, Alexander Baring stopped in London. He sounded out the Addington ministry,[35] for the government's concurrence was vital if gold were to be shipped out of the country. The Cabinet agreed to allow the deal to go through, although it obviously violated the usual rules of mercantilism as well as British regulations governing trade with the enemy in time of war. Why did they do so? Doubtless two chief reasons were the desire to make doubly sure that Bonaparte got no foothold in North America and to end the troublesome possibility that France might sell the stock in America and establish a fund for military purchases. In addition, the house of Baring was already preëminent in London finance, and its desires carried great weight, even though most of the elder Baring's friends sat on Opposition benches in the House of Commons. Finally, the bankers were in effect buying the stock at 78½,[36] thus depriving Bonaparte of almost one quarter of the principal and all of the interest that the United States had contracted to pay him. Since these varied considerations probably influenced the British government, it would be dangerous to say that the permission extended to the Barings was basically an act of good will towards the United States. Nevertheless, relations with America were doubtless considered. The United States was a friendly nation. The agreements concluded with Rufus King made closer ties a real possibility, and a further concession could certainly do no harm. This, and other important factors, justified granting an export permit even for so large an amount of specie as that which Baring proposed to ship to Paris.

Thus, by the sale of Louisiana, Bonaparte ended a serious quarrel with the United States and, with British connivance, gained a considerable installment of the sinews of war. At the same time, he ended for the moment all possibility of a military alliance between England and America. We cannot safely predict what would have happened if Bonaparte had made a different choice, if the autocrat of the Tuileries had decided to go through with his colonial venture or even merely to maintain title to Louisiana until a French victory in Europe should allow him once again to turn his attention to the trans-Atlantic arena.

We do know, however, that to protect the entrepôt of the American West Jefferson was ready to join Britain in a war against France and that the Addington ministry would have listened to his proposals with a receptive ear. While Bonaparte's reversal of French policy scotched this project almost before it got started, it still has importance as an index of Anglo-American relations. Republican sympathies for France seemed no longer to exist. Jefferson was willing to promise Britain not to make a separate peace; the Federalists had never gone that far during the quasi war. Particularly interesting is the fact that it was Jefferson himself who spoke of alliance in the strongest terms, for it was he, a supposed partisan of France, whose triumph in 1800 had caused doleful predictions in Britain and America. In 1798 Pitt and Grenville offered the United States cannon for the defense of Charleston, naval vessels for a price, convoys, and other assistance; in 1803 Addington and Hawkesbury were ready to make the United States a gift, albeit a gift of twice stolen property, of the American heartland. It would obviously be untrue to say that there was any philanthropy involved. In 1803, as in 1798, self-interest lay at the root of national policy. Yet at both times the coöperation proposed would not have been considered had not relations between the two countries been strong and satisfactory.

A survey of Republican diplomacy shows that, in their first two years in power, Jefferson and Madison did not significantly alter Federalist policy. They even allowed a member of the opposition party to remain at his post as American minister to Britain. The new regime adopted the approach of its predecessor with respect to the breakdown of the two Jay treaty commissions, and it watched with approval as Rufus King negotiated a settlement of this, the most important issue between England and America. The boundary discussions, too, were carried on in a conciliatory manner, and it must be repeated that in this instance, as in the case of the countervailing duties, the final repudiation of the diplomats' efforts came after the spring of 1803, after the resumption of European conflict altered the political situation. In May the boundary convention seemed a success, commercial legislation still possible. These prospective settlements, together with coöperation on such matters as the supply of American naval vessels cruising against Barbary and the return of the Maryland bank stock, strengthened international ties already improved by the debt commission settlement.

Basically, commercial relations were good. The trade depression in the United States, although in large part the result of a decline in the volume of trade with Britain, was obviously chiefly caused by loss of the reëxport trade, and England was not widely blamed for harsh commercial policy. As a matter of fact, despite the return of peace, American ships continued to trade with India in complete freedom, and the ports of the West Indies were not, for a number of reasons, closed against them. Anglo-American trade continued to bulk large in the economy of the United States, British manufactures maintained their dominant position, and both countries avoided outright commercial warfare. Even the *Anti-Jacobin Review,* surprisingly enough, commented favorably on the liberal policies of the London and Washington governments, emphasized the importance of good relations, and added its "trust [that] the rulers of the two countries will ever suffer these considerations to predominate in their minds, and to regulate their conduct."[37]

The cordial Anglo-American relationship in the first years of the nineteenth century owed much to the armistice in Europe. There were no seizures of American ships, and thus no quarrels over maritime rights. Impressment was in abeyance, and the diplomats barely discussed it until just before the resumption of war. Although these factors were soon to reappear against the backdrop of a new war, their temporary removal to the background combined with a number of positive developments to make the period of the Louisiana negotiations, the spring of 1803, one of the high points in the first rapprochement between the United States and Great Britain.

Two statements from sources not always known for their support of Anglo-American understanding illustrate the change that had taken place over the years. As hostilities reopened in Europe, Thomas Jefferson wrote, in language perhaps the stronger because addressed to an Englishman, "We see . . . with great concern the position in which Great Britain is placed, & should be seriously afflicted were any disaster to deprive mankind of the benefit of such a Bulwark against the torrent which has for some time been bearing down all before it." Six months earlier, the London *Times* had written:

Every British statesman must now be aware of the great importance of maintaining a good understanding with the United States of America. The two countries may be so mutually serviceable, or so mutually mischievous to each other, that the utmost pains should be employed to cultivate not only peace, but to improve every sentiment of kindness and affection.[38]

Ebb Tide **15**

UNFORTUNATELY, ALTHOUGH THE RENEWAL OF EUROPEAN HOSTILITIES in May 1803 was not immediately followed by quarrels between Britain and America, the Addington and Jefferson governments proved less successful in dealing with the vexations of war than the problems of peace. The resumption of war did not precipitate a violent party controversy in the United States as it had in 1793, largely because Americans fairly generally sided with England, although much of this feeling was a direct and transitory outgrowth of the Louisiana crisis. The Federalists still made no bones of the fact that they believed that only a British victory would assure the peace and prosperity of the world. The Republicans' attitude, on the other hand, had changed greatly since the days when Citizen Genêt was so boisterously received. Whereas just after the Jay treaty the *Aurora* had run articles on seizures sardonically entitled "Evidences of British Amity," in 1803 the *National Intelligencer*, the successor to Bache's paper as party spokesman, headed accounts of French captures with the words, "French Amity." Thomas Jefferson spoke of Britain as a "Bulwark against the torrent" and wrote that "The Events which have taken place in France have lessened in the American mind the motives of Interest which it felt in that Revolution, and its Amity towards that Country now rests on its Love of Peace and Commerce." Along the same lines, Edward Thornton predicted that "a predilection for France will not furnish any motive of action either in the government or in the country at large,"[1] a comment on the Jeffersonian regime few would have hazarded in 1800.

Rufus King's successor, James Monroe, did not reach London until July 1803, chiefly because his superiors took some time to decide between him and Robert R. Livingston. Monroe was not a good choice for the London post, although this did not become apparent immediately. His reputation as an ardent Francophile was harmful, though largely out of date, but Monroe's chief drawback was his manner of doing business. Despite a gentle hint from the Secretary of State, he dealt with the Foreign Office by note rather than personal interview, thus eliminating the informal give-and-take which had so often proved of great value during the time King was at London. Sometimes he bombarded Downing Street with garrulous memoranda; at others he preserved a deep silence, causing Lord Hawkesbury to remark that "so far as regards their office he might as well be in Virginia—"[2]

Monroe's spirit was not bad, and his earlier affections for France had disappeared along with those of so many of his fellow Republicans. In the fall of 1803 he reported to Jefferson that impressment was the only major issue between the two countries, endorsed English claims that most impressed seamen actually were British subjects, and said that a settlement of this problem was possible. Later in the year, Monroe expressed a belief that

this gov^t begins to see the folly of connecting itself with any party in America. It must perceive that it can preserve the most favorable relations with the existing government of our country that a just regard for its rights & interests will permit, peace, friendly intercourse, equality with other powers, &c. I think these truths are gaining strength daily here.[3]

Three weeks before Monroe wrote this letter, the new British minister arrived in the United States. He was Anthony Merry, a veteran diplomat who had been one of two nominees for the post in 1801 but whose departure had been postponed by important service during the Amiens negotiations. Merry was chosen largely because of the intervention of Rufus King, who believed that the other candidate, Francis James Jackson, would not further good relations, an analysis of Jackson's character abundantly confirmed a decade later. William Cobbett protested that Merry was too obscure a man to make a favorable impression on the Americans,[4] but the government was not moved by his argument, and Merry sailed for America late in September 1803. The absence of serious controversy is demonstrated by Hawkesbury's instructions, which laid down as Merry's chief task the preservation of the favored status granted by Britain by the Jay treaty and stated, "it is not probable that any new Circumstances should occur of a nature to create any serious Discussion between you and the American ministers.—I have therefore no particular Instructions . . . except that you endeavour to cultivate . . . good understanding."[5]

Merry's arrival in the United States roughly coincides with the beginning of deteriorating relations. The President received him in carpet slippers, and Merry's formal speech on good relations between the two countries, so carefully prepared during his voyage, was heard by an audience of just two—Jefferson and Madison. After his first official conversations with Madison, Merry reported to London that the United States hoped to take advantage of French successes in Europe to establish "a more convenient System of neutral Navigation than the Interests of the British Empire have hitherto allowed His Majesty to concur in."[6]

To Merry's diplomatic troubles, social ones were soon added. They arose out of the studied informality of manners practiced by Thomas Jefferson and his Cabinet, something which had been reported without disquiet by Thornton two years before. But Thornton was a bachelor and mere chargé, whereas Merry, the son of a wine merchant, fully appreciated his rise to ministerial rank and was married to a lady not inclined to allow real or fancied slights to pass unnoticed. The first dinner tendered to the Merrys by Jefferson was a trying affair, not least because the guest list was distinguished only by the inclusion of Monsieur Pichon, the French envoy. A dinner at the Madisons' was even more unpleasant, and the British minister was certain that this discourtesy was planned and not the manifestation of "Ignorance and Awkwardness (though God knows a great Deal of both as to Matters even of common Etiquette is to be seen at every step in this Part of the Country)."[7] It is not surprising that, for the remainder of his stay in America, Merry was not particularly useful, serving almost solely as a channel through which American protests were transmitted.

Instead of undertaking negotiations with Madison, Merry entered into secret relations with secessionist conspirators, notably Aaron Burr and disgruntled Federalists, who hoped to lead New England and New York out of the Union. The dream of a Northern Confederacy died with Burr's defeat in the New York gubernatorial election of 1804, but soon, through Colonel Charles Williamson, the Vice President offered to "lend his assistance to His Majesty's Government in any manner in which they may think fit to employ him, particularly in endeavoring to effect the separation of the Western Part of the United States."[8] Merry forwarded this offer to London, and in March and November 1805 he reported a series of interviews with Burr during which the former Vice President asked for British military and financial assistance. London wisely declined to support these projects.

An even greater part of Merry's voluminous correspondence was devoted to highly critical commentaries on the policy of Jefferson and his administration. For the first year, at least, these reports were overdrawn, although Edward Thornton supported and seconded them. This is not to say that American feeling for Britain had remained as it was in the spring of 1803, when there was no war and English assistance against France seemed to be in the offing. But the change was by no means as substantial as Merry and Thornton reported. The distorted picture of the American situation painted by them was the product of two factors. The first was the quarrel over Merry's social position, and the other was anti-impressment legislation introduced by Samuel Smith which authorized action against offending naval commanders and even against the nations which countenanced their activities. Merry and Thornton insisted that Smith's bill was an administration measure, although Jefferson and Madison actually thought the proposal poorly timed, since they had not given up hope of negotiating a settlement. Early in 1804, Wilson C. Nicholas announced in the Senate that he was authorized to say that "at no period of our Government has there subsisted so cordial a friendship between the government of this Country & that of . . . Great Britain as at this time, the newspaper publications to the contrary notwithstanding."[9] Nicholas' statement caused the Smith bill to be put over until December, but Merry virtually ignored this development in his official correspondence.

During the early months of 1804 little action was taken by the London government directly affecting the United States one way or the other, and William Pitt replaced Addington before "the Doctor" and Hawkesbury could carry out any change of policy as a result of the dispatches from Washington. The Addington ministry had been steadily losing strength since the resumption of war with France. Invasion was daily expected, and to oppose the legions of Bonaparte the government had only a small regular army and a proliferation of militia organizations, one commanded by Lord Grenville in his spare time. Pitt, the Grenvilles, and even the Whigs joined in attacking ministers who had allowed England to become so nearly defenseless. In April 1804 Pitt urged his sovereign to consider the need for broadening the government, and two days later Henry Addington handed in his resignation.

Henry Adams once wrote that the second Pitt government, which now came into office, represented "a state of feeling toward America very different from that which prevailed under the mild rule of Addington."[10] Although it is undeniable that relations deteriorated after May 1804, the reasons were more general than personal bias. The new Cabinet, though none too strong in Commons, was more energetic, more capable, more businesslike than its predecessor; inevitably this meant, in time, more conflict with America. Pitt and his cohorts returned to power with a program calling for all out prosecution of the war; as an American newspaper put it, "the reign of the last honest but imbecile administration is over, and more vigorous men are now calling the long dormant energies of the nation into action."[11] This too was bound to bring about quarrels with neutrals. Furthermore, the Grenvilles' refusal to enter the Cabinet meant that doctrinaire conservatives formed the backbone of the government.

Pitt's close friend, Dudley Ryder, now Lord Harrowby, succeeded Hawkesbury at the Foreign Office. Harrowby was a man of ability who was later offered the premiership several times, but he had almost no knowledge of foreign affairs. This troubled him, but Lord Malmesbury, drawing upon his own experience, assured the new Foreign Secretary that all that was necessary was to avoid saying anything definite to ambassadors, since their visits were usually made merely for the purpose of filling up a dispatch.[12]

Monroe was never able to bring the new Foreign Secretary to serious negotiations, and delays and evasions exasperated the Virginian. The handling of impressment illustrates the difficulties he faced. Early in 1804, Madison directed Monroe to negotiate an impressment convention closely patterned after that King had proposed, omitting mention of the Narrow Seas but making concessions to Britain in other regards, notably in provisions for the return of deserters. Monroe was unable to get any action out of Harrowby until fall, although in August he highlighted the seriousness of the problem by forwarding to the Foreign Office a list of fifteen hundred seamen taken since the press recommenced in March 1803, only four hundred of whom had been ordered released. In September, Harrowby finally condescended to comment on the American proposal, informing Monroe that no agreement could be expected in the immediate future.[13] Harrowby's decision was reinforced by the opinion of the Admiralty that the American proposals were "tantamount to establish in every American vessel an asylum from the Impress service," since the United States was not likely to carry out a promise to return deserters taking refuge under the American flag. Two months later, however, the Admiralty did order commanders on the American station "to observe the utmost Lenity in visiting Ships of the United States on the high Seas, and [though this directive should not have been needed] to abstain from impressments in the Ports of the United States."[14]

During most of this period, seizures were a less important American grievance than impressment. The Pitt government made no extensive alterations in the British maritime code, and American ships suffered little more than they had in the closing months of the previous war. Operating under the protection of the *Polly* decision, the American reëxport trade once again enjoyed a great boom. In July 1804 Monroe exulted, "The truth is that our commerce never enjoyed in any war, as much freedom, and indeed favor from this gov^t as it now does. The little bickerings produce no effect on the conduct of the gov^t in that respect."[15]

The prosperity of the American marine aroused much jealousy in Britain, and spokesmen for the maritime interest insisted that America's success had been gained at the expense of English shipowners. In February 1804 Lord Sheffield brought forth a pamphlet entitled *Strictures on the Necessity of Inviolably Maintaining the Navigation and Colonial System;* in sixty-five highly charged pages he argued that the ills of the British merchant marine could be cured by rigid enforcement of the Navigation Acts and particularly by ending the system of governors' proclamations which opened the West Indies to American shipping. Sheffield's pamphlet caused a great stir. *The Anti-Jacobin* and *Annual Register* were soon enlisted in his support, and their combined strength more than offset the answers to the *Strictures* written by representatives of colonial merchants and planters.[16]

Under this pressure, the Board of Trade began hearings in June. In September, it ordered the colonial governors to open their ports only in the most dire emergencies, under no circumstances to admit certain American products easily procured from the Empire, and particularly not to permit ships of the United States to trade with the islands on a more favorable basis than British merchantmen. Early in 1805, the Board urged that American vessels bringing anything except provisions to the West Indies be seized for violation of the Navigation Acts.[17] As usual, the attempt to tighten up the proclamation system was not completely successful, but the new regulations nevertheless aroused considerable apprehension in the

United States, particularly since Governor Nugent at Jamaica inaccurately announced that the government intended to bring all American trade with the West Indies to an end.[18]

Meanwhile, in the summer of 1804 a flagrant invasion of American rights had taken place in New York harbor. During an unsuccessful attempt to intercept Jérome Bonaparte, who was on the point of sailing for France, Captain Bradley of H. M. S. *Cambrian* searched a number of ships within American territorial waters. The *Cambrian* episode helped arouse public opinion in the United States. Jefferson wrote his Secretary of the Navy that if the gunboats then building were "now ready I should certainly make a proposition to send the whole to New York & to clear out the harbor."[19]

Resentment at Bradley's conduct, combined with gradually accumulating feelings on impressment and seizures, caused the government to abandon its opposition to retaliatory legislation, and a law of March 1805 authorized the President to take punitive action against naval officers who "commit[ted] any trespass or tort or any spoliation, on board any vessel of the United States."[20] But the situation did not yet appear to be desperate. In March, Madison wrote Monroe, who had gone to Spain on a special mission, approving of his conduct "in winking at . . . [Britain's] dilatory policy, and keeping the way open for a fair and friendly experiment on your return from Madrid."[21] A few months later Anthony Merry, who was not easy to please, found the attitudes of Jefferson and Madison relatively satisfactory.

A major factor retarding the deterioration of Anglo-American relations was the dispute that called James Monroe to Madrid. Monroe's appearance did little to lessen Spanish resentment at various American actions, particularly passage of the so-called Mobile Act, authorizing the incorporation into the United States of territory almost indisputably Spanish. War was considered likely, and Thomas Jefferson, ever the opportunist in foreign affairs, once again thought briefly of an alliance with Britain. In August of 1805 he wrote to Madison, "I think . . . we should take into consideration whether we ought not immediately to propose to England an eventual treaty of alliance, to come into force whenever (within   years) a war shall take place with Spain or France."[22] Papers were circulated through the Cabinet, but the project was never seriously considered. It demonstrates, however, that even as late as the summer of 1805 Jefferson at least temporarily regarded a controversy with the rickety Spanish monarchy as more important than disagreements with the Pitt government.

Upon his return to England in July, Monroe was confronted by a problem that had arisen during his absence, the spate of seizures brought on by the *Essex* decision. In 1799 this American ship carried wine from Barcelona to Salem. After complying with the bonding provisions of American customs law, she cleared for Havana with the same cargo. En route, she was intercepted by the privateer *Favourite*. Taken to New Providence, the *Essex* and her cargo were condemned by Judge John Kelsau, who ignored the *Polly* precedent and argued that the landing at Salem was designed solely to conceal a continuous voyage from Spain to Cuba:

I cannot hesitate in denying to a fradulently circuitous voyage, those immunities which are with held from a direct one. Without reference to any other principle, I consider this as actually a traffic between Spain and Cuba, and condemn the vessel and cargo accordingly.[23]

The *Essex* was then released on bail while her owners appealed the decision. She traded with the Middle East and achieved a gruesome notoriety when her captain, Joseph Orne, and her crew were massacred by Arab pirates in the Red Sea in 1806.

Before this, however, the *Essex* had achieved more permanent fame through the decision of the Lords Commissioners of Appeals, to which exalted body her owners had carried their protests. There were many delays in the appellate process, chiefly to allow the owners of the *Essex* to forward further proof of a bona fide importation into the United States. At last, in the spring of 1805,[24] a decision was handed down. Although Sir William Scott, Britain's foremost admiralty lawyer, was present and on the bench, the verdict was read by the Master of the Rolls, Sir William Grant, a prominent jurist but one who usually specialized in the common law and "had a leaning to the strict interpretation and undeviating rules of the common law courts."[25] Presumably since the Lords were in effect upholding Kelsau's reasoning and since the case had been discussed in earlier proceedings, the verdict was very brief:

The Lords having maturely deliberated pronounced the further proof of the duties that were paid . . . and of the certificates of the entries at the Custom House in America respecting the said Ship and cargo to be insufficient, and by interlocutory decree condemned the said ship and cargo as good and lawful prize to Charles Underwood commander of the private Ship of War Favourite.[26]

Later on, after American protests, the Master of the Rolls elucidated the *Essex* decision in the case of the *William*, Trefry:

The landing of the cargo [,] the entry at the custom-house, and the payment of such duties as the law of the place requires, *are necessary ingredients* in a genuine importation. . . . But in a fictitious importation they are mere voluntary *ceremonies* . . . resorted to . . . with a view of giving to the voyage which . . . [the owner] has resolved to continue, the appearance of being broken by an importation, which he has resolved not really to make.[27]

Further evidence of a bona fide importation was required, and the burden of proof lay with the shipowner. Grant noted that the case had been put over since 1803 to allow counsel for the *Essex* to gather evidence, but none was forthcoming, other than the fact that the goods had been landed and duties paid. (Actually, all but two hundred dollars was returned to the owner upon reëxportation.) Grant said that he had had no option but to confirm the decree of condemnation on the ground that, by participating in trade between Spain and Cuba, the *Essex* had violated the Rule of 1756.

There is much to be said for Sir William Grant's argument—if the Rule of 1756, unilaterally promulgated by Great Britain, is admitted to have force. American evasions of English rules for neutrals became more and more flagrant and more and more extensive as time went on, and they made a mockery of British attempts to stop the flow of goods between France and Spain and their colonies. It was left to Grant, in the *Essex* case, to overthrow the *Polly* decision and make British maritime policy effective once again.

Technically, Grant was right when he argued that the *Polly* decision had been distinguished and not reversed,[28] for in that case Sir William Scott carefully stated that landing and payment of duties were not the only tests of bona fide importation. Yet Scott also said that if these standards were not applied, "I should be at a loss to know what should be the test."[29] This observation, almost dictum in the case at hand, was given the stamp of government approval when an opinion endorsing the principle was handed to Rufus King for the information of his government. American shipowners, who were not likely to examine these papers in search of legal quibbles and qualifications, accepted them at face value. When Great Britain withdrew the permission which seemed to have been extended, the United States was naturally and rightly outraged. In sum, then, while Grant's opinion was logical and may have been, by British standards, good law, it was an entirely unexpected alteration of the base upon which American commerce rested and, as such, the ground for serious complaint.

Some of the trouble which subsequently arose could have been avoided if the enforcement of this decree had been suspended at least until the American merchant marine could learn of its existence. As Lord Holland later wrote, "The sudden and peremptory manner of enforcing" the new principle made it "yet more offensive." No new Orders in Council were issued, and Undersecretary Hammond said that he "could not conceive how an idea had gone abroad of any new order having been issued." The decision itself apparently was not published or even made public, and James Monroe could at first only protest against "the principles which appear to have been adopted in some late decisions of the Court of admiralty." Lord Mulgrave, who had succeeded Harrowby when the latter, while carrying dispatch boxes, fell down a flight of stairs at the Foreign Office and incapacitated himself for business, at first blandly denied that there had been any important change in British maritime policy.[30] Specific news of the *Essex* decision did not reach America until autumn. But long before that, officers of the Royal Navy, often informed of the decree by the attorneys who represented them in prize cases, had begun to seize scores of ships engaged in an indirect trade between Europe and the enemy islands in the Caribbean.

Some English voices questioned the wisdom and legal justification of the new policy which the Pitt government had allowed to grow out of the *Essex* decision. The Foreign Office asked Sir William Scott to prepare an answer to Monroe's extended and polemical protests, only to find that the jurist was "more afraid of the controversy, than of a Contest" with the United States. Scott's defense of the new departure was so weak that Mulgrave concluded, "It may . . . be dangerous . . . to drag our Friend into the fight like Sir Andrew Ague Cheek, when he requires so many Sir Toby's to hold up his sword for him—"[31] The Whig *Morning Chronicle* attacked a return to the policy of "hasty violence and tardy atonement," arguing that "we ought not, either in justice or in policy to drive America to measures of reprisal," but it was soon under heavy fire from the *Sun*, from Cobbett, and from its erstwhile ally, the *Morning Post*.[32]

Two new developments soon decided the issue once and for all. On October 21, Nelson smashed the Franco-Spanish line of battle and, at the cost of his own life, destroyed the fleet of Admiral Villeneuve at Trafalgar, thereby greatly reducing the necessity for Britain to conciliate neutrals. On the very same day, a pamphlet entitled *War in Disguise; Or, the Frauds of the Neutral Flags* appeared in London. The author, a lawyer named James Stephen, had previously submitted his manuscript to Sir William Scott, who consulted Pitt and advised Stephen to issue it privately as a pamphlet, both because the public needed educating on the "important Interests involved in the present questions, and because I think that if it sh[d] carry our Pretensions somewhat higher than the Convenience of Publick Affairs may allow, it will commit Government less" than if it seemed to have "any stamp of Official Communication upon It."[33]

Basically, *War in Disguise* was an expansion and reassertion of the principles lying at the heart of the *Essex* decision. Stephen complained that, though Britain was at war with all the other major European maritime powers, "the ocean does not sustain a single keel . . . in which we can find any merchandise that is allowed to be legitimate prize." The reason was that most of the so-called neutral trade, particularly the American, was fraudulently sheltering enemy property. Thus, "the encroachments and frauds of the neutral flags . . . [are the] channels of a revenue, which sustains the ambition of France, and prolongs the miseries of Europe." To prevent this, to deprive Napoleon of the sinews of war and the neutrals of their dishonest profits, Stephen urged rigorous execution of Britain's maritime code and a complete interruption of the enemy's colonial trade.[34]

War in Disguise crystallized British opinion, consolidated it behind a policy that showed little respect for neutrals. Liberal men like William Wilberforce, Alexander Baring, and the editors of the *Edinburgh Review* did not accept Stephen's conclusions, but even they had to admit the force of his arguments. In America, *War in Disguise* was widely read and almost universally condemned. Gouverneur Morris, Tench Coxe, and the Secretary of State himself composed counterblasts, and Madison's pamphlet was distributed gratis to members of Congress.[35] The *Essex* case and Stephen's polemic were too much for even the most extreme Federalists to stomach, although they pointed out that French outrages balanced those of England. "If the *Laws of Nations* have been violated," shrilled the *Columbian Centinel*, "let the Administration remonstrate to all the Powers who have violated these Laws.—If Justice be denied, let the LAST REASONING be resorted to."[36]

The ebb tide, which for some months had been flowing uncertainly and sporadically, began to run in earnest with the *Essex* case, the seizures of the summer of 1805, Trafalgar, and the appearance of *War in Disguise*. England and America were carried along into the tragedy of the War of 1812. In 1806, in the last full scale attempt at negotiation, Monroe and Pinkney failed to secure a treaty acceptable to Jefferson. Thereafter the current flowed steadily. Orders in Council . . . the *Chesapeake* . . . the Embargo . . . Erskine and Jackson . . . Tippecanoe . . . the War Hawk Congress—all followed one another in steady succession, and in June 1812 the United States declared war on Great Britain. War was not made inevitable in 1805, but it was certainly a less surprising development following the events of that year. A combination of inept statesmanship, mercantile greed, nationalistic ambitions, and the pressures of war made the good relations prevailing from 1795 to 1805 seem almost like a cruel joke of history.

Epilogue: The First Rapprochement

THE RECEDING TIDE OF 1804 AND 1805 LEFT THE BATTERED HULK OF cordiality stranded on the beach of the past. The ribs and braces of the vessel were visible, attesting to the skill of the shipwrights who had fashioned her, but it was to be many years before she was again a trim and seaworthy craft.

Inept pilotage, less expected after the generally able helmsmanship since 1794, was largely to blame. Jefferson and Madison, Addington and Hawkesbury were not unsuccessful in maintaining the system inherited from their predecessors as long as Europe was at peace. But neither they nor the members of the new Pitt ministry were able to meet the challenge provided by the second and more desperate act of the bloody European drama. It was perhaps fitting, if unfortunate, that at this time new envoys should replace Robert Liston and Rufus King. Merry, a disputative, pompous diplomat, was accompanied by a wife who compounded his faults, whereas Liston had been an imaginative and friendly minister. Like Merry, James Monroe was argumentative and lacking in diplomatic finesse; bludgeoning and repetition were his chief weapons in dealing with Downing Street, and he did not see, as had King, the importance of private conversation and personal contact.

By 1805, the term of the commercial articles of the Jay treaty was fast coming to an end. The United States sought their extension with some modifications, and James Monroe directed numerous notes on the subject to the Foreign Office. But neither Harrowby nor Mulgrave was willing to give the matter serious attention or to deputize anyone to negotiate with him, and the Board of Trade was almost equally somnolent. As a result, commercial relations between the two countries were allowed to rest upon the weak base of American law and an annual Act of Parliament. One of the most important sections of the Jay treaty, the fundamental underlying factor in the growth of respect after 1795, was allowed to atrophy and die.

Perhaps some conflict over the rights of neutral shipping was inevitable, since the enterprise of Yankee shipowners, encouraged by the loose requirements of American customs law and the moderate attitude of British courts and government down to 1801, drove them to the very limits of neutral practices, while Great Britain increasingly allowed the shrill voices of extreme nationalists like Stephen, Sheffield, and Cobbett to influence her policy. When the crisis did come, it was ineptly handled by the English government, in marked contrast to the days when Grenville was at the Foreign Office. The story of impressment is very similar. During the Pitt-Adams period, thanks to careful management on both sides of the Atlantic, the issue became relatively dormant. Now the fundamental conflict of views moved into the foreground, chiefly because London failed to resist the strident demands of war and to restrain the growing harshness of naval commanders. The impressment controversy burst upon the scene with such suddenness that one British historian has even been emboldened to claim that the whole matter was concocted by Jefferson and Madison for domestic political purposes.[1]

This poor management was the more to be regretted because of the substantial achievements of the preceding decade. The beneficial growth of Anglo-American trade had been encouraged by both governments, particularly the Pitt ministry, which not only permitted the West Indies to be opened and altered legislation to meet some of Rufus King's criticisms, but also fostered American intercourse with India by direct interference in court proceedings. Three problems growing out of the 1783 settlement—the frontier posts, St. Croix boundary, and pre-Revolutionary debts—were liquidated, though the last was solved only after an acid controversy brought to an end by the convention of 1802, second only to the Jay treaty in importance.

On the high seas, the release of Captain Lasker's *Polly* and the opinion of the King's Advocate established a tacit agreement on the rights of American merchantmen. Although this position was not fixed until seven years after the Jay treaty, even in the preceding period seizures were not as serious a problem as they had been or were to be in the future. Outside factors aided this development, of course, but government policy was decisive. Several times during the years down to 1805, for example, Britain suffered from a food shortage as acute as that of the spring of 1795, but never again were provision cargoes subject to forced sale in English ports. All in all, the British government seemed to recognize, as Henry Dundas worded it, that the "amity [of the United States] . . . is at least as desirable as that of any other nation,"[2] and both Federalist and Republican administrations were ready to meet England half way.

Relations with France played an important part in the development of the first rapprochement. The extensive record of coöperation during the naval war, particularly in dealing with Santo Domingo, and the effect of the Louisiana crisis were important not only in themselves, but also as an indication of the decline of Francophile sentiments in America. By the late nineties, even the Republicans could not ignore, though they might minimize, the diplomatic and domestic excesses of *La Grande Nation*. Shortly after the peace of Mortefontaine, James Madison wrote, "the confidence and cordiality which formerly subsisted have had a deep wound from the occurrences of the late years." The rise of Napoleon made this shift more obvious and more definite. In 1804 Jefferson remarked to

Senator John Quincy Adams "how *contrary to all expectation* this great *bouleversement* had turned out. . . . He thought it very much to be wished that they could now return to the Constitution of 1789, and call back *the Old Family.*" Commenting on the decline of American politicians who were "invariably the friends and panegyrists of France, and the foes and calumniators of Great Britain," the London *Times* noted that "The *revolutionary* disease, although not quite subdued, is disappearing fast."[3] The change, obvious to more acute observers for some time, helped to ease the way for the architects of reconciliation between the English-speaking powers.

One of the most delicate indicators of Anglo-American amity was the state of relations along the Canadian boundary, and in the decade after 1795 this barometer steadily forecast favorable weather. The transfer of the posts was effected in a handsome manner, and in 1796 Lord Dorchester was prevented from placing stringent controls on American trade with Canada since, as Liston put it, "no single portion of the Empire can with propriety impede the completion of a transaction calculated for the good of the whole."[4] The policy of the United States was equally correct. As a result, British trade with Indians of the Northwest expanded 50 per cent from 1796 to 1798, reaching a total value of one hundred thousand pounds. Down to the end of the century there was little interference with this commerce, and when General Wilkinson attempted to check it he was directed to withdraw his orders.[5] The closing of the newly acquired Louisiana province to British traders in 1805 signalized in one more field the end of the period of good relations.

Contact between armed forces along the frontier was generally friendly. The two officers who symbolized the asperities of 1794 ceased to trouble international relations, Simcoe because he was removed and Wayne because, during the few remaining months of his life, he adapted his tune to the one currently being played in Philadelphia. "General Waine," an anonymous correspondent informed the British government in 1796, seems "desirous by his conduct to conciliate the good dispositions of every description of persons." Harmony at Detroit did not end with Wayne's departure; in 1799 the British commandant at Amherstburg reported "a very good understanding" with the American colonel across the river. The same was true at other posts. At Niagara, Major Rivardi exchanged ceremonial visits with the commander of British works opposite his own and reported:

the Brittish Officers . . . come to see us whenever the river is free of Ice—the day before yesterday Most of them with their Ladies Spent the day with me & it is a truly pleasing circumstance To See the friendly unreserved intercourse which subsists between the two Garrisons.'

The political importance of the section protected by these garrisons grew steadily as settlement pushed westward; by 1802 there were already three states west of the Appalachians. This was something to be reckoned with, particularly since Westerners were by temperament bellicose and nationalistic. Furthermore, the frontiersman had not forgotten massacres carried out by Indians in the employ of England during the Revolution, Lord Dorchester's provocative speech to the tribes in 1794, or the building of a new fort on the Maumee in the same year. Yet for almost a decade the frontier was quiet, and by 1804 there were only 1,700 soldiers in Canada.[7] British policy scarcely justified further spasms of Anglophobia, and the greatest Western outcry during this period was not directed at England but at France, formerly a respected ally and sister republic. As subsequent events were to show, there remained a great deal of latent feeling against Britain. But for a decade the absence of conflict in the West, and consequently of sectional pressure upon the national government, was an important aspect of the rapprochement.

In one of the many notes punctuating the negotiations of 1794, John Jay urged haste upon Lord Grenville: "So mutable are human affairs, especially in these mutable Times, that the sooner the peace and Friendship of our two Countries, are put out of Hazard, the better—"[8] Jay and Grenville ended the immediate threat, and a reconciliation was built upon the foundation they laid. This real if temporary rapprochement was at least as firm and long-lived as any during the first century of separation. Long before the demise of the royal "tyrant" and many of the "rebels" who rose against him, the two nations came to respect one another and to recognize their joint interest in stable relations. For the first time, a fact was demonstrated that is today obvious but has too often been obscured—the strength of the forces working for comity between the United States and Britain.

At the same time, this epoch showed that a real rapprochement depended heavily upon capable diplomacy on both sides of the Atlantic, but especially in England, since it goes without saying that not all the factors in the international equation were favorable ones. Fortunately, the years from the Jay treaty to 1801 are almost a case study in competent diplomacy. At the height of the 1794 controversy, Fisher Ames wrote that "If John Bull is a blockhead, and puts himself on his pride to maintain what he has done, . . . it will, I think, be war."[9] Pitt and Grenville, whatever their failings, were not ignorant, nor in this instance were they unyielding. Britain's course changed abruptly, the Washington and Adams administrations reciprocated, and great progress was made, particularly during the time of America's naval war with France. When the fasces passed to new hands in 1801, the heirs of Pitt and Adams showed an equally friendly spirit; although less adroit than their predecessors, they were nevertheless able, until the resumption of European war altered the stage of diplomacy, to maintain and improve the cordiality that had developed.

At the opening of this auspicious decade, Talleyrand predicted that the United States would "be useful to England more than any other power and . . . this usefulness will increase in proportion as the English government abandons the *formes d'hauteur* which it uses in all its relations with America."[10] Nothing that occurred in the years from 1795 to 1804 invalidated the forecast of the ex-bishop of Autun.

Appendix

Statistical observations on (a) "An ACCOUNT . . . of the Several APPEALS against Decrees concerning Ships and Goods claimed by NEUTRALS," *Parliamentary Papers, 1801*, V, 227-305, a record of all cases before the High Court of Appeals, dated 25 March 1801, and (b) "An ACCOUNT . . . of the Several APPEALS against DECREES condemning Ships and Goods claimed by NEUTRALS," *ibid.*, 379-419, a list of cases still to be heard by the High Court of Appeals, dated 27 April 1801.

TABLE 1

APPELLATE VERDICTS OF HIGH COURT OF APPEALS

Court Reviewed	Verdict for Neutral			Verdict for Captor		
	Gain	Confirmed	Total	Gain	Confirmed	Total
HIGH COURT OF ADMIRALTY	6	5	11	3	8	11
Bermuda	51	2	53	2	4	6
Jamaica	25	0	25	0	10	10
St. Kitts	28	0	28	0	1	1
Dominica	26	0	26	0	1	1
Montserrat	12	0	12	0	0	0
Bahamas	1	0	1	6	5	11
Antigua	7	0	7	0	1	1
Tortola	6	0	6	0	0	0
Barbados	6	0	6	0	0	0
New Providence	2	1	3	1	3	4
Martinique	1	0	1	0	3	3
St. Vincents	1	0	1	0	0	0
Grenada	0	1	1	0	0	0
TOTAL WEST INDIES	166	4	170	9	29	38
Nova Scotia	8	0	8	1	3	4
Halifax	1	0	1	0	4	4
TOTAL NOVA SCOTIA	9	0	9	1	7	8

TABLE 2

DELAY BEFORE VERDICTS

Year of Lower Decision	Year of Appellate Verdict					
	1795	1796	1797	1798	1799	1800
1793	2	3	6	11	6	4
1794	5	3	11	59	43	16
1795	1	0	0	15	8	4
1796	0	0	0	6	4	14
1797	0	0	0	1	9	2
1798	0	0	0	0	0	2

This table can only be considered in conjunction with the following one.

TABLE 3

DATES OF ORIGIN OF CASES STILL PENDING, 1801

```
1793 ........................ 4
1794 ........................ 26
1795 ........................ 5
1796 ........................ 15
1797 ........................ 23
1798 ........................ 37
1799 ........................ 20
1800 ........................ 1
```

Many other appeals had not yet reached the docket of the High Court of Appeals.

Notes

PROLOGUE: THE JAY TREATY

1—5

1. Charlemont to Edmund Malone, 29 October 1794, John T. Gilbert, ed., *The Manuscripts and Correspondence of James, First Earl of Charlemont*, II (Historical Manuscripts Commission, *Thirteenth Report*, Appendix, Part VIII, London, 1894), 251.
2. Charles Maurice de Talleyrand-Périgord, "Les États-Unis et L'Angleterre en 1795," *Révue d'Histoire Diplomatique*, III (1889), 67, 75-76.
3. J. Hamilton to Henry Dundas, 30 November 1794, enclosed in J. King to George Aust, 5 March 1795, Foreign Office Records, Public Record Office, London, FO 5/12.
4. Baron Auckland to Lord Henry Spencer, 28 March 1794, Robert J. Eden, Lord Auckland, Bishop of Bath and Wells, ed., *The Journal and Correspondence of William, Lord Auckland*, III (London, 1862), 197.
5. J. Ross Robertson, ed., *The Diary of Mrs. John Graves Simcoe* (Toronto, 1911), p. 226 (16 May 1794).
6. George III to William Pitt, [date illegible], Pretyman MSS, Cambridge University Library (Add. MSS 6958), Vol. VIII; Dundas to John G. Simcoe, 4 July 1794, "Colonial Office Records," Michigan Pioneer and Historical Society, *Collections and Researches*, XXIV (Lansing, 1895), 678; Dundas to Dorchester, 5 July 1794, *ibid.*, pp. 679-82; Baron Grenville to Hammond, Secret and Confidential, 8 August 1794, FO 5/5.
7. John Nutt and William Molleson to Grenville, 13 September 1794, Chatham Papers, Public Record Office (PRO 30/8), Vol. CCCXLIV; "The Memorial, of the Merchants of London, trading to the Province of Canada" to the Duke of Portland, presented 20 November 1794, Portland MSS, University College, Nottingham, Miscellaneous 62. These thoughts had already been presented orally.
8. Memorandum of a conversation with Pitt and Dundas, 23 June 1794, Chatham MSS, Vol. CXCV.
9. "Projet of Heads of Proposals to be made to Mr. Jay," n. d. [1794], Papers of William Wyndham Grenville, Lord Grenville, at Boconnoc, Lostwithiel, Cornwall, America 1793-1803; Samuel F. Bemis, *Jay's Treaty, a Study in Commerce and Diplomacy* (New York, 1923), pp. 278-85.
10. Dundas to Grenville, n. d. [1794], Boconnoc MSS, Dundas 1793-98.
11. Hawkesbury memorandum on Grenville's "Heads of Proposals to be made to Mr. Jay," Liverpool Papers, British Museum (Add. MSS 38190-38489), Add. MSS 38354. This memorandum appears in Bradford Perkins, ed., "Lord Hawkesbury and the Jay-Grenville Negotiations," *Mississippi Valley Historical Review*, XL (1953-54), 291-304.
12. Hawkesbury to Grenville, 17 October 1794, Chatham MSS, Vol. CLII.
13. Grenville to Auckland, 4 March 1806, Auckland MSS, British Museum (Add. MSS 34412-34471), Add. MSS 34456.
14. *Connecticut Courant* (Hartford), 15 June 1795.
15. *True Briton* (London), 22 November 1794; *Sun* (London), 25 November 1794. For scoffing comment by Whig journals, see *Morning Post* (London), 18 October 1794; *Morning Chronicle* (London), 18 November 1794.

7—14

CHAPTER 1: TRANS-ATLANTIC TIES

1. William Reitzel, "The Purchasing of English Books in Philadelphia, 1790-1800," *Modern Philology*, XXXV (1937-38), 159.
2. James Greig, ed., *The Farington Diary*, II (London, 1923), 245 (31 May 1804). For the earlier comment, see James Greig, ed., *The Farington Diary*, I (London, 1922), 251 (8 December 1798).
3. *Morning Post*, 20 October 1794. The paper reported that this artist, Miss George, was urging her friends at home to join her in gathering the Yankee dollar. By the summer of 1795, Miss George had made three thousand pounds in the United States (*ibid.*, 28 August 1795). A somewhat less exceptional rate of pay was doubtless the £180 per week received by Mrs. Siddons' sister (William Priest, *Travels in the United States of America; Commencing in the Year 1793, and Ending in 1797* [London, 1802], pp. 157-58).
4. *Edinburgh Review*, II (1803), 448.
5. Cobbett to William Windham, 19 February 1801, Windham Papers, British Museum (Add. MSS 37842-37935), Add. MSS 37853; Hannah More to Martha More, n. d. [1795], William Roberts, ed., *Memoirs of the Life and Correspondence of Mrs. Hannah More* (London, 1834), II, 470; Cobbett to Windham, 19 February 1801, Windham MSS, Add. MSS 37853.
6. Allan Nevins, ed., *American Social History as Recorded by British Travellers* (London, 1924), p. 10.
7. Isaac Weld, Jr., *Travels Through the States of North America and the Provinces of Upper and Lower Canada During the Years 1795, 1796, and 1797* (London, 1799); John S. Hull, *Remarks on the United States of America* (Dublin, 1801); Thomas Moore, *Epistles, Odes, and Other Poems* (London, 1806), p. 177. (For a work of much the same purpose as Hull's, see George Henderson, *A Short View of the Administration in the Government of the United States* [London, 1802].) Richard Parkinson, *A Tour in America in 1798, 1799, and 1800* (London, 1805); *Edinburgh Review*, VII (1805), 29-42. For an example of the reaction to which the *Review* objected, see *Anti-Jacobin Review and Magazine; or, Monthly Political and Literary Censor* (London), XXII (1805), 22.
8. Henry Wansey, *An Excursion to the United States of North America in the Summer of 1794* (2nd ed., Salisbury, 1798); *Anti-Jacobin Review*, XIII (1802), 181; John Davis, *Travels of Four Years and a Half in the United States of America* (London, 1803); William Winterbotham, *View of the American United States and of the European Settlements in America and the West-Indies* (4 vols., London, 1795).
9. Liston to Grenville, 25 June 1798, FO 5/22.
10. *Porcupine* (London), 30 October 1800.
11. Talleyrand, "Les États-Unis et L'Angleterre," p. 74; Alexander Baring, *An Inquiry into the Causes and Consequences of the Orders in Council; and an Examination of the Conduct of Great Britain Towards the Neutral Commerce of America* (London, 1808), pp. 19-20.
12. Norman S. Buck, *The Development of the Organization of Anglo-American Trade, 1800-1850* (New Haven, 1925), pp. 12-13, 114-15, and *passim*; Ralph W. Hidy, *The House of Baring in American Trade and Finance* (Norman S. B. Gras and Henrietta Larson, eds., *Harvard Studies in Business History*, XIV, Cambridge, 1949), p. 30; Harry E. Wildes, *Lonely Midas: The Story of Stephen Girard* (New York, 1943), pp. 152-57; John B. McMaster, *The Life and Times of Stephen Girard* (Philadelphia, 1918), I, 431-33.
13. Hidy, *House of Baring*, pp. 28-29; Margaret L. Brown, "William Bingham, Eighteenth Century Magnate," *Pennsylvania Magazine of History and Biography*,

LXI (1937), 419-24. The amusing Knox-Bingham correspondence on the sale will be found in Knox Papers, Massachusetts Historical Society, Vols. XXXVIII-XL.

14. Helen I. Cowan, *Charles Williamson* (Rochester Historical Society, *Publications*, XIX, Rochester, 1941), p. 202 and *passim*.

15. Vancouver to the Earl of Warwick, 23 June 1804, Harrowby MSS, Sandon, Staffordshire, transcript.

16. King to John Laurance, 26 February 1798, Rufus King Papers, New-York Historical Society, Vol. LXXXVII.

17. Memorandum of Baring, 26 December 1803, Gallatin Papers, New-York Historical Society. For the effect of the Jay treaty, see the *Times* (London), 13 March 1795. The house of Baring also handled the official business of the United States after the failure of the firm of Bird, Savage & Bird in 1803 caused loss not only to the United States government but also to John and John Quincy Adams (Samuel F. Bemis, *John Quincy Adams and the Foundations of American Foreign Policy* [New York, 1949], pp. 114-15; Hidy, *House of Baring*, pp. 32-33).

18. James O. Wettereau, "New Light on the First Bank of the United States," *Pennsylvania Magazine of History and Biography*, LXI (1937), 269, 275; Timothy Pitkin, *A Statistical View of the Commerce of the United States of America* (2nd ed., New York, 1817), p. 333. It was even reported that George III owned a substantial amount of United States bonds (*Independent Chronicle and the Universal Advertiser* [Boston], 23 April 1795).

19. Charles H. Evans, ed., "Exports, Domestic, from the United States to All Countries from 1789 to 1883, Inclusive," 48th Congress, 1st Session, *House of Representatives Miscellaneous Document 49*, Part 2 (Washington, 1884), p. 28; Thomas Ellison, *The Cotton Trade of Great Britain* (London, 1886), pp. 85-86.

20. Pitkin, *Statistical View*, p. 218.

21. King to John Marshall, 13 December 1800, King MSS, Vol. LIII.

22. John Debrett, ed., *The Parliamentary Register*, LXXIII (London, 1800), 48-49.

23. Pitkin, *Statistical View*, pp. 251, 254; Adam Seybert, *Statistical Annals* (Philadelphia, 1818), p. 155.

24. Sir Frederick M. Eden, *Eight Letters on the Peace and on the Commerce and Manufactures of Great Britain* (London, 1802), p. 83; Seybert, *Statistical Annals*, pp. 254, 286; C. Northcote Parkinson, Arthur C. Wardle, and Charles M. MacInnes, "The Seaports," C. Northcote Parkinson, ed., *The Trade Winds, A Study of British Overseas Trade During the French Wars, 1793-1815* (London, 1948), pp. 63, 67; Pitkin, *Statistical View*, p. 251.

25. David MacPherson, *Annals of Commerce*, IV (London, 1805), 489; Herbert Heaton, "Yorkshire Cloth Traders in the United States 1770-1840," *Thoresby Miscellany*, XXXVII, part 3 (Leeds, 1944), 226, 243-45.

26. Ostensibly, the balance of trade ran heavily against the United States, but official American figures are open to serious question on two counts. They are based on prices in ports of the United States, thus including freight charges on imports but not on exports, and they ignore the income American shipowners gained while carrying cargoes owned by British citizens. The American merchant marine earned an estimated thirty-two million dollars annually from 1795 to 1801, the largest share of the total in trade with British possessions. The profit from the sale of goods which wartime relaxation of the Navigation Laws permitted to be carried from foreign possessions directly to England is incalculable. Between them, however, these factors must have gone far to wipe out the theoretical trade deficit (Seybert, *Statistical Annals*, pp. 212, 219, 266, 268, 270, 280, and *passim*). For the competitive positions of the British and

14—27

American marines, see John MacGregor, *Commercial Statistics*, III (London, 1843), 800.

27. Ames to Timothy Pickering, 5 November 1799, Pickering Papers, Massachusetts Historical Society, Vol. XXV.

28. *Annual Register*, XXXVI (London, 1799), 256; John B. Holroyd, Earl of Sheffield, *Strictures on the Necessity of Inviolably Maintaining the Navigation and Colonial System* (London, 1804), p. 47; Herbert Heaton, "The American Trade," Parkinson, ed., *Trade Winds*, p. 213; H. M. Bird to King, 2 June 1801, King MSS, Vol. XXXIV; Gerald B. Hertz, *The Manchester Politician, 1750-1812* (London, 1912), pp. 27-28.

29. Cobbett to William Gifford, 4 November 1799, Chatham MSS, Vol. CXXIV.

30. Baring, *Inquiry*, pp. 4-5.

31. Dundas to Grenville,—October 1800, Walter Fitzpatrick, ed., *Report on the Manuscripts of J. B. Fortescue, Esq., Preserved at Dropmore* (Historical Manuscripts Commission), VI (London, 1908), 370.

32. *Cobbett's Annual Register*, II, 6 (30 June-10 July 1802).

33. George Dangerfield, *The Era of Good Feelings* (New York, 1952), p. 254.

34. *Anti-Jacobin Review*, XIII (1802), 311.

35. Sinclair to Washington, 10 September 1796, printed as a preface to Sir John Sinclair, ed., *Letters from His Excellency George Washington, President of the United States of America, to Sir John Sinclair* (London, 1800), pp. 14-15.

CHAPTER 2: EMPIRE AND REPUBLIC

1. Arthur Bryant, *The Years of Endurance, 1793-1802* (London, 1942).

2. George Rose to Auckland, 7 April 1795, Auckland MSS, Add. MSS 34453.

3. George III to Grenville, 9 February 1796, Bonamy Dobrée, ed., *The Letters of George III* (London, 1935), p. 223; George III to Pitt, 4 March 1797, Pretyman MSS, Vol. XI; memorandum of—1797 (April-May), King MSS, Vol. LXXIII.

4. J. Holland Rose, "The Struggle with Revolutionary France," Sir Adolphus W. Ward and George P. Gooch, eds., *The Cambridge of British Foreign Policy 1783-1919* (Cambridge, 1939), p. 219; Wilberforce's "Sketch of Pitt," Anna M. Wilberforce, ed., *Private Papers of William Wilberforce* (London, 1897), p. 62. See also Keith G. Feiling, *The Second Tory Party, 1714-1832* (London, 1938), pp. 165-66.

5. Grenville to Marquis of Buckingham, 7 March 1807, Philip H. Stanhope, Earl Stanhope, *Life of the Right Honourable William Pitt*, II (London, 1861), 122; Grenville to Buckingham, 28 April 1797, Richard P. T. N. B. C. Grenville, Duke of Buckingham and Chandos, *Memoirs of the Court and Cabinets of George III*, II (2nd ed., London, 1853), 376; George M. Trevelyan, *Lord Grey of the Reform Bill* (London, 1920), p. 131.

6. Boconnoc MSS, Autobiography, p. 32 (written in 1810); Grenville to Auckland, 19 May 1806, Auckland MSS, Add. MSS 34456; Giles S. H. F. Strangways, Earl of Ilchester, ed., *The Journal of Elizabeth, Lady Holland (1793-1811)* (London, 1908), II, 191 (12 December 1806).

7. Charles Abbot, Lord Colchester, ed., *The Diary and Correspondence of Charles Abbot, Lord Colchester* (London, 1861), I, 22 (December 1795).

8. King to Williamson, 16 May 1803, Boconnoc MSS, America 1793-1803.

9. *Morning Chronicle*, 3 June 1796.

10. George III to Pitt, 30 October 1795, Chatham MSS, Vol. CIV; Trevelyan, *Grey*, p. 94; Granville Leveson-Gower to Lady Stafford, 9 November 1797, Castalia R. Leveson-Gower, Countess Granville, ed., *Lord Granville Leveson-Gower (First Earl Granville), Private Correspondence, 1781-1821* (London, 1916), I, 182.

11. In the House of Commons, 21 January 1794, quoted in Walter Sichel, *Sheridan*

(London, 1909), I, 121.

12. Augustus J. Foster to Lady Foster, 30 June 1805, Vere Foster, ed., *The Two Duchesses* (London, 1898), p. 227.

13. Jay to Tench Coxe, 18 December 1794, Henry P. Johnston, ed., *The Correspondence and Public Papers of John Jay*, IV (New York, 1893), 153; Jay to Washington, 6 March 1795, *ibid.*, p. 168; Charles F. Adams, ed., *Memoirs of John Quincy Adams*, I (Boston, 1874), 137-38 (24 November 1795); King to Washington, 6 February 1797, Charles R. King, *The Life and Correspondence of Rufus King*, II (New York, 1895), 143-44.

14. Liston to Hammond, 10 December 1796, Liston Manuscripts, Scottish National Library, Edinburgh, Accession 720, Vol. XII.

15. A. F. Freire to Henrietta Liston, 4 July 1799, *ibid.*, Vol. XIII.

16. Maitland to Dundas, Private, 20 April 1799, War Office Papers, Public Record Office, WO 1/71.

17. King to Pickering, 11 October 1799, King MSS, Vol. LXV.

18. Grenville to Liston, Private, 18 February [1800], Liston MSS, Vol. XIII, misplaced at 1799; Liston to Grenville, 7 May 1800, FO 5/29A.

19. William Tatham to J. King, 19 April 1798, James B. Wilbur, *Ira Allen, Founder of Vermont* (Cambridge, 1928), II, 169.

20. [Benjamin F. Bache], *The Foul Charges of the Tories against the Editor of the Aurora* (Philadelphia, 1798), p. 65.

21. Memoirs of Sir Edward Thornton, MSS, Library of Congress.

22. Adams to Abigail Adams, 29 January 1795, Charles F. Adams, ed., *Letters of John Adams, Addressed to His Wife* (Boston, 1841), II, 176.

23. Worthington C. Ford, "John Adams," Allen Johnson, ed., *Dictionary of American Biography*, I (New York, 1928), 81.

24. Adams to Abigail Adams, 19 June 1795, Adams, ed., *Adams Letters to His Wife*, II, 185; Adams to Abigail Adams, 9 April 1796, *ibid.*, p. 217; Adams to Elbridge Gerry, 13 February 1797, Charles F. Adams, ed., *The Works of John Adams*, VIII (Boston, 1853), 522.

25. Joseph Fauchet to Commissioner of Foreign Relations, 4 February 1795, Frederick J. Turner, ed., *Correspondence of the French Ministers to the United States, 1791-1797* (American Historical Association, *Annual Report for 1903*, II, Washington, 1904), p. 562. See also [Vicomte de Noailles?] to Windham, 1 June [1793], Archibald P. Primrose, Earl of Rosebery, ed., *The Windham Papers* (London, 1913), I, 125-26; Jefferson to William B. Giles, 31 December 1795, Andrew A. Lipscomb, ed., *The Writings of Thomas Jefferson* (*Memorial Edition*, Washington, 1905), IX, 315-17.

26. Henrietta Liston to James Jackson, 14 July 1797, Liston MSS, Vol. XIII; Hammond to Grenville, 5 January 1795, FO 5/8; Edward H. Phillips, "The Public Career of Timothy Pickering, Federalist, 1745-1802" (Unpublished Ph.D. dissertation, Harvard University, 1950), pp. 143-44; Dearborn to Pickering, 18 August 1798, Pickering MSS, Vol. XXIII.

27. Adams to James Lloyd, 21 February 1815, Charles F. Adams, ed., *The Works of John Adams*, X (Boston, 1856), 127-28; Hamilton to Pickering, 8 June 1798, Henry C. Lodge, ed., *The Works of Alexander Hamilton* (*Federal Edition*, New York, 1904), X, 294.

28. Jefferson to Giles, 27 April 1795, Paul L. Ford, ed., *The Writings of Thomas Jefferson*, VII (New York, 1896), 11-12.

29. Jefferson to Peregrine Fitzhugh, 23 December 1798, *ibid.*, p. 211.

30. "Notes on the United States. By the Right Hon. Sir Augustus J. Foster, Bart.," *Quarterly Review* (London), LXVIII (1841), 44.

THE FIRST RAPPROCHEMENT

27—38

31. Jefferson to Thomas Pinckney, 29 May 1797, Ford., ed., *Writings of Jefferson*, VII, 129.
32. Jefferson to Monroe, 5 May 1793, Lipscomb, ed., *Writings of Jefferson*, IX, 75-76; Liston to Grenville, 29 January 1799, FO 5/25A; Marshall to King, 20 September 1800, *American State Papers. Class I. Foreign Relations*, II (Washington, 1832), 487.
33. "Balance of Europe," March 1802, Seth Ames, ed., *Works of Fisher Ames* (Boston, 1854), II, 233-34. "The true interests, & independence of this country require, that those rival nations should be balanced" (Charles Carroll to James McHenry, 4 November 1800, Bernard C. Steiner, *The Life and Correspondence of James McHenry* [Cleveland, 1907], p. 474).
34. Louis-Guillaume Otto, "Considérations sur la conduite du Gouvernement des États-Unis vers la France depuis 1789 jusqu'en 1797," June-July 1797, E. Wilson Lyon, "The Directory and the United States," *American Historical Review*, XLIII (1937-38), 520.
35. Jefferson to John Gibson, 13 February 1798, Jefferson Papers, Library of Congress, Vol. CII.

CHAPTER 3: AMERICA ACCEPTS THE TREATY

1. *Aurora [and] General Advertiser* (Philadelphia), 7 February 1795.
2. Blaney to Jay, 20 September 1795, George Pellew, *John Jay* (Cambridge, 1890), pp. 304-5. See also *Connecticut Courant*, 16 March 1795.
3. Hammond to Grenville, 28 June 1795, FO 5/9; Fauchet, La Forest, and Petry to Committee of Public Safety, 9 June 1795, Turner, ed., *Correspondence of French Ministers*, p. 709.
4. Butler to Madison, 12 June 1795, Madison Papers, Library of Congress, Vol. XVIII.
5. *Journal of the Executive Proceedings of the Senate of the United States*, I (Washington, 1828), 181-82. Except where otherwise noted, *ibid.*, pp. 181-86, provides information used in the following account of the Senate proceedings.
6. Ralston Hayden, *The Senate and Treaties, 1789-1817* (New York, 1920), p. 76.
7. Gallatin to Hannah M. Gallatin, 29 June 1795, Henry Adams, *The Life of Albert Gallatin* (Philadelphia, 1879), p. 151.
8. Adet to Committee of Public Safety, 25 June 1795, Turner, ed., *Correspondence of French Ministers*, p. 738.
9. Tazewell to Monroe, 27 June 1795, Monroe Papers, Library of Congress, Vol. III.
10. *Columbian Centinel* (Boston), 30 May 1795.
11. *Aurora*, 29 June 1795; Gallatin to Hannah M. Gallatin, 29 June 1795, Adams, *Gallatin*, p. 151; Bernard Faÿ, *The Two Franklins* (Boston, 1933), pp. 239-40. Adet claimed credit for publication of the treaty (Adet to Committee of Public Safety, 3 July 1795, Turner, ed., *Correspondence of French Ministers*, p. 742).
12. Ames to Wolcott, 9 July 1795, George Gibbs, ed., *Memoirs of the Administrations of Washington and John Adams, Edited from the Papers of Oliver Wolcott, Secretary of the Treasury* (New York, 1846), I, 210. For the town meeting, see *Independent Chronicle*, 13 July 1795; *Connecticut Courant*, 20 July 1795.
13. *Ibid.*; Cabot to King, 14 August 1795, King MSS, Vol. VI. See also Higginson to Pickering, 14 July 1795, Pickering MSS, Vol. XX; Higginson to Pickering, 13 August 1795, J. Franklin Jameson, ed., "Letters of Stephen Higginson, 1783-1804," American Historical Association, *Annual Report for 1896*, I (Washington, 1897), 789-90. See also *Columbian Centinel*, 1 and 5 August 1795.
14. Jefferson to Madison, 3 August 1795, Madison MSS, Vol. XVIII. See also *Connecticut Courant*, 27 July 1795; King to Gore, 24 July 1798, King MSS, Vol. VI.
15. Hammond to Grenville, 14 August 1795, FO 5/9; *Aurora*, 27 July 1795; *Connecti-*

cut Courant, 3 August 1795; Hammond to Grenville, 14 August 1795, FO 5/9. Much of the preceding description of the reception of the Jay treaty rests on John B. McMaster, *A History of the People of the United States*, II (New York, 1885), 212 ff.

16. Washington to Randolph, 22 July 1795, John C. Fitzpatrick, ed., *The Writings of George Washington*, XXXIV (Washington, 1940), 244.

17. Portland to Lords of the Admiralty, 24 April 1795, Admiralty Papers, Public Record Office, London, Admy 1/4164. The provision order was first reported in the *Columbian Centinel*, 30 June 1795. For its effect, see, e.g., Elias Vanderhorst to Randolph, 23 May 1795, 17 June 1795, 29 July 1795, Department of State, Consular Despatches, National Archives, Bristol, Vol. I; William Symons to William A. Deas, 14 July 1795, 4 August 1795, *ibid.*, Plymouth, Vol. I; Thomas Auldjo to Randolph, 18 July 1795, 23 August 1795, *ibid.*, Southampton, Vol. I; Robert W. Fox to Randolph, 9 June 1795, *ibid.*, Falmouth, Vol. I .

18. Earl Spencer to Captain Sidney Smith, [7 June 1795], Julian S. Corbett, ed., *Private Papers of George, second Earl Spencer*, I (*Navy Records Society Publications*, XLVI, London, 1913), 82.

19. *Aurora*, 25 June 1795; Randolph to Washington, 12 July 1795, Worthington C. Ford, ed., "Edmund Randolph on the British Treaty, 1795," *American Historical Review*, XII (1906-7), 590-99; Hammond to Grenville, 18 July 1795, FO 5/9; Hamilton to Wolcott, 10 August 1795, Hamilton Papers, Library of Congress, Vol. XXV. For Wolcott's argument that the provision order had no connection with the treaty, see Wolcott to Hamilton, 30 July 1795, *ibid.*

20. Moncure D. Conway, *Omitted Chapters in History Disclosed in the Life and Papers of Edmund Randolph* (New York, 1888), p. 270; Liston to Grenville, Private, 6 February 1800, Liston MSS, Vol. XXXV; William Sullivan, *The Public Men of the Revolution* (Philadelphia, 1847), p. 97; Grenville to Hammond, 9 May 1795, FO 5/9.

21. Pickering and Wolcott had some difficulty reading the French. The original dispatch is now in the Pickering MSS, as is Pickering's translation. The latter has many interlineations marked "Col°. A. Hamilton's corrections" (Pickering MSS, Vol. XLI).

22. "Mr. Jay's British Treaty," n. d. [1826?], Pickering MSS, Vol. XLVI; Conway, *Omitted Chapters*, pp. 270-71, 285-87; Pickering to Washington, Private, 31 July 1795, Pickering MSS, Vol. VI; Washington to Secretaries of State and War and (?) Attorney General, n. d. [August 1795], Fitzpatrick, ed., *Writings of Washington*, XXXIV, 275-76.

23. Pickering to Phineas Bond, 2 September 1795 [not sent], Pickering MSS, Vol. VI; Captain Rodham Home to Evan Nepean, 7 September 1795, Admy 1/493; Home to Admiral William Parker, 22 February 1796, enclosed in Lords of the Admiralty to Grenville, 8 June 1796, FO 5/16.

24. Hamilton to Washington, 5 November 1795, Lodge, ed., *Works of Hamilton*, X, 131-32; Higginson to Pickering, 30 December 1795, Charles W. Upham, *The Life of Timothy Pickering*, III (Boston, 1873), 252. See also Pickering to Hamilton, 17 November 1795, Pickering MSS, Vol. VI.

25. Pickering to J. Q. Adams, 25 August 1795, *ibid.*, Vol. XXXV. In actual fact, the provision order was revoked in September as food supplies increased (Grenville to Lords of the Admiralty, 9 September 1795, Admy 1/4165).

26. Deas to Pickering, 28 October 1795, King MSS, Vol. XLVIII. Deas' share in the exchange was his last important function at London. Soon afterwards, Lord Grenville let the United States know that, because of his intemperate protests against the provision order, he would never again be acceptable to His Majesty's Government as chargé d'affaires (Grenville to Liston, 18 March 1796, FO 5/14).

38—44

27. Portland to Dorchester, 15 January 1796, Brig.-Gen. Ernest A. Cruikshank, ed., *The Correspondence of Lieut. Governor John Graves Simcoe*, IV (Toronto, 1925), 170-71. See also Grenville to Bond, 18 January 1796, FO 115/5; Grenville to Liston, 18 March 1796, FO 5/14. The full Cabinet endorsed this policy (minute of Cabinet, 14 March 1796, FO 5/16).

28. Madison to [Dallas], 23 August 1795, Madison MSS, Vol. XVIII; Jefferson to Coxe, 10 September 1795, Jefferson MSS, Vol. XCIX; *Independent Chronicle*, 14 December 1795; Ames to Jeremiah Smith, 18 January 1796, Ames, ed., *Works of Ames*, I, 183; Jefferson to Madison, 21 September 1795, Jefferson MSS, Vol. XCIX. See also *Aurora*, 2 December 1795. As late as 1800 Republican journals were still scoffing at the verbosity of the *Camillus* letters (*ibid.*, 7 June 1800).

29. Pickering to J. Q. Adams, Private, 10 September 1795, Pickering MSS, Vol. VI; Pickering to Thomas Pinckney, Private, 24 September 1795, *ibid.*; King to Noah Webster, 20 December 1795, Emily E. F. Ford, ed., *Notes on the Life of Noah Webster* (New York, 1912), I, 403; Washington to Gouverneur Morris, 4 March 1796, Jared Sparks, *The Life of Gouverneur Morris* (Boston, 1832), III, 80; Adet to Commissioner of Foreign Relations, 30 January 1796, Turner, ed., *Correspondence of French Ministers*, pp. 823-24; Bond to Simcoe, 15 February 1796, Cruikshank, ed., *Correspondence of Simcoe*, IV, 194-95.

30. *Aurora*, 14 March 1796; Jefferson to Monroe, 21 March 1796, Monroe MSS, Vol. IV; James Winchester to McHenry, 22 April 1796, Bernard C. Steiner, ed., "Maryland Politics in 1796—McHenry Letters," Southern History Association, *Publications*, IX (1905), 376. See also Henry to Elizabeth Aylett, 20 August 1796, William W. Henry, *Patrick Henry* (New York, 1891), II, 569; *National Intelligencer, and Washington Advertiser*, 7 November 1800, where it is asserted that this struggle restored the constitutional position of the House. The succeeding description of the debate, except where otherwise noted, rests on the report printed in *Annals of the Congress of the United States, 4th Congress, 1st Session* (Washington, 1849), pp. 426-783, 940-1292.

31. "Remarks on the Jay treaty," 7 March 1796, Gallatin MSS; *Annals of Congress, 4th Congress, 1st Session*, pp. 487-95; Ames to Christopher Gore, 11 March 1796, Ames, ed., *Works of Ames*, I, 189; Madison to Jefferson, 13 March 1796, Madison MSS, Vol. XIX; *Annals of Congress, 4th Congress, 1st Session*, pp. 759-60.

32. James D. Richardson, ed., *Messages and Papers of the Presidents*, I (Washington, 1896), 194-96. See also Washington to Secretaries of State, Treasury, and War, and Attorney General, 25 March 1796, Fitzpatrick, ed., *Letters of Washington*, XXXIV, 505; *ibid.*, p. 505n; Hamilton to Washington, 25 and 28 March 1796, Hamilton MSS, Vol. XXVIII; Hamilton to King, 16 March 1796, King MSS, Vol. XXVIII.

33. *Annals of Congress, 4th Congress, 1st Session*, pp. 772-82; Irving Brant, *James Madison, Father of the Constitution, 1787-1800* (Indianapolis, 1950), pp. 436-37. See also *Aurora*, 1 April 1796.

34. Bond to Grenville, 31 March 1796, FO 5/13.

35. Alexander Addison to Gallatin, 7 April 1796, Gallatin MSS. See also John Johnston *et al.* to Gallatin, 21 March 1796, *ibid.*; John McMillen to Gallatin, 5 May 1796, *ibid.*; John Badollet to Gallatin, 18 May 1796, *ibid.*; *Pennsylvania Gazette* (Philadelphia), 23 March 1796.

36. John Marshall to Hamilton, 25 April 1796, Hamilton MSS, Vol. XXVIII.

37. *Columbian Centinel*, 23 April 1796. See also Hamilton to Wolcott, 20 April 1796, Lodge, ed., *Works of Hamilton*, X, 162; *Philadelphia Gazette*, 20 April and 4 May 1796; *Connecticut Courant*, 25 April and 2 May 1796; *Independent Chronicle*,

28 April 1796. Virtually every issue of the newspapers at this time contains an account of some meeting which endorsed the treaty.

38. Hamilton to Wolcott, 20 April 1796, Lodge, ed., *Works of Hamilton*, X, 162.

39. *Connecticut Courant*, 25 April 1796.

40. *Independent Chronicle*, 28 April 1796; *Aurora*, 19 April 1796. These Republican papers frequently printed accounts of protreaty meetings and petitions during this period.

41. *Annals of Congress, 4th Congress, 1st Session*, pp. 957-58.

42. Hamilton to King, 15 April 1796, Lodge, ed., *Works of Hamilton*, X, 157-60.

43. Ames, ed., *Works of Ames*, II, 37-71. For comment, see *Aurora*, 29 April 1796.

44. Muhlenberg not only was never reëlected to the House of Representatives, but a few days later he was attacked and stabbed by his brother-in-law. Paul A. W. Wallace, *The Muhlenbergs of Pennsylvania* (Philadelphia, 1950), pp. 285-86, 291; Liston to Grenville, 13 October 1796, FO 5/14. The Republicans claimed that if all absentees had been present the result would have been reversed (*Independent Chronicle*, 9 May 1796).

45. *Annals of Congress, 4th Congress, 1st Session*, p. 1291; Robert G. Harper to his constituents, 2 May 1796, Elizabeth Donnan, ed., *Papers of James A. Bayard, 1796-1815* (American Historical Association, *Annual Report for 1913*, II, Washington, 1915), pp. 21-22; Madison to Jefferson, 1 May 1796, Madison MSS, Vol. XIX. The treaty bill passed the Senate without difficulty and became law on the sixth of May (*Annals of Congress, 4th Congress, 1st Session*, pp. 77-78, 80; Bond to Liston, 9 May 1796, Liston MSS, Vol. XII).

46. Bond to Pickering, 26 March 1796, William R. Manning, ed., *Diplomatic Correspondence of the United States. Canadian Relations, 1784-1860*, I (Washington, 1940), 466-68; Bond to Grenville, 17 April 1796, FO 5/13; Hamilton to Wolcott, 20 April 1796, Hamilton MSS, Vol. XXVIII; Wolcott to Hamilton, 29 April 1796, *ibid.*

47. Bond to Grenville, 6 May 1796, FO 5/13; *Senate Executive Journal*, I, 207; Bond to Grenville, 9 May 1796, FO 5/13.

CHAPTER 4: 1796: NEW ENVOYS, NEW POLICIES

1. Jay to Grenville, Private, 22 November 1794, Boconnoc MSS, Hammond and Bond, 1791-97. For other statements of this nature, by men who were not enemies of an Anglo-American understanding, see Wolcott to Oliver Wolcott, Sr., 14 April 1794, Gibbs, ed., *Administrations of Washington and Adams*, I, 133; Sir John Temple to Pitt, 12 December 1795 [1794?], Chatham MSS, Vol. CLXXXII.

2. Grenville to Hammond, Private, 9 December 1794, Boconnoc MSS, America 1793-1803. Hammond apparently harbored no grudge against America; years later, he regretted that "during . . . my residence . . . I was necessarily . . . much engaged in hostile and irritating discussions" (Hammond to William Hamilton, 30 April 1814, Papers of George Hammond, Foxholm, Cobham, Surrey). Hammond's companion at the Foreign Office, George Canning, was also never known as a friend of the United States, but he too gave no indication of anti-American bias during this period. In fact, he twice expressed admiration for the American form of government, once praising it as, at least potentially, perhaps the finest in the world (Canning to Reverend John Sneyd, 12 December [1792], Josceline Bagot, ed., *George Canning and His Friends* [London, 1909], I, 37; Canning to Pitt, 7 December 1799, Chatham MSS, Vol. CXX). The Canning Papers are closed, and most of Hammond's correspondence has been lost, so any estimate of the opinions of these two men is necessarily tentative.

3. Jay to Grenville, 21 March 1795, Walter Fitzpatrick, ed., *Report on the Manuscripts of J. B. Fortescue, Esq., Preserved at Dropmore* (Historical Manu-

44—57

scripts Commission), III (London, 1899), 39; Grenville to Liston, 4 August 1795, Liston MSS, Vol. XII; Liston to Henry Cunningham, n. d., Beckles Willson, *Friendly Relations* (Boston, 1934), p. 19.

4. Liston to Grenville, 9 May 1796, FO 5/14.
5. Henrietta Liston to Jackson, 8 May 1796, Liston MSS, Vol. XII; Robert Troup to Williamson, 30[?] May 1796, Cowan, *Williamson*, p. 190.
6. Bond to Liston, 5 May 1796, Liston MSS, Vol. XII.
7. Thomas Pinckney to Pickering, 7 March 1796, Manning, ed., *Diplomatic Correspondence, Canadian Relations*, I, 465-66; William Smith to King, 2 April 1797, King, *King*, II, 165. For Adet's comment, see Adet to Foreign Minister, 31 March 1797, Turner, ed., *Correspondence of French Ministers*, p. 1005.
8. Pickering to Liston, 13 March 1798, Pickering MSS, Vol. VIII. In 1800, Pickering was taken in when Republican papers printed an intercepted letter written by Liston, distorting what was intended as sarcasm into an apparent claim that Britain ran the American government from the background. Pickering confessed that he had always had a much higher opinion of Liston than the letter appeared to justify (Pickering to Jacob Wagner, 12 June 1800, *ibid.*, Vol. XIII).
9. Liston to Coutts, 10 May 1796, Liston MSS, Vol. XII; Liston to Hammond, 31 May 1796, *ibid.*
10. Hamilton to Pickering, 10 May 1796, Pickering MSS, Vol. XX.
11. Grenville to King, Private, 29 March 1798, Boconnoc MSS, America 1793-1803; King to Grenville, Private, 30 March 1798, *ibid.*
12. Liston to Grenville, 3 July 1796, 13 August 1796, and 6 September 1796, FO 5/14.
13. Grenville to Bond, January 1796, FO 5/13; Thomas Pinckney to Grenville, 25 April 1796, FO 5/16; John King to Hammond, 2 May 1796, *ibid.*
14. Benjamin Moodie to George Miller, 14 May 1796, FO 5/15; Thomas MacDonough to Sir James Bland Burges, 12 January 1796, *ibid.*; Liston to Pickering, 29 June 1796, Department of State, Notes, Great Britain, Vol. II; Liston to Grenville, 3 July 1796, FO 5/14.
15. Bond to Grenville, 9 May 1796, FO 5/13; Dorchester to Liston, 6 June 1796, "Colonial Office Records," Michigan Pioneer and Historical Society, *Collections and Researches*, XXV (Lansing, 1896), 123.
16. Wayne to McHenry, 24 February 1796, "Selections from the McHenry Papers," *The Historical Magazine*, New Series, II (1867), 362. For details of the evacuation of Detroit, see Louise P. Kellogg, *The British Regime in Wisconsin and the Northwest* (Joseph L. Schafer, ed., *Publications of the State Historical Society of Wisconsin*, Madison, 1935), p. 234; Howard L. Osgood, "The British Evacuation of the United States," Rochester Historical Society, *Publication Fund Series*, VI (1927), 62; Charles B. Slocum, *The Ohio Country* (New York, 1910), p. 149. These works also describe transfer of the other posts.
17. Peter Russell to Portland, 20 August 1796, Brig.-Gen. Ernest A. Cruikshank and Andrew F. Hunter, eds., *The Correspondence of the Honourable Peter Russell*, I (Toronto, 1932), 28.
18. Wayne to Captain William Mayne, 3 October 1796, *ibid.*, p. 58.
19. *Columbian Centinel*, 3 August 1796 (for a good example of Republican scoffing, see *Independent Chronicle*, 11 August 1796); Pickering to King, 29 August 1796, Manning, ed., *Diplomatic Correspondence, Canadian Relations*, I, 100; Grenville to Liston, 7 October 1796, Liston MSS, Vol. XXXVI.
20. For a highly detailed discussion in which relevant documents are reproduced, see John B. Moore, ed., *International Adjudications, Modern Series*, I-II (New York, 1929-30).
21. Pickering to Washington, 20 May 1796, Pickering MSS, XXXVI. See also Knox to Pickering, Private, 14 April 1796, *ibid.*, Vol. XX.

22. Pickering to Hamilton, 28 March 1796, *ibid*, Vol. XXXVI.
23. Barclay to John Turner, 18 October 1796, George L. Rives, ed., *Selections from the Correspondence of Thomas Barclay* (New York, 1894), pp. 62-63.
24. Bond to Liston, 28 August 1796, Liston MSS, Vol. XII. Since the St. Croix commission operated in virtual isolation from the other diplomatic problems of the period, whereas the debt and seizure commissions formed an integral part of the broader story, the examination of its activities will be completed before the study of events in 1796 is resumed.
25. Barclay to Liston, 10 May 1798, Rives, ed., *Correspondence of Barclay*, pp. 83-86; Grenville to King, 5 February 1798, King MSS, Vol. LII; Grenville to King, 8 March 1798, FO 5/24; King to Pickering, 14 March 1798, King MSS, Vol. LII.
26. Pickering to Sullivan, 5 October 1798, Pickering MSS, Vol. IX. For British feelings, see Sir John Wentworth to Edward Winslow, 4 April 1798, William O. Raymond, ed., *Winslow Papers, A. D. 1776-1826* (St. John's, New Brunswick, 1901), p. 428; Grenville to Liston, 19 January 1799, FO 115/7.
27. Howell to Pickering, Confidential, 3 January 1799, *ibid.*, Vol. XXIV. See also Liston to Grenville, 6 November 1798, FO 5/22; Chipman to Dorchester, 29 October 1798, enclosed in John King to Hammond, 14 June 1799, FO 5/27.
28. Howell to Pickering, Confidential, 3 January 1799, Pickering MSS, Vol. XXIV.
29. Winslow to Edward G. Lutwyche, n. d. [1799], Raymond, ed., *Winslow Papers*, p. 436.
30. King to Pickering, 12 November 1796, King MSS, Vol. LI.
31. Macdonald and Rich to Grenville, 9 January 1797, FO 5/20.
32. Pinkney to McHenry, 21 March 1796, James McHenry MSS, Library of Congress, unnumbered volume of photostats. John B. Moore, ed., *International Adjudications, Modern Series*, Vol. IV (New York, 1931) describes the proceedings of the commission.
33. Grenville to Jay, 9 July 1796, Boconnoc MSS, Private Correspondence Sent 1796; Gore to Higginson, 5 July 1796, Pickering MSS, Vol. XX.
34. Bond to Grenville, 3 May 1796, FO 5/13; unsigned memorandum, n. d. [1796], *ibid.*
35. King's endorsement on Samuel Williams to King, 14 November 1800, King MSS, Vol. XLIII.
36. Trumbull to Nicholl, Anstey, Gore, and Pinkney, 26 August 1796, John Trumbull Letterbook, 1796-1802, New-York Historical Society.
37. King to Pickering, 26 February 1797, King MSS, Vol. LI. This dispatch is King's report on the entire affair.
38. Memorandum of 16 December 1796, *ibid.*, Vol. LXXIII.
39. King to Pickering, 26 February 1797, *ibid.*, Vol. LI.
40. Memorandum of 26 December 1796, *ibid.*, Vol. LXXIII.
41. In instructions handed to Liston before his departure, Grenville authorized him, if the treaty caused a clash between France and the United States, to declare that Britain would "make common Cause against an Attack which can be dictated by no other motive than by a desire, to prevent the Establishment of a good understanding between Great Britain and the United States" (Grenville to Liston, Secret, 18 March 1796, FO 5/14).
42. Morris to Washington, 19 December 1795, Anne C. Morris, ed., *The Diary and Letters of Gouverneur Morris* (New York, 1888), II, 143-44.
43. Monroe to Madison, 1 September 1796, Stanislaus M. Hamilton, ed., *The Writings of James Monroe, III* (New York, 1900), 52-53.
44. *Connecticut Courant*, 14 November 1796; *American State Papers. Class I. Foreign Relations*, I (Washington, 1833), p. 37. Some Republicans denied that the

57—71

French appeal had any connection with the election (*Aurora*, 16 and 18 November 1796).

45. *Morning Chronicle*, 9 and 11 November 1796.
46. *Sun*, 9 November 1796; *True Briton*, 10 November 1796.
47. *Times*, 11 November 1796.
48. Liston to Grenville, 17 November 1796, FO 5/14.
49. *Times*, 12 November 1796.
50. *Morning Chronicle*, 21 January 1797. The Opposition journals never completely and enthusiastically endorsed Jefferson.
51. Liston to Grenville, 18 March and 13 February 1797, FO 5/18. Cf. Adet: "Jefferson . . . is an American and, as such, he cannot be our sincere friend. An American is the born enemy of all European peoples" (Adet to Foreign Minister, 21 December 1796, Turner, ed., *Correspondence of French Ministers*, p. 983).

CHAPTER 5: THE PRESS GANGS

1. Captain Joseph Hammell to Nepean, 27 January 1799, Admy 1/1847.
2. Memorandum of 28 February 1803, John K. Laughton, ed., *Letters and Dispatches of Horatio, Viscount Nelson, K. B.* (London, 1886), p. 301.
3. Barclay to Grenville, 8 August 1799, FO 5/26.
4. Sir William Scott, quoted by James F. Zimmerman, *Impressment of American Seamen* (*Columbia University Studies in History, Economics and Public Law*, CXVIII, No. 1, New York, 1925), p. 20; Grenville to Thomas Pinckney, 16 June 1795, FO 5/16. In a private letter written in 1801, Jefferson stated a position which was the exact opposite of Britain's claims:

   The persons on board a vessel traversing the ocean, carry with them the laws of their nation, have among themselves a jurisdiction, a police, not established by their individual will, but by the authority of their nation, of whose territory their vessel still seems to compose a part, so long as it does not enter the exclusive territory of another (*Jefferson to Robert R. Livingston, 9 September 1801, Paul L. Ford, ed.,* The Writings of Thomas Jefferson, *VIII* [*New York, 1897*], 89-90).

   This principle did not, however, become official American policy at this time. It was stated by Daniel Webster to Lord Ashburton in 1842 (Zimmerman, *Impressment*, pp. 19-22). But Madison at least strongly stated the arguments in favor of this position in 1804 (Irving Brant, *James Madison, Secretary of State, 1801-1809* [Indianapolis, 1953], pp. 173-74, 256-58).
5. Endorsement on Lieutenant H. N. Nicholas to Nepean, 14 May 1800, Admy 1/3406.
6. Liston to Grenville, 30 August 1797, FO 5/18. A short time later, Liston reported that the United States had never asked the discharge of immigrants who came to America after 1783 (Liston to Grenville, 28 October 1797, *ibid.*). For a Republican protest against American acceptance of the indefeasible allegiance doctrine, see *Aurora*, 17 May 1795.
7. David Lenox to Nepean, 15 July 1797, Admy 1/3850. Of course appeals for release lagged far behind actual impressment. This fact does not, however, affect the inference that impressment was not a diplomatic problem of the first magnitude in the years before 1796. Pinckney appealed for the release of three men in 1793, eighteen in 1794, and eleven in 1795.
8. Liston to Grenville, 6 September 1796, FO 5/14.
9. *Independent Chronicle*, 17 March 1796.
10. *Annals of Congress, 4th Congress, 1st Session*, pp. 104-5, 802-20; Zimmerman, *Impressment*, pp. 56-60.
11. Grenville to King, 3 November 1796, King MSS, Vol. LI. See also Grenville to Pinckney, 13 July 1796, FO 5/16.

12. Grenville to Lords of the Admiralty, 28 August 1797, Admy 1/4173.
13. Pickering to Talbot, 31 August 1796, Pickering MSS, Vol. XXXVI.
14. Parker to Talbot, 12 October 1796, Department of State, Consular Despatches, Kingston, Jamaica, Vol. I. This volume, and Pickering's report to Congress, *Annals of Congress, 5th Congress, 3rd Session* (Washington, 1851), pp. 3294-3308, are the chief sources of information on Talbot's mission.
15. Talbot to Pickering, 22 April and 29 May 1797, Department of State, Consular Despatches, Kingston, Vol. I.
16. Parker to Captains of H. M. Ships, 8 May 1797, *ibid.*; Parker to Talbot, 3 March 1797, *ibid.*
17. Talbot to Pickering, 4 July 1797, *ibid.*
18. Savage to Pickering, 1 November 1800, *ibid.* See also a statement by Savage, *National Intelligencer,* 7 August 1801.
19. King to Pickering, 26 June 1797, King MSS, Vol. LI; Zimmerman, *Impressment,* pp. 71-73; Lenox to Pickering, 13 December 1797 and 1 March 1798, Department of State, Consular Despatches, London, Vol. VIII.
20. "Reply to the Appeal of the Massachusetts Federalists," Henry Adams, ed., *Documents Relating to New-England Federalism, 1800-1815* (Boston, 1877), p. 179.
21. The chart is dated 15 September 1801 (King MSS, Vol. XXXV).

Original applications		2059
Renewed applications		159
		——
TOTAL APPLICATIONS		2218
Discharged	464	
Ordered discharged	578	
	——	
Total discharged or to be discharged		1042
Insufficient proof		624
Accepted King's Bounty		201
Proved British subjects		102
Miscellaneous, denied		249
		——
TOTAL CASES		2218

   For the huge applications mentioned above, see Lenox to Nepean, 15 July 1797, Admy 1/3850; Lenox to Nepean, 23 October 1801, Admy 1/3852.
22. King to Pickering, 16 October 1796, King MSS, Vol. LI.
23. Projet enclosed in Grenville to Liston, 5 July 1797, FO 115/5.
24. Grenville to Liston, 9 January 1798, FO 5/22. For Liston's reports on Federalist feeling, see Liston to Grenville, 3 and 28 October 1797, FO 5/18.
25. Liston to Grenville, 30 May 1800, and enclosure, FO 5/29A.
26. Liston to Grenville, 15 August 1800, *ibid.*; Marshall to King, 20 September 1800, Department of State, Instructions to Ministers, Vol. V.

CHAPTER 6: MERCHANTMEN AND MERCHANT COMMERCE

1. D. Hunter Miller, ed., *Treaties and Other International Acts of the United States of America,* II (Washington, 1931), 255-56. Two valuable studies of the whole subject of American trade with India are Holden Furber, "The Beginnings of American Trade with India, 1784-1812," *New England Quarterly,* XI (1938), 235-65, and Wilson H. Elkins, "British Policy in Its Relation to the Commerce and Navigation of the United States of America from 1794 to 1807" (Unpublished Oxford University thesis, 1936), pp. 49-92, 144-72.
2. *Morning Chronicle,* 18 August 1795.

71—83

3. Cyril H. Phillips, *The East India Company, 1784-1834* (*University of Manchester Publications*, CCLXX, Manchester, 1940), pp. 82-83.
4. Dundas to Hugh Inglis, 14 June 1797, India Office, Home Series, Miscellaneous, Commonwealth Relations Office, Vol. CCCXXXVII.
5. William Fawkener to Board of Control, 9 May 1797, *ibid.*, Vol. CDXXXIX.
6. Decision in *Wilson* v. *Marryat*, filed in *ibid.*, Vol. CCCXXXVII. A preliminary decision in the Court of King's Bench had already upheld the right of American ships to go indirectly to India, but the *Argonaut* was not freed because she sailed from America before the treaty was ratified (*Times*, 13 June 1798). For Grenville's opinion, see Grenville to Loughborough, 23 November 1797, FO 5/21.
7. Elkins, "British Policy", pp. 72-74.
8. Grenville memorandum of 6 November 1799, India Office, Home Miscellaneous, Vol. CCCXXXVII; Dundas to Grenville, 10 November 1799, *ibid.*; Dundas to Grenville, "Sunday Morning," [12 or 19 October 1800], Boconnoc MSS, Dundas 1799-1801.
9. Memorandum of G. Udny, 15 September 1800, Robert R. Pearce, ed., *Memoirs and Correspondence of the Most Noble Richard Marquess Wellesley* (London, 1846), I, 396-406; Wellesley to Court of Directors, 30 September 1800, Wellesley MSS, British Museum (Add. MSS 12564-13915, 37274-37318), Add. MSS 13447; Philips, *East India Company*, p. 106; Furber, "Beginnings of American Trade," pp. 248 and 248n-49n.
10. *Independent Chronicle*, 10 October 1796.
11. These figures are adapted from Elkins, "British Policy," p. 70.
12. Lowell J. Ragatz, *The Fall of the Planter Class in the British Caribbean* (New York, 1928), p. 231.
13. Elkins, "British Policy," pp. 93-96; S. Cock, *An Answer to Lord Sheffield's Pamphlet on the Subject of the Navigation System* (London, 1804), Table B.
14. Circular to Governors in the West Indies, 1 July 1799, Colonial Office Papers, Public Record Office, CO 5/267. This order reinforces the order of 9 December 1796, which is not preserved in this volume.
15. Pitkin, *Statistical View*, p. 167. See also Elkins, "British Policy," pp. 97-103; Ragatz, *Fall of the Planter Class*, pp. 234-35.
16. Harold A. Innis, *The Cod Fisheries* (James T. Shotwell, ed., *The Relations of Canada and the United States*, New Haven, 1940), p. 221; *Journals of the House of Commons*, LXI (1806), 713-15.
17. Pickering to King, 8 June 1796, Pickering MSS, Vol. XXXVI.
18. Board of Trade Minutes, 1793-1805, Public Record Office, BT 5/11, 17-19 (15 November 1795); *Journals of the House of Commons*, LIV (1798-99), 69; *ibid.*, LV (1800), 357-451, *passim*; Holroyd, *Strictures*, pp. 5-10; William E. Lingelbach, "England and Neutral Trade," *Military Historian & Economist*, II (1917), 156.
19. Dundas' memorandum of 11 January 1801, Pretyman MSS, Vol. XV.
20. Miller, ed., *Treaties*, II, 257-58.
21. King to Pickering, 13 April 1797, King MSS, Vol. LI; King to Grenville, Private, 9 May 1797, FO 5/20. For the Board's calculations, see BT 5/10, *passim*.
22. King to Grenville, 21 May 1797, King MSS, Vol. LI; King to Grenville, 24 May 1797, FO 5/20; King to Grenville, 1 June 1797, FO 5/21; King to Canning, 8 June 1797, *ibid.*; King to Pickering, 12 June 1797, King MSS, Vol. LI.
23. King to Pickering, 4 July 1797, *ibid.*
24. *Oracle and Public Advertiser* (London), 31 May 1797.
25. *True Briton*, 1 June 1797; John Debrett, ed., *Parliamentary Register*, LXIV (London, 1797), 666-67; *Journals of the House of Commons*, LII (1797), 529-690, *passim*; Grenville to King, 21 June 1797, FO 5/21.

26. Jefferson to Madison, 22 February 1798, Madison MSS, Vol. XX. See also *Aurora,* 28 February and 3 November 1798.
27. King to Pickering 17 March 1798, King MSS, Vol. VII.
28. King to Pickering, 1 June 1798, *ibid.,* Vol. LII. See also Boconnoc MSS, Minute Book, May 1798 (25 May 1798).
29. Rose to King, Private, 22 June 1798, King MSS, Vol. LII.
30. King to Pickering, 23 June 1798, *ibid.;* footnote to memorandum of 25 May 1798, *ibid.,* Vol. LXXIII.
31. *Columbian Centinel,* 22 September 1798.
32. MacPherson, *Annals of Commerce,* IV, 333, 369, 400, 439, 467, 492, 505.
33. Pitkin, *Statistical View,* p. 201; MacPherson, *Annals of Commerce,* IV, 332, 370, 399, 438, 466, 491, 536.
34. Rose to King, Private, 22 June 1798, King MSS, Vol. LII.

CHAPTER 7: BRITANNIA'S RULE OF THE WAVES

1. Anne Fremantle, ed., *The Wynne Diaries,* II (London, 1937), 166 (5 February 1796).
2. *Aurora,* 21 May 1794.
3. Washington to Morris, 22 December 1795, Fitzpatrick, ed., *Writings of Washington,* XXXIV, 399; J. Q. Adams to King, 3 October 1796, Worthington C. Ford, ed., *Writings of John Quincy Adams,* II (New York, 1913), 33.
4. Pickering to Edward Stevens, 5 September 1799, Pickering MSS, Vol. XII.
5. Thornton to Hawkesbury, 10 August 1801, FO 5/32.
6. In a perspicacious study, a Danish historian has emphasized the mercantilist aspects of the policies of the belligerents, pointing out that both frequently permitted violation of general principles in the interest of commercial gain (Eli F. Heckscher, *The Continental System: An Economic Interpretation* [Oxford, 1922], pp. 33-42 and *passim*).
7. *Ibid., p.* 103; Victor S. Clark, *History of Manufactures in the United States, 1607-1860* (Carnegie Institution of Washington, *Publication No. 215B,* Washington, 1916), pp. 238, 245.
8. George Vandeput to Nepean, 6 December 1797, Admy 1/494; Pickering to Hamilton, 9 June 1798, John C. Hamilton, ed., *The Works of Alexander Hamilton,* VI (New York, 1851), 303-4.
9. *Maryland Gazette* (Annapolis), 12 May 1796.
10. "An ACCOUNT . . . of the Several APPEALS against DECREES concerning Ships and Goods claimed by NEUTRALS . . . ," *Parliamentary Papers, 1801,* V, 227-305. The statements in this and the following paragraph are based on a careful examination of this document and "An ACCOUNT . . . of the Several APPEALS against DECREES condemning Ships and Goods claimed by NEUTRALS . . . ,"*ibid.,* pp. 379-419, a list of cases still to be heard by the High Court of Appeals. See Appendix.
11. Auckland to [Earl of Chatham?], Private, 18 September 1797, Auckland MSS, Add. MSS 34454.
12. Hawkesbury memorandum on Grenville's "Projet of Heads of Proposals to be made to Mr. Jay," n. d. [1794], Liverpool MSS, Add. MSS 38354.
13. Pickering to King, Private, 6 February 1799, Pickering MSS, Vol. X; King to Hammond, 14 September 1799, King MSS, Vol. LIII; King to Grenville, 18 November 1799, FO 5/28; Marshall to King, 20 September 1800, Department of State, Instructions to Ministers, Vol. V.
14. Pickering to King, 11 May 1799, Pickering MSS, Vol. XI; Marshall to King,

83—97

20 September 1800, Department of State, Instructions to Ministers, Vol. V; King to Madison, 10 May 1803, King MSS, Vol. LV.

15. Liston to Grenville, 3 July 1796, FO 5/14; Nelson to Addington, 27 May 1801, Laughton, ed., *Letters and Dispatches of Nelson*, p. 278.

16. Grenville to Lords of the Admiralty, 23 November 1799, FO 95/358; Christopher Robinson, ed., *Reports of Cases Argued and Determined in the High Court of Admiralty*, I (London, 1799), 334; King to Hawkesbury, 18 August 1801, FO 5/34; King to Madison, 23 December 1801, King MSS, Vol. LIV.

17. King to Marshall, 19 May 1801, *ibid.*

18. Grenville to Portland, 9 November 1794, Fitzpatrick, ed., *Dropmore MSS*, III, 533; Lords of the Admiralty to Portland, 28 April 1795, enclosed in J. King to George Aust, 11 May 1795, FO 5/12; Grenville to Jay, 11 May 1795, Boconnoc MSS, America 1793-1805.

19. Pickering to King, 5 December 1797, Pickering MSS, Vol. XXXVII. For the British response, see J. King to King, 9 April 1798, King MSS, Vol. VII. See also *Maryland Gazette*, 8 October 1798.

20. St. Vincent to Erskine, 13 March 1801, David B. Smith, ed., *Letters of Admiral of the Fleet the Earl of St. Vincent whilst First Lord of the Admiralty*, I (*Navy Records Society Publications*, LV, London, 1921), 290; Scott to King, 19 April and 21 May 1801, King MSS, Vol. LIV.

21. John Debrett, ed., *The Parliamentary Register*, LXXVII (London, 1802), 176-83.

22. G. W. Jordan to Hawkesbury, 14 May 1801, FO 5/34; Jefferson to John Breckenridge, 29 July 1801, Jefferson MSS, Vol. CXV; Thornton to Hawkesbury, 10 August 1801, FO 5/32.

23. St. Vincent to Nelson, Secret, 21 January 1801, St. Vincent MSS, British Museum (Add. MSS 31158-31193), Add. MSS 31167; *Morning Chronicle*, 20 January 1801.

24. King to Grenville, 6 September 1798, FO 5/24; Grenville to Loughborough, 11 October 1798, Boconnoc MSS, Cabinet 1784-1801; King to Pickering, 6 and 16 October 1798, King MSS, Vol. LII. For a complaint that Marriott compounded incapacity with harshness, see *Independent Chronicle*, 31 October 1796.

25. Cecilia A. Baring, ed., *The Diary of the Right Hon. William Windham* (London, 1866), p. 386 (11 January 1798).

26. Anna C. Clauder, *American Commerce as Affected by the Wars of the French Revolution and Napoleon, 1793-1810* (Philadelphia, 1932), [p. 9]; Lingelbach, "England and Neutral Trade," p. 156; Baring, ed., *Diary of Windham*, p. 382 (30 November 1797); W. Alison Phillips and Arthur H. Reede, *Neutrality, Its History, Economics and Law*, II (New York, 1936), 117. For trade with enemy areas, see sources cited above, n 18, chap. 6.

27. Robert G. Albion, "Maritime Adventures in New York in the Napoleonic Era," *Essays in Modern English History in Honor of Wilbur Cortez Abbot* (Cambridge, 1941), p. 318; Herbert W. Briggs, *The Doctrine of Continuous Voyage* (*Johns Hopkins University Studies in Historical and Political Science*, Series XLIV, No. 2, Baltimore, 1926), p. 18.

28. Chatham to Pitt, 20 May 1799, Pretyman MSS, Vol. XIII.

29. For Scott's decision, see Christopher Robinson, ed., *Reports of Cases Argued and Determined in the High Court of Admiralty*, II (London, 1801), 194-206.

30. Case of the *Polly*, *ibid.*, pp. 361-72.

31. Nichol to Grenville, 28 July 1800, enclosed in Grenville to Lords of the Admiralty, 4 August 1800, Admy 1/4184.

32. Report of the King's Advocate, 16 March 1801, enclosed in J. King to Hammond, 31 March 1801, FO 5/34. This was not quite an accurate paraphrase of Scott's decision.

33. *Connecticut Courant*, 18 July 1796; *Independent Chronicle*, 10 October 1796; Hamilton to King, 15 February 1797, King MSS, Vol. XLI. For Republican arguments that American toleration of British outrages forced France to retaliate, see *Aurora*, 7 and 9 March 1798.
34. Grenville to Liston, 15 January 1798, FO 5/22. For provisions of the French decrees, see Clauder, *American Commerce*, [p. 11].
35. Pickering to J. Q. Adams, Private, 26 May 1798, Pickering MSS, Vol. VIII.
36. Jay to Grenville, 22 November 1794, Boconnoc MSS, America 1793-1803.

CHAPTER 8: FOES OF FRANCE

1. Henrietta Liston to Jackson, 8 April 1797, Liston MSS, Vol. XIII; Liston to Hammond, 19 April 1797, *ibid.*, Vol. XXXV.
2. Liston to Grenville, 13 July 1797, FO 5/18.
3. Grenville to Liston, 15 January 1798, FO 5/22.
4. Harper to constituents, 9 March 1798, Donnan, ed., *Papers of Bayard*, p. 51; Jonathan Mason, Jr., to Harrison G. Otis, 30 March 1798, Samuel E. Morison, *The Life and Letters of Harrison Gray Otis* (Boston, 1913), I, 93.
5. *Aurora*, 6 April 1798; *Independent Chronicle*, 12 April 1798; *Connecticut Courant*, 19 November 1798; *Independent Chronicle*, 10 May 1798.
6. Henrietta Liston to Jackson, 3 May 1798, Liston MSS, Vol. XIII; Liston to Grenville, 2 May 1798, FO 5/22.
7. William E. H. Lecky, *A History of England in the Eighteenth Century*, VIII (London, 1890), 125-28; memorandum of May 1798, King MSS, Vol. LXXIII.
8. *Morning Chronicle*, 15 and 18 May 1798; *The Anti-Jacobin; or, Weekly Examiner* (London), p. 216 (14 May 1798) ; *Times*, 16 May 1798
9. Memorandum of 25 May 1798, Boconnoc MSS, Minute Book May 1798; memorandum of 24 January 1798, King MSS, Vol. LXXIII.
10. J. Bartlet Brebner, *North Atlantic Triangle* (James T. Shotwell, ed., *The Relations of Canada and the United States*, New Haven, 1945), p. 72.
11. Liston to Grenville, 12 June 1798, FO 5/22.
12. Liston to Pickering, 10 September 1798, Department of State, Notes, Great Britain, Vol. II. Portland ordered the transfer of the cannon before it became known in London that Edward had handed them over (Portland to Wentworth, 3 September 1798, Douglas Brymner, ed., "Calendar of Papers relating to Nova Scotia," *Report on Canadian Archives for 1894* [Ottawa, 1895], p. 549).
13. Pickering to Adams, 14 September 1798, Pickering MSS, Vol. XXXVII.
14. Grenville to Liston, 8 June 1798, FO 5/22.
15. Stephen Cottrell to King, 19 May 1798, King MSS, Vol. VII; Thomas Dickinson & Co. to King, 19 September 1798, *ibid.*; John & Francis Baring & Co. to King, 15 November 1798, *ibid.*, Vol. XXXIX; Dudley W. Knox, ed., *Naval Documents Related to the Quasi-War Between the United States and France*, II (Washington, 1935), 147-97; Maury to King, 4 October 1798, Department of State, Consular Despatches, Liverpool, Vol. I.
16. King to Wolcott, 5 November 1798, King MSS, Vol. LII. Weaver to King, 20 May 1800, *ibid.*, Vol. LIII, states that sixteen thousand stand of arms were transferred under this agreement.
17. Cottrell to King, 20 December 1798, *ibid.*, Vol. VII.
18. [Richard Alsop, Lemuel Hopkins, Theodore Dwight], *The Political Green-House, for the Year 1798* (Hartford, 1799), p. 24.
19. *Sun*, 16 August 1798.
20. Grenville to Liston, 27 January 1797, FO 5/18; Liston to Grenville, 18 April 1797, *ibid.*

97—109

21. Nepean to Canning, 31 May 1797, FO 5/20.
22. Grenville to Lords of the Admiralty, 8 February 1798, Admy 1/4175; King to consuls, 13 February 1798, King MSS, Vol. LII; Lords of the Admiralty to Captain Francis Pender, 23 February 1798, Admy 2/1099. See also *Maryland Gazette*, 19 April 1798.
23. Cabot to King, 21 March 1798, King MSS, Vol. XLI.
24. This paragraph is based on Admiralty records, particularly Admy 2/1099-1100, devoted exclusively to convoys, and in-letters from admirals, with their endorsements, in Admy 1 series, searched with the aid of Ind series. There is some further information in Dudley W. Knox, ed., *Naval Documents Related to the Quasi-War Between the United States and France* (7 vols., Washington, 1935-38) and in American consular dispatches. For the purported order of Vandeput, see Admiral Sir William Parker to Nepean, 23 August 1800, extract, enclosed in Lords of the Admiralty to Grenville, 23 September 1800, FO 5/31. For a Republican hint that Britain hoped, by extending convoy protection, to inveigle the United States into "one more treaty—a treaty of exclusive commerce, and of alliance offensive and defensive," see *Aurora*, 3 November 1798.
25. Liston to Grenville, 2 April 1799, FO 5/25A.
26. Benjamin Stoddert to Murray, 21 September 1798, Dudley W. Knox, ed., *Naval Documents Related to the Quasi-War Between the United States and France*, I (Washington, 1935), 433. For the stations of the American navy, see Gardner W. Allen, *Our Naval War with France* (Boston, 1909), *passim*.
27. Pickering to Liston, 18 July 1798, Pickering MSS, Vol. IX; Vandeput to Nepean, 9 November 1798, Admy 1/494.
28. *Independent Chronicle*, 1 July 1799, quoting *Aurora*.
29. King to Pickering, 15 March 1799, King MSS, Vol. LIII; Alan C. Appel, "The Undeclared Naval War Between France and the United States, 1798-1801" (Unpublished Senior thesis, Princeton University, 1941), pp. 53-56, 69; *Columbian Centinel*, 30 January 1799.
30. Liston to Grenville, 16 March 1797, FO 5/18. See also Liston to Grenville, 13 February 1797, *ibid*.
31. Grenville to Liston, 8 April 1797, FO 115/5.
32. Liston to Pickering, 2 July 1797, *American State Papers, Foreign Relations*, II, 71; Richardson, ed., *Messages and Papers*, I, 248.
33. Liston to Pickering, 15 July 1797, Department of State, Notes, Great Britain, Vol. II.
34. Monroe to Pickering, 21 September 1796, Manning, ed., *Diplomatic Correspondence, Canadian Relations*, I, 477.
35. Liston to Grenville, 6 May 1799, FO 5/25A; P. Selby to Russell, 23 January 1799, Michigan Pioneer and Historical Society, *Collections*, XXV, 185.
36. Liston to Grenville, 25 January 1797, FO 5/18.
37. Pickering to King, 20 June 1797, King MSS, Vol. XLV. Anglophobes claimed that McLean's sentence—to be hanged, drawn, and quartered—was more cruel than oriental punishments (*Independent Chronicle*, 7 August 1797).
38. Thornton to Grenville, 9 February 1801, FO 5/32.
39. Pickering to King, and Pickering to King, Private, 6 April 1796, King MSS, Vol. XLV; Pickering to King, 16 June 1797, *ibid*. For the most detailed account of this affair, though heavily biased in Allen's favor, see Wilbur, *Allen*, Vol. II, *passim*.
40. Grenville to Liston, 9 May 1800, FO 115/8. For the Bowles episode, see Arthur P. Whitaker, *The Mississippi Question, 1795-1803* (New York, 1934), pp. 162-75. When Bowles fell into Spanish hands in 1803, William Cobbett bitterly attacked

the Pitt government for failing to support the former and thus obtain "possession of that country, which France has now made the means of striking a mortal blow at our connexion with the United States of America" (*Cobbett's Annual Register*, IV, 447-48 [24 September 1803]). See also Liston to Grenville, 13 December 1799, FO 5/25A; Windham MSS, Add. MSS 37878, *passim*.

41. Morris, ed., *Diary and Letters of Morris*, II, 102 (14 July 1795).
42. Burges to Grenville, 28 June 1795, Boconnoc MSS, Sir J. Burges 1791-1794.
43. [Morris] to Grenville, 5 October 1796, Fitzpatrick, ed., *Dropmore MSS*, III, 258; [Morris] to Grenville, 6 November 1796, *ibid.*, p. 266.
44. J. Q. Adams to Adams, 31 January 1798, Ford, ed., *Writings of John Quincy Adams*, II, 251-52.
45. King to Murray, 16 August 1798, Fitzpatrick, ed., *Dropmore* MSS, IV, 365; Grenville to King, Private, 6 November 1798, Boconnoc MSS, America 1798-1803. The deciphered dispatches are to be found in America 1780-1841, Deciphers of Diplomatic Papers, LI, British Museum, Add. MSS 32303.
46. Simcoe to Portland, 20 December 1794, Brig.-Gen. Ernest A. Cruikshank, ed., *The Correspondence of Lieut. Governor John Graves Simcoe*, III (Toronto, 1925), 233.

CHAPTER 9: TOUSSAINT, MIRANDA, ALLIANCE

1. Dundas to Grenville, 8 November 1797, Fitzpatrick, ed., *Dropmore MSS*, III, 390-91.
2. Liston to Grenville, Confidential, 12 June 1798, and endorsement, FO 5/22; King to Pickering, 14 July 1798, King MSS, Vol. LII. During a summer visit to Braintree, Liston soon learned that the President himself shared Pickering's views (Liston to Grenville, 27 September 1798, FO 5/22).
3. Secret Conventions, 31 August 1798, WO 1/70. This document has been published, translated from the French, by a close student of the whole question: Rayford W. Logan, *The Diplomatic Relations of the United States with Haiti, 1776-1891* (Chapel Hill, 1941), pp. 65-66.
4. King to Grenville, 1 December 1798, Boconnoc MSS, America 1793-1803.
5. Dundas to King, 9 December 1798, enclosed in Grenville to Liston, 11 December 1798, FO 115/6. See also memorandum of 6 December 1798, King MSS, Vol. LXXIII; King to Dundas, 8 December 1798, *ibid.*, Vol. XLIV.
6. Grenville to King, 9 January 1799, and enclosures, Boconnoc MSS, America 1793-1803.
7. Memorandum of 10 January 1799, King MSS, Vol. LXXIII; King to Pickering, 10 January 1799, *ibid.*, Vol. LIII.
8. Dundas to Maitland, Secret, 26 January 1799, WO 1/71. Similar instructions were sent to Liston, who was ordered to coöperate with Maitland (Grenville to Liston, 19 January 1799, FO 115/7).
9. Pickering to Jacob Mayer, Private, 30 November 1798, Department of State, Consular Despatches, Cape Haytien, Vol. I.
10. Liston to Grenville, 18 February 1799, FO 5/25A. See also Liston to Grenville, 31 January 1799, *ibid.*
11. *Columbian Centinel*, 13 February 1799.
12. "Heads of Regulations to be proposed by Brigadier General Maitland to General Toussaint, to be established by the authority of the latter; and to which it is understood that the American Government will assent," and "Points on which there is an understanding between the Government of Great Britain and the United States of America, in consequence of the foregoing proposed regulations,"

20 April 1799, Department of State, Consular Despatches, Cape Haytien, Vol. I.
13. Liston to Grenville, 20 April 1799, FO 5/25A.
14. Maitland to Grenville, 20 April 1799, *ibid.;* Maitland to Dundas, 20 April 1799, WO 1/71.
15. Pickering to Stevens, 20 April 1799, Department of State, Consular Despatches, Cape Haytien, Vol. I.
16. Stevens to Pickering, 23 June 1799, *ibid.* This letter describes the entire negotiations. Pickering approved Stevens' action and ordered him to show Toussaint that he must cultivate better relations with England (Pickering to Stevens, 5 September 1799, Dudley W. Knox, ed., *Naval Documents Related to the Quasi-War Between the United States and France,* IV [Washington, 1936], 157-58).
17. These arose primarily out of Britain's unwillingness to see Toussaint achieve a complete victory over his mulatto rival, Rigaud, and Edward Stevens' issue of passports to ships owned by residents of Santo Domingo, a plain violation of the Anglo-American agreement. See Logan, *Diplomatic Relations with Haiti,* pp. 104-5; Dundas to Grenville, 23 January [1800], Boconnoc MSS, Dundas 1799-1801; Liston to Grenville, 4 November 1800, FO 5/29A.
18. King to Hamilton, 31 July 1798, King MSS, Vol. XLIV. The standard treatment of Miranda's career is William S. Robertson, *The Life of Miranda* (2 vols., Chapel Hill, 1929). For Hamiltonian references to Latin America, see, e. g., Hamilton to Gunn, 22 December 1798, John C. Hamilton, ed., *The Works of Alexander Hamilton,* V (New York, 1851), 184; Hamilton to McHenry, 27 June 1799, Lodge, ed., *Works of Hamilton,* VII, 97. An interesting consideration of one aspect of this question is Marshall Smelser, "George Washington Declines the Part of El Libertador," *William and Mary Quarterly,* Third Series, XI (1954), 42-51.
19. King to Pickering, 26 February 1798, King MSS, Vol. LII.
20. Memorandum of Dundas to Cabinet, 2 October 1799, and Grenville's endorsement, Charles W. Vane, Marquess of Londonderry, ed., *Memoirs and Correspondence of Viscount Castlereagh, Second Marquess of Londonderry,* VII (London, 1851), 284-85; memorandum of 5 October 1799, Windham MSS, Add. MSS 37878.
21. Adams to Pickering, 3 October 1798, Pickering MSS, Vol. XXIII; Adams to James Lloyd, 29 March 1815, Adams, ed., *Works of Adams,* X, 148-49.
22. Hamilton to Miranda, 22 August 1798, Hamilton MSS, Vol. XXXII. Among those who did not feel this way was Adams' son-in-law, William Stephens Smith, who provided financial backing for Miranda's ill-fated expedition in 1806. The ex-president's grandson, William Steuben Smith, actually sailed with the filibusterers.
23. *Cobbett's Annual Register,* I, 201-2 (2 March 1802).
24. Adams to Cabinet, 24 January 1798, Adams, ed., *Works of Adams,* VIII, 561-62.
25. Hamilton to McHenry, n. d. [January-February 1798], Steiner, *McHenry,* pp. 291-95; Adams, ed., *Works of Adams,* VIII, 562n; Pickering to Hamilton, 25 March 1798, Pickering MSS, Vol. VIII.
26. Pickering to King, 2 April 1798, King MSS, Vol. XLV.
27. Grenville to Liston, 8 June 1798, FO 5/22. Pitt apparently hoped that the ships-for-seamen trade would go through, for he discussed the accretion to the Mediterranean fleet which it might make possible (Pitt to Grenville, 5 July 1798, Walter Fitzpatrick, ed., *Report on the Manuscripts of J. B. Fortescue, Esq., Preserved at Dropmore,* IV [London, 1903], 245).
28. Liston to Grenville, 27 September 1798, FO 5/22.
29. *Independent Chronicle,* 5 April 1798; Pickering to Washington, 27 October 1798, Pickering MSS, Vol. IX.

30. Grenville to Liston, 8 December 1798, FO 115/6. For Liston's inquiry, see Liston to Hammond, Private, 10 October 1798, Liston MSS, Vol. XXXV.
31. *Columbian Centinel*, 24 November 1798; Murray to J. Q. Adams, 5 October 1798, Worthington C. Ford, ed., "Letters of William Vans Murray to John Quincy Adams, 1797-1803," American Historical Association, *Annual Report for 1912* (Washington, 1914), p. 479. See also Liston to Grenville, 29 January 1799, FO 5/25A.
32. *Independent Chronicle*, 25 October 1798.

CHAPTER 10: A BRIEF DRIFT APART

1. John Trumbull, *Autobiography, Reminiscences, and Letters of John Trumbull* (New Haven, 1841), pp. 196-218.
2. Nichol and Anstey to Grenville, 10 May 1798, FO 5/24; Francis Moore to Grenville, 20 June 1798, *ibid.*
3. King to Pickering, 3 August 1798, King MSS, Vol. LII.
4. Liston to Grenville, 27 June 1797, FO 5/18.
5. Memorial of Macdonald, 25 July 1798, FO 5/24. It should be noted that many Loyalists attempted to recover their property through the Philadelphia commission. This, too, was made easier by Macdonald's memorandum, and, although never mentioned, doubtless contributed to the anger of the Americans.
6. Minutes of the board, 6 and 8 August 1798, King MSS, Vol. XL; Guillemard to Hammond, 3 August 1799, FO 5/27; Pickering to FitzSimons and Sitgreaves, 21 September 1798, Pickering MSS, Vol. XXXVII; Pickering to Sitgreaves, 24 October 1798, *ibid.*
7. FitzSimons and Sitgreaves to Pickering, 12 March 1799, King MSS, Vol. XLII.
8. Guillemard to Hammond, 3 August 1799, FO 5/27; John B. Moore, ed., *International Adjudications, Modern Series*, III (New York, 1931), 238-62. Most of the documents bearing on the board's activities will be found in this volume of Moore's work.
9. Guillemard to Hammond, 3 August 1799, FO 5/27; Pickering to Gore, Private, 3 January 1800, Pickering MSS, Vol. XIII; Liston to Grenville, 4 August 1799, FO 5/25A.
10. *Independent Chronicle*, 1 April 1799, citing the *Richmond Examiner*. See also *Aurora*, 18 July 1799.
11. Liston to Grenville, 4 August 1799, FO 5/25A; Pickering to King, 7 February 1800, Pickering MSS, Vol. XXXVIII; Jay to Pickering, 23 December 1797, *ibid.*, Vol. XXI. The *Aurora*, determined that no Federalists should emerge with credit from the affair, for once agreed with Liston and stated that fear of the public reaction had alone caused Sitgreaves and FitzSimons to refuse to permit the British commissioners to have their way (*Aurora*, 13 August 1799).
12. Grenville to Liston, 22 October 1799, FO 115/7.
13. *Anti-Jacobin Review*, IV (1799), 123-27. For the President's view, see Adams to Lloyd, 31 March 1815, Adams, ed., *Works of Adams*, X, 153.
14. King to Pickering, 25 May 1799, King MSS, Vol. LIII.
15. Grenville to King, Private, 9 April 1800, *ibid.* For the presentation of Pickering's proposal, see King to Grenville, 18 February 1800, *ibid.*
16. King to Pickering, 22 April 1800, *ibid.*
17. Marshall to King, 23 August 1800, Department of State, Instructions to Ministers, Vol. V. See also Adams to Marshall, 11 August 1800, Charles F. Adams, ed., *The Works of John Adams*, IX (Boston, 1854), 74. It is interesting to note that the President felt that if no other way out could be found "good faith will oblige us to try another board; and I have so little objection to the modes of

121—134

appointing a new board . . . that I am content to leave it to Mr. King to do the best he can" (Adams to Marshall, 1 August 1800, *ibid.*, pp. 68-69). The idea of new personnel was first suggested by Grenville (Grenville to King, Private, 6 April 1800, King MSS, Vol. LIII).

18. *Anti-Jacobin Review*, V (1800), 357; *Connecticut Courant*, 8 July 1799.

19. *Anti-Jacobin Review*, III (1799), 109-111; King to Pickering, 11 October 1799, King MSS, Vol. LXV.

20. Pickering to Washington, Private, 9 October 1799, Pickering MSS, Vol. XII. Although Pickering, with rare moderation, credited Adams with believing that the French would not offer acceptable terms, he was fearful that this would not be the case and that war with England would result (Pickering to Ames, Private, 20 November 1799, *ibid.*). After Adams' decision to dispatch the mission, in an effort to lessen British resentment, Pickering showed Liston parts of the envoys' instructions (Liston to Grenville, 4 November 1799, FO 5/25A). He also sent a "private and confidential" letter to King which put the best possible light on the situation (Pickering to King, Private and Confidential, 7 November 1799, King MSS, Vol. XLV).

21. Adams to Pickering, 12 May 1800, Adams, ed., *Works of Adams*, IX, 55; *Aurora*, 9 May 1800.

22. Pickering to McHenry, 13 February 1811, Steiner, *McHenry*, p. 568.

23. See below, pp. 124-25.

24. Goodhue to Pickering, 26 October 1798, Henry C. Lodge, *The Life and Letters of George Cabot* (Boston, 1877), p. 179n; *Sun*, 26 June 1800; *Morning Post*, 28 June 1800; *Times*, 30 June 1800. Thomas Macdonald prepared a memorandum for Grenville analyzing the change in similar terms (Macdonald to Grenville, 29 October 1800, Boconnoc MSS, America 1793-1803).

25. Sedgwick to King, 11 February 1800, King MSS, Vol. XXXI.

26. Maitland to Dundas, Private, 20 April 1799, WO 1/71; *Times*, 24 May 1799; *Anti-Jacobin Review*, IV (1799), 121-28; Grenville to Liston, Private, 28 February [1800], Liston MSS, Vol. XIII.

27. Liston to Grenville, Private, 7 May 1800, FO 5/29A.

28. Liston to Pickering, 23 May 1799, Department of State, Notes, Great Britain, Vol. II; Pickering to Liston, 4 June 1799, Pickering MSS, Vol. XXXVII; *Connecticut Courant*, 19 August 1799. In 1798, at British request, Captain Truxtun searched the *Constellation* for one of the mutineers. He was discovered and turned over to the Royal Navy for trial. There was no large-scale protest (Truxtun's journal, 31 August 1798, Knox, ed., *Naval Documents*, I, 365; Liston to Grenville, 27 September 1798, FO 5/22).

29. *Aurora*, 22 August 1799; Samuel E. Forman, "The Political Activities of Philip Freneau," *Johns Hopkins University Studies in Historical and Political Science*, Series XX, Nos. 9-10 (Baltimore, 1902), 83-85.

30. *Annals of Congress, 6th Congress* (Washington, 1851), pp. 596-618. The Republican motion was defeated, 61-35, on March 8 (*ibid.*, pp. 618-20).

31. King to Hamilton, 6 February 1797, King, *King*, II, 142; Liston to Grenville, 21 December 1799, FO 5/25A.

32. Cobbett to Thornton, 20 January 1800, George D. H. Cole, ed., *Letters from William Cobbett to Edward Thornton Written in the Years 1797 to 1800* (London, 1937), p. 38; *Anti-Jacobin Review*, VI (1800), 534.

33. King to Pickering. 28 February 1800, King MSS, Vol. LIII.

34. *Morning Post*, 24 January 1800; *Morning Chronicle*, 24 January 1800. The third quoted sentence was, of course, intended to reflect on Pitt.

35. *Times*, 24 January 1800. See also *Sun*, 24 January 1800; *True Briton*, 31 January 1800.

36. King to Marshall, 15 January 1801, King MSS, Vol. LIV. See also Marshall to King, 20 September 1800, Department of State, Instructions to Ministers, Vol. V.
37. Jefferson to Madison, 19 December 1800, Ford, ed., *Writings of Jefferson*, VII, 471.
38. *Porcupine*, 30 October 1800; *Times*, 27 October 1800. See also *Sun*, 7 October 1800; *True Briton*, 7 October 1800. The *Times* later somewhat revised its position, expressing concern that the convention might pave the way for more unfavorable developments (*Times*, 31 October 1800).
39. King to Marshall, 31 October 1800, King MSS, Vol. LIII.
40. Macdonald to Grenville, 29 October 1800, Boconnoc MSS, America 1793-1803.
41. King to Marshall, 22 November 1800, Charles R. King, *The Life and Correspondence of Rufus King*, III (New York, 1896), 334.
42. *British Magazine*, I (1800), 82-83.

CHAPTER 11: JEFFERSON AND ADDINGTON STEP FORWARD

1. Matthew Davis to Gallatin, 1 May 1800, Gallatin MSS; Liston to Grenville, 6 May 1800, FO 5/29A.
2. Liston to Grenville, 6 November and 8 October 1800, *ibid.*
3. *Anti-Jacobin Review*, VII (1801), xi-xii; *Times*, 20 January 1801.
4. *National Intelligencer*, 7 and 21 November 1800.
5. *Aurora*, 29 January 1800. See also *ibid.*, 25 and 30 January 1800. For a weak Republican defense of Bonaparte's action, see *Independent Chronicle*, 23 January 1800.
6. Thornton to Grenville, 7 March 1801, FO 5/32. See also Thornton to Grenville, 28 February 1800, *ibid.*
7. Madison to Monroe, 25 July 1801, Madison MSS, Vol. XXIV. See also Madison to King, 24 July 1801, Department of State, Instructions to Ministers, Vol. V.
8. Memorandum of 31 January 1801, King MSS, Vol. LXXIII. See also St. Vincent to Nelson, Secret, 21 January 1801, St. Vincent MSS, Add. MSS 31167; *Columbian Centinel*, 15 and 22 April 1801. For evidences of succeeding shifts in British feelings, see, e.g., *Times*, 20 August 1801; *Morning Chronicle*, 22 January 1802.
9. Wilson C. Nicholas to Jefferson, 30 October 1801, Jefferson MSS, Vol. CXXVII.
10. Lady Malmesbury to Sneyd, 13 February 1801, Bagot, ed., *Canning and His Friends*, I, 127.
11. *Times*, 14 February 1801; Grenville to Earl of Carysfort, 16 March 1801, Fitzpatrick, ed., *Dropmore MSS*, VI, 473. See also *Morning Post*, 9 February 1801; *Sun*, 11 February 1801; *National Intelligencer*, 30 March 1801.
12. Greig, ed., *Farington Diary*, II, 80 (13 February 1801). For Addington's position in 1812, see George Pellew, *The Life and Correspondence of the Right Honble Henry Addington, First Viscount Sidmouth* (London, 1847), III, 85.
13. Keith G. Feiling, *Sketches in Nineteenth Century Biography* (London, 1930), p. 20.
14. Henry Brougham to James Loch, 12 December 1803, R. H. M. Buddle Atkinson and G. A. Jackson, eds., *Brougham and His Early Friends* (London, 1908), II, 99; Leveson V. Harcourt, ed., *The Diaries and Correspondence of the Right Hon. George Rose* (London, 1860), II, 46-47 (20-23 August 1803). See also Comte de Wedel Jarlsburg to Comte de Bernsdorf, 1 January 1802, Liverpool MSS, Add. MSS 38237.
15. King to Marshall, 25 February 1801, Department of State, Despatches from Great Britain, Vol. IX; memorandum of 8 April 1801, King MSS, Vol. LXXIII.
16. Dearborn to James Bowdoin, 20 April 1802, *The Bowdoin and Temple Papers, Part II* (Massachusetts Historical Society, *Collections*, Seventh Series, VI, Boston, 1907), p. 229. For a similar opinion expressed by Rufus King, see Gallatin

134—144

to Jefferson, 18 August 1803, Henry Adams, ed., *The Writings of Albert Gallatin* (Philadelphia, 1879), I, 141.

17. Madison to Monroe, 8 March 1804, Madison MSS, Vol. XXVII.
18. King to Nicholas Low, 7 July 1800, King, *King,* III, 269.
19. Grenville to Liston, 28 February 1800, FO 115/8; Grenville to Liston, Private, 28 February 1800, Liston MSS, Vol. XIII. The rest of Liston's distinguished service was in European capitals. In due course he was knighted and made a member of the Privy Council, although the King complained that Liston, "who had formerly had a very just reputation for conduct and firmness, seemed to have been quite altered by his abode in America, for at the Northern Courts he had always been recommending concession and giving way" (Francis Bickley, ed., *The Diaries of Sylvester Douglas [Lord Glenbervie]* [London, 1928], I, 393 [19 January 1804]).
20. Liston to Pickering, 10 December 1800, Pickering MSS, Vol. XXVI.
21. *Anti-Jacobin Review,* VII (1801), xvi; Elizabeth Merry to Thomas Moore, n. d. [1804], Lord John Russell, ed., *Memoirs, Journal, and Correspondence of Thomas Moore,* VIII (London, 1856), 51; Cole, ed., *Cobbett-Thornton Letters,* p. xxiii, quoting *Aurora.*
22. Marquis Cornwallis to Admiral William Cornwallis, 16 December 1800, Walter Fitzpatrick, ed., "The Manuscripts of Cornwallis Wykeham-Martin, Esquire," Historical Manuscripts Commission, *Report on Manuscripts in Various Collections,* VI (Dublin, 1909), 394.
23. King to Madison, 2 November 1801, King MSS, Vol. LIV.
24. *Columbian Centinel,* 21 November 1801; Joseph Lee, Jr., to Andrew Smith, 19 January 1802, Kenneth W. Porter, ed., *The Jacksons and the Lees* (Cambridge, 1937), I, 517.
25. MacGregor, *Commercial Statistics,* III, 800.
26. Heckscher, *Continental System,* p. 103; Pitkin, *Statistical View,* p. 167; Mac-Gregor, *Commercial Statistics,* III, 800.
27. *The Diary of William Bentley, D. D.,* II (Salem, 1907), 403 (16 November 1801).

CHAPTER 12: TWO CONVENTIONS

1. Monroe to Jefferson, 29 April 1801, Hamilton, ed., *Writings of Monroe,* III, 279; Monroe to Jefferson, 30 April 1801 [not sent], *ibid.,* pp. 281n-82n; Monroe to Jefferson, 4 May 1801, *ibid.,* pp. 279-81.
2. Anstey memorandum for Hawkesbury, n. d. [January 1801], Boconnoc MSS, America 1793-1803; King to Marshall, 1 May 1801, Department of State, Despatches from Great Britain, Vol. IX.
3. Levi Lincoln to King, 25 April 1801, *ibid.,* Instructions to Ministers, Vol. V; Franklin B. Sawvel, ed., *The Complete Anas of Thomas Jefferson* (New York, 1903), p. 216 (13 June 1801); Madison to King, 15 June 1801, *American State Papers, Foreign Relations,* II, 389-90.
4. Addington to King, 16 July 1801, King MSS, Vol. LIV; King to Madison, 24 August 1801, Department of State, Despatches from Great Britain, Vol. IX.
5. Hawkesbury to George III, [14 September 1801], Liverpool MSS, Add. MSS 38237.
6. Memorandum of 19 August 1801, enclosed in King to Madison, 4 October 1801, Department of State, Despatches from Great Britain, Vol. IX; King to Madison, 20 October 1801, *ibid.*
7. Nutt and Molleson to Hawkesbury, 10 November 1801, FO 5/34; Henry Glassford to Hawkesbury, 22 November 1801, *ibid.*; King to Madison, Private, 11 January 1802, Department of State, Despatches from Great Britain, Vol. IX.

8. Memorandum of 15 December 1801, King MSS, Vol. LXXIII.
9. Miller, ed., *Treaties*, II, 488-90.
10. King to Adams, 12 January 1802, King MSS, Vol. LV. See also King to Marshall, 12 January 1802, *ibid.*
11. Memorandum of February 1802, *ibid.*, Vol. LXXIII; *Cobbett's Annual Register*, II, 45 (10-17 July 1802); *Morning Post*, 28 January 1802. See also *True Briton*, 18 January 1802; *Morning Chronicle*, 18 January 1802; *Times*, 29 January 1802; *Sun*, 29 January 1802.
12. King to Marshall, 5 August 1802, King MSS, Vol. LV. Of the agreement, Jefferson wrote:

    it would be very ill judged not to close, for it would revive their claim of twenty odd millions of dollars awarded by the commissioners, which they would hold as a rod forever over our heads, to operate on our seaport towns, and even on Congress at will. it is now settled by our predecessors. if the bargain be hard, it is their work. that it is not more hard has been the effect of our measures. if this be given up it can never be settled but by war (Jefferson to Monroe, 31 March 1802, Jefferson MSS, Vol. CXXIII).

    The commission had not awarded twenty million dollars, of course. Jefferson was probably referring to claims before the board. The *National Intelligencer*, the administration's spokesman, printed an outline of the convention (26 March 1801), its text (7 April 1802), and news of the resumption of the London commission (19 April 1802) without once expressing an opinion on the merits of the agreement.
13. *Columbian Centinel*, 28 April 1802.
14. For Senate proceedings, see *Senate Executive Journal*, I, 415, 417-22.
15. Macdonald, Rich, and Guillemard to Earl of Harrowby, 3 September 1804, FO 5/44; Macdonald, Rich, and Guillemard to Baron Mulgrave, 20 November 1805, FO 5/47.
16. King to Madison, 25 March 1803, Department of State, Despatches from Great Britain, Vol. X.
17. King to Madison, 30 April 1803, *ibid.* See also King to Madison, 23 April 1803, *ibid.* The Lord Chancellor at this time was Lord Eldon, who had succeeded Loughborough.
18. Gore to King, 29 February 1804, King MSS, Vol. X.
19. Christopher Gore calculated awards to Americans as follows:

		Cases	Amount (£)		
By Scott and Nicholl, 1797-98		96	59,102	15	10
By commission before suspension		40	91,358	18	10
By commission after resumption		328	1,222,580	12	2
Recovered directly from captors		—	240,000	0	0
Under provision order	est.	120	720,000	0	0
			2,333,042	6	10

    (Memorandum received from Gore, 18 February 1814, Pickering MSS, Vol. LIV.) John Trumbull's figures are slightly different, but he agrees that the total compensation was about two and a third millions (Trumbull, *Autobiography*, pp. 237-38).
20. King to Madison, 31 December 1801, Department of State, Despatches from Great Britain, Vol. IX.
21. Sullivan to Madison, 20 May 1802, *American State Papers, Foreign Relations*, II, 586; Madison to King, 8 June 1802, Department of State, Instructions to Ministers, Vol. VI.

145—159

22. Memorandum of 20 April 1802, King MSS, Vol. LXXIII. For Thornton's dispatch, see Thornton to Hawkesbury, 6 March 1802, FO 5/35.
23. Gore to Madison, 6 October 1802, *American State Papers, Foreign Relations*, II, 587-88.
24. King to Madison, 28 February 1803, Department of State, Despatches from Great Britain, Vol. X; Barclay to Hammond, 16 February 1803, FO 5/40.
25. King to Madison, 28 February 1803, Department of State, Despatches from Great Britain, Vol. X.
26. Hammond to King, 11 May 1803, King MSS, Vol. LV; King to Madison, 13 May 1803, Department of State, Despatches from Great Britain, Vol. X. For the text of the convention, see Manning, ed., *Diplomatic Correspondence, Canadian Relations*, I, 555n-57n.
27. Hawkesbury to Merry, 16 September 1803, FO 115/11.
28. Gallatin to Jefferson, n. d. [received 4 October 1803], Adams, ed., *Writings of Gallatin*, I, 159; Richardson, ed. *Messages and Papers*, I, 359. See also *National Intelligencer*, 19 October 1803, where the convention is mildly praised.
29. *Annals of Congress, 8th Congress, 2nd Session* (Washington, 1852), p. 1253. Cf. Bemis, *Adams*, 125-26. See also King to Madison, 9 December 1803, King MSS, Vol. IX.
30. Merry to Hawkesbury, 30 January 1804, FO 5/41; *Senate Executive Journal*, I, 463-64; Pickering to Jefferson (2), 18 January 1804, Charles W. Upham, *The Life of Timothy Pickering*, IV (Boston, 1873), 86-87. Brant, *Madison, Secretary of State*, pp. 170-71, suggests that, by bluntly stating that the boundary was designed to give Britain access to the Mississippi, Merry destroyed the possibility of unconditional ratification. But objection to Article V arose before Merry's statement, and the article apparently was doomed from the first. For discussions of Senate action on the convention, see Alfred L. Burt, *The United States, Great Britain, and British North America from the Revolution to the Establishment of Peace after the War of 1812* (James T. Shotwell, ed., *The Relations of Canada and the United States*, New Haven, 1940), pp. 194-96; W. Stull Holt, *Treaties Defeated by the Senate* (Baltimore, 1933), pp. 19-21.
31. Merry to Hawkesbury, 1 March 1804, FO 5/41.

CHAPTER 13: RUFUS KING CLOSES HIS MISSION

1. Madison to King, 10 December 1801, Department of State, Instructions to Ministers, Vol. VI. In a memorandum presented to Hawkesbury, King pointed out that the British duties were heaviest on the bulk cargoes exported from the United States to England, the field in which maritime competition was most intense (enclosure in King to Hawkesbury, 3 February 1802, FO 5/37).
2. Thornton to Hawkesbury, 18 December 1801, FO 5/23. This dispatch reached London on 3 February 1802.
3. King to Madison, 5 February 1802, Department of State, Despatches from Great Britain, Vol. X; King to Madison, Private, 13 February 1802, *ibid*; King to Hawkesbury, 9 February 1802, FO 5/37.
4. *Cobbett's Annual Register*, I, 138n-39n (13-20 February 1802).
5. King to Madison, 5 March 1802, King MSS, Vol. LV. See also Vansittart to King, 26 February 1802, *ibid.*, Vol. VIII.
6. John Debrett, ed., *The Parliamentary Register*, LXXIX (London, 1805), 147-48. For reports of the debate, see *ibid.*, pp. 130-48; John Wright, ed., *The Parliamentary History of England*, XXXVI (London, 1820), 351-60; *Morning Chronicle*, 6 March 1802; *Cobbett's Annual Register*, I, 229-33 (6-13 March 1802); *National Intelligencer*, 30 April 1802.

7. Sheffield to Vansittart, 22 March 1802, Papers of Nicholas Vansittart, Lord Bexley, British Museum (Add. MSS 31229-31237), Add. MSS 31229.
8. Madison to King, 7 April 1802, Department of State, Instructions to Ministers, Vol. VI.
9. Richardson, ed., *Messages and Papers*, I, 343; Thornton to Hawkesbury, 31 December 1802, FO 5/35.
10. *Columbian Centinel*, 29 January 1803; Bowdoin to Henry Dearborn, n. d. [April 1802], *Bowdoin-Temple Papers, Part II*, pp. 231-32.
11. *American State Papers. Class IV. Commerce and Navigation*, I (Washington, 1832), 502-4. The Chambers of Commerce of New York and Philadelphia petitioned Congress to reject the report (*National Intelligencer*, 24 and 26 January 1803), and on February 12 Smith admitted defeat (*ibid.*, 14 February 1803).
12. For King's final success with respect to the New Orleans entrepôt, see above, p. 83.
13. Hawkesbury to King, 25 April 1803, and enclosure, Department of State, Despatches from Great Britain, Vol. X. See also King to Madison, 1 May 1803, *ibid.*; John Munro to King, 17 August 1804, King MSS, Vol. X.
14. Thornton to Hawkesbury, 10 May 1801, FO 5/32; memorandum of 24 May 1801, King MSS, Vol. LXXIII.
15. Jefferson to Butler, 27 July 1801, Jefferson MSS, Vol. CXIV. See also Madison to Monroe, 25 July 1801, Madison MSS, Vol. XXIV.
16. *Connecticut Courant*, 17 July 1805.
17. Memorandum of 25 September 1801, King MSS, Vol. LXXIII; King to Madison, Private, 8 October 1801, Department of State, Despatches from Great Britain, Vol. IX; King to Hawkesbury, 7 May 1803, FO 5/40.
18. *Ibid.*
19. St. Vincent to Hawkesbury, 10 May 1803, St. Vincent MSS, Add. MSS 31169; St. Vincent to King, 10 May 1803, King MSS, Vol. XXX.
20. King to St. Vincent, 15 May 1803, *ibid.*, Vol. IX; King to St. Vincent, 17 May 1803, FO 5/40; St. Vincent to King, 17 May 1803, King MSS, Vol. XXX.
21. King to Madison,—July 1803, *ibid.*, Vol. LV.
22. King to St. Vincent, 18 May 1803, *ibid.*, Vol. XXX.
23. Vansittart to King, 19 May 1803, *ibid.* See also Hammond to King, 19 May 1803, *ibid.*
24. Gallatin to Jefferson, 18 August 1803, Adams, ed., *Writings of Gallatin*, I, 141. Thornton later reported that Gallatin would probably have accepted the Narrow Seas proposal (Thornton to Hawkesbury, 1 November 1803, FO 5/38).
25. King to Marshall, 5 August 1802, King MSS, Vol. LV. See also *Connecticut Courant*, 8 April 1802; King to Madison, 5 August 1802, Department of State, Despatches from Great Britain, Vol. X.
26. *Times*, 28 March 1803. See also *True Briton*, 30 March 1803.
27. King to Madison, 16 May 1803, King MSS, Vol. IX.
28. Gallatin to Jefferson, 18 August 1803, Adams, ed., *Writings of Gallatin*, I, 140-41.
29. Edward Channing, *A History of the United States*, IV (Rev. ed., New York, 1927), 353.
30. *Morning Chronicle*, 28 March 1803.

CHAPTER 14: LOUISIANA

1. Memorandum of 22 September 1798, King MSS, Vol. LXXIII.
2. King to Madison, 1 June 1801, Department of State, Despatches from Great Britain, Vol. IX.
3. Madison to Hamilton, 26 May 1801, Hamilton MSS, Vol. LXXXIII. See also

160—174

Madison to Nicholas, 10 July 1801, Gaillard Hunt, ed., *The Writings of James Madison*, VI (New York, 1906), 427n.

4. King to Madison, 20 November 1801, Department of State, Despatches from Great Britain, Vol. IX.

5. Thornton to Hawkesbury, 6 March 1802, FO 5/35.

6. Jefferson to Livingston, 18 April 1802, Ford, ed., *Writings of Jefferson*, VIII, 145. Madison had already expressed the idea in less striking language; Madison to Livingston, 28 September 1801, quoted in Brant, *Madison, Secretary of State*, p. 71.

7. Jefferson to du Pont de Nemours, 25 April 1802, Lipscomb, ed., *Writings of Jefferson*, X, 317.

8. Thornton to Hawkesbury, 3 July and 3 August 1802, FO 5/35.

9. Madison to Livingston, 1 May 1802, Department of State, Instructions to Ministers, Vol. VI.

10. *Cobbett's Annual Register*, I, 44-46 (16-30 January 1802).

11. Windham to [Addington], 3 November 1802, Windham MSS, Add. MSS 37881.

12. George Orr, *The Possession of Louisiana by the French Considered* (London, 1803), *passim*.

13. *Times*, 13 May 1802. The paper added, "It was on this principle that some of our Politicians of the old school entertained the opinion, that we might attribute the loss of the American Colonies to our retention of Canada after the seven years war."

14. *Ibid.*, 8 February 1803.

15. Memorandum of 25 November 1801, King MSS, Vol. LXXIII.

16. *National Intelligencer*, 6 December 1802; Bond to Hawkesbury, 2 January 1803, FO 5/39; Thornton to Hawkesbury, 3 January 1803, FO 5/38.

17. Jefferson to Monroe, 10 January 1803, Monroe MSS, Vol. VII. See also Jefferson to Monroe, 13 January 1803, "State Papers and Correspondence Bearing upon the Purchase of the Territory of Louisiana," 57th Congress, 2nd Session, *House of Representatives Document 431* (Washington, 1903), pp. 68-69. John Randolph attacked the hypocrisy of the Federalists, pointing out that those who had never before shown much concern for the West "were arrogating to themselves all the zeal excited by the sensibility of the American nation on this important subject" (*National Intelligencer*, 7 January 1803).

18. Thornton to Hawkesbury, 31 January 1803, FO 5/38. See also Madison to Livingston and Monroe, 2 March 1803, Department of State, Instructions to Ministers, Vol. VI.

19. Thornton to Hawkesbury, 9 March 1803, FO 5/38.

20. Sawvel, ed., *The Anas of Jefferson*, pp. 218-19 (8 April 1803).

21. Madison to Monroe and Livingston, 18 April 1803, Department of State, Instructions to Ministers, Vol. VI.

22. Whitworth to Hawkesbury, 4 January and 7 February 1803, FO 27/67; Frere to Hawkesbury, Private, 25 February 1803, Liverpool MSS, Add. MSS 38238.

23. Thornton to Hawkesbury, 3 January 1803, FO 5/38; endorsed received 13 February 1803.

24. James H. Harris, Earl of Malmesbury, ed., *Diaries and Correspondence of James Harris, Earl of Malmesbury* (London, 1844), IV, 203 (16 February 1803).

25. King to Livingston, 11 March 1803, King MSS, Vol. LV.

26. Malmesbury to Pelham, 20 March 1803, Pelham MSS, British Museum (Add. MSS 33100-33130), Add. MSS 33110.

27. King to Madison, 2 April 1803, Department of State, Despatches from · Great Britain, Vol. XI. Madison easily saw that self-interest was at the root of the British offer to seize New Orleans; it was, he wrote, "calculated to decoy us into the war" (Madison to Monroe, Private, 31 May 1803, quoted in Brant,

Madison, Secretary of State, p. 131). On the other hand, he did not reject the offer for this reason, and even hoped that the threat it posed would strengthen the diplomatic armory of Livingston and Monroe. Before the American government could follow up this new approach, word reached Washington that Louisiana had been sold to the United States.

28. Whitworth to Hawkesbury, 14 April 1803, FO 27/68.
29. *Morning Chronicle,* 25 April 1803; "To the Rt. Hon. Ld. Hawkesbury, &c.," *Cobbett's Annual Register,* III, 801-10 (4 June 1803). For other comment, see *Morning Chronicle,* 18 and 19 May 1803; *Morning Post,* 20 May 1803; *Times,* 18 May 1803; *Sun,* 20 May 1803.
30. Hawkesbury to King, 19 May 1803, King MSS, Vol. LV; memorandum of 9 December 1821, Pickering MSS, Vol. LI; Monroe to Madison, Private, 25 November 1803, Monroe MSS, Vol. IX.
31. Livingston to John Armstrong, 1 September 1803, Armstrong Papers, Historical Society of Pennsylvania, transcript. Actually, France feared that Britain might seize Louisiana and transfer it to the United States before payment was completed (Brant, *Madison, Secretary of State,* p. 143).
32. Richardson, ed., *Messages and Papers,* I, 358; *Annals of Congress, 8th Congress, 1st Session,* pp. 445, 452. For the entire debate, see *ibid.,* pp. 432-89.
33. Thornton to Hawkesbury, 6 September 1803, FO 5/38; G. Labouchère, "L'Annexion de la Louisiane aux États-Unis et les Maisons Hope et Baring," *Révue d'Histoire Diplomatique,* XXX (1916), 441-42; Hidy, *House of Baring,* p. 33; Barbé-Marbois to Livingston and Monroe, 28 May 1803, Louisiana Papers, Treasury Department.
34. For the text of the agreement, see James E. Winston and R. W. Colomb, "How the Louisiana Purchase was Financed," *Louisiana Historical Quarterly,* XII (1929), 215-18.
35. Thornton to Hawkesbury, 31 October 1803, FO 5/38.
36. Gallatin to Jefferson, 31 August 1803, Adams, ed., *Writings of Gallatin,* I, 151.
37. *Anti-Jacobin Review,* XIII (1802), 311.
38. Jefferson to Sinclair, [30 June 1803], enclosed in Barclay to Hawkesbury, 2 December 1803, FO 5/40; *Times,* 27 November 1802.

CHAPTER 15: EBB TIDE

1. Jefferson to Sinclair, [30 June 1803], enclosed in Barclay to Hawkesbury, 2 December 1803, FO 5/40; Thornton to Hawkesbury, 5 May 1803, FO 5/38. See also Pichon to Talleyrand, 3 June 1803, Henry Adams, *History of the United States During the First Administration of Thomas Jefferson,* II (*History of the United States,* II, New York, 1889), 354.
2. Gore to King, 21 November 1803, King MSS, Vol. IX.
3. Monroe to Madison, Private, 25 November 1803, Monroe MSS, Vol. IX. For the earlier letter, see Monroe to Jefferson, 25 September 1803, Jefferson MSS, Vol. CXLIII.
4. *Cobbett's Annual Register,* III, 571-72 (16 April 1803), 628-29 (30 April 1803).
5. Hawkesbury to Merry, 16 September 1803, FO 115/11.
6. Merry to Hawkesbury, 6 December 1803, FO 5/41.
7. Merry to Hammond, 7 December 1803, *ibid.*
8. Merry to Harrowby, 7 August 1804, FO 5/42. For later interviews, see Merry to Harrowby, 29 March 1805, FO 5/45; Merry to Mulgrave, 25 November 1805, *ibid.* In justice to Merry, it should be noted that he recognized the real possibility that Burr was playing a double game. This does not, however, lessen the anti-American aspect of the minister's intriguing.
9. Everett S. Brown, ed., *William Plumer's Memorandum of Proceedings in the*

175—184

United States Senate, 1803-1807 (New York, 1923), p. 146 (28 February 1804). See also Merry to Hawkesbury, 20 January 1804, FO 5/41; Madison to Monroe, Private, 8 April 1804, Madison MSS, Vol. XXVII.

10. Adams, *First Jeffersonian Administration*, II, 396.

11. *Columbian Centinel*, 7 July 1804.

12. Harris, ed., *Diaries and Correspondence of Malmesbury*, IV, 311-14 (20 May 1804).

13. Madison to Monroe, 5 January 1804, Department of State, Instructions to Ministers, Vol. VI; memorandum of George W. Erving, 21 August 1804, enclosed in Hammond to William Marsden, 10 September 1804, Admy 1/4197; Monroe to Madison, 8 September 1804, Department of State, Despatches from Great Britain, Vol. XII.

14. Earl Melville (Dundas) to Harrowby, 6 September 1804, Harrowby MSS, transcript; Marsden to Hammond, 20 November 1804, FO 5/44.

15. Monroe to Madison, 1 July 1804, Stanislaus M. Hamilton, ed., *The Writings of James Monroe*, IV (New York, 1900), 218.

16. Holroyd, *Strictures, passim; Anti-Jacobin Review*, XVII (1804), 433; *Cobbett's Annual Register*, VI, 196-202 (11 August 1804); Cock, *Answer to Sheffield*; Gibbs W. Jordan, *The Claim of the West India Colonists to the Right of Obtaining Necessary Supplies in America* (London, 1804). Some of Jordan's comments were reprinted by the *National Intelligencer*, 17 July 1805.

17. BT 5/14, 310 (22 June 1804), 332-37 (4 July 1804), 359-63 (14 July 1804); BT 5/15, 2-5 (1 January 1805).

18. Merry to Harrowby, 25 January 1805, FO 5/45.

19. Jefferson to Robert Smith, 6 September 1804, Jefferson MSS, Vol. CXLIII.

20. Zimmerman, *Impressment*, p. 104.

21. Madison to Monroe, 6 March 1805, Gaillard Hunt, ed., *The Writings of James Madison*, VII (New York, 1908), 168. See also Merry to Mulgrave, 2 June 1805, FO 5/45.

22. Jefferson to Madison, 4 August 1805, Madison MSS, Vol. XXIX. See also Jefferson to Madison, 7 August 1805, Jefferson MSS, Vol. CLI; Jefferson to Robert Smith, 7 August 1805, *ibid.*; Jefferson to Madison, 25 August 1805, *ibid.*, Vol. CLII.

23. "Sentence of the Vice-Admiralty Court of Nassau, New Providence in the case of the Brig Essex, Joseph Orne Master," enclosed in Monroe to Madison, 18 October 1805, Department of State, Despatches from Great Britain, Vol. XII.

24. There is some confusion as to the exact date of the decision (Lingelbach, "England and Neutral Trade," 158n). A contemporary, James Stephen, *War in Disguise; Or, the Frauds of the Neutral Flags* (London, 1805), p. 60, gives the date as 22 May. But "Confirmation of the foregoing Sentence by the Lords Commissioners of Appeals," enclosed in Monroe to Madison, 18 October 1805, Department of State, Despatches from Great Britain, Vol. XII, gives the date as 22 June. This would scarcely allow time for the large number of seizures reported in July.

25. William C. Townshend, *The Lives of Twelve Eminent Judges* (London, 1846), II, 227-28.

26. "Confirmation of the foregoing Sentence by the Lords Commissioners of Appeals," enclosed in Monroe to Madison, 18 October 1805, Department of State, Despatches from Great Britain, Vol. XII.

27. Christopher Robinson, ed., *Reports of Cases Argued and Determined in the High Court of Admiralty*, V (London, 1806), 396-97. Robinson printed this decision of 1806 because it summarized previous cases, including the *Essex*. Its inclusion in a volume otherwise devoted to Scott's decisions in the High Court of Ad-

miralty apparently explains the frequently seen statement that it was Scott who made the decision in the *Essex* case.

28. This was not true, however, to the extent that Grant shifted the burden of proof from the captor, where it had been placed by Scott, to the shipowner. This aspect has seldom been emphasized, but it was very important. Rufus King believed that this was the most threatening part of the decision; King to Gore, 28 October 1806, King MSS, Vol. X.

29. Robinson, ed., *Reports*, II, 369.

30. Henry R. Fox, Lord Holland, *Memoirs of the Whig Party*, II (London, 1854), 100; "Minute of a Conversation between M[r] Erving & M[r] Hammond. August the 30, 1805," Department of State, Despatches from Great Britain, Vol. XII; Monroe to Mulgrave, 31 July 1805, enclosed in Monroe to Madison, 6 August 1805, *ibid.*; Mulgrave to Monroe, 9 August 1805, *ibid.*

31. Mulgrave to Pitt, 11 October 1805, Pretyman MSS, Vol. XVII. However, as had Sir Andrew, Scott put up a brave front. In the case of the ship *Maria*, he noted that "The *Essex*, Orne, was . . . the first case which called for the decision of the Superior Court" on this principle, adding that "the same doctrine would have been held in any other case, if such a case had occurred at an earlier period" (Robinson, ed., *Reports*, V, 368).

32. *Morning Chronicle*, 19 October 1805; *Cobbett's Annual Register*, VII, 660-67 (19 October 1805); *Morning Post*, 21 October 1805; *Sun*, 22 October 1805.

33. Scott to Pitt, 25 August 1805, Chatham MSS, Vol. CLXXVI.

34. Stephen, *War in Disguise*, pp. 93, 4-5, and *passim*.

35. Wilberforce to King, 7 November 1805, King MSS, Vol. X; Baring, *Inquiry*, pp. 2-3; *Edinburgh Review*, VIII (1806), 1-35; [Gouverneur Morris], *An Answer to War in Disguise* (New York, 1806); Tench Coxe (Juriscola, pseud.), *An Examination of the Conduct of Great Britain, Respecting Neutrals* (Philadelphia, 1807); [James Madison], *An Examination of the British Doctrine, which Subjects to Capture a Neutral Trade, not Open in Time of Peace* (Philadelphia [?], 1806); Merry to Mulgrave, 2 February 1806, FO 5/48. Madison's pamphlet actually was composed before *War in Disguise* reached this country but still served as an answer to it.

36. *Columbian Centinel*, 21 September 1805.

EPILOGUE: THE FIRST RAPPROCHEMENT

1. Anthony Steel, "Anthony Merry and the Anglo-American Dispute about Impressment, 1803-1806," *Cambridge Historical Journal*, IX (1947-49), 338-39 and *passim*.

2. Dundas to Inglis, 14 June 1797, India Office, Home Miscellaneous, Vol. CCCXXXVII.

3. Madison to Charles Pinckney, 9 June 1801, "Louisiana State Papers," p. 5; Adams, ed., *Memoirs of John Quincy Adams*, I, 316 (23 November 1804); *Times*, 11 August 1804.

4. Liston to Grenville, 3 July 1796, FO 5/14.

5. R. Hamilton, "Observations on the Trade of Upper Canada," 24 September 1798, Michigan Pioneer and Historical Society, *Collections*, XXV, 202-5; Liston to Russell, 3 April 1798, Brig.-Gen. Ernest A. Cruikshank and Andrew F. Hunter, eds., *The Correspondence of the Honourable Peter Russell*, II (Toronto, 1935), 134.

6. — to —, 13 November 1796, Michigan Pioneer and Historical Society, *Collections*, XXV, 135; Hector McLean to James Green, 21 March 1799, Brig.-Gen. Ernest A. Cruikshank and Andrew F. Hunter, eds., *The Correspondence of the Honourable Peter Russell*, III (Toronto, 1936), 145; Major J. J. Ulrich Rivardi

185—186

to Hamilton, 3 April 1799, Hamilton MSS, Vol. XXXVIII. Rivardi, who served at various posts along the frontier throughout this period, frequently reported such incidents.

7. Memorandum of 22 November 1804, Liverpool MSS, Add. MSS 38358.
8. Jay to Grenville, 30 September 1794, Boconnoc MSS, America 1793-1803.
9. Ames to Gore, 26 March 1794, Ames, ed., *Works of Ames*, 1, 140.
10. Talleyrand, "Les États-Unis et L'Angleterre," p. 77.

Selective Bibliography

This study rests chiefly upon an extensive examination of primary sources, although secondary works have also been consulted. Available materials, particularly on the American side, are so extensive that they cannot all be mentioned here; a few primary sources and many secondary treatments have been omitted. In addition to those cited below, the footnotes contain references to others which touch briefly on specific aspects of the topic. A more exhaustive bibliography and further documentation (pp. 719-41), as well as a more detailed examination of the whole subject, will be found in the author's *The First Anglo-American Rapprochement, 1795-1805*, deposited in the Widener Library, Harvard University, 1952, and also available on microfilm at the Alderman Library, University of Virginia.

I. PRIMARY SOURCES

A. GOVERNMENT PAPERS

1. American, manuscript

Houghton Library, Harvard University
> Opinions filed by the Commissioners acting under the VII. Article of the Treaty of Amity, Commerce and Navigation between Great Britain and the United States of America. 2 vols. Presented by Christopher Gore.

Library of Congress
> Baring Letters to the Treasury.
> United States Eastern Boundary, 1796-98. 2 vols. Minutes of the St. Croix commission and the evidence presented to it.

National Archives
> Department of State
>> Consular Despatches, Aux Cayes, Vol. I; Bristol, Vols. I-II; Cape Haytien, Vols. I-IV; Cork, Vol. I; Dublin, Vol. I; Falmouth, Vol. II; Gibraltar, Vols. I-II; Glasgow, Vol. I; Kingston, Jamaica, Vol. I; Leith, Vol. I; Liverpool, Vols. I-II; London, Vols. VII-IX; Malta, Vol. I; Plymouth, Vol. I; Southampton, Vol. I. These volumes provided interesting and valuable sidelights on commerce, seizures, and impressment. The Haitian volumes contain important material on negotiations with Toussaint.
>> Despatches from the United States Minister to Great Britain, Vols. IX-XII.
>> Instructions to Ministers, Vols. V-VI.

Notes to Foreign Legations, Notes from Missing Vol. I.
Notes from the British Legation, Vol. IA.
Notes, Great Britain, Vol. II.
Notes, British Legation, Vol. III.
War Department
Secretary of War, Letters Received, 1777-97, and Book II. War Department records were gutted by fire, and these files are consequently very incomplete.
Treasury Department
Louisiana Papers. Formal correspondence on the financing of the Louisiana Purchase.

2. American, printed

American State Papers. Class I. Foreign Relations, Vols. I-III. Washington, 1832-33. An extensive collection, but unreliably edited, so that it by no means obviates the necessity of examining manuscript sources.

American State Papers. Class II. Indian Affairs, Vol. I. Washington, 1832.

American State Papers. Class IV. Commerce and Navigation, Vol. I. Washington, 1832.

Knox, Dudley W., ed. *Naval Documents Related to the Quasi-War Between the United States and France.* 7 vols. Washington, 1935-38. An excellent compilation which provides much information on British-American naval coöperation.

Manning, William R., ed. *Diplomatic Correspondence of the United States. Canadian Relations, 1784-1860,* Vol. I. Washington, 1940. The concept of Canadian relations is so broad that there is a wealth of material in this volume.

3. British, manuscript

British Museum
America, 1780-1841. Deciphers of Diplomatic Papers, Vol. LI. Add. MSS 32303.

Commonwealth Relations Office
India Office, Home Series, Miscellaneous, Vols. CCCXXXVII, CDV, CDXXXIX, CDXCI, CDXCIV, DCV. Information on American trade with India.

Public Record Office
Admiralty
Admy 1/various. Searched with the aid of the Ind series. Correspondence with other departments, foreign officials, and naval officers. Very valuable for a study of impressment and British maritime policy, these records have been insufficiently examined by American historians. The indexing system is complex, cumbersome, and complete.
Admy 2/1099-1100. Convoys.

Admy 7/303.
Admy 106/2225-2229.
Board of Trade
BT 5/9-15. Minutes of the Committee of Trade, 1793-1805.
Foreign Office
FO 5/5-51. United States, 1794-1806. For each year, there are one
or two volumes of correspondence between the Foreign Office and
the legation in America, one volume of consular reports from the
United States, and one volume titled "Domestic," which contains
interdepartmental correspondence, memorials to the government,
etc. The latter volumes are often particularly valuable, throwing
light on the formulation of policy.
FO 27/65-59. France, 1802-3. These volumes contain comments on
the Louisiana negotiations.
FO 83/1-4. Interdepartmental correspondence, 1794-1805.
FO 95/-
357-59. Letterbooks, Admiralty, 1794-1805.
513. Article VI commission.
514. King-Anstey correspondence.
FO 115/4-14. Archives of the American legation, 1794-1805.
These volumes are almost identical with those in FO 5 devoted to
correspondence with the legation, but FO 5 includes a number of
incoming enclosurs omitted in FO 115, which in turn includes many
outgoing enclosures not preserved in FO 5.
FO 304/-
19-24. Minute books of the Article VII commission.
25-27. Awards of the Article VII commission.
34. Minute book of the Article V commission.
War Office
WO 1/69-73. San Domingo, 1796-1801.

4. British, printed

Brymner, Douglas, Arthur G. Doughty, and Gustave Lanctot, eds. *Report
on Canadian Archives.* Ottawa, 1872-.
"Colonial Office Records," Michigan Pioneer and Historical Society, *Col-
lections and Researches,* Vols. XXIV-XXV. Lansing, 1895-96.
Ells, Margaret, ed. *A Calendar of Official Correspondence and Legislative
Papers, Nova Scotia, 1802-1815* (Public Archives of Nova Scotia,
Publication No. 3). Halifax, 1936.
Mayo, Bernard, ed. *Instructions to the British Ministers to the United
States, 1791-1812* (American Historical Association, *Annual Report
for 1936,* Vol. III). Washington, 1941. A work of the very first quality,
save for the index.
Robinson, Christopher, ed. *Reports of Cases Argued and Determined in
the High Court of Admiralty.* 6 vols. London, 1799-1808. These volumes

are a compilation of the decisions of Sir William Scott, but also contain Grant's decision in the case of the *William*.

5. Miscellaneous, printed

Turner, Frederick J., ed. *Correspondence of the French Ministers to the United States, 1791-1797* (American Historical Association, *Annual Report for 1903*, Vol. II). Washington, 1904.

B. Private Papers and Memoirs

1. American, manuscript

Cabot, Samuel, MSS, Massachusetts Historical Society.

Gallatin Papers, New-York Historical Society. Only about half the material in this collection has been arranged for the use of scholars, and, for the period covered by this study, most of the organized material is incoming letters. Despite these qualifications, valuable information on the Republican attitude may be found in these papers.

Gates Papers, New-York Historical Society.

Hamilton, Alexander, MSS, Library of Congress. This huge collection has by no means been exhausted by the Hamilton and Lodge editions of Alexander Hamilton's writings. Much outgoing correspondence, almost all of the letters received, and masses of military papers are to be found only in manuscript form, and in this collection.

Jefferson, Thomas, Papers, Library of Congress. With the Madison and Monroe collections, fundamental for an understanding of Republican attitudes before 1801 and of American policy thereafter.

King, Rufus, Papers, New-York Historical Society. Probably the most important single source for this study. King carefully preserved not only his entire official correspondence, but also copies of that of his predecessor provided by the Department of State and most of his own extensive private correspondence. The few volumes of memoranda are particularly important.

Knox Papers, Massachusetts Historical Society.

Madison, James, Papers, Library of Congress.

Marshall, John, MSS, Library of Congress.

McHenry, James, MSS, Library of Congress.

Monroe, James, Papers, Library of Congress.

Pickering Papers, Massachusetts Historical Society. Private and public correspondence carefully preserved, as well as numerous memoranda, usually acid, composed by Pickering later in life.

Sedgwick Papers, Massachusetts Historical Society.

Trumbull, John, Letterbook, 1796-1802, New-York Historical Society.

Trumbull, John, Memorandum Book, 1792-1799, Library of Congress.

Washington, George, Letters to Sir John Sinclair, British Museum, Add. MSS 5757.

2. American, printed

Adams, Charles F., ed. *Letters of John Adams, Addressed to His Wife.* 2 vols. Boston, 1842.

——. *Memoirs of John Quincy Adams,* Vol. I. Philadelphia, 1874. This famous diary is disappointingly weak on the period of Adams' service in the Senate, but there are some interesting observations on his short mission to London.

——. *The Works of John Adams,* Vols. VIII-X. Boston, 1853-56.

Adams, Henry, ed. *Documents Relating to New-England Federalism, 1800-1815.* Boston, 1877.

Ames, Seth, ed. *Works of Fisher Ames.* 2 vols. Boston, 1854. The character of Ames is not hidden despite the heavy editing.

Bowdoin and Temple Papers, Part II (Massachusetts Historical Society, *Collections,* Seventh Series, Vol. VI). Boston, 1907.

Brown, Everett S., ed. *William Plumer's Memorandum of Proceedings in the United States Senate, 1803-1807.* New York, 1923.

Cole, George D. H., ed. *Letters from William Cobbett to Edward Thornton written in the Years 1797 to 1800.* London, 1937. Cole provides an excellent introduction setting the American stage.

Diary of William Bentley, D. D., Vols. II-III. Salem, 1907-11.

Donnan, Elizabeth, ed. *Papers of James A. Bayard, 1796-1815* (American Historical Association, *Annual Report for 1913,* Vol. II). Washington, 1915.

Fitzpatrick, John- C., ed. *The Writings of George Washington,* Vols. XXXIV-XXXVII. Washington, 1940-41. There are some errors of transcription in this set, but it is an exhaustive and generally excellent job.

Ford, Paul L., ed. *The Writings of Thomas Jefferson (Federal Edition),* Vols. VII-VIIᵀ New York, 1896-97.

Ford, Worthington C., ed. "Edmund Randolph on the British Treaty, 1795." *American Historical Review,* XII (1906-7), 587-99.

——. "Letters of William Vans Murray to John Quincy Adams, 1797-1803," American Historical Association, *Annual Report for 1912* (Washington, 1914), pp. 347-408. Includes also some interesting correspondence with Timothy Pickering.

——. *Writings of John Quincy Adams,* Vols. I-III. New York, 1913-14.

Gibbs, George, ed. *Memoirs of the Administrations of Washington and John Adams, Edited from the Papers of Oliver Wolcott, Secretary of the Treasury.* 2 vols. New York, 1846. This is a Hamiltonian Federalist tract, bitterly anti-Adams, with little on relations with England after 1795.

Hamilton, John C., ed. *The Works of Alexander Hamilton,* Vols. V-VI. New York, 1851.

Hamilton, Stanislaus M., ed. *The Writings of James Monroe*, Vols. II-IV. New York, 1899-1900.

Hunt, Gaillard, ed. *The Writings of James Madison*, Vols. VI-VII. New York, 1906-8.

Jameson, J. Franklin, ed. "Letters of Stephen Higginson, 1783-1804," American Historical Association, *Annual Report for 1896*, I (Washington, 1897), 704-841.

Jay, William, ed. *The Life of John Jay*, Vol. II. New York, 1833.

Johnston, Henry P., ed. *The Correspondence and Public Papers of John Jay*, Vol. IV. New York, 1893.

Lipscomb, Andrew A., ed. *The Writings of Thomas Jefferson (Memorial Edition)*, Vols. IX-XI. Washington, 1905.

Lodge, Henry C., ed. *The Works of Alexander Hamilton (Federal Edition)*, Vols. V, VII, X. New York, 1904. Heavily biased editing; confusing because of topical rather than chronological arrangement.

Morris, Anne C., ed. *The Diary and Letters of Gouverneur Morris*, Vol. II. New York, 1888.

Reitzel, William, ed. *The Autobiography of William Cobbett*. London, 1947.

Sawvel, Franklin B., ed. *The Complete Anas of Thomas Jefferson*. New York, 1903.

Sparks, Jared, ed. *The Life of Gouverneur Morris*, Vols. II-III. Boston, 1832.

Thomas Jefferson Papers (Massachusetts Historical Society, *Collections*, Seventh Series, Vol. I). Boston, 1900.

Warren, Charles, ed. *Jacobin and Junto or Early American Politics as Viewed in the Diary of Dr. Nathaniel Ames, 1758-1822*. Cambridge, 1931.

3. British, manuscript

Auckland MSS, British Museum Add. MSS 34412-34471.

Boconnoc MSS, Papers of William Wyndham Grenville, Lord Grenville, now in the possession of George Grenville Fortescue, Boconnoc, Lostwithiel, Cornwall. Vitally important for this study, this collection has not previously been examined by an American scholar. The printed selections (Fitzpatrick, ed., *Dropmore MSS*), voluminous as they are, merely scratch the surface, particularly in so far as American relations are concerned. The box, America 1793-1803, is very valuable, but others, particularly those containing correspondence with the King and Cabinet and the few memorandum volumes, also repay examination. Unfortunately, the boxes of correspondence with William Pitt were not available when the author examined the collection, but some of these letters are in America 1793-1803 and many others are included in the printed selections.

Chatham Papers, Second Series, Public Record Office 30/8, Vols. CI-

CCCLXIII. Correspondence, chiefly incoming, of William Pitt the Younger. Arranged alphabetically according to correspondent.

Cobbett Letters, British Museum Add. MSS 22906-22907. For the years 1800-1810, chiefly business letters, but some interesting political comments.

Foster, Augustus John, Papers, Library of Congress.

Hammond, George, Papers, in the possession of Colonel Anthony Barnes, Foxholm, Cobham, Surrey. Very little correspondence still preserved.

Harrowby Papers, in the possession of the Earl of Harrowby, Sandon, Staffordshire. Transcripts of the few letters bearing on American relations provided by Viscount Sandon.

Liston MSS, Scottish National Library, Edinburgh, Accession 720. This recent acquisition, never before seriously examined, has not been completely organized by the Scottish National Library, and the box numbers cited in the footnotes are thus necessarily subject to change. Liston's private letters and those of his wife are particularly interesting, and there are also a few very important unofficial letters from Lord Grenville which, contrary to the usual practice, do not appear in FO 5 or FO 115. This collection is now available on microfilm at the Library of Congress.

Liverpool Papers, British Museum Add. MSS 38190-38489, 38564-38581. There is a great deal of important information in this collection, particularly the elder Hawkesbury's memorandum on Grenville's projet for Jay, but it is extremely difficult to find because of the tremendous bulk of the whole. Papers of both the first and second Earls of Liverpool are included.

Melville Papers, British Museum Add. MSS 40100-40102, 41079-41085.

Portland MSS, University College, Nottingham.

Pretyman Papers, Cambridge University Add. MSS 6958. Transcripts of the letters in the Chatham MSS, but organized chronologically.

St. Vincent Papers, British Museum Add. MSS 31158-31193.

Thornton, Sir Edward, Memoirs, Library of Congress.

Vansittart, Nicholas, Lord Bexley, Papers, British Museum Add. MSS 31229-31237.

Wellesley Papers, British Museum Add. MSS 12564-13915, 37274-37318.

Windham Papers, British Museum Add. MSS 37842-37935.

4. British, printed

Abbot, Charles, Lord Colchester, ed. *The Diary and Correspondence of Charles Abbot, Lord Colchester,* Vols. I-II. London, 1861.

Bagot, Josceline, ed. *George Canning and His Friends.* 2 vols. London, 1909.

Baring, Cecilia A., ed. *The Diary of the Right Hon. William Windham.* London, 1866.

Bickley, Francis, ed. *The Diaries of Sylvester Douglas (Lord Glenbervie)*. 2 vols. London, 1928.

Corbett, Julian S., ed. *Private Papers of George, second Earl Spencer*, Vol. I (*Navy Records Society Publications*, Vol. XLVI). London, 1913.

Cruikshank, Brig.-Gen. Ernest A., and Andrew F. Hunter, eds. *The Correspondence of the Honourable Peter Russell*. 3 vols. Toronto, 1932-36.

Cruikshank, Brig.-Gen. Ernest A., ed. *The Correspondence of Lieut. Governor John Graves Simcoe*, Vols. III-IV. Toronto, 1925-31.

Dobrée, Bonamy, ed. *The Letters of George III*. London, 1935. Very limited, but there is no better collection of the King's writings for this period. Sympathetically edited.

Eden, Robert J., Lord Auckland, Bishop of Bath and Wells, ed. *The Journal and Correspondence of William, Lord Auckland*. 4 vols. London, 1861-62.

Fitzpatrick, Walter, ed. *Report on the Manuscripts of J. B. Fortescue, Esq., Preserved at Dropmore* (Historical Manuscripts Commission), Vols. I-VI. London, 1892-98. Introductory notes relate almost exclusively to the European scene, and America is given short shrift in the letters selected for publication. The index identifies the writers of a number of anonymous letters, particularly Gouverneur Morris.

[Foster, Augustus J.] "Notes on the United States. By the Right Hon. Sir Augustus J. Foster, Bart.," *The Quarterly Review*, LXVIII (1841), 20-57. Ostensibly a review of an unpublished manuscript, actually almost exclusively quotations.

Fox, Henry R., Lord Holland. *Memoirs of the Whig Party*. 2 vols. London, 1852-54.

Greig, James, ed. *The Farington Diary*, Vols. I-III. London, 1922-24. Comments of interest, particularly by Trumbull, West, and Copley, are scattered through this diary of a member of the Royal Academy.

Harcourt, Leveson V., ed. *The Diaries and Correspondence of the Right Hon. George Rose*. 2 vols. London, 1860.

Harris, James H., Earl of Malmesbury, ed. *Diaries and Correspondence of James Harris, First Earl of Malmesbury*. 4 vols. London, 1844.

————. *Letters of the First Earl of Malmesbury*. 2 vols. London, 1870.

Laughton, John K., ed. *Letters and Dispatches of Horatio, Viscount Nelson, K. B.* London, 1886.

————. *Letters and Papers of Charles, Lord Barham*, Vols. II-III (*Navy Records Society Publications*, Vols. XXXVIII, XXXIX). London, 1910-11.

Martin, Montgomery, ed. *The Despatches, Minutes, and Correspondence of the Marquess Wellesley, K.G. During his Administration in India*. 5 vols. London, 1836-37.

Pearce, Robert R., ed. *Memoirs and Correspondence of the Most Noble Richard Marquess Wellesley*, I-II. London, 1846. Some information on American trade with India.

Perkins, Bradford, ed. "A Diplomat's Wife in Philadelphia: Letters of Henrietta Liston, 1796-1800," *William and Mary Quarterly*, Third Series, XI (1954), 592-632.

————, ed. "Lord Hawkesbury and the Jay-Grenville Negotiations," *Mississippi Valley Historical Review*, XL (1953-54), 291-304.

Primrose, Archibald P., Earl of Rosebery, ed. *The Windham Papers*. 2 vols. London, 1913.

Rives, George L., ed. *Selections from the Correspondence of Thomas Barclay*. New York, 1894.

Russell, Lord John, ed. *Memoirs, Journal and Correspondence of Thomas Moore*, Vols. I, VIII. London, 1853-56.

————. *Memorials and Correspondence of Charles James Fox*, II-IV. London, 1853-57. Almost no mention of America in this period.

Smith, David B., ed. *Letters of Admiral of the Fleet the Earl of St. Vincent whilst First Lord of the Admiralty, 1801-1804* (*Navy Records Society Publications*, Vols. LV, LXI). 2 vols. London, 1922-27.

5. Miscellaneous, printed

Archivo del General Miranda, Vols. VI-VII, XIII, XVI-XVII. Caracas and Habana, 1930-50. Very inaccurately edited.

C. TRAVELERS' REPORTS
1. American

Austin, William. *Letters from London: Written During the Years 1802 & 1803*. Boston, 1804.

Silliman, Benjamin. *A Journal of Travels in England, Holland, and Scotland . . . in the Years 1805 and 1806*. 2 vols. 2nd ed., Boston, 1812.

2. British

Baily, Francis. *Journal of a Tour in Unsettled Parts of North America in 1796 & 1797*. Augustus de Morgan, ed. London, 1856.

Bernard, John. *Retrospections of America, 1797-1811*. Mrs. W. Bayle, ed. New York, 1887.

Burnaby, Rev. Andrew. *Travels Through the Middle Settlements in North America, in the Years 1759 and 1760*. New ed., London, 1798.

Davis, John. *Travels of Four Years and a Half in the United States of America*. London, 1803.

Hull, John S. *Remarks on the United States of America*. Dublin, 1801.

Moore, Thomas. *Epistles, Odes, and Other Poems*. London, 1806.

Nevins, Allan, ed. *American Social History as Recorded by British Travellers*. London, 1924.

Parkinson, Richard. *A Tour in America in 1798, 1799, & 1800*. London, 1805.

Priest, William. *Travels in the United States of America; Commencing in the Year 1793, and Ending in 1797*. London, 1802.

Sutcliff, Robert. *Travels in Some Parts of North America in the Years 1804, 1805, & 1806.* York, 1811.

Twining, Thomas. *Travels in America 100 Years Ago.* New York, 1893.

Wansey, Henry. *An Excursion to the United States of North America in the Summer of 1794.* 2nd ed., Salisbury, 1798.

Weld, Isaac, Jr. *Travels Through the States of North America and the Provinces of Upper and Lower Canada During the Years 1795, 1796, and 1797.* London, 1799.

Winterbotham, William. *View of the American United States and of the European Settlements in America and the West-Indies.* 4 vols. London, 1795.

3. Miscellaneous

Talleyrand-Périgord, Charles Maurice de. "Les États-Unis et L'Angleterre en 1795," *Révue d'Histoire Diplomatique,* III (1889), 64-77.

D. PAMPHLETS

1. American

Alsop, Richard, Lemuel Hopkins, and Theodore Dwight. *The Political Green-House, for the Year 1798.* Hartford, 1799.

"American Independence." *In Vindication of the President's Nomination of a New Embassy to France.* Boston, 1799.

An Attempt to Vindicate the American Character, Being Principally a Reply to the Intemperate Animadversions of Thomas Moore Esq. Philadelphia,, 1806.

Bache, Benjamin F. *The Foul Charges of the Tories Against the Editor of the Aurora.* Philadelphia, 1798.

————. *Remarks Occasioned by the Late Conduct of Mr. Washington.* Philadelphia, 1798.

Carey, Matthew, ed. *The American Remembrancer; Or, an Impartial Collection of Essays, Resolves, Speeches, &c. Relative, or Having Affinity, to the Treaty with Great Britain.* 3 vols. Philadelphia, 1795. Despite Carey's personal prejudice, this is the best collection of contemporary arguments on the Jay treaty, presenting both sides of the question.

Carey, Matthew. *Plumb Pudding for the Humane, Chaste, Valiant, Enlightened Peter Porcupine.* Philadelphia, 1799.

————. *The Porcupiniad.* 2nd ed., Philadelphia, 1799.

Cobbett, William (Peter Porcupine, *pseud.*). *Plain English.* Philadelphia, 1795.

————. *A Prospect from the Congress-Gallery, During the Session Begun December 7, 1795,* Philadelphia, 1796.

————. *Works of Peter Porcupine.* 12 vols. London, 1801.

Cooper, Thomas. *Political Essays.* 2nd ed., Philadelphia, 1800.

Coxe, Tench. *A brief Examination of Lord Sheffield's Observations on the commerce of the United States.* Philadelphia, 1791.

———— (Juriscola, *pseud.*). *An Examination of the Conduct of Great Britain, Respecting Neutrals.* Philadelphia, 1807.

"Friend to Regular Government, A," *British Honour and Humanity; or the Wonders of American Patience.* Philadelphia, 1796.

————. *British Honour, as Exemplified in the Modest Publications, and Universal Applause of Mr. William Cobbett. . . .* Philadelphia, 1796.

Gore, Christopher (Manlius, *pseud.*), *Letters of Manlius.* Boston, 1794.

Impartial Examination of the Case of Captain Isaac Phillips, An. Baltimore, 1825.

Last Confession and Dying Speech of Peter Porcupine, The. 2nd ed., Philadelphia, 1797.

Madison, James. *An Examination of the British Doctrine, Which Subjects to Capture a Neutral Trade, not Open in Time of Peace.* Philadelphia [?], 1806.

"Member of the Old Congress, A," *Sketches of French and English Politicks in America in May, 1797.* Charleston, 1797.

Monroe, James. *A View of the Conduct of the Executive in the Foreign Affairs of the United States.* Philadelphia, 1797. President Washington's copy, containing his extensive comments, is in the Houghton Library, Harvard University.

Morris, Gouverneur. *An Answer to War in Disguise.* New York, 1806.

Smith, William L. (Phocion, *pseud.*). *American Arguments for British Rights.* London, 1806. This is a British reprint of American newspaper articles.

Wolcott, Oliver, Jr. *British Influence on the Affairs of the United States Proved and Explained.* Boston, 1804.

2. British

Baring, Alexander. *An Inquiry into the Causes and Consequences of the Orders in Council; and an Examination of the Conduct of Great Britain towards the Neutral Commerce of America.* London, 1808.

Bosanquet, Charles. *A Letter to W. Manning, on the Causes of the Rapid and Progressive Depreciation of West India Property.* 2nd ed., London, 1807.

Case of the Owners of the British Ships, The. London, 1803.

Cock, S. [Simon?]. *An Answer to Lord Sheffield's Pamphlet on the Subject of the Navigation System.* London, 1804.

Eden, Sir Frederick M. *Eight Letters on the Peace and on the Commerce and Manufactures of Great Britain.* London, 1802.

"Englishman, An." *The Speech of Thomas Jefferson, Esq., on the 4th of March 1801. With a Few Remarks on its Probable Effects.* London, 1801.

Henderson, George. *A Short View of the Administrations in the Government of the United States, under the Former Presidents, the Late General*

Washington and John Adams; and of the Present Administration under Thomas Jefferson. . . . London, 1802.

Holroyd, John B., Earl of Sheffield. *Observations on the Commerce of the American States.* Rev. ed., London, 1784.

—————. *Strictures on the Necessity of Inviolably Maintaining the Navigation and Colonial System.* London, 1804.

Jordan, Gibbs W. *The Claim of the West India Colonists to the Right of Obtaining Necessary Supplies in America.* London, 1804.

Orr, George. *The Possession of Louisiana by the French Considered.* London, 1803.

Stephen, James. *War in Disguise; Or, the Frauds of the Neutral Flags.* London, 1805.

—————. *Observations on the Speech of the Hon. John Randolph* . . . *on a Motion for the Non-Importation of British Merchandize.* London, 1806.

E. NEWSPAPERS AND PERIODICALS
1. American

Aurora [and] General Advertiser (Philadelphia). Entitled *General Advertiser* until 7 November 1794. 1794-1800.

Columbian Centinel (Boston). Becomes *Columbian Centinel & Massachusetts Federalist,* 5 October 1799. Returns to original title, 5 July 1800. Resumes as *Columbian Centinel; and Massachusetts Federalist,* 4 May 1803. 1794-1805.

Connecticut Courant (Hartford). 1795-1805.

Independent Chronicle and the Universal Advertiser (Boston). 1795-1800.

Maryland Gazette (Annapolis). 1795-1805.

National Intelligencer, and Washington Advertiser. 1800-1805.

Pennsylvania Gazette (Philadelphia). 1795-96.

2. British

Annual Register (London), for 1794-1805. 1799-1807.

Anti-Jacobin; Or, Weekly Examiner (London). 1797-98.

Anti-Jacobin Review and Magazine; Or, Monthly Political and Literary Censor (London), Vols. I-XXII. 1799-1805.

British Magazine (London). 1800.

Caledonian Mercury (Edinburgh). 1794-1805.

Cobbett's Annual Register (London). Becomes *Cobbett's Political Register,* 1804. 1802-5.

Daily Advertiser and Oracle (London). Becomes *Daily Advertiser, Oracle, and True Briton,* 16 April 1804. 1804-5.

Edinburgh Evening Courant. 1799-1805.

Edinburgh Review, Vols. I-VII. 1802-5.

Gore's General Advertiser (Liverpool). 1800, 1805.

Liverpool Trade List, Nos. 234-305. 1798-1800.

Morning Chronicle (London). 1794-1805.

Morning Post (London). Becomes *Morning Post and Fashionable World*, 5 July 1794; *Morning Post [and] Gazetteer*, 2 October 1797; *Morning Post*, 3 January 1803. 1794-1805.

Oracle and Public Advertiser (London). 1794-1805.

Porcupine (London). 1800-1801.

Sun (London). 1794-1805.

Times (London). 1794-1805.

True Briton (London). Becomes *True Briton and Porcupine*, 1 January 1802. 1794-1803.

F. LEGISLATIVE RECORDS
1. American

Annals of the Congress of the United States, 3rd Congress-9th Congress, 1st Session. Washington, 1849-52.

Journal of the Executive Proceedings of the Senate of the United States, Vols. I-II. Washington, 1828.

2. British

Debrett, John, and John Stockdale, eds. *The Parliamentary Register*, Vols. LIV-XCII. London, 1794-1806.

Hansard, Thomas C., ed. *The Parliamentary Debates*, Vols. I-VII. London, 1803-1806.

Journals of the House of Commons, Vols. XLIX-LXI and various.

Parliamentary Papers. Various.

Wright, John, ed. *The Parliamentary History of England*, Vols. XXX-XXXVI. London, 1812-20.

G. STATISTICAL COLLECTIONS
1. American

Evans, Charles H., ed. "Exports, Domestic, from the United States to All Countries from 1789 to 1883, Inclusive," *48th Congress, 1st Session, House of Representatives, Miscellaneous Document 49*, Part 2 (Washington, 1884), 9-251.

Pitkin, Timothy. *A Statistical View of the Commerce of the United States of America*. 2nd ed., New York, 1817.

Seybert, Adam. *Statistical Annals*. Philadelphia, 1818.

United States Bureau of the Census, *Historical Statistics of the United States, 1789-1945*. Washington, 1949.

2. British

MacGregor, John. *Commercial Statistics*, Vol. III. London, 1847.

MacPherson, David. *Annals of Commerce*, Vol. IV. London, 1805.

Porter, George R. *The Progress of the Nation*. F. W. Hirst, ed. Rev. ed., London, 1912.

H. MAPS AND ATLASES

Mitchell, John. *A Map of the British Colonies in North America*. 2nd ed.,

1775 [1782?]. The so-called Oswald and Franklin copies in the British Museum and New-York Historical Society respectively are marked with the famous "red lines," but the lines are so broad, reworked, smudged, and altered that a precise estimate of the intention of the negotiators at Paris is difficult. Their general intent, however, is made clear.

Paullin, Charles O. *Atlas of the Historical Geography of the United States* (Carnegie Institution of Washington, *Publication No. 401*). Baltimore, 1932.

II. SECONDARY MATERIAL

Adams, Henry. *History of the United States of America During the First Administration of Thomas Jefferson (History of the United States,* Vols. I-II). 2 vols. New York, 1889. Adams is bitterly and sometimes unfairly anti-Jefferson, as for example in accepting Merry's version of the social controversy with Jefferson. This classic work is well written, backed by extensive research, with a good grasp of the period.

————. *The Life of Albert Gallatin.* Philadelphia, 1879. Includes many letters not in the *Writings.*

Albion, Robert G. *Forests and Sea Power (Harvard Economic Studies,* XXIX). Cambridge, 1926.

————. "Maritime Adventures in New York in the Napoleonic Era," *Essays in Modern English History in Honor of Wilbur Cortez Abbott* (Cambridge, 1941), pp. 314-44.

Allen, Gardner W. *Our Naval War with France.* Boston, 1909. Narrow and inadequate, but the only existing study in print.

Appel, Alan C. "The Undeclared War Between France and the United States, 1798-1801." Unpublished Senior thesis, Princeton University, 1941. The information is almost exclusively drawn from Knox, *Naval Documents,* but this study nevertheless adds a few details.

Bemis, Samuel F. *Jay's Treaty, A Study in Commerce and Diplomacy.* New York, 1923. This is a very valuable pioneer study, based chiefly on a thorough examination of official correspondence, but subject to some emendations, particularly because the private papers of Grenville and Hawkesbury were not examined by the author.

————. *John Quincy Adams and the Foundations of American Foreign Policy.* New York, 1949.

————. "The London Mission of Thomas Pinckney, 1792-1796." *American Historical Review,* XXVIII (1922-23), 228-47.

Benjamin, Lewis S. (Lewis Melville, *pseud.*). *The Life and Letters of William Cobbett in England and America.* 2 vols. London, 1913.

Beveridge, Albert J. *The Life of John Marshall,* Vol. II. Boston, 1916.

Bond, Beverly W., Jr. *The Monroe Mission to France, 1794-1796* (J. H. Vincent, J. H. Hollander, W. W. Willoughby, eds., *Johns Hopkins*

University Studies in Historical and Political Science, Series XXV, Nos. 2-3). Baltimore, 1907.

Brant, Irving. *James Madison, Father of the Constitution, 1787-1800.* Indianapolis, 1950.

―――――. *James Madison, Secretary of State, 1801-1809.* Indianapolis, 1953. Brant's two volumes, ably written and resting on substantial research in American materials, form parts of what will doubtless be a standard biography. They are very friendly to the subject.

Briggs, Herbert W. *The Doctrine of Continuous Voyage (Johns Hopkins University Studies in Historical and Political Science*, Series XLIV, No. 2). Baltimore, 1926.

Bryant, Arthur. *The Years of Endurance, 1793-1802.* London, 1942.

―――――. *Years of Victory, 1802-1812.* London, 1944. Bryant's two volumes are excellent popular histories of the period. The judgment of English political figures is generally deft. American relations get little attention, and the temptation to construct a parallel between these years and the years of writing sometimes weakens the work.

Buck, Norman S. *The Development of the Organization of Anglo-American Trade, 1800-1850.* New Haven, 1925. Although this work sticks very narrowly to the subject and does not consider trade in its broader aspects, it is still helpful and contains a fine bibliography.

Burt, Alfred L. *The United States, Great Britain, and British North America from the Revolution to the Establishment of Peace after the War of 1812* (James T. Shotwell, ed., *The Relations of Canada and the United States*). New Haven, 1940. An excellent study of this aspect of Anglo-American relations, based primarily on the *American State Papers* and Canadian archives including transcripts from London.

Chinard, Gilbert. *Thomas Jefferson: The Apostle of Americanism.* Boston, 1929. A sympathetic biography, with emphasis on the influence of French thought.

Clark, Mary E. *Peter Porcupine in America: the Career of William Cobbett, 1792-1800.* Philadelphia, 1939. Very little assessment of Cobbett's position, but almost every detail of his career in the United States seems to have been included.

Clauder, Anna C. *American Commerce as Affected by the Wars of the French Revolution and Napoleon, 1793-1810.* Philadelphia, 1932. On the whole, this work is disappointing, but the comprehensive summary of the decrees of the rival powers is useful.

Conway, Moncure D. *Omitted Chapters of History Disclosed in the Life and Papers of Edmund Randolph.* New York, 1888. Conway pasted together a defense of the Virginian, made up chiefly of excerpts from his correspondence.

Cowan, Helen I. *Charles Williamson* (Rochester Historical Society, *Publications*, XIX). Rochester, 1941. Well-written analysis of Williamson's career as a land agent in the United States, drawing heavily from business records. Shows the methods of one of the more enlightened groups of British land speculators and, to some degree, the connection with American politics.

Dallas, George M. *Life and Writings of Alexander James Dallas*. Philadelphia, 1871.

Elkins, Wilson H. "British Policy in its Relation to the Commerce of the United States of America from 1794 to 1807." Unpublished thesis, Oxford University, 1936. By an American who studied at Oxford. The research, particularly in the British manuscript sources, is extensive and capable, and the study as a whole is very valuable. The organization and style are somewhat uneven.

Elliott, Charles B. "The Doctrine of Continuous Voyage," *American Journal of International Law*, I (1907), 61-104.

Fäy, Bernard. *The Two Franklins*. Boston, 1933. The second Franklin is Benjamin Franklin Bache. Fäy's work is very tendentious, sometimes inaccurate, and often repetitive, yet remains lively, and the range of research, particularly in periodicals, is wide.

Fitzmaurice, Edmond G. P., Baron Fitzmaurice. *Life of William, Earl of Shelburne*. 3 vols. London, 1875-76.

Furber, Holden. "The Beginnings of American Trade with India, 1784-1812," *New England Quarterly*, XI (1938), 235-65.

Galpin, W. Freeman. *The Grain Supply of England During the Napoleonic Period*. New York, 1925.

Graham, Gerald S. *Sea Power and British North America, 1783-1820* (*Harvard Historical Studies*, XLVI). Cambridge, 1941.

Heaton, Herbert. "Yorkshire Cloth Traders in the United States, 1770-1840," *Thoresby Miscellany*, XXXVII (Leeds, 1944), 225-87.

Heckscher, Eli F. *The Continental System: an Economic Interpretation*. Oxford, 1922. This excellent study casts much light on the motives and policies of the European belligerents, but most of the volume deals with the years after 1806. The statistical tables are particularly valuable.

Hidy, Ralph W. *The House of Baring in American Trade and Finance* (Norman S. B. Gras and Henrietta Larson, eds., *Harvard Studies in Business History*, Vol. XIV). Cambridge, 1949.

Holt, W. Stull. *Treaties Defeated by the Senate*. Baltimore, 1933. The brief notes on the Jay treaty and boundary convention show the difficulty of studies of Senate action in this period.

Jay, William. *The Life of John Jay*, Vol. I. New York, 1833. A son's tribute to his father.

Jenks, Leland H. *The Migration of British Capital to 1875*. New York, 1927. Unfortunately for the purposes of this study, the volume deals almost entirely with the years after 1815.

Kellogg, Louise P. *The British Régime in Wisconsin and the Northwest* (Joseph Schafer, ed., *Publications of the State Historical Society of Wisconsin*). Madison, 1935.

King, Charles R. *The Life and Correspondence of Rufus King,* Vols. II-IV. New York, 1893-97. This work is valuable almost exclusively for the letters it contains, and the editing, done by King's grandson, is very biased and not always accurate.

Labouchère, G. "L'Annexion de la Louisiane aux États-Unis et les Maisons Hope et Baring," *Révue d'Histoire Diplomatique,* XXX (1916), 423-55.

Laing, Lionel H. "Nova Scotia's Admiralty Court as a Problem of Colonial Administration," *Canadian Historical Review,* XVI (1935), 151-61.

Lingelbach, William E. "England and Neutral Trade," *Military Historian & Economist,* II (1917), 153-78. An interesting defense of the logic of the *Essex* decision is included in this discussion, which, perhaps because of the time of its writing, is not overly harsh on the assumption of rights by belligerents. One of the best brief treatments of the problem.

Lodge, Henry C. *Life and Letters of George Cabot.* Boston, 1877. This is a highly colored defense of the ultra-Federalist. Since Cabot destroyed most of his papers, Lodge was forced to depend upon printed works and the private collections of Cabot's contemporaries.

Logan, Rayford W. *The Diplomatic Relations of the United States with Haiti, 1776-1891.* Chapel Hill, 1941. Extensive work in the documentary sources, a very detailed treatment, but somewhat inclined in favor of the Haitian point of view. Logan does not recognize the existence of a real Anglo-American concert at the time of the negotiations with Toussaint.

Lyon, E. Wilson. "The Directory and the United States," *American Historical Review,* XLIII (1937-38), 514-32.

—————. *Louisiana in French Diplomacy, 1759-1804.* Norman, Oklahoma, 1934.

McMaster, John B. *A History of the People of the United States,* Vols. II-III. New York, 1885-92. Valuable for its discussion of public opinion, but to be used with caution.

—————. *The Life and Times of Stephen Girard.* 2 vols. Philadelphia, 1918. This authorized biography is made up largely of excerpts from the huge collection of Girard correspondence placed at the disposal of McMaster.

Monaghan, Frank. *John Jay.* New York, 1935.

Montague, Ludwell L. *Haiti and the United States, 1714-1938.* Durham, 1940.

Moore, John B. *International Adjudications, Modern Series,* Vols. I-IV. New York, 1929-31. These volumes cover the activities of the Jay treaty commissions in exhaustive detail. Virtually all the important American documents, as well as many on the British side, are reproduced.

Morison, Samuel E. *The Life and Letters of Harrison Gray Otis.* 2 vols. Boston, 1913. A well-written, not unsympathetic biography, with large quantities of valuable letters printed at the close of each chapter.

————. *The Maritime History of Massachusetts, 1783-1860.* Cambridge, 1921.

Newcomb, Josiah T. "New Light on Jay's Treaty," *American Journal of International Law,* XXVIII (1934), 685-92. On the secret provision order.

Osgood, Howard L. "The British Evacuation of the United States," Rochester Historical Society, *Publication Fund Series,* VI (1927), 9-30.

Parkinson, C. Northcote. *Trade in the Eastern Seas.* Cambridge, England, 1937.

————, ed. *The Trade Winds, A Study of British Overseas Trade During the French Wars, 1793-1815.* London, 1948. A coöperative work, perhaps overly compartmentalized, but generally of a high standard. See especially the chapter on American trade by Herbert Heaton.

Pellew, George. *John Jay* (John T. Morse, ed., *American Statesmen Series*). Cambridge, 1890.

Pellew, George. *The Life and Correspondence of the Right Honble Henry Addington, First Viscount Sidmouth.* 3 vols. London, 1847. Chiefly correspondence, arranged so as to give the most favorable impression of Addington.

Philips, Cyril H. *The East India Company, 1784-1834 (Publications of the University of Manchester,* Vol. CCLXX). Manchester, 1940.

Phillips, Edward H. "The Public Career of Timothy Pickering, Federalist, 1745-1802." Unpublished Ph.D. dissertation, Harvard University, 1950.

Phillips, W. Alison, and Arthur H. Reede. *Neutrality, Its History, Economics and Law.* Volume II: *The Napoleonic Period.* New York, 1936. A well-written, well-conceived study.

Primrose, Archibald P., Earl of Rosebery. *Pitt.* London, 1891.

Ragatz, Lowell J. *The Fall of the Planter Class in the British Caribbean, 1763-1833.* New York, 1928. This work is very helpful, particularly on the opening of the islands by the governor's proclamations.

Riddell, William R. *The Life of John Graves Simcoe.* Toronto, 1926. A defense.

————. "When International Arbitration Failed," *Canadian Law Times,* XL (1919-20), 351-60. A capable brief survey of the activities of the debt commission meeting in Philadelphia.

Robertson, William S. *The Life of Miranda.* 2 vols. Chapel Hill, 1929. Explores every facet of Miranda's career, resting heavily on the correspondence of the adventurer, which was first discovered by the author.

Rose, J. Holland. *Life of William Pitt.* 2 vols. London, 1911. A very capable study.

Russell, Nelson V. *The British Regime in Michigan and the Old Northwest, 1760-1796.* Northfield, Minnesota, 1939.

Schachner, Nathan. *Thomas Jefferson.* 2 vols. New York, 1951.

Scott, Duncan C. *John Graves Simcoe* (Duncan C. Scott and Pelham Edgar, eds., *The Makers of Canada*). Toronto, 1905.

Setser, Vernon G. *The Commercial Reciprocity Policy of the United States, 1774-1829.* Philadelphia, 1937. The study is fairly technical and largely devoted to the period after 1815, but still useful.

Sherrard, Owen A. *A Life of Lord St. Vincent.* London, 1933.

Spiller, Robert E. *The American in England.* New York 1926.

Stanhope, Philip H., Earl Stanhope. *Life of the Right Honourable William Pitt.* 4 vols. London, 1860-62. In the absence of any edition of Pitt's correspondence, the extensive quotations in this work must serve as the chief printed source of his letters. The biography is highly partisan.

Steel, Anthony. "Anthony Merry and the Anglo-American Dispute about Impressment, 1803-1806," *Cambridge Historical Journal* IX (1947-49), 331-51.

————. "Impressment in the Monroe-Pinkney Negotiations," *American Historical Review*, LVII (1951-52), 353-69. Steel's two articles purport to show that the impressment controversy was chiefly the result of American domestic political influences and that the British government exercised commendable moderation. He attacks Zimmerman for using only American manuscript materials, but has himself examined only Foreign Office records, and as a result his picture is distorted.

Steiner, Bernard C. *The Life and Correspondence of James McHenry.* Cleveland, 1907.

Tansill, Charles C. *The United States and Santo Domingo.* Baltimore, 1938.

Thompson, Isabel. "The Blount Conspiracy," *East Tennessee Historical Society Publications*, No. 2 (1930), 3-21.

Turner, Frederick J. "The Policy of France toward the Mississippi Valley in the Period of Washington and Adams," *American Historical Review*, X (1905-6), 249-79.

Tsiang, I-Mien, *The Question of Expatriation in America Prior to 1907* (*Johns Hopkins University Studies in History and Political Science*, Series LX, No. 3), Baltimore, 1942.

Upham, Charles W. *The Life of Timothy Pickering*, Vols. III-IV. Boston, 1873. These two volumes, a continuation of the work begun by Octavius Pickering, consist largely of excerpts from Pickering's correspondence but do not by any means exhaust the interest of his papers. Furthermore, the Federalist tinge is so pronounced as to limit the usefulness of the work.

Wheaton, Henry. *Some Account of the Life, Writings, and Speeches of William Pinkney.* Boston, 1826.

Whitaker, Arthur P. *The Mississippi Question, 1795-1803.* New York, 1934. This very capable study is useful for the discussion of Blount, Hamilton, and Bowles.

White, Kate, "John Chisholm, Soldier of Fortune," *East Tennessee Historical Society Publications*, No. 1 (1929), 60-66. Lacks footnotes.

239

Wilbur, James B. *Ira Allen, Founder of Vermont,* Vol. II. Cambridge, 1928. This biography is very much slanted in Allen's favor.

Wildes, Harry E. *Lonely Midas: The Story of Stephen Girard.* New York, 1943.

Willson, Beckles. *America's Ambassadors to England, 1783-1928.* London, 1928.

————. *Friendly Relations.* Boston, 1934. Sketches of British envoys to America.

Winston, James E., and R. W. Colomb. "How the Louisiana Purchase Was Financed," *Louisiana Historical Quarterly,* XII (1929), 189-237.

Yonge, Charles D. *The Life and Administration of Robert Banks, Second Earl of Liverpool.* 3 vols. London, 1868. One of the worst of the authorized correspondence-plus-text biographies.

Zimmerman, James F. *Impressment of American Seamen (Columbia University Studies in History, Economics and Public Law,* CXVIII, No. 1). New York, 1925. This standard work on the subject is none too detailed. Zimmerman did not examine British sources, and a complete study of impressment will not be written until both the Foreign Office and Admiralty records are examined.

Index

Abukir, Nelson's victory, hailed in United States, 114-15; effect in Britain, 123

Act of Union, passed by Pitt, 132

Adams, Abijah, Republican editor, 93

Adams, Henry, on second Pitt ministry, 175

Adams, John, 14, 29, 31, 42, 140, 158, 191*n*; character, 24-25; criticizes Hamilton, 26; questioned by St. Croix commission, 51; disliked by French, 56; becomes President, 58-60; analysis by Liston, 58-59; sends XYZ mission to France, 92; becomes genuinely popular, 93-94; Blount conspiracy, 100; Santo Domingo, 108-9; Miranda, 112; opposes Anglo-American alliance, 112-15; describes difficulty of claims negotiations, 120; leaves office, 120; seeks peace with France, 121; orders new mission to France, 121-22; dismisses Pickering and McHenry, 122; loses Federalist support, 122; names Marshall Secretary of State, 123; challenges Federalists, 123; orders mutineer surrender to Britain, 124-25; defeated for Presidency, 129-30; willing to reconstitute debt commission, 209*n*-210*n*; criticized by Pickering, 210*n*

Adams, John Quincy, 22, 90, 105, 183-84, 191*n*; John Adams, 25; ordered to London, 37; says impressment reduced, 65; criticizes British maritime policy, 80; negotiates treaty with Prussia, 83; rumored to marry British princess, 114; reports for Senate committee on boundary commission, 147

Adams administration, policy on trade, 78-79; policy toward Britain, 90, 185; policy toward Santo Domingo, 106-10; policy toward Miranda, 111-12; attacked by *Anti-Jacobin Review*, 120; success in Anglo-American relations, 128; policy continued by Republicans, 170. *See also* Adams, John; France; Marshall, John; Pickering, Timothy; Trade

Addington, Henry, 10; welcomes Ellsworth, 127; character, 132-33; forms ministry, 132-34; friendly toward America, 133; claims convention, 138-39; favors duty repeal, 151; offers aid to United States Navy, 154; at dinner for Rufus King, 157; resigns, 175; fails to meet problems of war, 182

Addington ministry, and American trade, 15, 150-53; relaxes blockade, 84; endorses *Polly* decision, 88-89, 179; weakness, 132-33; American attitude toward, 133-34; friendly toward America, 133-34; negotiates peace with France, 136; claims and boundary conventions, 138-49; delays, 139, 142-43, 146, 162-63; delays defeat boundary convention, 148; offers aid to United States Navy, 153-54; analyzed by Rufus King, 157; policy on Louisiana, 161-63, 165-67; plans expedition to New Orleans, 166-67; permits Baring to finance Louisiana Purchase, 169; fails to preserve comity, 172-74; assessed by Monroe, 173; resigns, 175; policy toward United States, 185. *See also* Addington, Henry; Hawkesbury, Lord; Impressment; Trade

Adet, Pierre A., French minister, 57-58; on Senate and Jay treaty, 32; feels Jay treaty gaining support, 38-39; fears Liston, 45; announces own recall, 56; intrigues, 101; analysis of Jefferson, 200*n*

Admiralty, British, 155; and American seamen, 63, 65; considers requests for release of seamen, 66; reform of admiralty courts, 84-85; directed to tolerate reëxport trade, 89; ordered to convoy American ships, 97; opposes concession on impressment, 176; orders care on impressment and seizures, 176. *See also* Impressment; Seamen

Admiralty, High Court of, Marriott removed, 86; cases, 87-88; cited, 89

Admiralty courts, reforms of, 14, 84-86; and American ships, 82; delays, 82; and Ira Allen, 102-3; record, 187-88

Africa, H. M. S., chases Fauchet, 37

Agents for seamen, authorized, 62-63; British policy toward, 63-64; careers, 63-66

Algiers, American treaty with, 41

Alien and Sedition Acts, distorted by

Fauchet, Joseph, French minister to United States, 122; intercepted dispatch, 36-37

Federalists, and business, 14, 23; control Congress, 26; and neutrality, 27; and French Revolution, 28; support Jay treaty, 30-33, 40-42; win election of 1796, 58; oppose Act for Relief and Protection of American Seamen, 62-63; attitude on impressment, 68-69; for war with France, 93; oppose Anglo-American alliance, 112-13; Liston criticizes, 119; oppose negotiations with France, 121-22; criticize Marshall, 123; split, 122; decline, 123; support surrender of Nash, 125; lose election of 1800, 129-30: and claims convention, 140-41; oppose duty repeal, 152; try to exploit Louisiana crisis, 163-64; plan secession, 174; criticize *Essex* and *War In Disguise*, 181; attacked by John Randolph, 216*n*

Fenner, Arthur, Governor of Rhode Island, resists British, 37

FitzSimons, Thomas. *See* Debt commission

Florida, feared transferred to France, 159, 161, 165; William A. Bowles, 103

Foodstuffs, British need, 12-13, 34-35; British West Indies' imports, 12, 73-75

Ford, Worthington C., on John Adams, 24-25

Foster, Augustus J., British diplomat, on Charles J. Fox, 21; describes Madison, 27

Fox, H. M. S., lands Bowles in Florida, 103

Fox, Charles J., 29; on Jay treaty, 5; attitude toward United States, 21. *See also* Opposition

France, Republicans lose affection for, 28-29, 130-31, 161, 183-84; American trade, 35; undeclared war, 43, 56, 60, 68-69, 92-112; maritime policy, 89-90; Anglo-American coöperation against, 95-115; intrigues in America, 101-3; Miranda, 111; peace, 121-23, 126-27, 129; Louisiana, 159-70. *See also* Amiens, Peace of

Freire, A. F., Portuguese diplomat's wife, on British policy, 22

French Revolution, Washington's attitude, 24; John Adams' attitude, 25; Jefferson favorably inclined, 27; Madison and, 27; Federalists cease to approve, 28; Rufus King and Grenville oppose, 46-47

French West Indies, American trade with. *See* Trade, American reëxport; Trade, American neutral

Freneau, Philip, Republican poet, 125

Frere, John Hookham, British diplomat, 165-66

Frontier posts. *See* Posts, frontier

Gallatin, Albert, 40; on Senate, 32; speaks against Jay treaty, 39; condemns France, 93; boundary convention, 147; receives report from Rufus King, 157; impressment negotiations, 215*n*

Gascoyne, Isaac, M. P. from Liverpool, opposes duty repeal, 151

Genesagernagumsis, Lake. *See* St. Croix commission

Genêt, Edmond, French minister to United States, 27, 172

George III, 46, 114; on Jay negotiations, 2; supports Benjamin West, 7; position and character, 17-18; on United States, 18; on Washington, 18; on Opposition 21; praises American firmness, 94; popular, 125; court ignores death of Washington, 125; fall of Pitt, 132; backs Addington, 136; asked to approve claims convention, 139; on Anglo-American relations, 157; fall of Addington, 175; owns United States Securities, 191*n*; criticizes Liston, 212*n*

George, Miss ———, British actress in United States, 190*n*

Gerry, Elbridge, American envoy to France, 92-93

Gibraltar, American squadron visits, 154

Girard, Stephen, American merchant, 11

Goddard, Captain ———, saves intercepted dispatches, 36

Goodhue, Benjamin, Senator from Massachusetts, criticizes Marshall, 123

Gore, Christopher, 155; Hawkesbury refuses to negotiate with, 146. *See also* Seizure commission

Gostling, Nathaniel, British proctor, 55

Grant, Sir William, *Essex* decision of, 1, 178-79

Great Britain, opinion of America, 10; American supplies, 12-13; situation, 17, 123, 135-36; John Adams dislikes, 25; Pickering's original hatred, 25-26; Hamilton favors, 27; Jefferson and Madison distrust, 27; Federalists support, 28; Republicans oppose, 28; discusses Farewell Address, 57; citizenship, 61-62; policy toward ships at sea, 61; American agent for seamen in, 62, 65-66; policy toward trade, 70-79, 176-83; reaction to XYZ affair, 94; effect of American negotiations with France, 121, 123-24,

126-28; regrets Pickering's replacement by Marshall, 123; reaction to death of Washington, 125-26; Republican attitude toward, changes, 131-32; opinion of claims convention, 140; praised by Monroe, 176; assesses Louisiana Purchase, 167-68; endorses *War in Disguise*, 180-81; relations with United States, analyzed, 182-86. *See also* Anglo-American relations; Impressment; Pitt ministry; Pitt ministry, second; Trade

Greenville, Treaty of, 41; delays ratification of Jay treaty, 38; difficulty cleared away, 43

Grenville, Baron, 29, 42-43, 60, 65, 70, 91, 99, 133, 183, 185; negotiations with Jay, 2-5; on trade with British West Indies, 4-5; character, 18-19; relations with Pitt, 19; attitude toward United States, 19; forwards intercepted dispatch, 36; exchanges ratifications of Jay treaty, 38; recalls Hammond, 44; relations with Rufus King, 46-47; pleased by transfer of posts, 48; negotiates modification of Jay treaty, 51; chooses debt commissioners 53; chooses seizure commissioners, 54; moderate on seizure commission controversy, 55; rights of ships, 61; objects to agent for seamen, 63; ends acceptance of American protections for seamen, 63; return of deserters, 67-68; aids American trade with India, 72; evades negotiations on trade with British West Indies, 75; trade legislation, 76-77; discusses New Orleans deposit, 83; orders more lenient treatment of American ships, 84; reform of Admiralty Courts, 85; expects Franco-American war, 90; Franco - American relations, 93; doubts Franco-American war, 94; offers convoys, 97; Blount conspiracy, 100; Ira Allen, 102; disavows William A. Bowles, 103; provides United States with information, 104; Gouverneur Morris, 104-5; Santo Domingo, 106-10; Miranda, 111-12; favors American attack on Louisiana, 113; debt commission breakdown, 117, 120; suspends London commission, 119; considers new policy towards United States, 124; moderate on Mortefontaine convention, 127; on Addington ministry, 132; authorizes Liston's return, 134; opposes Addington, 136; supports Rufus King with Hawkesbury, 139; Louisiana, 159; in militia, 175; criticizes Deas, 195n; offers aid against France, 199n

Griswold, Roger, Congressman from Connecticut, opposes Act for Relief and Protection of American Seamen, 62

Guillemard, John. *See* Debt Commission

Gunn, James, Senator from Georgia, favors Jay treaty, 31-32

"Hail Columbia," written, 93.

Hamilton, Alexander, 42; policy, 14, 23; influence, 26; urges conditional ratification of Jay treaty, 31; supports Jay treaty, 33-34; criticizes Provision Order, 36; on choice of Secretary of State, 37; *Camillus* letters defend Jay treaty, 38; opposes providing information on treaty, 40; feels Jay treaty gaining, 40; plans countermeasures against Republicans, 41; praises Rufus King, 46; considered for claims commission, 54; opposes concession on impressment, 68; comments on anti-French feeling, 90; Miranda, 111-12; opposes Anglo-American alliance, 112-13; opposes John Adams, 122, 129

Hammond, George, 35-36, 42, 83, 92, 114, 120, 155; restrained by Grenville, 2-3; and Cobbett, 10; on Timothy Pickering, 25; accused of bribery, 32; windows broken by mob, 34; feels Jay treaty gaining support, 38-39; recalled as minister to United States, 44; unpopular in America, 45; doubts Franco-American war, 94; mission to Berlin, 104; and boundary convention, 144-46; denies new Orders in Council, 179; attitude toward United States, 197n

Hamtramck, Colonel John, occupies frontier posts, 47-48

Harper, Robert G., Congressman from South Carolina, supports Jay treaty, 41; for war with France, 93

Harrowby, Earl of, formerly Dudley Ryder, 179, 182; on trade with United States, 76-77; as Foreign Secretary, rejects amended boundary convention, 148-49; negotiates with Monroe, 175-76

Harvey, Admiral Henry, moderate on impressment, 64-65

Hawkesbury, Baron, later first Earl of Liverpool, 22, 133; Jay treaty, 3-4; favors bounty on American foodstuffs, 13; Grenville on, 19; character, 20; defends Navigation Acts, 70; against United States trade with British West Indies, 73; opposes definition of contraband, 83.

Hawkesbury, Baron, later second Earl

of Liverpool, son of Baron Hawkesbury, first Earl of Liverpool, 10; confirms *Polly* principle, 89; becomes
Foreign Secretary, 132; character,
133; friendly toward United States,
133-34; negotiates peace with France,
136; negotiates claims convention,
138-40; opposes interest on claims,
141-42; negotiates boundary convention, 143-46; expects ratification of
boundary convention, 147; and
countervailing duties, 150-53; praises
Jeffersonian government, 151 - 52;
Maryland bank stock, 153; offers aid
to United States Navy, 154; negotiates on impressment, 154-56; respects
Rufus King, 158; Louisiana, 159-63,
165-70; Louisiana Purchase, 167-68;
criticizes Monroe, 172; sees no Anglo-
American issues, 173
Hédouville, ———, F r e n c h agent,
ousted from Santo Domingo, 108
Henry, Patrick, offered position as Sec-
retary of State, 37
Hermione, H. M. S., seamen released,
64; mutiny, 124
Higginson, Stephen, American mer-
chant, supports Jay treaty, 33; cau-
tions Pickering, 37
High Court of Admiralty. *See* Admiral-
ty, High Court of
High Court of Appeals. *See* Appeals,
Lords Commissioners of
Hobart, Lord, undersecretary in For-
eign Office, fetes Rufus King, 157
Holland, Baron, 21; protests against
seizures, 179
Holland, American payments, 47; Anti-
French underground, 105
Home, Captain Rodham, pursues Fau-
chet, 37
Hope & Company, finances Louisiana
Purchase, 12, 169
House of Commons. *See* Commons,
House of
House of Representatives. *See* Repre-
sentatives, House of
Howell, David. *See* St. Croix commis-
sion
Hull, John S., British traveler, on
United States, 9
Huskisson, William, British official, 107

Immanuel case, and continuous voyage, 87
Importation, bona fide, 88-89, 177-79
Imports, British, from America. *See*
Trade, American, with Britain
Impressment of American seamen, 90,
131, 138; omitted from Jay treaty,
5; Liston checks, 47; discussed, 60-
69; fluctuating incidence, 65, 201n;

negotiations, 67-69, 154-56, 175-76;
effectiveness of American policy toward, 69; from United States Navy,
99, 154; excused by Monroe, 173;
American legislation, 174; renewal,
175-76; analysis, 183. *See also* Nash,
Thomas; Seamen
Independence, American, date disputed,
118-19
Independent Chronicle, Boston newspaper, scoffs at Hamilton, 38; opposes Jay treaty, 41; praises Robert
R. Livingston, 62; predicts American
dominance of trade with India, 73;
criticizes seizure of American ships,
89; excuses France, 93; rumor of
Anglo-American alliance, 114; exe-
cution of McLean, 206n
India Act of 1784, British, 71
India, American trade with, 13-14, 171,
183; Jay treaty, 3, 5; development,
70-73, 202n; complaints of East India
Company, 70-72
Indians, American, war with United
States, 2, 23, 185; trade regulated,
42; Blount conspiracy, 99-100;
French intrigues, 101; William A.
Bowles, 103; British trade, 184. *See
also* Greenville, treaty of
Inglis, Charles, claim, 118-19
Innes, James. *See* Debt commission
Intelligence, Anglo-American coöpera-
tion, 99-105
Ireland, effect of XYZ affair, 94; fall
of Pitt, 132
Isolation. *See* Alliance, Anglo-Ameri-
can; Neutrality, American
Jackson, Francis J., British minister to
United States, 173, 181
Jackson, James, Senator from Georgia,
opposes Jay treaty, 31-32
Jay, John, 42, 43, 54, 85, 158; on
British policy, 22; John Adams on,
25; at Bath, 30; burned in effigy, 34;
criticizes Hammond, 44; urges capable envoy, 44; hopes for Anglo-American friendship, 91; warns of danger
of delay, 185. *See also* Jay treaty
Jay treaty, 14, 23-25, 46, 59, 75, 90,
119, 123-24, 183-85; reverses trend
toward war, 1; controversy preceding,
2; negotiation, 2-5, 83; terms, 5;
British reaction, 5; effect on security
market, 12; reaches America, 30;
conditionally approved by Senate, 30-
32; terms revealed, 33; ratification,
34, 36-38; American reaction, 33-34,
38-41; before House of Representatives, 38-42; explanatory article, 42,
47; weighed, 42-43; enforced, 47;
further modified, 51; effect of ratification delay, 53-54; angers France,

56; trade with India, 70-72; regulates commerce with British Isles, 76; effect on trade debated, 77; claimed to improve British courts, 82; blamed for troubles with France, 89-90, 93; not infringed by Mortefontaine, 127; incompletely executed, 143; commercial articles expire, 182. *See also* Arbitration; Debt commission; Seizure commission; St. Croix commission

Jean Bart, French ship, captured with dispatches, 36

Jefferson, Thomas, 9, 38, 51, 127, 158, 182; Cobbett on, 10; and Anglo-American trade, 14; on Charles J. Fox, 21; on Edmund Randolph, 25; character and attitude, 26-27; considers alliance with Britain, 28, 160-61, 164-65, 170, 177; dislikes Britain, 28; on treaty-making power, 39; defeated in election of 1796, 56-58; Adet on, 58, 200n; impressment, 69; criticizes British legislation, 77-78; welcomes reform of admiralty courts, 85; reports Anglo-American alliance, 113; fears effect of Mortefontaine, 127; elected President, 129-30; transformation of attitude toward Britain, 130-32, 171-72; visited by Liston, 134; and Thornton, 135; expects opposition to claims convention, 141; indiscretion, 144-45; boundary convention, 144-48; criticized by Pickering, 148; endorses duty repeal, 152-53; feels Britain friendly, 154; and Tripoli, 154; appoints Monroe, 163-64; praises France for sale of Louisiana, 168; and Merry, 173-74; approves retaliation against Britain, 177; wants to clear New York harbor, 177; favors restoration of Bourbons, 183-84; on claims convention, 213n

Jefferson administration, Grenville criticizes, 19; members praise Addington government, 133-34; claims and boundary conventions, 138-39; Hawkesbury on friendliness of, 151-52; and Louisiana Purchase, 159-70; continues Federalist policy, 170; fails to preserve comity, 172-81; criticized by Merry, 174; policy toward Britain, 185. *See also* Impressment; Jefferson, Thomas; Madison, James; Trade

Jeffersonians. *See* Republicans

Kenyon, Baron, British Chief Justice, decision in *Argonaut* case 72, 202n; welcomes Ellsworth, 127

Kelsau, John, admiralty judge, condemns *Essex,* 178

King, Rufus, 14, 48, 49, 66, 68, 72, 89,

90, 94, 96, 99, 127, 131, 136, 182; on land sales, 11; on British food shortage, 13; on Dundas, 20; on British policy, 22; interview with Grenville, 23; in Senate, 30-31; supports Jay treaty, 33-34; declines to become Secretary of State, 37; becomes minister to England, 46-47; relations with Grenville, 46-47; negotiates modification of Jay treaty, 51; on Macdonald and Rich, 53; seizure commission, 55, 141-43; impressment, 63, 65, 67, 154-56; trade with British West Indies, 75; secures changes in British legislation, 76-78; deposit at New Orleans, 83; influences reform of admiralty courts, 85; secures ouster of judge, 86; convoys, 97; Ira Allen, 102-3; aids Britain, 104-5; Santo Domingo, 107-8; Miranda, 111-12; efforts for Anglo-American coöperation, 113-15; praises British government, 117; negotiates claims and boundary conventions, 120, 135, 138-49, 170; reports British coolness, 121; on popularity of Washington in Britain, 125; on British mourning for Washington, 126; reassures Grenville on Jefferson, 131; regrets fall of Pitt ministry, 133; criticizes Hawkesbury, 133; expects removal, 134; serves Jefferson administration, 138-58; skill in negotiation, 138, 142-43, 172; on reception of claims convention, 140; Presidential possibility, 148; seeks reduction of countervailing duties, 150, 214n; secures return of Maryland bank stock, 153; leaves London, 155-57; criticizes Jefferson administration, 156-57; analyzes Addington ministry, 157; analysis of success, 157-58; Louisiana, 159-61, 166-67; urges appointment of Merry, 173

King - Hawkesbury conventions. *See* Boundary convention; Claims convention

Knox, General Henry, American land speculator, 11; considered for boundary commission, 49

Labouchère, P. C., finances Louisiana Purchase, 169

Lake of the Woods, boundary near. *See* Boundary convention

Land, British purchases of, in America, 11

Langdon, John, Senator from New Hampshire, opposes Jay treaty, 31-32

Lansdowne, Marquis of, formerly Earl of Shelburne, and peace of 1783, 19; and America, 21; receives portrait of

Privateers, British, complaints against, 83-84. *See also* Seizures, British, of American ships; Trade, American neutral

Protections, for American seamen, 62-63; not accepted by Britain, 63

Provision Order, British, American protests against, 26, 37-38; delays ratification of Jay treaty, 34-36; claims for damages under, 53-54, 116

Pulteney, Sir William, 15; invests in American lands, 11

Purviance, Samuel, Representative from North Carolina on Louisiana Purchase, 168

Ragatz, Lowell J, on American trade with British West Indies, 74

Randolph, Edmund, 34; character, 25; receives Jay treaty, 30; criticizes Provision Order, 35; and Fauchet, 36; resigns as Secretary of State, 36-37; attacks Federalists, 216*n*

Read, Jacob, Senator from South Carolina, opposes Jay treaty, 31-32

Rebates, American, on reëxports, 177-79, 182. *See also* Trade, American reëxport

Recognition signals, Anglo-American, 98

Reëxport trade. *See* Trade, American reëxport

Relief and Protection of American Seamen, Act for, passed, 62-63; results, 63

Representatives, House of, composition, 26; approves Jay treaty, 38-42; votes agents for seamen, 62-63; debates surrender of deserter, 125; and repeal of duties, 150-53; debates Louisiana Purchase, 168-69; criticizes Bonaparte, 168-69. *See also* Congress

Republicans, 58, 158; on Washington, 24; attitude toward Britain, 28, 130-32, 172; oppose Jay treaty, 31-34, 39-40; criticize Provision Order, 35; urge agents for seamen, 62; warn against French resentment, 89-90; oppose war with France, 93; Blount conspiracy, 100; condemn surrender of deserter, 125; in election of 1800, 129-30; claims convention, 140-41; boundary convention, 147-48; shift of feeling toward France, 160, 183-84. *See also* Jefferson administration

Revolution, Anglo-American hatred of, 111-12

Rich, Henry Pye, 61. *See also* Debt commission

Richmond, Virginia, supports Jay treaty, 40

Right of search, Britain maintains, 98; America contests, 200*n*

Rivardi, Major J. J. Ulrich, on frontier, 184

Robbins, Jonathan. *See* Nash, Thomas

Robinson, Christopher, King's Advocate, paraphrases *Polly* decision, 89; *Reports*, source of confusion, 218*n*-219*n*

Robinson, Moses, Senator from Vermont, opposes Jay treaty, 31-32

Rose, George, British Treasury official, drafts legislation, 77; favors understanding with America, 78

Rose, J. Holland, on Pitt, 18

Rowson, Henrietta, novelist, 8

Royal Navy, threat to America, 28; moderation, 37, 42-43; criticized by Trumbull, 55; conditions in, 60-61; aids United States, 96; strengthening in American waters sought, 113; recovers deserter, 125, 210*n*. *See also* Impressment; Seamen; Seizures, British, of American ships

Rule of the War of 1756, British policy, 3, 81, 86-89, 177-79

Ryder, Dudley. *See* Harrowby, Earl of

St. Croix commission, success of, 48-53, 116, 134, 143, 183

St. John River, 49

St. Vincent, Earl of, aids American ships, 84; plans reform in admiralty courts, 85; fears Armed Neutrality, 131; First Lord of the Admiralty, 132; negotiates on impressment, 133, 154-55

San Ildefonso, treaty of, 159-60

Santo Domingo, 85, 131; Anglo-American relations, 106-10, 135, 183; British hopes for conquest, 113; French forces in, 165

Savage, William, agent for seamen, 65

Schoodiac River. *See* St. Croix commission

Scott, Sir William, M. P. and judge, friend of Rufus King, 46; awards to United States, 54, 142; decision favors United States, 84; bill for reform of admiralty courts, 85-86; on maritime policy, 86; doctrine of continuous voyage, 87-89, 178-79; on Ira Allen, 103; ends negotiations on impressment, 155-56; doubts *Essex* decision correct, 180; endorses *War in Disguise*, 180

Seamen, British, in American ships, 61, 124; American, sought by Britain, 113-14, 208*n*. *See also* Impressment

Secession, New England, agitated, 174

Securities, American, held in Britain, 12; in Europe, 169